grab your boarding pass

A Daily Devotional
for Juniors / Earliteens

Kalie Kelch

REVIEW AND HERALD® PUBLISHING ASSOCIATION
Since 1861 | www.reviewandherald.com

Copyright © 2013 by Review and Herald® Publishing Association

Published by Review and Herald® Publishing Association, Hagerstown, MD 21741-1119

The author assumes full responsibility for the accuracy of all facts and quotations as cited in this book.

Unless otherwise noted, Bible texts in this book are from the *Holy Bible, New International Version.* Copyright © 1973, 1978, 1984, 2011 by Biblica, Inc. Used by permission. All rights reserved worldwide.

Scripture quotations marked NASB are from the *New American Standard Bible,* copyright © 1960, 1962, 1963, 1968, 1971, 1972, 1973, 1975, 1977, 1995 by The Lockman Foundation. Used by permission.

Texts credited to NKJV are from the New King James Version. Copyright © 1979, 1980, 1982 by Thomas Nelson, Inc. Used by permission. All rights reserved.

Scripture quotations marked NLT are taken from the *Holy Bible,* New Living Translation, copyright © 1996, 2004, 2007 by Tyndale House Foundation. Used by permission of Tyndale House Publishers, Inc., Carol Stream, Illinois 60188. All rights reserved.

Bible texts credited to TEV are from the *Good News Bible*—Old Testament: Copyright © American Bible Society 1976, 1992; New Testament: Copyright © American Bible Society 1966, 1971, 1976, 1992.

Statements in this volume attributed to other speakers/writers are included for the value of the individaul statements only. No endorsement of those speakers'/writers' other works or statements is intended or implied.

This book was
Edited by JoAlyce Waugh
Copyedited by Vesna Mirkovich
Designed by Emily Ford / Review and Herald® Design Center
Cover art by Emily Ford / © Thinkstock.com
Typeset: Minion Pro 11/13

PRINTED IN U.S.A.

17 16 15 14 13   5 4 3 2 1

Library of Congress Cataloging-in-Publication Data
Kelch, Kalie, 1977-
  Grab Your Boarding Pass! : A daily devotional for juniors / Kalie Kelch.
     pages cm
  ISBN 978-0-8280-2747-2
  1. Preteens--Prayers and devotions--Juvenile literature. 2. Devotional calendars--
Seventh-Day Adventists--Juvenile literature. I. Title.
  BV4870.K44 2014
  242'.62--dc23
                        2013014177

ISBN 978-0-8280-2747-2

Dedication

TO JESUS, for pushing me to do things I never would have dreamed possible and for giving me the talents I need to get each job done. I'm so glad I'm Your daughter!

TO MY HUSBAND, Randy, for being my best friend and partner in ministry, for supporting me in all the projects I get involved in, and for believing in me as a mom, writer, and editor.

TO MY KIDS, Katelyn and Ryan, for having a sense of adventure as we explore new places and learn new things as a family, for reading the Bible together each night and helping me think about God's Word in a fresh new way, and for inspiring me to be the best mom I can be.

TO MY MOM, Sue, for teaching me to have faith in God, for cheering me on in all my endeavors, and for involving me in church ministry at an early age.

TO THE TEACHERS, PASTORS, AND FRIENDS who have helped me grow as a Christian, for studying God's Word and talking about spiritual matters together, for sharing the good and bad times and bearing one another's burdens, and for praying together as sisters and brothers in Christ.

About the Author

K alie Kelch has been involved in church ministry since she was 10 years old, helping with music and/or children's ministries for as long as she can remember. She has a deep desire to help kids use their talents for Jesus and make the Bible practical and real. Kalie and her husband, Randy, are dedicated to helping their children, Katelyn and Ryan, and other kids develop a friendship with Jesus and find their place in church ministry while they are young.

Introduction

I love to travel. I love everything about it. I love planning where to go and what to do, and I love reading about places I've never been to and finding out the cool things to see and do in that area. After I've planned a family vacation, I can't wait for the months to pass before we actually leave.

In fact, as our departure date draws closer, I start setting aside things we'll need for the trip—tickets, books, games, clothes, camping equipment, etc.—sometimes as much as a month in advance. My husband laughs at me, but I like to be prepared. Part of the excitement of the trip is anticipating the fun we'll have, the places we'll see, and the people we'll meet. Because I'm prepared, I feel more relaxed when our vacation starts; I know there's a plan, and I know what to expect.

My love for travel and adventure made me think about my relationship with God and the things I need to do now to prepare for the biggest trip I'll ever take—a trip through the clouds at Jesus' second coming. Heaven is the final destination on my boarding pass, but I need to have my bags packed and ready to go if I'm going to catch my flight.

For the next 365 days we are going to travel to each of the 50 states in America, the 10 provinces and three territories in Canada, and Bermuda and Guam in search of spiritual lessons that will prepare us for heaven. So pack your bag, grab your phone (make sure you have Google Maps on it!), and jump on board for a whirlwind tour. Oh, and don't forget to bring your GPS—otherwise known as your Bible. You'll need it!

PS: EACH OF THESE LOCATIONS is part of the North American Division of Seventh-day Adventists. You may want to ask your parents for a map so you can keep track of the states and provinces and territories we visit on our trek. Have a safe trip!

An Epic Adventure

All these people [Abel, Enoch, Noah, Abraham, and Sarah]
were still living by faith when they died. They did not receive the
things promised; they only saw them and welcomed them from a distance,
admitting that they were foreigners and strangers on earth. **Hebrews 11:13.**

A few summers ago our family planned an epic trip out west. From Maryland we traveled to South Dakota, Wyoming, Utah, Arizona, Colorado, and back across the Midwest to home, sweet home. Six thousand miles and three weeks later we parked our dirty Honda Odyssey in our garage and enjoyed a good night's sleep in our comfy beds. What an adventure!

We camped and hiked, we saw waterfalls and wildlife, and we spent fun-filled hours making memories as a family. But our trip didn't happen just because we jumped into our van one day and decided to see the countryside. No, it took months of planning—trust me. We mapped out a route that took us in a complete circle, stopping at all the destinations we wanted to visit in an orderly manner.

It would have been chaotic and ridiculous—and also would have cost a lot of money for gas—to have driven from Maryland to Colorado, up to South Dakota, down to Arizona, and then back up to Wyoming. (Grab a map if you're foggy on your geography; you'll quickly see that this plan would be silly.)

Without a plan our trip could have been a disaster, and no one would have had fun.

Many people compare life to that of a journey, a trip. Your life started when you were born, and the final destination of your journey, the place you want to end up, is heaven.

So how do you get ready for heaven? All you have to do is ask Jesus to forgive you of your sins and accept His free gift of salvation. By faith you are saved and assured of your final destination—heaven. And as you stay focused on God, you'll live your life for Him.

The Bible characters in today's text made sure they were on the right path. They were strangers in this land because they knew where their final destination was. Their boarding pass had "HEAVEN" emblazoned on it.

Where are you headed? Is heaven your final destination? I hope so, because God wants you there more than anything in the world.

NEXT STOP: Eastport, Maine

January 2

Let There Be Light

And God said, "Let there be lights in the vault of the sky to separate
the day from the night, and let them serve as signs to mark sacred times
and days and years, and let them be lights in the vault of the sky
to give light on the earth." And it was so. **Genesis 1:14, 15.**

North America is the third-largest continent in the world, and this year we are going to be traveling to hundreds of locations throughout the United States and Canada. Our first stop is the town of Eastport, Maine. Consisting entirely of islands, the town had a population of 1,331 at the 2010 census.

What makes Eastport unique is that it is the first city in the United States to receive the golden rays of morning sun as it peeks over the horizon. Each morning the sunlight greets this sleepy town before the rest of the country awakes from its slumber.

Can you imagine what it was like when God created the sun? Talk about an intense, blinding light. It is hard to think about a time when there was no sun to warm the earth or provide light to help us see. The Bible tells us that the earth was shapeless and dark until God created light on the first day. But He wasn't finished providing His children with light for their new world. No, on the fourth day He created the sun and gave it the job of marking the days, months, years, and seasons.

The sun also provides us with warmth, helps our gardens grow, and gives us the vitamin D we need to stay healthy. It helps us know what time it is and faithfully marks the beginning and ending of each day.

Just as God gave the sun a specific job to do, He gives each one of us a job that is unique to our talents and abilities. The sun can never become the moon and shine at night. No! God placed it in the sky to shine during the day. Likewise, He has placed you in your family, school, church, and community for a special job that only you can do. You just have to discover what that job is and then, as the sun, shine boldly for God.

NEXT STOP: Maine Blueberry Farm

Blue Tastiness

Kind words are like honey—sweet to the soul and healthy for the body. **Proverbs 16:24, NLT.**

Maine is known for its blueberries. In fact, it is the largest producer of the juicy little berries in the United States, with 99 percent of all the blueberries in the country coming from Maine. Maybe you have another favorite fruit, but blueberries are high on my list. I love them in muffins, oatmeal, cobblers, pies, and ice cream.

My family's favorite blueberry recipe is called Blueberry Buckle. It's similar to a coffee cake but is topped with blueberries and a crumbly butter, flour, and sugar topping that melts in your mouth. We reserve this special treat for Sabbath breakfast and special occasions such as birthdays, anniversaries, or holidays. Everyone starts licking their lips when they find out that we are having Blueberry Buckle for Sabbath breakfast.

Just as blueberries taste sweet when you pop them into your mouth, wise King Solomon told us that pleasant words have the same effect. Pleasant words are sweet like honey, and they make you healthy. Did you know that your words could make you and those around you healthy? Can they give you vitamins like those you get from eating blueberries? In a way they can. Think about it. When you speak kindly to your brother or sister, you are building up your sibling and making them happy. When you are polite to your teacher, you are giving them strength to make it through another day. Happiness and a positive attitude can help us stay healthy.

On the other hand, when you tease a kid at school who dresses differently than you, you're leaving a rotten taste in their mouth. Anger, hatred, and bitterness are the result of mean words, which are definitely the opposite of sweetness. These feelings can lead to sickness of mind and body.

Make sure your words today are as sweet as a blueberry—or honey, as King Solomon wrote.

NEXT STOP: Portland, Maine

January 4

Hello out there!

Where It All Began

Listen to my words: "When there is a prophet among you, I . . . reveal myself to them in visions, I speak to them in dreams." **Numbers 12:6.**

Ellen G. Harmon was born on November 26, 1827, along with her twin sister, Elizabeth, near the village of Gorham, Maine. A few years later her family moved to the city of Portland, Maine, where she lived until she married James White in 1846.

There in Portland, in 1840 and again in 1842, Ellen and her family attended meetings that presented the ideas of William Miller and his associates, who proclaimed that Christ would return in 1844. The Harmon family believed, as did many other people, that the second coming of Christ was to take place on October 22, 1844. Unfortunately, Ellen and hundreds of other believers were disappointed when the clock struck midnight on October 23, 1844, and Jesus had not returned.

The believers who chose not to abandon their faith spent the following days and weeks praying and studying, seeking guidance from the Holy Spirit. God answered their honest prayers in the form of a vision given to Ellen.

In December 1844, at the home of a believer in south Portland, Ellen and four other women had gathered to study and pray together. While they were worshipping together, Ellen was shown a vision of heaven and the Advent people's journey to the holy city. At just 17 years of age, Ellen was reluctant to share the vision with others, but God had called her to serve as His prophet and He promised to give her strength.

Ellen accepted God's call and became one of the founding pioneers of the Seventh-day Adventist Church. God spoke to Ellen White through visions and dreams, as He had to Moses, Daniel, and the countless prophets before her. And like Moses and Daniel, she faithfully served God until the day she died.

God desires to make Himself known to His people. Whether through visions, the Bible, His prophets, godly parents and teachers, or nature, God *will* reveal Himself to you if you look for Him and honestly seek His truths.

NEXT STOP: The Maine Coast

Let It Shine, Let It Shine, Let It Shine

In the same way, let your light shine before others, that they may see your good deeds and glorify your Father in heaven. **Matthew 5:16.**

More than 60 lighthouses dot the coast of Maine's approximately 5,000 miles of shoreline. When you think of being on the ocean, you probably think of beaches and sand and shells. Not in Maine! If you haven't visited Maine, you might be surprised to learn that its shoreline is made up of jagged, rocky cliffs. Although there are some sandy beaches, the majority of Maine's shoreline consists of rock. Because of the cliffs, lighthouses are a necessity; without them many sailors would be in danger of crashing their boats to pieces against the rocks in a storm.

I've photographed a number of Maine lighthouses, and they come in different sizes, shapes, and colors. Most are white, but the West Quoddy Head lighthouse is red-and-white-striped. Others are not painted at all, revealing the dark-gray weathered stone that they are made of. The shortest lighthouse is six feet tall, while the tallest lighthouse soars more than 133 feet into the air.

In spite of the differences between the lighthouses, they all perform one important function: they shine their light through the darkness so that ship captains know where the shoreline is. The lighthouses serve as a guiding light, protecting ships from unseen danger.

As followers of Christ, you and I are lighthouses. Like Maine's lighthouses, we come in different shapes and sizes and colors. We have different talents and abilities. You might be good with technology and helping run sound at church, while others are good at singing or telling the children's story. However, like the lighthouse, we all have one thing in common. We are on a mission to save people from the dangers of sin and Satan. We are on a mission to let God's love shine through us so that people will follow Him and get ready for heaven.

Did you ever sing "This Little Light of Mine" when you were in kindergarten Sabbath school? Time for a pop quiz. Do you remember all of the words? Go ahead: sing it out loud or in your head. Done? What is the main phrase that is repeated again and again? That's right, "I'm gonna let it shine" is the key phrase and the most important thing to remember from that song. Is your light shining today?

NEXT STOP: Acadia National Park, Maine

Hello out there!

January 6

Thunder Hole

When the people saw the thunder and lightning and heard the trumpet and saw the mountain in smoke, they trembled with fear. They stayed at a distance. **Exodus 20:18.**

Thunder Hole is a popular attraction in Acadia National Park. From the parking lot you can hear the ocean waves crashing on the rocks. After you hike a short distance through the woods, you'll find that the trees give way to rocky cliffs and the ocean. A set of stairs descends toward the Atlantic Ocean and takes you out onto a rock ledge. As you stand on the secure walkway, you wait, along with many other tourists, for a wave to roll into a narrow rocky inlet. As water fills the inlet and crashes against the back wall, it has nowhere to go but up, sometimes shooting water 40 feet in the air with a thunderous *boom*.

The stairs and walkway near Thunder Hole are usually very wet from the water sprayed from the waves, which soaks everything in sight. Because the concrete and rocks surrounding the area are so slippery, there are signs cautioning visitors to stay behind the rails. No climbing on the rocks is allowed. Of course, not everyone heeds the warning, and people in search of a closer look or a better picture have tumbled into the ocean and been smashed against the rocks, losing their lives in an instant because of a poor choice.

When the Israelites heard the thunder, saw the lightning, and listened to the trumpets while standing near Mount Sinai, they were scared. Like visiting Thunder Hole for the first time and not knowing how loud it will be or if the wave will crash over the railing and soak you, the Israelites didn't know what to expect after hearing God speak the Ten Commandments to them. They must have realized their own insignificance and how much they had messed up. I wonder if they worried about how they would measure up to God's standards.

Unfortunately, what they were missing was a relationship with God. They trembled in fear because they didn't know who He was. The last ruler they had served was a dictator—the unbending, uncaring pharaoh who had ruled their lives. They had to learn to trust their new leader—a loving and caring God who had their best interest in mind. If they had known God, I don't think they would have trembled in fear at the sound of the thunder and the trumpets. Instead, they would have fallen on their knees in worship and in awe of His power and majesty.

NEXT STOP: New Hampshire

January 7

Going Against the Flow

Noah was a righteous man, blameless among the people of his time, and he walked faithfully with God. **Genesis 6:9.** Now the earth was corrupt in God's sight and was full of violence. **Verse 11.**

New Hampshire was one of the original 13 colonies that decided they were through living under the rule of England. They were tired of the taxes and the lack of representation. They were tired of the king's iron fist. They wanted to do things their way!

But did you know that New Hampshire, the first colony to declare its independence from England, did so a full six months before the signing of the Declaration of Independence? Most people go along with the motto that there is safety in numbers. The colonial leaders knew that they could be hanged for treason, so they stuck together. But the leaders of New Hampshire didn't wait around for the rest of the group to make a decision. Instead, they took their stand regardless of what the other colonies were doing.

The Bible talks about a man who took a stand for right in spite of the fact that other people thought he was crazy. Noah was not afraid to follow his convictions, what he knew to be right. Surrounded by evil on all sides—lying, murder, adultery, and other horrible acts—Noah and his family followed God's instructions to build the ark. Although Noah did not enjoy safety in numbers in earthly terms, he had a host of angels and God Himself on his side.

Every day (for more than 40,000 days) Noah tried to reason with the people. He encouraged them to give up their evil ways and be saved in the ark, but they laughed at him, teased him, and told him he was nuts. Fortunately, Noah's best friend was God. No doubt he shared his hurt feelings and doubts with God, and God gave Noah the strength to keep preaching and building until the day when it was time to enter the ark.

Have you ever stood up for a classmate who was being picked on when no one else would? Have you ever volunteered to help out at your church's cleaning bee when none of your friends signed up because they wanted to sleep in and watch TV? Have you ever felt as if you were going against the flow and swimming upstream? Don't worry—you aren't alone. Noah and a number of other Bible characters faced the same challenges. Keep your head up and keep doing what is right. Your reward is waiting in heaven!

NEXT STOP: Mount Washington, New Hampshire

15

January 8

Hello out there!

A Tad Windy

And the Lord said to Moses, "Stretch out your hand over Egypt
so that locusts will swarm over the land and devour everything growing
in the fields, everything left by the hail." **Exodus 10:12.**

Mount Washington, located in the White Mountains of New Hampshire, is the highest peak in the Northeast, rising to 6,288 feet. But its height is not what gives Mount Washington its claim to fame. No, it's the mountain's erratic weather and extremely high winds that make scientists and adventurers stop and take note. The second-highest recorded wind gust on the earth's surface was registered at Mount Washington.

On April 11, 1934, a ridge of high pressure was building to the north and east, and a system of low pressure was building to the west. The pressure system converged on Mount Washington, resulting in the air rushing quickly from high to low pressure, thus causing hurricane-force winds registering at 136 miles per hour. On April 12, 1934, the winds continued to grow stronger until, at 1:21 p.m., they reached an all-time high of 231 miles per hour!

The wind must have sounded like a freight train barreling down on the mountain. Have you ever gotten nervous when the wind howls and the house seems to shake because of 60-mile-per-hour wind gusts in a bad thunderstorm? Now quadruple that to nearly equal the world record wind gust on Mount Washington. Yikes!

Wind is a powerful force of nature that makes you stop and realize how small and defenseless you are. It is only through God's mercy that we can withstand the powers of nature.

If only Pharaoh had recognized God's power and control over nature, he and his countrymen would not have ended up at the bottom of the Red Sea (see Exodus 14). You see, God used a great wind to try to get Pharaoh's attention when He sent locusts as the eighth plague. "So Moses stretched out his staff over Egypt, and the Lord made an east wind blow across the land all that day and all that night. By morning the wind had brought the locusts; they invaded all Egypt and settled down in every area of the country in great numbers. Never before had there been such a plague of locusts, nor will there ever be again" (Exodus 10:13, 14).

Sadly, Pharaoh still didn't listen, and he lost everything. Are you listening?

NEXT STOP: Franconia, New Hampshire

Built on Solid Rock

The Lord is my rock, my fortress and my deliverer; my God is my rock, in whom I take refuge. He is my shield and the horn of my salvation, my stronghold. **Psalm 18:2.**

Today we are visiting the town of Franconia, near the base of Cannon Mountain in the White Mountains of New Hampshire. In 1805 a cliff was discovered there, and the rock formation was named Old Man of the Mountain. Nowadays all you will see is a granite cliff, but there used to be a series of five granite ledges that looked like a man's face when viewed from the north.

Years later, in 1945, the rock formation became the state emblem. It was used on New Hampshire's license plates, state route signs, and on the back of its statehood quarter. Unfortunately, the rock formation couldn't hold up to the elements and the constant freezing and thawing of water that settled in the crack on the Old Man of the Mountain's forehead. By the 1920s the crack had to be mended with chains to hold it together. Then in 1957 New Hampshire's legislature allocated $25,000 to protect the cliff by pouring quick-drying cement in the crack, driving steel rods in place, and building cement gutters to divert water so it wouldn't settle in the crack and freeze.

In spite of all these efforts, the Old Man of the Mountain collapsed on May 3, 2003. Saddened that their state symbol was gone, many people left flowers at the base of the cliff in honor of the rock formation that had been the state's identifying feature for 58 years.

What is your identity? Are you Alex, the basketball star, or Jenny, the singer? Are you Sabrina, the artist, or Tim, the computer geek? Are you Liz, the class clown, or Nathan, the straight-A student? If those talents were stripped away, who would you be?

The residents of New Hampshire had based their identity on something temporary, something that shattered and broke. If you base your identity on your talents or what your friends think of you or who your parents want you to be, you're eventually going to break. But when you base your identity on God and your self-worth on who you are in His eyes, you'll never fall apart. You are His son or daughter. You are heir to His kingdom. You are on a journey to heaven. And although the world may crumble around you, your identity is planted on the solid, immovable rock of Jesus.

NEXT STOP: Concord, New Hampshire

Hello out there!

Heavenly Rewards

For the living know that they will die, but the dead know nothing;
they have no further reward, and even their name is forgotten. Their love,
their hate and their jealousy have long since vanished; never again will
they have a part in anything that happens under the sun. **Ecclesiastes 9:5, 6.**

In 1985 Christa McAuliffe, a social studies teacher at Concord High School in Concord, New Hampshire, was chosen from more than 11,000 applicants to take part in the NASA Teacher in Space Project. She was to be the first teacher in space, where she would conduct experiments and teach two lessons from the space shuttle *Challenger*. Unfortunately, her dreams never became a reality. On January 28, 1986, 73 seconds after the launch of *Challenger,* the spacecraft blew up, instantly killing Christa and the six other crew members on board.

I lived in Florida at the time, and I was at a friend's house that day when I looked out the window and saw a huge orange-and-white cloud in the sky with a white tail behind it and what looked like two puffy white trails shooting in opposite directions out of the top of the fireball. I didn't know what had happened at the time, but even though I was only 8 years old, I knew something was wrong. Later we learned the news about the space shuttle.

In honor of Christa's death more than 40 schools around the world have been named after her, and her home state of New Hampshire built the Christa McAuliffe Planetarium/McAuliffe-Shepard Discovery Center in Concord. In addition, a number of scholarships have been set up in her memory. On July 23, 2004, Christa and the other 13 astronauts who died in the *Challenger* and *Columbia* disasters received, posthumously, the Congressional Space Medal of Honor, which was awarded by the former president George W. Bush.

Although these honors are nice, Christa has no idea that people are paying tribute to her. As King Solomon pointed out in today's text, "the dead know nothing; they have no further reward." People who die cannot claim any further rewards on this earth. All their earthly treasures are gone. What really matters is how they lived their lives and whether they accepted Jesus' gift of salvation and stored up their treasures in heaven. What are you living for?

NEXT STOP: Peterborough, New Hampshire

Calling All Bookworms

Then the dragon was enraged at the woman and went off
to wage war against the rest of her offspring—those who keep
God's commandments and hold fast their testimony about Jesus. **Revelation 12:17.**

Do you have a library card? My daughter, a self-proclaimed bookworm, got her own library card when she was 9 years old. She smiled at me, and her eyes sparkled as the librarian handed her the plastic card.

"How many books can I check out at one time?" she asked.

I looked at the pamphlet that listed the policies for the library. "You can have a total of 50 items checked out at one time," I replied.

Her eyes grew wide at the idea of having 50 books to read all at once, but then she said, "I think that would be a little much."

If you enjoy reading, then you probably love the library. Our country was built on the philosophy that all people are free to learn and make a better life for themselves, and libraries are a part of that idea. In 1833 New Hampshire was the first state to establish a publicly funded library, which was opened in Peterborough.

Our country thrives on the fact that, as citizens of the United States, we have the freedom to read what we want, say what we want, go where we want, worship when and how we want, and do what we want. However, we know that these freedoms will disappear at the end of time. The very ideas our country was founded on will be stripped away and replaced with a new set of rules that will force people to worship as the government dictates.

But we don't have to be surprised when we see these things happen, because God has told us what is to come. According to the book of Revelation, the conflict will be between Christians and the rest of the world. Because the dragon, or Satan, hates God's people, he makes war against those who obey God's commandments and follow Him.

Fortunately, we need not fear. Read Revelation 22:7-21 to see how the story ends. All of the tens of thousands of books in the library cannot compare to the Bible. God's Word is the only thing you'll need to beat Satan. Check it out; you'll be glad you did.

NEXT STOP: Vermont

January 12

Hello out there!

Caught in the Middle

Let one of us sit at your right
and the other at your left in your glory. **Mark 10:37.**

Welcome to Vermont! This is the home of skiing in the winter, sugaring (making maple syrup) in the early spring, hiking in the summer, and leaf peeping in the fall. Vermont is sandwiched between New Hampshire and New York with a maximum east-to-west width of 89 miles (145 kilometers) and a maximum north-to-south width of 159 miles (260 kilometers).

Except for Alaska and Hawaii, all states share a border with at least one other state, but most share a border with two or more states. Vermont is no different than other states in that regard. However, Vermont was "caught in the middle" and fought over by its neighbors. At various times throughout its early history, Vermont was claimed by both New Hampshire and New York. Finally, in July 1777, the Constitution of Vermont was drafted, and the state enjoyed its own rights and freedoms.

Are you ever stuck in the middle of family arguments or disagreements between your friends at school? It's very uncomfortable, isn't it? I've been in the middle of other people's problems numerous times in elementary school, high school, and even as an adult, and it never gets easier. It makes for very awkward situations.

Did you know that James and John created an awkward situation for Jesus? Leading up to their request, which is our text for today, they said, "Teacher . . . we want you to do for us whatever we ask" (Mark 10:35). Talk about being pushy and demanding. James and John felt they were more deserving than the other disciples to receive special treatment from Jesus. They tried to put Jesus in an uncomfortable position by making Him choose between His disciples.

So how did Jesus deal with their request and the fight that almost ensued because of their question? Keep reading in Mark 10: "When the ten heard about this, they became indignant with James and John. Jesus called them together and said, '. . . Instead, whoever wants to become great among you must be your servant, and whoever wants to be first must be slave of all. For even the Son of Man did not come to be served, but to serve, and to give his life as a ransom for many'" (verses 41-45).

I hope you choose to serve others instead of putting people in the middle of a conflict.

NEXT STOP: Waterbury, Vermont

20

January 13

I Scream, You Scream

Woe to those who call evil good and good evil, who put darkness for light and light for darkness, who put bitter for sweet and sweet for bitter. Isaiah 5:20.

Any guesses about what we're going to talk about, from today's title? No, we're not talking about roller coaster rides. We're talking about ice cream! As the saying goes: "I scream, you scream; we all scream for ice cream!"

In 1978 two friends, Ben Cohen and Jerry Greenfield, opened an ice-cream shop in a remodeled gas station in Burlington, Vermont, and began selling the Ben & Jerry's ice cream we all know today. On the one-year anniversary of the opening of their little store, they held a Free Cone Day event, during which they gave away free scoops of ice cream all day to everyone who visited their store. Two years later they began making and packaging their ice cream to sell to restaurants and small grocery stores in the area. In 1981 they opened a small manufacturing facility to increase their ice-cream production. Then, in 1985, they moved into their permanent manufacturing plant and company headquarters in Waterbury, Vermont.

Bordering on bizarre sometimes, the names of their flavors are unique: Chubby Hubby, Chunky Monkey, Fair Goodness Cake, Jamaican Me Crazy, or Vermonster. So what's your favorite ice-cream flavor? You might prefer vanilla or mint chocolate chip or plain chocolate to Ben & Jerry's fancy creations. But regardless of your favorite ice cream, one thing is certain—it's sweet.

You wouldn't eat ice cream that was bitter, would you? Of course not! Adding a bitter ingredient (such as radishes) to ice cream would ruin it. But what would be even worse is if the person eating it claimed that the bitter radish ice cream was actually really sweet.

The same goes for sin. Isaiah warns us that trouble will come to anyone who looks at things that are evil and calls them good. If you lie and marvel at how you tricked your parents, or if your friend steals something and you applaud him or her for not getting caught, you are falling into the trap of dismissing evil and saying it is good. Somewhere along the line you've stopped listening to your conscience and have become so comfortable with evil that you don't even recognize it as evil. Instead, you think that it is good. Don't let yourself be deceived!

Make sure you are always eating sweet ice cream—doing what is right. If you start eating radish ice cream—doing evil—and think that it is good, you're in trouble!

NEXT STOP: A Sugar Bush Farm in Vermont

January 14

Hello out there!

Sugar Water

How sweet your words taste to me;
they are sweeter than honey. **Psalm 119:103, NLT.**

What is your favorite topping for pancakes or waffles? Fruit, peanut butter, applesauce, syrup? I like my pancakes with nothing but maple syrup on them, and I don't mean the stuff that is flavored to taste like maple syrup. I mean the real deal—the expensive stuff you get from Vermont, the largest producer of maple syrup in the United States.

Aunt Jemima syrup costs approximately $3 for a 12-ounce bottle. On the other hand, the same quantity of _pure_ maple syrup costs almost $8. So what's the difference? A lot of it has to do with the time it takes to make maple syrup and the quantity that is produced from the collected sap. Let's take a trip to a sugar bush, a maple syrup production farm.

First, the farmer must tap the trees in mid- to late winter. To tap the tree, the farmer drills a small hole in the base of the trunk on the sunniest side of the tree so that the sap will flow freely from the hole. After a hole is created, the famer inserts a spile, a small metal shaft with a spout on the front, into the hole so that the sap can drip off the spout and into the bucket hanging below the spile. A cover is then placed over the bucket to prevent rain, bark, and other debris from mixing with the sap. Once sap accumulates in the bucket, it is collected and boiled for hours until the water has evaporated, leaving the sugary sweet maple syrup behind.

Although that may not sound like a lot of work, the catch is that the farmer has to collect 40 gallons of sap to produce one gallon of maple syrup! That's why the real deal is so expensive. The length of time it takes to make a gallon of syrup increases the value of the product.

King David knew the value of God's Word. He knew that the truths of Scripture are more valuable than riches, fame, good food, friends, or even family.

What value do you place on the Word of God? Are you willing to dig through the Bible to find the sweet truths that God wants to reveal to you? It may take you a while to read through the Bible (like collecting 40 gallons of sap), but in the end you will be left with _pure_ truth (like the real maple syrup). Trust me: it's worth it!

NEXT STOP: Dummerston, Vermont

Buried in Snow

"Come now, let us settle the matter," says the Lord.
"Though your sins are like scarlet, they shall be as white as snow;
though they are red as crimson, they shall be like wool." **Isaiah 1:18.**

On average, the northeastern part of Vermont gets approximately 80 inches (more than six feet) of snow each year. With 20 ski resorts in the state, many people enjoy winter sports such as skiing, snowboarding, snowmobiling, cross-country skiing, and snowshoeing. But what about golf?

Rudyard Kipling, author of *The Jungle Book*, lived in Dummerston, Vermont, in the 1890s. A man who enjoyed the gentlemen's game of golf, Kipling found the sport relaxing, especially while writing his book. But he had to figure out what to do in the winter when there were feet of snow on the ground and no green grass for miles on which to play golf.

His solution? He decided to simply play in the snow. I'm sure you're wondering how he could possibly find a small, white golf ball in a field of snow. Well, he painted his golf balls red and placed red cups in the snow as holes to aim for.

And believe it or not, Kipling's backyard game turned into an honest-to-goodness modern-day sport in the 1990s. The annual world ice golf championship has been held in Greenland since 1997, and the first two-day European championship in snow golf was held in Switzerland in January 2011.

I don't know if today's modern snow golfers paint their golf balls red, but even if they do, I can only imagine how many golf balls have been lost in the snow that aren't found until the snow golf course thaws in the spring.

If you look at today's verse, God promises us that He will wash away our sins, which He compares to the color red, and make us as white as snow. Just as the snow swallows up the red golf balls and hides them from the golfer's view, our sins are covered by God's perfect love.

Are there any sins in your life that you haven't confessed to the Lord? If so, take the time right now to talk to God and ask Him to make your heart as white as snow.

NEXT STOP: Stowe, Vermont

January 16

Hello out there!

Fleeing for Their Lives

> Saul was told that David had gone to Keilah, and he said, "God has delivered him into my hands, for David has imprisoned himself by entering a town with gates and bars." And Saul called up all his forces for battle, to go down to Keilah to besiege David and his men. **I Samuel 23:7, 8.**

The Trapp Family Lodge is a mountain resort located in Stowe, Vermont, that features an alpine lodge, guest chalets, and villas modeled after Austrian architecture. You see, the von Trapp family was originally from Austria. The family immigrated to the United States in 1939 after leaving Nazi-occupied Austria, settling in Pennsylvania for three years before purchasing a farm in Stowe that reminded them of the homeland they dearly missed.

Their family story became famous when a Broadway musical was written about their escape from Austria. Six years later the movie *The Sound of Music* was released, which fictionalized the story of Maria, who came to live with the von Trapp family to serve as a governess, or nanny, to Baron Georg von Trapp's seven children after their mother died. As the movie unfolds, Georg watches Maria work with the children, he falls in love with her, and she with him. They flee their home almost immediately after their marriage. In real life, the von Trapp family left Austria 11 years after Georg and Maria wed.

The von Trapp family is not the only family in history to have fled from their homeland. King David, before he became king, spent years running from King Saul. In 1 Samuel 23 we read the story of one such pursuit. David had been running from Saul, but Saul's informers told him that David was staying in the city of Keilah. So Saul assembled his army and marched toward Keilah. When David heard this, he immediately prayed about the situation and asked for God's advice. The Lord made it very clear to David that it was not safe to remain in Keilah. So "David stayed in the wilderness strongholds and in the hills of the Desert of Ziph. Day after day Saul searched for him, but God did not give David into his hands" (verse 14).

Did you catch the last part of that verse? "God did not give David into his hands." God had a plan, and that plan was to keep David safe until he could be king. That didn't mean that David's life was easy, but God was in control, and David submitted his life to the Lord. Are you doing the same thing?

NEXT STOP: Pleasant Bay, Nova Scotia, Canada

I See One!

Now the Lord provided a great fish to swallow Jonah,
and Jonah was in the belly of the fish three days and three nights. **Jonah 1:17.**

Get your passport ready! We are leaving the United States for a few weeks and crossing the border into the country of Canada. If you didn't already know this, Canada is not made up of states. It is divided into 10 provinces and 3 territories. Our first stop in Canada is Nova Scotia, a beautiful destination whose slogan is "Canada's Ocean Playground." Nova Scotia is almost completely surrounded by water, so there is plenty of ocean to play in!

Located at the northern tip of Nova Scotia is the town of Pleasant Bay. On a sunny day in July (it rained the other three days we spent in Nova Scotia), our family drove to Pleasant Bay, where we boarded a boat that took us out in the Gulf of Saint Lawrence in search of whales. I had always wanted to go on a whale-watching tour, so I was very excited! We didn't see a humpback or blue whale or any of their large cousins, but we saw a lot of pilot whales, which are a member of the dolphin family. Dark gray or black in color, pilot whales usually measure between 18 and 21 feet in length and are extremely social and friendly. We saw large pods swimming and playing together, and a mama and baby swam within two feet of the boat!

I couldn't stop snapping pictures and scanning the horizon for the next pod. Although these whales are friendly, I wouldn't have wanted to get in the water with them. I would have been scared to swim with creatures so much larger than I was.

Have you ever thought about how Jonah must have felt being swallowed by a great fish? I can't imagine how frightened he must have been as something dark and mysterious swam toward him and opened its giant mouth. Maybe he gulped in a big breath of air before the rush of water propelled him toward the creature's stomach. The Bible doesn't tell us exactly how it happened. But what we do know is that Jonah had a long talk with God while in the belly of the great fish, where he stayed for three days and three nights.

Like Jonah, do you pray only when you're stuck in a rotten situation? Or do you talk to God during the good and bad times? I hope you talk to Him all the time! He's listening right now, so tell Him what you're thinking and feeling as you start a new day.

NEXT STOP: Baddeck, Nova Scotia

Hello out there!

Ring, Ring

One day Jesus was praying in a certain place. When he finished, one of his disciples said to him, "Lord, teach us to pray, just as John taught his disciples." **Luke 11:1.**

Today we are visiting the small village of Baddeck, where Alexander Graham Bell built a summer home and laboratory in 1886. Over the next 30 years of his life, his stays at his estate in Baddeck lengthened beyond just the summer months as he absorbed himself in his experiments.

During his lifetime Bell was granted 30 patents, 18 with his name on them and 12 in collaboration with other inventors. These patents covered such things as aerial vehicles, hydroplanes, a phonograph, telegraphs, and telephones. He even invented an audiometer, which is used to detect hearing problems. Although he invented countless machines and dedicated a great deal of his career to developing methods of teaching deaf people how to speak, he is best known for his invention of the telephone—a device that transformed how people communicated.

Can you imagine a world without telephones? Phones, especially cell phones, are a part of our daily existence. You don't think anything about picking up the phone to call your friends and plan a Sabbath-afternoon hike or discuss a homework assignment. And even if you won't admit it, I bet it makes you feel better to know that your parents are only a phone call away when you're on a school outing or Pathfinder campout. Think about it: If you got hurt on a Pathfinder campout, your director could quickly call your parents to come pick you up and take you home. It's comforting to know that someone who loves you is only a phone call away.

But there is Someone else who is only a "phone" call away. That's right. Jesus is available 24/7 through a direct line called prayer.

Jesus knew the power of prayer. He spent hours praying to God the Father. Jesus knew He couldn't make it through the day without asking God for guidance, strength, wisdom, or whatever else He needed. Although His disciples missed some things, they recognized the importance of staying connected to God, and they asked Jesus to teach them how to pray. You can read the Lord's Prayer in Luke 11:2-4. In fact, read through verse 13. Jesus not only teaches His disciples how to pray, but also assures them, and us, that God is listening and will answer our prayers as only a loving Father can. Remember, God is only a "phone" call away.

NEXT STOP: Louisbourg, Nova Scotia

A Mighty Fortress

Find rest in God; my hope comes from him. Truly He, is my rock and my salvation; he is my fortress, I will not be shaken. My salvation and my honor depend on God; he is my mighty rock, my refuge. **Psalm 62:5-7.**

The Fortress of Louisbourg loomed in the distance as our tour bus bumped along a winding dirt road from the visitors' center to the site of the original fortress, which was now a living history village with blacksmiths, bakers, musicians, soldiers, and street vendors dressed in costumes and portraying life as it was in the 1740s.

As we walked through the enormous wooden gates, two soldiers welcomed us to the fortress. The fog was heavy, and a light rain fell as we made our way through the muddy streets, stopping in houses and shops and walking through carefully designed vegetable gardens filled with leafy greens. (We noticed that there were no tomato plants, so we asked an interpreter why no tomatoes were being grown, and we learned that the French thought tomatoes were poisonous. Bet you didn't know that!)

French people built the Fortress of Louisbourg in 1713, and it quickly became a bustling fishing and commercial port. As it grew in importance, its residents constructed the wall surrounding the town to protect it from attack. Nevertheless, British colonists captured the fortress in 1745. Then it was returned to French control in 1748. However, 10 years later British forces once again attacked and captured the fortress, at which time they began destroying it.

The fortress had a strong defense along the Atlantic Ocean, but it was built on low-lying ground and was weak if attacked on land. The British knew this and used it to their advantage.

Satan knows where you are weak, too. Do you struggle with lying, cheating, getting angry, eating too much food, keeping secrets from your parents, holding grudges? He will tempt you and push your buttons until he breaks down your wall and gets you to fall. But we have to remember that we have a secret weapon. If we build our lives on the Rock, we will not be shaken. As King David wrote, God is our fortress, our Rock, our refuge, and our salvation. When the enemy is beating against you and you feel like you're going to lose, remember that God is on your side. Ask Him for help! He's always ready and willing to rescue His children.

NEXT STOP: Bay of Fundy, Nova Scotia

January 20

Hello out there!

Rising Waters

Then Moses stretched out his hand over the sea, and all that night the Lord drove the sea back with a strong east wind and turned it into dry land. The waters were divided, and the Israelites went through the sea on dry ground, with a wall of water on their right and on their left. **Exodus 14:21, 22.**

Have you ever been to a beach on vacation and seen signs posted displaying information about the high and low tides? Lifeguards post the high and low tide times so that swimmers, and surfers on some beaches, aren't caught off guard when the sea levels start to rise or fall, a phenomenon caused by the gravitational forces of the moon and the sun and the rotation of the earth.

The average tidal change on most beaches is a couple of feet, but not so in the Bay of Fundy, which holds the *Guinness Book of World Records* title for the highest tides, ranging from 47.5 to 53.5 feet. The power of nature is evident each day as the waters recede at low tide, leaving rocks, pebbles, seaweed, and small creatures such as scallops exposed on the bottom of the sea.

Curious tourists wishing to explore the Bay of Fundy at low tide must be alert to the start of the high tide because the water can return as quickly as 32 feet per minute! You definitely don't want to be far from shore when the water begins rising and flowing back into the bay! Being caught off guard in the Bay of Fundy could spell disaster.

Just as God is in control of the oceans' tidal streams, He was in control thousands of years ago when He instructed Moses to stretch out his hand over the Red Sea, which God then miraculously parted so the children of Israel could cross to safety.

However, like the foolish tourist who wanders too far from shore and is caught by the high tide, Pharaoh and the Egyptians realized too late whom they were really fighting against—the King of the universe. "During the last watch of the night the Lord looked down from the pillar of fire and cloud at the Egyptian army and threw it into confusion. . . . And the Egyptians said, 'Let's get away from the Israelites! The Lord is fighting for them against Egypt'" (Exodus 14:24, 25). At that moment the Lord instructed Moses to stretch out his hand, and the waters crashed down on the Egyptian army, killing every single man.

Don't be caught off guard by ignoring God's instructions. His ways are good!

NEXT STOP: Cape Breton Island, Nova Scotia

Throwing a Party

In the same way, I tell you, there is rejoicing in the presence of the angels of God over one sinner who repents. **Luke 15:10.**

Cape Breton Island is connected to Nova Scotia by a 4,544-foot rock causeway. The island is made up of lakes, rocky shores, glacial valleys, mountains, woodlands, and areas of farmland. The island is also home to many different types of animals, including moose (they claim to have a large population, but they were apparently playing hide-and-seek when we were looking for them), bald eagles, fox, snowshoe hare, and Canada lynx. The tree-covered mountains, plunging valleys, and rocky coastline are beautiful.

It was raining on our last day on the island, and we decided to stroll through the gift shops in the little town near where we were staying. As we prepared to leave one store and run through the rain to the next shop up the street, a man gave us a flyer and invited us to an event featuring Gaelic folk music—the island has embraced its heritage and tried to revive some of the Scottish culture, including the Gaelic language and music.

On the flyer the event was spelled *ceilidh*, but the man pronounced it "Kaylee," which is my name—Kalie—only spelled differently. I was startled to hear him say my name when the word on the piece of paper looked nothing like my name. When we asked about the meaning, he said *ceilidh* meant a party. Later I looked up the word and discovered that there are a number of different meanings, including a visit, party, concert, or social gathering. Regardless of the meaning you select, my name in Gaelic is associated with a celebration. I like that!

But when I stop and think about it, every single person's name on this planet is associated with a celebration—a celebration in heaven. In the parable of the lost coin Jesus in Luke 15:10 tells His listening audience what the woman's great rejoicing represents. There is a *ceilidh*, a party, in heaven each time someone gives his or her heart to God. Has heaven thrown a party for you? I hope so.

NEXT STOP: Prince Edward Island, Canada

January 22

God Is Great

The disciples were amazed. "Who is this man?" they asked. "Even the winds and waves obey him!" **Matthew 8:27, NLT**.

Welcome to Prince Edward Island, the smallest of Canada's provinces in terms of area and population. This beautiful little island features rolling hills, farmland, and miles of coastline with small coves and reddish-colored sandy beaches. The island, which is also known by the name PEI, is west of Cape Breton Island, Nova Scotia, in the Gulf of St. Lawrence.

The motto of the island is "the small under the protection of the great." If you aren't sure what a motto is, it is a short phrase that sums up the beliefs or ideals of a group of people. I don't know if the leaders who chose the motto for PEI were religious or not, but when I read the motto, I immediately thought about God. "The small" stands for *us*, and we are "under the protection of the great," which is God.

Can you think of some Bible stories in which God showed His people that He was watching out for them and protecting them? There are so many! The Bible is full of stories of God's protection and guidance, but today I want to look at the story of Jesus calming the storm in Matthew 8:23-27.

Jesus had spent a busy day healing people and preaching. I'm sure He was tired and worn out from all the walking and constant crowds pressing in around Him. As the crowd squeezed in tighter around Jesus, He decided it was time to leave, so He got in a boat with His disciples and ordered them to cross the lake. Once settled in the boat, Jesus fell asleep. Then the Bible tells us that without warning "a fierce storm struck the lake, with waves breaking into the boat. But Jesus was sleeping" (verse 24). This doesn't sound like a little rain shower. This sounds like a dangerous storm, especially if you're in the middle of a lake without any shelter!

The disciples were afraid—as I would have been—but Jesus took care of His friends, who were small compared to His greatness. He "got up and rebuked the wind and waves, and suddenly there was a great calm" (verse 26). He fixed the problem. He protected the people He loved.

Jesus is the same yesterday, today, and forever! He will protect you just as He protected His disciples.

NEXT STOP: Charlottetown, PEI

The Beauty of Sand

Charm is deceptive, and beauty does not last; but a woman who fears the Lord will be greatly praised. **Proverbs 31:30, NLT.**

Prince Edward Island is known for its red sand that is visible on the dirt roads, beaches, and cliffs around the island. The rocks and sand are a beautiful shade of rusty red that makes PEI unique.

In the capital city of Charlottetown, sand sculptors use tons of this reddish-brown sand to create the most amazing sand sculptures you have ever seen. Ask your parents to do a Google search for "PEI sand sculptures" so that you can see some of the life-size sculptures that depict what it is like to live on PEI. From farming and fishing, to potatoes and the characters from the book *Anne of Green Gables*, the red sand makes the sculptures stand out in contrast to their surroundings.

Similar to how the red sand stands out against the blue sky or water or the green fields, someone who is like Jesus stands out in contrast to the world around them.

Today's text specifically addresses women, but it can be applied to everyone. Boys and girls, men and women, can be charming and attractive, but that doesn't last. People get old, and looks change. But a person who is kind and loving will never go out of style.

Have you ever tried to become friends with the cute boy in your class or the pretty girl at school only to find out that when you get to know them, they demand things from you, gossip about you, or treat you as if you were scum? Do those kinds of people make you want to stay friends with them? Do they look so cute or beautiful when they treat you so poorly?

Make sure you are beautiful on the *inside*, not just the outside. It's what's on the inside that matters in your journey to heaven. Make sure your inner beauty matches God's outline of a gorgeous person according to the Bible.

NEXT STOP: Alberton, PEI

January 24

Protect the Crops

*The Lord said to Moses, "Speak to the Israelites and say to them:
'When you cross the Jordan into Canaan, drive out all the inhabitants
of the land before you. Destroy all their carved images and their cast idols,
and demolish all their high places.'"* **Numbers 33:50-52.**

The town of Alberton is on the far west coast of Prince Edward Island. Like many of the towns on the island, Alberton is a farming community, and its staple crop is potatoes, used to make French fries and potato chips or to sell for general cooking. This small island produces 2.8 billion pounds of potatoes each year! That's a lot of spuds!

The government of PEI takes its potato crops seriously. Because potatoes are a major source of cash for the residents of the island, the government does everything they can to make sure the crops succeed and produce well. One way PEI protects its crops is by not allowing anyone to bring potatoes in from another country.

When we crossed the border into Canada on our trip to Prince Edward Island, the border patrol asked us where we were going. When we told the officer we were driving to PEI, he asked if we had any potatoes with us. I thought that was a strange question until I learned the reasoning behind it. If we had brought potatoes onto the island, they could have been carrying a disease or bug that could have affected the crops. Therefore, to be safe, they don't allow any potatoes that are not grown on PEI to come onto the island.

In the same way, God tried to protect the children of Israel from being affected by the heathen people in the land of Canaan by having the Israelites drive out all of the inhabitants and destroy all of their idols. God knew the weaknesses of the Israelites, and He was trying to protect them from becoming infected by idol worship. God even warned them about the problems that would beset them if they didn't follow His command. "But if you do not drive out the inhabitants of the land, those you allow to remain will become barbs in your eyes and thorns in your sides. They will give you trouble in the land where you will live" (Numbers 33:55).

Unfortunately, the Israelites did not follow God's instructions, and they suffered for years to come because of their bad choices. Are you following God's instructions? Do you protect yourself from being infected by the things of this world? Think about it.

NEXT STOP: Cavendish, PEI

A Picture of Heaven

Instead, they were longing for a better country—
a heavenly one. Therefore God is not ashamed to be called their God,
for he has prepared a city for them. **Hebrews 11:16.**

Have you ever heard of the book *Anne of Green Gables*? Even if you haven't heard of it, everyone on Prince Edward Island has! The author, Lucy Maud Montgomery, was born and raised on Prince Edward Island and spent most of her time in Cavendish. Published in 1908, *Anne of Green Gables* has sold more than 50 million copies since then.

For those of you who have not read the book, the main character, Anne Shirley, is a redheaded orphan who comes to live at Green Gables with Matthew and Marilla Cuthbert, a brother and sister who are in their 50s. The Cuthberts wanted to adopt a boy to help with the chores, but after a week or so of having Anne around on a trial basis, they decide to keep her. Anne is extremely talkative and has an imagination that runs wild with ideas and stories.

Anne's imagination causes her to look at her surroundings differently than those who have lived in the town all their lives. Her excitement over having a real home brings out the best of her creativity. On their way to Green Gables from the train station, Anne and Matthew are riding in the buggy when they turn down a lane lined with apple trees that are covered with white blossoms. She asks the name of the road, and Matthew tells her that it is called the Avenue. She informs him that that is too common a name, so she renames it the White Way of Delight. On their ride, they also pass a pond, the name of which she changes to the Lake of Shining Waters. In her mind, the places are too beautiful to have ordinary names.

What do you imagine heaven will be like? I think the sea of glass definitely qualifies as a lake of shining waters! It's hard to picture streets of gold, a sea of glass, the tree of life, pearl gates, or mansions on every corner. But God has promised us that He is preparing heaven for us to enjoy. Let your imagination run wild today, and dream about heaven. Think about the things you will eat, the interesting people you will meet, the animals you will play with, and the most important person there, Jesus, who wants to sit and talk to *you*!

NEXT STOP: Confederation Bridge, PEI

January 26

Hello out there!

Connections

"Yes, I am the vine; you are the branches. Those who remain in me, and I in them, will produce much fruit. For apart from me you can do nothing." **John 15:5, NLT.**

Today we are leaving Prince Edward Island and traveling to the province of New Brunswick, which we will be touring for the next five days. However, we are on an island, so how are we getting off? Before 1997 the only way to get on and off the island was by ferry. Today the island is connected to the mainland of Canada by the Confederation Bridge, an eight-mile-long bridge!

The next time you get in the car, ask your mom or dad to pay attention to the mileage and tell you when you have driven eight miles. It's a long, long, long bridge! If you get nervous crossing bridges, being suspended over water and not being able to see land, this bridge is not for you.

Although people may get nervous on the bridge, it serves as an important connection between PEI and the rest of Canada. Once isolated and harder to reach, PEI is now easier to travel to thanks to this impressive concrete structure.

Just as the Confederation Bridge connects two pieces of land, a relationship with Jesus connects us to God and helps us to grow in the image of our Creator. In today's text Jesus uses the example of a vine to represent Himself and its branches to represent us. If we stay connected to Jesus, we will be the person He wants us to be, but apart from Him, we will be nothing.

The verse also says that we will bear fruit if we are connected to Jesus. That means that people will know we are Christians by our actions. When you mow the lawn without being asked or help unload the dishwasher as a surprise for your mom, you are letting Jesus shine through you. When you volunteer to collect the offering or read the Bible story in the Beginners' Sabbath school, you are bearing good fruit. When you help clean up the classroom after school or clear tables after potluck, you are showing others that God lives in you.

The character traits of kindness and thoughtfulness that Jesus demonstrated when He was growing up are visible in your life when you stay connected to the vine. Think about the fruit you are bearing as you go through your day.

NEXT STOP: New Brunswick, Canada

Two Sides

*It would have been better for us to serve the Egyptians
than to die in the desert!* **Exodus 14:12.**

Welcome to New Brunswick, Canada, home of the warmest saltwater beaches north of Virginia and one of the longest snowmobiling seasons south of the Arctic. "What?" you're probably asking. "Did you write that correctly?" Yes, I did.

Although it doesn't seem possible, that's what New Brunswick offers Canadians and tourists who want the best of both worlds as far as summer and winter outdoor activities are concerned.

Do you ever want the best of both worlds? You want to play on the school's soccer team and be in band, but they meet at the same time. You want to play on the computer, but you want a good grade on your history test tomorrow. What should you do?

As you think about that, let's read about the Israelites and their desire for the best of both worlds. In Exodus 2 the Israelites cried out to God to deliver them from their horrible living conditions: "The Israelites groaned in their slavery and cried out, and their cry for help because of their slavery went up to God. God heard their groaning and he remembered his covenant with Abraham, with Isaac and with Jacob" (verses 23, 24). That's when God sent Moses to represent Him before Pharaoh and demand that the children of Israel be released.

Now fast-forward to their wandering in the desert. Although they were free and their enemies had been destroyed in the Red Sea, the people said to Moses, "Was it because there were no graves in Egypt that you brought us to the desert to die? What have you done to us by bringing us out of Egypt? Didn't we say to you in Egypt, 'Leave us alone; let us serve the Egyptians'? It would have been better for us to serve the Egyptians than to die in the desert!" (Exodus 14:11, 12).

The children of Israel wanted the best of both worlds. They wanted a home and the security of food and water in Egypt, but they wanted to be free from slavery, which required them to leave the life they knew. If they had only trusted in God, they would have been OK.

So when you are faced with the dilemma between deciding between the best of both worlds, ask God for His opinion. And then be willing to follow His advice.

NEXT STOP: Deer Island, New Brunswick

January 28

Hello out there!

Giant Sucking Noises

Rescue me from the mire, do not let me sink; deliver me from those who hate me, from the deep waters. Do not let the floodwaters engulf me or the depths swallow me up or the pit close its mouth over me. **Psalm 69:14, 15.**

Today we are visiting Deer Island, New Brunswick, and the largest tidal whirlpool in the Western Hemisphere. A whirlpool is similar to a tornado, but in water. (Fill your bathtub and then unplug the drain; the water near the drain will turn into a small whirlpool, which produces a funnel or tornado effect.) The name of the whirlpool is Old Sow, because the story goes that it sounds like a pig when the water is really churning, making a giant sucking sound. The whirlpool is approximately 250 feet in diameter—way bigger than you can recreate in your bathtub!

This unique natural phenomenon is caused by the tidal streams we learned about the other day when we visited the Bay of Fundy. As you can imagine, if you got sucked into the whirlpool, you probably wouldn't make it out. The forces of nature would be too strong and would pull you into the funnel and bury you in a cyclone of water.

Although you would never be so foolish as to swim in the water near Old Sow, do you stay far away from sin? Satan is in the habit of sucking us into bad habits or situations and trying to drown us. For example, at first you might watch a TV show in which there is an occasional bad word. You know you shouldn't talk that way, so you reason that it won't affect you. But before you know it, you're watching other shows where the characters use more and more bad language. Then you start to slip further with shows that feature lying, theft, murder, adultery . . . the list can go on and on.

You see, Satan knows that if he can get us to try something and compromise our standards now, we will be more likely to compromise them further in the future. If you were to get in the water at the edge of the whirlpool, you might be able to swim for a while. But soon you would get tired and would drift closer to the funnel as the current pulled you along.

Sin is the same way. Your safest location is on the shore with Jesus by your side. What sins are you struggling with? What bad habits are sucking you toward bigger problems? Get out while you can. Ask Jesus to rescue you. He's the best lifeguard you could ever meet!

NEXT STOP: St. Stephen, New Brunswick

January 29

Surprise!

Once when Zechariah's division was on duty and he was serving as priest before God, he was chosen by lot, according to the custom of the priesthood, to go into the temple of the Lord and burn incense. **Luke 1:8, 9.** *Then an angel of the Lord appeared to him. . . . When Zechariah saw him, he was startled and was gripped with fear.* **Verses 11, 12.**

The oldest candy company in Canada is located in St. Stephen, New Brunswick. Ganong Bros., Ltd., was founded by two brothers in 1873, and to this day the company makes boxed chocolates. Ganong Bros. was the first company in North America to create a heart-shaped box filled with chocolates. The special box soon found a spot on store shelves on Valentine's Day, making it an immediate hit with customers.

What is your favorite boxed chocolate? Do you like the caramel kind? Or the ones with nuts? What about the creamy fruit-flavored chocolates? Do you like to just pick one and be surprised, or do you grab the chart that usually comes with a box of chocolates and look to see what flavor each candy is before you pop one into your mouth?

I prefer not to be surprised when I open a box of chocolates because I really don't like the fruit-flavored ones. I avoid them at all costs! But sometimes we can't avoid surprises, and when they are surprises from God, we would be smart to follow God's lead.

Throughout earth's history, God has surprised a number of His followers, including Zechariah, who is the focus of today's text. God sent an angel to Zechariah to share with him the good news that he and Elizabeth would have a very special baby boy. Zechariah was so surprised and shocked by the angel's announcement that he asked, "How can I be sure of this? I am an old man and my wife is well along in years" (Luke 1:18).

In response to Zechariah's doubt, the angel answered, "I am Gabriel. I stand in the presence of God, and I have been sent to speak to you and to tell you this good news. And now you will be silent and not able to speak until the day this happens, because you did not believe my words, which will come true at their appointed time" (verses 19, 20).

So although you may not like surprises, learn from Zechariah, and if Jesus surprises you with a special mission or calling, listen and do what He asks. You won't regret it!

NEXT STOP: Magnetic Hill, New Brunswick

January 30

Hello out there!

Magic Tricks

In the morning his mind was troubled,
so he sent for all the magicians and wise men of Egypt. Pharaoh told them
his dreams, but no one could interpret them for him. **Genesis 41:8.**

If your parents drove to the bottom of a hill and put the car in neutral, could it roll back up the hill? I can hear you saying, "Of course not. That's impossible." Well, not if you visit Magnetic Hill near the city of Moncton in New Brunswick. For a small fee, tourists can drive their car to the end of the road, place it in neutral, and the vehicle will roll backwards, which appears to be uphill. Some call it magic, while others know it is an optical illusion.

The slope of Magnetic Hill, which is also known as a gravity hill, is so slight that drivers can't tell the angle of the road. This illusion is often caused by a hidden horizon. Without a defined horizon it is difficult to judge the slope of the road, thus creating the illusion of a magnetic hill that pulls cars back up to the top of the hill once they are at the bottom.

Even though I know it is an optical illusion, it is amazing to watch cars roll "uphill"—it certainly plays tricks on your mind.

Although I do not believe in magic, many people around the world do. People have believed in the power of magic for thousands of years. Take, for example, the Egyptians. The pharaohs could not operate without magicians and wise men in their courts. They called on them regularly to give them advice and ask them to interpret dreams.

In today's text we learn that Pharaoh had a dream, which he asked his magicians and wise men to interpret. But they couldn't do it! Why? Because there wasn't anything magical about them. They didn't possess special superhero mind-reading powers.

Pharaoh then finds out that there is a young Hebrew who can interpret dreams, so he calls for Joseph. Did Joseph possess any magical powers? No, not of his own, but with God, he had power. "Pharaoh said to Joseph, 'I had a dream, and no one can interpret it. But I have heard it said of you that when you hear a dream you can interpret it.' 'I cannot do it,' Joseph replied to Pharaoh, 'but God will give Pharaoh the answer he desires'" (Genesis 41:15, 16).

Joseph was quick to give credit where credit was due—God had the power, not he. If you let God work through you, you *can* do powerful things for Him.

NEXT STOP: Saint John, New Brunswick

38

Stand Still

The sun stopped in the middle of the sky and delayed going down about a full day. There has never been a day like it before or since, a day when the Lord listened to a human being. Surely the Lord was fighting for Israel! **Joshua 10:13, 14.**

Today we are traveling to Saint John where another interesting act of nature, called Reversing Falls, takes place on the Saint John River. Do you get the feeling that things in New Brunswick go in the wrong direction? It's kind of humorous.

Reversing Falls is caused by—surprise, surprise—the tides from the Bay of Fundy. The drastic changes in low tide and high tide affect a lot of the waterways in New Brunswick that feed into the bay. Here is how it works. When the tide in the bay is low, the river empties into the bay, creating a series of rapids and whirlpools through a narrow gorge near the Reversing Falls Bridge. Then, at high tide the river slowly changes courses, during which there is a short period of time where the water is level and there are no rapids. However, that quickly changes as the tide continues to rise to a level that is 14 feet higher than the river, thus reversing the flow of the river and creating a "reverse" waterfall near the bridge. This natural wonder occurs about every 12½ hours.

The power of nature causes Reversing Falls, but God, the most powerful natural force in the universe, can override the laws of nature when needed. For instance, look at the story of Joshua when he marched to Gibeon to fight the Amorites. After an all-night march, Joshua took the enemy by surprise and defeated them at Gibeon, sending them running. The Israelite army pursued the Amorites. It was then that God helped the Israelites by hurling hailstones down on the enemy, which killed more than had died from the Israelites' swords! Talk about using natural forces to your advantage! But the best was yet to come.

Joshua and his army were still pursuing their enemies, but since it was getting late in the day, Joshua prayed and asked the Lord to make the sun stand still. And the Lord did as Joshua requested. Read today's text again. This Bible story confirms that God has all authority over nature and will use it to help His children. Just as God fought for Israel back then, He fights for us today.

NEXT STOP: Newfoundland and Labrador, Canada

February 1

Hello out there!

A Thousand Steps

But I do not consider my life of any account as dear to myself, so that
I may finish my course and the ministry which I received from the Lord Jesus,
to testify solemnly of the gospel of the grace of God. **Acts 20:24, NASB.**

Welcome to Newfoundland and Labrador, a unique Canadian province that is made up of two separate landmasses. Newfoundland is an island surrounded by the Atlantic Ocean, while Labrador is connected to the mainland of Canada. The two areas of land are separated by the Strait of Belle Isle. Although much of its landmass is tundra, which means that not many trees grow because of cold temperatures and short growing seasons, a well-known mountain region runs up the western coast of Newfoundland, linking it to the United States.

This mountain range begins in Alabama and runs up the East Coast of the United States, ending in Newfoundland. Ever heard of the Appalachian Mountain range?

Winding through the mountain range is the famous Appalachian Trail that many people attempt to hike each year, hoping to complete the entire trail in five to seven months. The trail begins in Maine and ends in Georgia, or vice versa if you are going from south to north. The total length of the trail is about 2,200 miles.

In 2003 a proposal was submitted to extend the trail to include Newfoundland. Thus, the International Appalachian Trail would add many more miles to an already long hike.

Of the people who attempt to hike the entire trail in one season, only 29 percent of thru-hikers accomplish their goal (as of 2006). I'm guessing that number will be even lower when the International Appalachian Trail is open. So what happens to the other 71 percent who drop out and don't finish the hike?

As Paul says, only those who finish the race of life will receive a crown of glory in heaven. Is your goal to finish the race and be with Jesus in heaven? If so, what are you doing to train for the hike of your life? Are you filling your mind with godly thoughts, images, and words? Are you helping other people and showing them God's love? Or are you sitting on the couch hoping you'll make it? It's your choice. But for me, I plan to grab my hiking boots and get out there. I've got a trail to conquer, and a goal to reach—heaven!

NEXT STOP: The Island of Newfoundland

No Snakes!

Now the serpent was more crafty than any of the wild animals
the Lord God had made. He said to the woman, "Did God really say,
'You must not eat from any tree in the garden'?" **Genesis 3:1.**

You may love snakes, and that's fine, but I don't like them. They scare me to death! When I'm hiking in the woods and see one on the trail, I make sure I go *way* around it. They make my skin crawl, and I never know which ones are poisonous and which ones are not, so I reason that it's better to stay away from all of them.

Up until a few years ago Newfoundland didn't have any snakes on the island, which I think isn't a bad thing! But in recent years, wildlife officials have found garter snakes on the island, which they believe are getting to the island by hitchhiking inside shipments of farm equipment. Regardless of the fact that some people would prefer keeping Newfoundland snake-free, introducing a new species to an environment can mess with the ecosystem and possibly bring in diseases that weren't there before.

I want you to imagine what would have happened if Satan hadn't worked through a snake, or serpent, and tricked Eve. Where would we be if Adam and Eve had never sinned? Could God have created the Garden of Eden without serpents? Sure He could have, but Satan would have found another way to tempt Eve.

God gives each of us the freedom to choose whether we will follow Him or Satan. God could have eliminated Satan from the world, but He gave him the same privilege He gives us—the power to decide whether we are going to obey His commands or do our own thing.

Although we wish life could be easy and we would never have to face temptations or hard decisions, the fact of the matter is that we live in a sinful world where Satan prowls like a lion, seeking to eat us for supper. God will not remove Satan so that we don't stumble and fall, but He does promise to help us if we ask.

Don't be like Eve, who fell for Satan's lies. Eliminate the snakes from your life and follow Jesus!

NEXT STOP: Channel-Port aux Basques, Newfoundland

February 3

Hello out there!

Saved

Now swear to me by the Lord that you will be kind to me and my family since I have helped you. Give me some guarantee that when Jericho is conquered, you will let me live, along with my father and mother, my brothers and sisters, and all their families. **Joshua 2:12, 13, NLT.**

A native of Newfoundland from the town of Channel-Port aux Basques, Jack Ford lived and worked for the Newfoundland Railway in a remote settlement in 1940. At that time World War II was heating up, and 21-year-old Jack enlisted in the military.

Jack quickly experienced the horrors of war. On his way to England his boat was attacked several times by German submarines. Over the next five years Jack served his country and fought for freedom; unfortunately, he was eventually captured by the enemy and sent to a prison camp in Japan. As a prisoner of war, he faced the harsh reality that he might not make it back home again.

Then, on August 9, 1945, life changed for the world when the atomic bomb was dropped on Nagasaki, Japan. In an instant, 30,000 to 40,000 people died, but not Jack. Quartered just four miles from the site where the bomb exploded, Jack survived and eventually returned home to Newfoundland.

I can't imagine what he saw as he looked at the land around him after the bomb exploded. The power of the atomic bomb completely wiped out houses, schools, hospitals, trees, parks—everything. The destruction was unlike anything anyone had ever seen before. But Jack survived.

Similarly, Rahab survived the destruction of Jericho. After hiding the Israelite spies on her rooftop, she asked them for a sign that she and her family would be safe when the army attacked the city. The spies assured her that if she placed a scarlet cord in her window, she and all her family in her house with her would be safe.

I'm sure Rahab was grateful to be saved, along with her family, when the walls of Jericho crumbled around her, but I wonder if she was also a little bit sad. Sad to think that so many people died who didn't know about the God of Israel. Tell someone about Jesus today so that they won't die without knowing about His amazing love.

NEXT STOP: Gander, Newfoundland

Being Prepared Pays Off

Then the kingdom of heaven shall be likened to ten virgins
who took their lamps and went out to meet the bridegroom.
Now five of them were wise, and five *were* foolish. **Matthew 25:1, 2, NKJV.**

In the late 1990s the world began panicking that when the clock struck midnight on January 1, 2000, all computer systems would crash, planes would fall from the sky, hospital equipment would stop working, and chaos would erupt. The problem had to do with computer coding and the changeover from x99 to x00, for 2000. Called Y2K for short, governments and companies spent billions of dollars to fix the problem and upgrade all equipment that ran on computer systems.

A lot of people were anxious about Y2K, but January 1, 2000, came and went, and the predicted problems never happened. Some people teased those who had prepared for the worst, but in the end, the people who prepared were ready for a crisis that took place nearly two years later. On September 11, 2001, two planes flew into the World Trade Center towers in New York City. In the hours after the accident, all planes were told to land wherever they could as quickly as possible. Dozens of flights crossing the Atlantic Ocean headed toward North America were rerouted to Gander International Airport in Gander, Newfoundland.

Air traffic controllers at the airport used their emergency Y2K plans to help safely land all of the flights that came to their airport. Although many people laughed at the Y2K emergency plans, being prepared may have saved hundreds of lives on September 11.

That reminds me of the parable of the 10 virgins. Five were foolish and did not have enough oil in their lamps to last until the bridegroom came, while the five wise virgins had extra oil that enabled them to refill their lamps in preparation for the bridegroom's arrival.

Sometimes we get discouraged and wonder if Jesus is ever going to come again. We may be tempted to stop studying our Bible or attending church or worshipping God, thinking that we have plenty of time to get ready for Jesus' second coming. But we don't know the day or hour of His return, so we need to be ready every day to meet Him. Make sure you are wise. You don't want to be a foolish person left trembling in fear when Jesus returns because you waited too long.

NEXT STOP: Terra Nova National Park, Newfoundland and Labrador

February 5

Hello out there!

Rare Treasure

A house is built by wisdom and becomes strong
through good sense. Through knowledge its rooms
are filled with all sorts of precious riches and valuables. **Proverbs 24:3, 4, NLT.**

It may be hard to believe that a rare flower could grow near the Arctic Circle in the cold climate of Newfoundland and Labrador, but the pink lady's slipper does. A rare, very delicate member of the orchid family, it is endangered in some regions in the United States. However, the species is still common in parts of the northern United States and Canada.

Ask your parents to help you look up a picture of this beautiful flower, which looks like a tiny slipper you could gently slide onto a doll's foot. Like its name, the flower is pink but ranges in shades from almost white to a deep magenta color.

Picking the flower before it has a chance to go through its blooming cycle will cause the plant not to regenerate or reseed so that it can grow the next year. So if you find one of these beautiful flowers in the woods, never pick it, or you could be causing the flower to become extinct.

King Solomon wrote a proverb, a simple statement that expresses a truth, about the rare and beautiful treasure of knowledge. Read the text again. Look at each part and see what it means to you.

To me, it means that if I am wise, I will build my life on God's Word. If I study and seek to understand things, my life (house) will be strong. Then as I continue to study, I will gain more and more knowledge. That knowledge will fill every corner of my life (rooms) like rare and beautiful treasures.

Knowing God and sharing your life with Him is the best treasure of all. He died for you because He loves you more than anything in the world. You are a rare treasure like the pink lady's slipper. And if you follow Him and don't allow yourself to get "picked" by Satan or destroyed in a storm or trampled by wild animals, God will "pick" you Himself when He returns.

NEXT STOP: Lake Manicouagan, Quebec, Canada

44

The "Eye of Quebec"

Open my eyes that I may see wonderful things in your law. **Psalm 119:18.**

Lake Manicouagan is the result of an asteroid that hit earth and created an impact crater, which is basically a hole in the ground that results from the asteroid slamming into the earth. The interesting thing about this lake is that there is an island in the middle of it. The lake flows around the island, which from space looks like an eye. The crater was originally 62 miles wide, but because of erosion and soil deposits, the current diameter is 45 miles, which is still quite large.

So if an asteroid hit the earth and created a huge hole, how is there an island in the middle of the lake? The answer is very scientific, but in a nutshell, the earth's crust bounced back after the crater hit, thus forming Mount Babel with a ring around it, which is the outer edge of the crater. At some point and time in history (which I do not believe happened millions of years ago, as scientists claim), the crater filled with water and formed Lake Manicouagan.

The really cool thing about this lake is that it is visible from space. It is such a distinct shape that you can't miss it. I don't know of many lakes that circle a mountain peak, so it definitely stands out.

But let's face it. If you were blind, it doesn't matter how visible it is from the ground, from an airplane, or from space, because you wouldn't be able to see it.

King David recognized that if his eyes weren't open to God's law, then he was spiritually blind, meaning that if he wasn't reading God's Word and looking for truths about His law, then he was in the dark about what God wanted him to do. King David viewed God's laws as a good thing. He realized that God's laws are designed to protect us from harm and the evil tricks that Satan throws our way.

Unfortunately, we often view God's laws as a burden and something we have to obey if we want to go to heaven. If that's what you think, I have to tell you that you've got it all wrong. Get to know Jesus first. Spend time reading about Him and talking to Him. I promise you that if you do that, you will see the "wonderful things" in God's law as David did.

NEXT STOP: Montreal, Quebec

February 7

Confusion

At one time all the people of the world spoke the same language and used the same words. **Genesis 11:1, NLT.**

Bonjour, aujourd'hui nous allons voyager à Montréal. C'est la deuxième plus grande ville de la langue française au monde, après Paris, France. C'est une ville bien animée. Les gens viennent à Montréal pour les divertissement des arts visuels, du théâtre, de la musique et de la danse. En été, le centre-ville de Montréal a beaucoup de festivals en plein air qui attirent les visiteurs du monde entier."

Any clue as to what I wrote in the first paragraph? I'm hoping you recognize a few words: Montreal, Paris, France, arts, festivals. However, those words alone aren't enough for you to piece together a whole paragraph and be able to tell me the main point. So here is the paragraph in English:

"Hello, today we are traveling to Montreal. It is the second-largest French-speaking city in the world, second to Paris, France. It's considered a very lively city. People come to Montreal to be entertained by the visual arts, theater, music, and dance. In the summer, Montreal's downtown area features countless outdoor festivals that attract visitors from around the world."

It's pretty tough when you don't speak someone's language and they are trying to share an important message with you. Imagine that you are trying to build a birdhouse with a friend who speaks only French and doesn't understand any English. Would that be somewhat of a challenge? You bet! You could use your hands to show them what to do, or you could draw pictures as to what steps need to be taken. But no matter how much you try, it will take you twice as long because of your limited communication skills.

After the Flood all the inhabitants of the earth spoke one language. But a number of people decided that they didn't trust God's promise that He would never send another flood, so they developed a plan to build a tower reaching to heaven. That way, if another flood came, they could run up the tower and escape the water. But God put a stop to their foolish plan. "Come, let us go down and confuse their language so they will not understand each other" (Genesis 11:7). Their building project came to a screeching halt when they couldn't communicate with one another. When people try to make their own plans and defy God's promises, they are always in for trouble!

NEXT STOP: Cap-Chat, Quebec

Hold On to Your Hat

Then a great and powerful wind tore the mountains apart. . . .
After the wind there was an earthquake. . . . After the earthquake
came a fire. And after the fire came a gentle whisper. I Kings 19:11, 12.

Today we are traveling to Cap-Chat, Quebec, a beautiful town on the banks of the Gulf of St. Lawrence. Rolling hills, towering evergreens, majestic mountains, clear water, and wind generators make up the scenery in this bayside town. Did your picture of the beautiful landscape change when you read about wind generators? Amid the beauty of nature stand 76 modern-day windmills.

Wind is a very powerful natural resource that many businesses are working to harness and convert into electricity. And because it doesn't hurt the environment (other than the fact that you have to get used to looking at the huge wind turbines), it is a good source of power.

God knows all about the power of wind because He created it. In fact, He used wind at various times in the Bible to save His children or teach them a lesson, such as when He sent the wind to part the Red Sea and send it crashing down again on the Egyptian army or when He allowed a storm to toss about the disciples' boat so that they would learn to trust Him.

In today's Bible text we read about how God used the wind and other natural resources to demonstrate His power to Elijah. Elijah had just won a showdown with the prophets of Baal on Mount Carmel, where God had sent fire from heaven to burn up the sacrifice, wood, altar, and water after Elijah prayed to Him and asked Him to show His power to the people of Israel. Immediately after this victory, Elijah fled to Horeb out of fear that Jezebel would kill him.

And this is where God had a talk with His prophet. He told Elijah to go stand on the mountain. First a powerful wind ripped apart the mountain and shattered rocks, then an earthquake shook the ground, and finally fire burned the area, but God was not in any of these displays of power. Instead, He then spoke to Elijah in a "gentle whisper."

God controls the world and can display His power in the forces of nature, but ultimately, He wants to draw near to us in gentleness and speak to us in a still small voice. Listen for Him today.

NEXT STOP: Forests of Quebec

February 9

Hello out there!

Timber!

> One day the group of prophets came to Elisha and told him, "As you can see, this place where we meet with you is too small. Let's go down to the Jordan River, where there are plenty of logs. There we can build a new place for us to meet." "All right," he told them, "go ahead." **2 Kings 6:1, 2, NLT.**

Quebec's forests represent 20 percent of Canada's forests, covering more than 760,000 square kilometers, which is equal to the size of Sweden and Norway combined. That's a lot of wood in one province! Approximately 70 percent of Quebec's forest is maintained by logging companies who cut the wood for timber and pulp and paper products and replant for future growth.

Wood is an essential resource that the world relies on for building purposes, even today when many structures are built out of steel and concrete block. But what about during the early years of the settlement of North America? What about during Bible times? What significance did wood play then? Of course, wood was even more important then. Wood was used to build houses, wagons, carts, furniture, boats, and utensils. Can you think of any other uses for wood?

Today's Bible story centers on trees and the wood that was needed to build a meeting place for the school of the prophets. It sounds like the building also served as their living quarters. Prophet Elisha approved of the idea to build a new meeting place, so he went with his students to the Jordan River, where they began to cut down trees.

Wood chips flew as each man picked a tree and began chopping. The steady rhythm of chopping could be heard throughout the forest, but suddenly a splash was heard near the riverbank, and then one man cried out, "Oh, Sir!" . . . "It was a borrowed ax!" (2 Kings 6:5, NLT). The iron axhead had flown off the ax he had been using and landed in the water. It seemed hopeless that he would get it back, but Elisha asked him where the axhead had fallen in. He then "cut a stick and threw it into the water at that spot. Then the ax head floated to the surface" (verse 6).

When was the last time you felt discouraged because something bad happened at school or at home and you didn't see how the situation could possibly be fixed? What was your first response? Did you pray or pout and cry? The next time you are faced with an impossible situation, ask God to help you instead of focusing on how bad the situation is.

NEXT STOP: Quebec City, Quebec

Ultimate Protection

"Don't be afraid," the prophet answered. "Those who are with us are more than those who are with them." 2 Kings 6:16.

Quebec City can lay claim to the fact that it is the only city in North America north of Mexico that is still surrounded by fortified city walls. This stone wall encircles most of Old Quebec, a historic neighborhood in Quebec City.

Of course, Old Quebec doesn't need the walls for protection today, but years ago the wall was its main source of protection and defense. In Bible times and the early years of Canadian and American history, cities were only as strong as the walls that surrounded them.

Yesterday we read about Elisha and the miracle of the floating axhead. Today we find Elisha again relying on God to provide for his needs. But as you'll learn, Elisha didn't rely on the strength of the walled city of Dothan to save him. He trusted in God for ultimate protection.

The story goes like this. "The king of Aram was at war with Israel. After conferring with his officers, he said, 'I will set up my camp in such and such a place'" (2 Kings 6:8). But God showed Elisha where the king of Aram was, so Elisha warned the king of Israel to not go near that place. Each time the king of Aram would make plans to attack the Israelites, God would send Elisha a message so that he could warn the king of Israel. This made the king of Aram really mad. He was so angry that he accused his own men of being traitors, but his officers told him that it was Elisha who was ruining his plans. So the king of Aram ordered his men to find Elisha and report back to him so that he could go capture him. Once Elisha was located, the king stormed down to Dothan with horses and chariots and surrounded the city, planning to take Elisha hostage.

The next morning Elisha woke up to a panicking servant and an army of horses and chariots surrounding the city. But was Elisha afraid? Nope! He had complete trust in God. In fact, the Lord let Elisha physically see God's protection, at which point Elisha prayed that his servant might also see and believe. "Then the Lord opened the servant's eyes, and he looked and saw the hills full of horses and chariots of fire all around Elisha" (verse 17).

God is more powerful than anything Satan can throw at us. Ask God to surround you with His wall of protection today and every day.

NEXT STOP: Hampton, New York

Hello out there!

February 11

Don't Run!

> The Lord gave this message to Jonah son of Amittai: "Get up and go to the great city of Nineveh. Announce my judgment against it...." But Jonah got up and went in the opposite direction to get away from the Lord. **Jonah 1:1-3, NLT.**

We've left Canada and returned to the United States. Now we're in New York, and over the next few months we will travel south until we reach Florida. Our first stop in the great state of New York is the home of William Miller, an important Advent preacher.

Born in 1782, William grew up doubting that God created everything or cared about humanity. With only 18 months of formal education, William taught himself everything he should've learned in school. At the age of 21 William married Lucy Smith. Nine years later he fought in the War of 1812 against the British. After the war he moved his family to Low Hampton, New York, where he bought a farm.

About this time God was working on his heart, and William became a Christian in 1816. He then set out on a quest to learn all he could from the Bible. He studied every day for two years, comparing scripture with scripture if he didn't understand a passage. While studying the book of Daniel, he pieced together the various dates and meaning of the prophecy until he came to the conclusion that Jesus would return to earth in 1843 or 1844. But he was afraid to tell anyone other than his family. All this time he kept studying the Bible. He told himself that he was a farmer, not a preacher. But God had plans for William Miller.

One day William prayed and told God that he would preach if someone asked him to. Shortly after his prayer there was a knock at the door and a young man asked him to preach at his family's church the next day. William did not even respond to the young man; he stomped out of the house and headed for a grove of maple trees on his property. There he prayed to God and reminded Him that he was only a farmer, not a preacher.

Fortunately, William did not run as Jonah did. God called Jonah, and Jonah turned the other way and ran. God called William, and although William wanted to run, he quickly changed his mind and trusted God to help him. Are you running from something God has asked you to do? Who do you want to be like, William Miller or Jonah? It's up to you to decide.

NEXT STOP: Ascension Rock, William Miller Farm, New York

A Very Sad Day

My tears have been my food day and night, while people say to me all day long, "Where is your God?" **Psalm 42:3.**

After William Miller responded to God's call, he poured his whole heart into telling others about Jesus. He first preached in August 1831, and for the next 13 years he told people about Jesus' soon return. More and more people began studying their Bibles and believing in William's message. Then one day someone set a date for Jesus' coming—October 22, 1844.

With each passing month October 22, 1844, grew closer and closer. Can you imagine the excitement of those who believed in Jesus' return on that date as the sun set on October 21, 1844? I doubt anyone slept that night as they waited for the clock to strike midnight, signaling the day of Christ's return.

On October 22 a number of people gathered at William's farm to wait for Jesus to come in the clouds. In fact, many of them waited outside on an outcropping of flat, black rocks behind the barn through a grove of trees. The rocks are now known as ascension rock.

I wonder if they began to grow anxious as each passing hour ticked by and the sun began to set on October 22. I imagine they kept telling themselves that Jesus still had a few more hours to return before midnight, but as we all know, Jesus did not return.

The Advent believers must have cried bucketfuls of tears, as King David did in today's text. And people teased them like crazy. "Where is your God?" they asked. "Why didn't He return as you thought He would?" But they didn't have answers. This was a huge test of their faith. Some stopped believing in God, but others kept studying until they understood the Bible more clearly and saw their mistake. Through their disappointment, they held on to God's promises.

What do you do when you are faced with disappointment? Do your friends ever tease you for your faith in God or for going to church on Saturday? If so, do you stand taller and stronger? Or do you start to lose your desire to follow God? As the end of the world grows closer, our faith in God will be tested. We have to stand firm today if we are going to stand firm in the end. Don't let go of God. Dry your tears and keep fighting back against Satan!

NEXT STOP: Lake Placid, New York

Hello out there!

The Underdogs

Thus David prevailed over the Philistine with a sling and a stone, and he struck the Philistine and killed him; but there was no sword in David's hand. **I Samuel 17:50, NASB.**

Lake Placid, New York, hosted the 1980 Winter Olympics. A small town in the Adirondack Mountains, Lake Placid welcomed the world to its winter wonderland. Thirty-seven countries were represented at the games, and as with any sporting event, certain teams or individuals were favored to win in their events.

One such team that was favored to win was the Soviet Union (now Russia) men's hockey team. The Soviet Union had always dominated on the ice, and this year was to be no exception. In fact, the Soviet Union had won the gold medal in ice hockey every Winter Olympic Games since 1964. Talk about a winning streak!

Not favored to win any medal, the United States slowly picked off each team in their group until they found themselves playing in the gold medal round against the Soviet Union. They still were not considered a threat. Dave Anderson, a columnist for the New York *Times*, wrote, "Unless the ice melts, or unless the United States team or another team performs a miracle . . . the Russians are expected to easily win the Olympic gold medal for the sixth time in the last seven tournaments."

The United States team was clearly the underdog. Early in the first period, the Americans fell behind, but by the end of the period the two teams were tied, 2–2. By the end of the second period, the Soviet Union was ahead by one point, 3–2. In the third period, the American team managed to tie the game, and then, with exactly 10 minutes left on the clock, the American team scored a goal and took the lead for the first time! As the minutes ticked away, they managed to block every shot the Soviet Union players fired on their goal, and they pulled out the win, 4–3!

There is always something in this life that seems to be against us. But we can beat the odds because God is on our side. David learned this firsthand when he faced Goliath. He was definitely not the favorite in that battle. Everyone thought Goliath would crush David under his pinky finger. But David trusted God—"All those gathered here will know that it is not by sword or spear that the Lord saves; for the battle is the Lord's, and he will give all of you into our hands" (1 Samuel 17:47)—and God rewarded his faith with an amazing victory!

NEXT STOP: Heart Island, New York

Shattered Dreams

"Do not store up for yourselves treasures on earth,
where moth and rust destroy, and where thieves break in and steal.
But store up for yourselves treasures in heaven, where neither moth nor rust
destroys, and where thieves do not break in or steal." **Matthew 6:19, 20, NASB.**

In celebration of Valentine's Day, we are touring Heart Island. Yup, there's an island in the Saint Lawrence River along the northern border of New York State that is named Heart Island. And there's even a castle built on it!

George Boldt was the general manager of a very fancy hotel in New York City. After vacationing in the area, he and his family fell in love with one of the islands, and in 1900 he decided to build a huge six-story stone structure that resembled a castle. Money was not an obstacle, and grand plans were laid for a magnificent staircase and ballroom, along with guest rooms, and a proposed pool and bowling lanes in the basement. George adored his wife and was building this grand home for her to enjoy.

Unfortunately, in 1904 George's wife died, and all work on Boldt Castle was immediately stopped. For the next 73 years the castle remained untouched. The harsh winter weather and occasional vandalism left the castle in ruins. Then in 1977 the Thousand Islands Bridge Authority bought Heart Island for one dollar and began restoring the buildings and completing the construction project that had begun so long ago.

Boldt Castle is now open to tourists, who can travel to the island by ferry and wander through the rooms and lush gardens surrounding the castle.

It would appear that George Boldt had it all. By human standards he was very wealthy, and he could have anything he wanted. But George's "treasures" quickly lost importance when tragedy struck. All of the money he spent did not preserve his castle or make him happy.

The Bible teaches us to store up our treasures in heaven, but we live in a world that teaches us the opposite. Every commercial on TV is designed to convince us that we need the latest and greatest electronic gadget, new food product, and so on. But God warns us that the things we want won't last forever. That's why He tells us to focus on what will last forever, such as heaven and helping our friends and neighbors get there.

NEXT STOP: Ellis Island, New York

February 15

Hello out there!

A New Start

Then Moses said to the people, "Commemorate this day,
the day you came out of Egypt, out of the land of slavery, because the Lord
brought you out of it with a mighty hand." **Exodus 13:3.**

We often take for granted the freedoms we enjoy in the United States, but people who emigrated from other countries, meaning they left their homes and came to America, often cherish the freedoms we have because they remember what it was like not to be free.

On January 1, 1892, the United States government opened Ellis Island, the first federal immigration station, on an island in New York Harbor. That day three ships landed, and 700 immigrants began a new life in America. In the first year that it was open, 450,000 immigrants filed the necessary paperwork to enter the United States.

As I walked through the massive two-story main hall where the immigrants waited in line for their paperwork to be completed and their medical clearance issued, stating that they weren't sick or carrying any diseases, I wondered how they felt about starting over in a new country. Even though they were free, I'm sure they were scared of the unknown. As a young boy, my grandfather stood in that same main room with his father and sisters waiting to enter America. Although he was young, I wonder if he was nervous because he didn't speak the language or know his way around.

Sometimes change can be scary. As the children of Israel left Egypt, I'm sure they cheered and shouted. They were finally free! But their song quickly changed when they ran out of food and water. They even told Moses that they wished they had never left Egypt!

Crazy, right? Why would anyone want to go back to being a slave? But they were so afraid of the unknown they decided they would rather be miserable and know what to expect—working long hours, being whipped, etc.—than to trust God and move forward.

Maybe your family has to move. Or maybe you're starting at a new school. Maybe someone you love has died. Or maybe your best friend won't speak to you anymore. Whatever change you are facing, you don't have to face it alone. Jesus will lead you to your own Promised Land, but you have to trust Him. Instead of running from the change or whining about it, embrace it, and God will help you adjust to whatever the change may be.

NEXT STOP: Liberty Island, New York

Symbol of Freedom

So now I am giving you a new commandment: Love each other.
Just as I have loved you, you should love each other. Your love for one another
will prove to the world that you are my disciples. **John 13:34, 35, NLT.**

If you asked people what one symbol represents America, many people would answer, "The Statue of Liberty." Located on Liberty Island in New York Harbor, the 151-foot statue is a symbol of freedom and liberty. Designed by a French sculptor, Frédéric Bartholdi, the statue was a gift from the people of France to the United States.

The statue is a robed female figure similar to the Roman goddess Libertas, who was representative of freedom in Roman history. Lady Liberty holds a torch in her right hand, a symbol of enlightenment or the spreading of knowledge to the world, and a tablet representing law in her left hand. On the tablet is inscribed the date of the American Declaration of Independence, July 4, 1776.

If the Statue of Liberty is a national symbol of America, what is the symbol of Christianity? Some would say the cross or the Christian fish. Seventh-day Adventists might say the Sabbath. But Jesus is pretty clear about how people will tell that we are His followers. Let's look at our Bible text for the day: "A new command I give you: Love one another. As I have loved you, so you must love one another. By this everyone will know that you are my disciples, if you love one another" (John 13:34, 35).

People will know we are Christians by our love. Sounds easy, right? Not always! It's hard to love the classmate who teases you and calls you names. It's hard to love your brother and sister when they break your stuff. It's hard to love your mom or dad when they yell at you because they've had a bad day.

But if we are going to be like Christ and show others that we follow Him, we have to love the people around us who aren't always lovable. So when someone is hard to love, take a deep breath, say a quick prayer (you don't even have to close your eyes—just talk to God in your head), and surprise the person who is being annoying or has hurt your feelings by loving them.

NEXT STOP: Times Square, New York City, New York

Hello out there!

February 17

Glitz! Glamour! Problems!

So they made an idol shaped like a calf, and they sacrificed to it and celebrated over this thing they had made. **Acts 7:41, NLT.**

We've spent the last two days in New York Harbor, and today we are heading to Manhattan, the most densely populated area of New York City. The streets of Manhattan are crowded with people heading in all different directions. As you walk the city blocks, skyscrapers tower overhead, blocking the sun and casting long shadows on the streets. Not only are there offices and apartments in these skyscrapers but there are *tons* of stores. You could shop till you dropped in New York City.

In midtown Manhattan there is an intersection called Times Square. With giant billboards, video screens flashing ads and messages, street vendors trying to sell tickets to the latest Broadway musical, and restaurants, hotels, and stores within walking distance on every side, Times Square overwhelms your senses. Its popularity as a tourist destination has made it the world's most visited attraction, with more than 39 million people visiting it annually, according to an October 2011 survey.

But beyond the shops, glitz, and glamour, one event attracts approximately 1 million visitors in one night—New Year's Eve. Every year since 1907 people cram into Times Square to witness the dropping of the ball. It's a huge celebration with music, noisemakers, celebrity guests, and *lots* of people.

There is nothing wrong with celebrating and throwing a party, but when you're having fun with your friends, what is your focus? Is God still a part of what you're doing, or have you pushed Him aside in the name of fun?

The children of Israel were celebrating when Moses was up on the mountain. They asked Aaron to make them a god they could worship, stating that they didn't know what had "become of this Moses" (Acts 7:40, NLT). Talk about an excuse! And, boy, was it the wrong type of celebration.

So celebrate life! Have friends over and throw a party, but remember to invite Jesus to your party.

NEXT STOP: Oneida, New York

Everywhere You Go

All this took place to fulfill what the Lord had said through the prophet: "The virgin will conceive and give birth to a son, and they will call him Immanuel" (which means "God with us"). **Matthew 1:22, 23.**

Grab your life jacket and a paddle; we're going to church! Today we are visiting the world's smallest church in Oneida, New York. Built in 1989, the church is located on a wooden platform in the center of a small pond and is accessible only by boat. The church is 28.69 square feet and can seat two people. That's cozy!

Apparently, years ago a wedding took place in the church, which could only hold the minister and the bride and groom. The rest of the guests had to sit in small boats on the pond or stand on the shore.

Churches come in all shapes and sizes. Obviously this one has earned the title as the smallest, while the largest church in the world, St. Peter's Basilica, a Roman Catholic church in Vatican City, can hold approximately 60,000 people.

Some people believe you can talk to God only when you are in a church. Other religions teach that you must travel to holy locations to be near God. However, the Bible tells us that God is with us. Before Jesus' birth, the prophets predicted His arrival, saying that a virgin would have a baby boy and call Him Immanuel, meaning "God with us."

Think about that for a minute. God sent His Son to be with people, to walk and talk with them, to heal them and save them. And when Jesus returned to heaven, He promised that the Holy Spirit would be with us. In John 14:26 Jesus said, "But the Advocate, the Holy Spirit, whom the Father will send in my name, will teach you all things and will remind you of everything I have said to you."

He didn't tell the disciples they had to go to the synagogue to talk to God. The Holy Spirit was with them wherever they went. That doesn't mean they didn't go to church to worship God and preach, but unlike some religions that say you can talk to their gods only in the temple, we know we serve a living God who is with us wherever we go. He isn't confined to a church, however big or small it may be.

NEXT STOP: Fairhaven, Massachusetts

February 19

Hello out there!

Sea Captain to Preacher

But Moses pleaded with the Lord, "O Lord, I'm not very good with words. I never have been, and I'm not now, even though you have spoken to me. I get tongue-tied, and my words get tangled." Then the Lord asked Moses, "Who makes a person's mouth? Who decides whether people speak or do not speak, hear or do not hear, see or do not see? Is it not I, the Lord? Now go! I will be with you as you speak, and I will instruct you in what to say." **Exodus 4:10-12, NLT.**

Today we're visiting the home of another Adventist pioneer: Joseph Bates. Living in the seaside village of Fairhaven, Massachusetts, Joseph grew up on the water. At age 14 he went to sea as a cabin boy.

After becoming a captain of his own ship, he required his men to behave on board. He didn't allow any drinking of alcohol or swearing on his ship. In 1818 Joseph married Prudence Nye, and before he left on one of his voyages, she packed a small New Testament Bible in his trunk. While at sea, he found the Bible and began reading it. He soon decided to follow Jesus.

Years later he heard William Miller preach about Jesus' second coming. Joseph believed the message and also began preaching. Like everyone else, Bates was disappointed when Jesus didn't return, but unlike many, he kept reading his Bible. That's when he discovered a very important truth! He learned about the seventh-day Sabbath and began telling others about what he had read. For the rest of his life, he preached and told people about God's love and His Sabbath.

Isn't it amazing to see whom God chooses to work for Him? He chose a sea captain to spread the word about the Sabbath, and He chose a weak girl, Ellen (Harmon) White, to help found the Seventh-day Adventist Church, along with countless other early Adventist pioneers.

The Bible is full of stories of ordinary people whom God used to work for Him. Moses was one of them, and he tried to get out of it. He came up with every excuse he could think of, including saying that he wasn't good at talking in front of people. And what was God's response? "Who do you think gave people the ability to talk? Who gives people the ability to see? I do, of course. I'll be with you and help you say the right things."

What is God calling you to do? Just remember, trust Him! The promise He made to Moses, He will keep with you. He'll help you know the right things to do and say.

NEXT STOP: Wareham, Massachusetts

February 20

Red as Blood

Moses and Aaron did just as the Lord had commanded. He raised his staff in the presence of Pharaoh and his officials and struck the water of the Nile, and all the water was changed into blood. **Exodus 7:20.**

Cranberries! Red. Juicy. Sweet! Not! Have you ever tasted a cranberry? Pop one into your mouth, and your jaw will tighten up as you pucker from the intense sour flavor. But throw a little sugar on them, and they are mighty tasty. Cranberries are good in juice, especially when they are mixed with other sweeter fruits, such as grapes. Some people like cranberry salads, especially at Thanksgiving and Christmas. And they are also good dried.

Today we are in Wareham, Massachusetts, at a cranberry bog. In fact, we are visiting a cranberry bog that sells their cranberries to Ocean Spray. Have you ever seen the Ocean Spray commercials where two men are standing in a pond, the water up to their waist and red cranberries floating all around them? They are standing in a bog.

Here's how it works. Cranberries grow on shrubs or vines in a field that has been dug out to make a dyke, which is a bank that surrounds the field on four sides and looks like a huge swimming pool when filled with water. When it is time to harvest the berries, the farmer floods the field and drives a special harvester through the water to remove the berries from the plants. The berries then float to the top of the water and the workers suck the berries up with a huge "vacuum" that pumps the cranberries up out of the water into a waiting truck to be taken to the factory.

As I watched the workers harvest the cranberries, it looked as if they were standing in a sea of blood—the water looked so red because of all the berries floating on top of it.

Can you imagine if the water you bathed in, got food from, and played in really turned to blood? Talk about disgusting and smelly! It must have been horrible when this first plague fell on the Egyptians. If only they had listened to God, history may have been totally different. But they chose to ignore Moses' requests, and they faced the consequences of their actions.

Consequences are a part of life, but you can choose to eliminate bad consequences by making good choices. Don't end up in a sea of blood—or cranberries! Make wise choices.

NEXT STOP: Plymouth, Massachusetts

59

February 21

Hello out there!

Broken but Not Forgotten

It is time for the Lord to act, for they have broken Your law. Therefore I love Your commandments above gold, yes, above fine gold. Therefore I esteem right all Your precepts concerning everything, I hate every false way. **Psalm 119:126-128, NASB.**

My mom warned me that Plymouth Rock was not that special, but since I was sightseeing in Boston, I decided to take a trip down to Plymouth to see the approximate location where the Mayflower landed and the Pilgrims established Plymouth Colony in 1620. We pulled up in our minivan, found a place to park, and walked a short distance to the monument near the water's edge. The monument is a large open structure with columns on all sides. In the center of the structure is a hole surrounded by an iron fence that opens to the sand below and . . . Plymouth Rock. About the size of a coffee table, the rock has the year 1620 inscribed on the top of it.

The rock used to be larger, but over the years it was broken, dragged around town by an ox to inspire the colonists fighting in the Revolution, and chipped away by people wanting a souvenir. Now preserved, the rock serves to remind us of a piece of American history.

God's law is kind of like Plymouth Rock. Sometimes it is broken, dragged around, and chipped away at. Throughout earth's history, people have tried to change God's law. King David wrote about God's law being broken.

We can't change how other people view God's law. We can't change the fact that people have attempted to change God's holy day from Sabbath to Sunday. We can't change the fact that some people choose to lie because they are helping out a friend or steal because their family needs money.

But we can change how *we* view God's law. God's law isn't meant to hit you over the head with the things you should or shouldn't do. God's law is there to protect you and help you live the best life possible. As Jesus becomes your best friend, you will want to follow the law because you love Him, not because it's in the Bible and you're told to obey. When you love someone, you want to make that person happy. The same idea applies to your relationship with God.

NEXT STOP: Plymouth Plantation, Massachusetts

A Day of Thanks

Give thanks to the Lord, for he is good!
His faithful love endures forever. **1 Chronicles 16:34, NLT.**

Thanksgiving is nine months away, but since we're in Plymouth, we're going to talk about this historic event even though it's February and not November.

Did you know that there are actually arguments among historians as to the origin of the first Thanksgiving in the United States? Some say that the first thanksgiving celebration took place in the Virginia Colony in 1619, while others believe that the Pilgrims held the first thanksgiving feast in 1621. Regardless of who celebrated first, the point is that the settlers were very thankful for surviving in their new home, and it was a cause for celebration. In the case of the Pilgrims, they did not have enough food to feed the colonists who were working hard to build shelters and gather and grow food to provide for their families.

If it hadn't been for the kindness of the Wampanoag Native Americans, who provided the Pilgrims with seed and taught them how to fish, many of the colonists would have died from starvation. As the Pilgrims brought in the harvest from the crops the Native Americans had helped them plant, they thanked God and held a feast in celebration of the harvest.

Today we celebrate Thanksgiving on the fourth Thursday in November in remembrance of God's providence, His protection and care, and the struggles the early settlers faced. But shouldn't we celebrate Thanksgiving every day? OK, maybe not with all of the food. (Your mom would never leave the kitchen if every day was Thanksgiving!) But think about it. If Thanksgiving is a day to remember how God has taken care of us, shouldn't we think about that every day?

Our Bible text tells us to thank the Lord for the good things He gives us. Stop right now and take a few minutes to thank God for at least five good things He has given you. Now read the rest of the verse, "His love endures forever," meaning His love for us will never run out or stop because of our mistakes. That's amazing love! That should be enough to make us stop again and thank Him for His never-ending love.

Just as your friends and family like to hear you say thank you for things they do for you, God smiles when you take the time to talk to Him and thank Him for all He does for you.

NEXT STOP: Boston Navy Yard, Massachusetts

February 23

Hello out there!

No ID, No Entry

Not everyone who says to me, "Lord, Lord," will enter the kingdom of heaven, but only the one who does the will of my Father who is in heaven. **Matthew 7:21.**

The U.S.S. *Constitution*, also known as Old Ironsides, is the oldest commissioned naval vessel afloat, having been launched in 1797. Fully commissioned to this day, the U.S. Navy ship has a crew of 60 officers and sailors who serve on the ship during ceremonies, educational programs, tours, and other special events.

Currently docked in the Boston Navy Yard, the U.S.S. *Constitution* was named by President George Washington in recognition of the Constitution of the United States of America. The ship's first duty was to provide protection for merchant ships crossing the Atlantic Ocean to trade goods with other countries. Then, in 1812, the ship fought against Great Britain in the War of 1812. This is when it earned its nickname, because cannonballs and gunfire seemed to bounce off the sides of the boat. It appeared to be unsinkable!

A few years ago my husband and I took our kids on a history field trip to Boston, and of course, one of our stops was the U.S.S. *Constitution*. When we reached the front of the line, a military private greeted us and asked to see our ID, either a driver's license or passport. Unfortunately, I didn't have my purse with me. All I had taken with me that day was my camera bag and two credit cards. I asked the private if my credit card with my name on it would work. But he said no. The only way I could board the ship was to prove with a photo ID that I was Kalie Kelch.

So I gave the camera to my husband, and he and our two kids toured the ship without me. I was disappointed, but it wasn't a life-or-death situation. However, we will one day face a life-and-death situation. When Jesus returns, there will be people who will feel as if they know Him. They will say, "Lord, Lord, we've done all these great things for You." But His response will surprise them—"I do not know you."

Unless your heart, which serves as your photo ID for heaven, is truly seeking God, you do not know Him. You can act like you do by going to church, helping other people, and reading your Bible, but unless you desire to follow Him, you're just playing the part of a Christian. Make sure you have your photo ID ready so that the Lord will recognize you when He comes!

NEXT STOP: Boston Harbor

February 24

Hidden Identity

So Saul disguised himself, putting on other clothes,
and at night he and two men went to the woman. "Consult a spirit for me,"
he said, "and bring up for me the one I name." **I Samuel 28:8.**

The Boston Tea Party was probably the first costume party in the colonies. However, everyone was dressed the same—as Mohawk Indians. Thirty to 130 men disguised as Indians boarded three ships anchored in Boston Harbor and tossed 342 chests of tea into the water in protest to the Tea Act that King George had signed into law on May 10, 1773.

The colonists were tired of paying taxes on whatever England dictated they should pay on, so they decided it was time to stand up for their rights. They wanted a say in deciding the laws for the colonies, and they figured they would make a statement by ruining the tea that England was trying to collect taxes on. Although these men wanted to take a stand for their rights, they were afraid of what might happen to them if someone found out about their rebellion against the crown, so they disguised themselves and tried to hide their identity.

When people disguise themselves, it's usually not a good thing. It usually means one of two things: that they are trying to trick someone else or that they are trying to hide their actions because they know they are doing something wrong.

Take a look at the story of King Saul and the witch of Endor. Saul disguised himself because he knew he was doing something wrong. His army was assembled against the Philistines, and he was scared. He had asked God for directions, but God hadn't responded. That's when Saul messed up. Instead of repenting of his past sins and making things right with God, Saul turned to the dark side. But even then, he knew he was stepping across the line into the camp of the enemy, so he disguised himself to hide from his own shame and guilt. And then he visited the witch of Endor and asked her to call up Samuel from the grave so that Samuel could give him advice. This event was Saul's last mistake, for the next day he died in battle.

The moral of the story is never to disguise yourself to do something you know is wrong. You can't hide from God, and your sins will find you out. Also, never, never, play around with the occult. Satan would love nothing more than for you to open the door to the spirit world, but once you let him in, it takes a miracle of God to rescue you from his grasp.

NEXT STOP: Boston, Massachusetts

63

February 25

Hello out there!

An Important Trade

*About that time, serious trouble developed ...
concerning the Way.* **Acts 19:23, NLT.**

What is the first thing you think of when you hear the name Paul Revere? I would guess you probably thought of his midnight ride to warn the Colonial militia that the British troops were marching on Lexington and Concord. Am I right? That's what most people remember about Paul Revere, but do you know what he did for work—what his trade was? He was a well-known silversmith in Boston.

At age 13 Paul dropped out of school and became an apprentice in his father's silver shop. As an apprentice he began learning the trade of crafting silver into utensils, silverware, dishes, bowls, buttons, rings, and decorative household pieces. A few years after his father died, Paul took over the family silver shop. The business grew because of his quality work and the fact that he could also engrave his own silver pieces, a skill most silversmiths did not possess.

Being a silversmith takes skill, and if you are good at it, you can make a lot of money. Paul Revere seemed to do well for himself, but from the stories we know about his life, he didn't seem motivated by greed. On the flip side, the Bible talks about a well-known silversmith in the city of Ephesus who was very motivated by greed. His name was Demetrius, and he built silver shrines to the god Artemis, which was a very profitable business.

However, his business began to decline when the apostle Paul came to Ephesus and began preaching about Jesus and telling people that "handmade gods aren't really gods at all" (Acts 19:26, NLT). This made Demetrius very mad. In fact, he was so angry that he finally called a meeting with his fellow craftsmen and stirred them up against Paul. Before long there was a riot in the city, and for two hours the mob shouted in unison, "Great is Artemis of the Ephesians!" (verse 34, NLT).

They were so consumed with making money that they missed out on the greatest treasure—a saving relationship with Jesus. They traded in the God of heaven for a false god, Artemis, and earthly wealth. What a foolish choice.

What motivates you? Fame, fortune, trendy stuff, or being like Jesus? Think about which way your life is headed. You're never too young to make a decision about where you're going to spend eternity.

NEXT STOP: Cambridge, Massachusetts

February 26

Know-it-all

The fear of the Lord is the beginning of knowledge, but fools despise wisdom and instruction. Listen, my son, to your father's instruction and do not forsake your mother's teaching. **Proverbs 1:7, 8.**

Cambridge, Massachusetts, is home to the first college in the United States. Harvard University was established in 1636 as a private institution of higher education. It is a highly respected institution for training thinkers and important people. Eight United States presidents have graduated from Harvard, and 62 living billionaires received their degrees from the university.

Harvard has a reputation of excellence to maintain. For these reasons the faculty expect students to push themselves and go beyond what is asked of them. Gaining knowledge and learning how to solve problems are the keys to success at Harvard.

But some people think that Harvard University is snotty and stuck up. They feel that it is full of rich people who can afford to pay the high price of tuition. They feel that the institution caters to the elite class. The funny thing is that there are thousands of Harvard graduates who don't become president of the United States, or a billionaire, or even a millionaire. Going to an elite school doesn't mean you will become elite.

But students strive to enroll at Harvard (paying more than $50,000 in tuition and room and board for one year), hoping to gain knowledge that will open up more opportunities for better pay and more important positions after graduation.

There is nothing wrong with attending Harvard and seeking knowledge, but "the fear of the Lord," meaning being serious about a relationship with God, is where knowledge begins. When you realize that all of your smarts come from God, you are headed in the right direction, and you will be open to God teaching you His ways.

King Solomon, the wisest person ever to live, wrote about this idea. He also made a point of reminding all of us that we should listen to our parents. They have been through things we haven't, so they can offer good advice on how to deal with the school bully, what to do when your best friend stops talking to you, and many more life situations. Talk to God, and follow His Word. Talk to your parents and listen to their advice. If you do, you will be wise indeed!

NEXT STOP: Rockport, Massachusetts

GYBP-3

65

Hello out there!

Don't Hide the Truth

Judah said to his brothers, "What will we gain if we kill our brother
and cover up his blood? Come, let's sell him to the Ishmaelites
and not lay our hands on him; after all, he is our brother,
our own flesh and blood." His brothers agreed. **Genesis 37:26, 27.**

Today we are visiting an unusual attraction—a house made out of newspapers! Built in 1924 by Elis Stenman, the man who designed the machines that make paper clips, the house is still standing. Although the framework to the house is made of wood, including a wooden floor and roof, the rest of the house is constructed out of newspapers. The walls are about an inch thick and are made up of layers of newspaper, glue, and varnish, a sticky liquid that forms a hard, clear, and shiny surface when it dries.

Over the years, the caretakers of the house have added layers of extra varnish on the exterior walls to protect them from the rain and snow, but they have tried not to add too much varnish on the inside walls, since it takes away from the design and unique beauty of the rooms. It also makes it too dark to read the stories on the walls, which is part of the unique character of the house. Too much varnish on the inside would make it dark and unattractive.

The same idea applies to our lives. We are beautiful the way God created us. But each time we sin, it is as if we are adding a layer of varnish over our hearts. Over time we notice that we are ugly and dark because of our sins.

Joseph's brothers found themselves in a sticky situation when they were given the opportunity to do away with their annoying younger brother. Although they didn't kill him, they had to come up with a story to tell their father after they sold Joseph to the Ishmaelites. One lie led to another, until a thick layer of varnish covered their lives. They lived with the guilt and shame of their lies until they finally came face to face with Joseph years later and were able to repent of their sins and ask for his forgiveness.

Fortunately, varnish can be removed with a special chemical product that causes the varnish to bubble up on the surface so that you can scrape it off. Likewise, sin can be removed from our lives with the blood of Jesus. Our acceptance of His sacrifice scrapes off the layers of sin that have built up on our heart, and He gives us a clean heart. How awesome is that?

NEXT STOP: Rhode Island

It's All Yours

After Lot had gone, the Lord said to Abram, "Look as far as you can see in every direction—north and south, east and west." **Genesis 13:14, NLT.**

Rhode Island has the distinction of being the smallest state in America. From north to south it is 48 miles in length, and from east to west the state measures 37 miles across. Compared to larger states such as Texas, California, or Alaska, Rhode Island is teeny-weeny. But what if you owned the whole state of Rhode Island? Would it seem big then? What would you do if you could do whatever you wanted with the land?

I wonder how big an area of land Abram could see when God showed him the land that Abram's offspring would someday own. Take a look as the story continues in Genesis 13:15-17, NLT: "I am giving all this land, as far as you can see, to you and your descendants as a permanent possession. And I will give you so many descendants that, like the dust of the earth, they cannot be counted! Go and walk through the land in every direction, for I am giving it to you."

What a promise! If God gave you Rhode Island and told you that someday your children, grandchildren, and great-grandchildren would live there, would you be shocked? I think it would take a while for that kind of news to sink in.

I don't know how long Abram stood there staring at the land that God was giving him, but I imagine he might have daydreamed a little about what the future held for him and his family. What we do know is that "So Abram moved his camp to Hebron and settled near the oak grove belonging to Mamre. There he built another altar to the Lord" (verse 18, NLT).

Do you notice anything special in verse 18 about what Abram did once he moved? That's right, he built an altar and worshipped God. Abram kept God at the center of his life, and God called him righteous (see Genesis 15:6).

As you start another day (or end it, if you have worship at night), make sure God is at the center of your life. Make sure you are putting Him first in all you do and say. And watch for His blessings!

NEXT STOP: Providence, Rhode Island

March 1

Hello out there!

It's the Law

"Caesar's," they replied. "Well, then," he said, "give to Caesar what belongs to Caesar, and give to God what belongs to God." **Matthew 22:21, NLT.**

Roger Williams was born in London, England, in 1603. At age 11 he was converted and decided to study to become a clergyman for the Church of England. However, before graduating from Cambridge, Roger became a Puritan and then a Separatist. He felt that the Church of England was corrupt and was not following the Bible. So he separated from the church and boarded a ship to the New World in 1630.

He and his wife arrived in Massachusetts, but he didn't feel that the churches in Plymouth had separated enough from the Church of England, so in 1636 he and a number of his followers moved to a new land that he named Providence because he felt that God had led him there. For many years the Providence Plantation provided a place of refuge for people suffering from religious oppression. In addition to fighting for religious freedom, Roger fought for the separation of church and state and for fair dealings with the Native Americans.

Religious freedom is very important and something worth fighting for, but what are we supposed to do if we don't agree with the government?

The Pharisees tried to trap Jesus with a question about authority and the ruling government of their day. "They sent some of their disciples, along with the supporters of Herod, to meet with him. 'Teacher,' they said, 'we know how honest you are. You teach the way of God truthfully. . . . Now tell us what you think about this: Is it right to pay taxes to Caesar or not?'" (Matthew 22:16, 17, NLT).

But Jesus saw through their trick, and He told them to return to Caesar what is Caesar's, and to God what is God's. In this response Jesus instructed us to obey the laws of the land while still obeying God's laws. However, when the laws of the land go against God's laws, which we know will happen at the end of time when the government will try to force people to worship on Sunday, we will need to stand as firm as the three Hebrews who were thrown into the fiery furnace.

If there is ever a question, we must follow God's laws. But otherwise, God calls us to obey the laws of the land and be good citizens.

NEXT STOP: Little Compton, Rhode Island

Cluck, Cluck

Jerusalem, Jerusalem, you who kill the prophets and stone those sent to you, how often I have longed to gather your children together, as a hen gathers her chicks under her wings, and you were not willing. **Matthew 23:37.**

Little Compton is home to the Rhode Island Red, a breed of chicken that is a deep reddish-brown color and is known for its hardiness and egg-producing capabilities. It is also raised as meat. But it is the chicken's unique color that makes it easy to spot. All across the country, many people raise this breed of chicken for its many desirable traits.

In honor of the chicken with Rhode Island as its namesake, the Rhode Island Red Club of America (yes, there is a club for everything) donated money to build a monument to the Rhode Island Red in Little Compton. Now Little Compton can boast that it is the only town in the United States with a monument dedicated to a chicken.

Silly, right? Not if you think that Jesus brought attention to chickens in the Bible when He used a mother hen as an example in Matthew 23. In this chapter Jesus didn't hold anything back. He told the Pharisees exactly what they were doing wrong. He called them hypocrites six times. A hypocrite is someone who says one thing but does something else. The Pharisees were good at looking perfect on the outside and telling the people all of the laws they should obey, while being wicked on the inside and not being willing to help someone in need.

Jesus ended His speech to the Pharisees by reminding them how much He loved them and desired for them to follow Him (Matthew 23:37). Even though the people of Jerusalem had killed the prophets sent by God, He still "longed to gather" them "as a hen gathers her chicks." He wanted to protect them and show them His love, but they refused. God's love for us is out of this world. Make sure you don't turn Him away as did the Pharisees. He can't protect you if you aren't under His "wings." Think about where you want to run to be safe.

NEXT STOP: Newport, Rhode Island

March 3

Hello out there!

Jewish Heritage

For the Jews there was light and gladness and joy and honor. **Esther 8:16, NASB.**

As we learned a couple days ago, Roger Williams established Rhode Island as a refuge for people of different religions. And in 1658 a group of Jews took advantage of this safe haven when they settled in Newport after fleeing religious persecution in Spain and Portugal.

The Jews settled in Newport and established a congregation. Today they are called the Congregation Jeshuat Israel, which is the second oldest Jewish congregation in the United States. In 1763 the congregation built the Touro Synagogue, which is "the oldest surviving Jewish synagogue in North America and the only surviving synagogue building in the U.S. dating to the colonial era," according to Wikipedia.

The Jews who moved to Rhode Island were definitely not the first Jews to be persecuted for their faith. The Bible contains many stories of the Jews' struggle for freedom and acceptance. One such story is found in the book of Esther. In fact, the whole book describes one man's hatred for the Jews and his strategic plan to eliminate them. And Haman's plan would have worked had God not intervened, giving Esther courage to act and causing King Xerxes to look upon Esther with compassion instead of contempt when she broke the law and entered his chamber without being invited.

As you may know, when Mordecai asked Esther to go before the king, she basically told him he was crazy. But after he pleaded with her and reminded her that maybe God, in His wisdom, had placed her in the palace for that moment in time, she agreed to fast and pray about the situation and then go before the king.

The Bible then details the two banquets that Esther threw for the king and Haman before revealing her request, at which point Haman was executed. But the king's original edict, or law, still stood—the Jews were to be killed on the "thirteenth day of the twelfth month" (Esther 3:13, NASB), so King Xerxes allowed Mordecai to draft a new edict stating that the Jews could fight back and kill and destroy anyone who tried to hurt them.

In the midst of persecution, God is still in control, which He has proved again and again throughout history. You can trust Him with your life!

NEXT STOP: Hartford, Connecticut

March 4

You Can't Do What?

When Moses went and told the people all the Lord's words and laws, they responded with one voice, "Everything the Lord has said we will do." **Exodus 24:3.**

Welcome to Hartford, Connecticut, the city where you aren't allowed to cross the street while walking on your hands. What? Yep, you read it correctly. That is a real law on the books of the city of Hartford. I'm not sure what the penalty is for breaking that law, but it is legally on the books.

Here's another silly law in Hartford: You may not educate dogs. I'm not sure if they feel that dog obedience school counts as educating a dog or if they don't want them sitting in on lectures at the local high school. Also, it is illegal for a man to kiss his wife on Sunday. I wonder how many men have been fined or arrested for breaking that law!

These laws really make you wonder what the lawmakers were thinking when they wrote them. They just aren't logical. I mean, why can a man kiss his wife on Monday but not on Sunday? It doesn't make sense.

Fortunately, we serve a God whose laws are just and fair and logical. In Exodus 20 God gave the children of Israel the Ten Commandments as guidelines for them to follow to keep them from falling into sin. Then in Exodus 21 through 24, He spelled out in detail more laws that specifically cover how to treat God and others as outlined in the Ten Commandments.

Here are two examples: "Whoever steals an ox or a sheep and slaughters it or sells it must pay back five head of cattle for the ox and four sheep for the sheep" (Exodus 22:1). "Do not spread false reports. Do not help a guilty person by being a malicious witness" (Exodus 23:1).

Those seem like good laws, right? If you steal something, you have to repay it, plus give back extra as a way of saying that you're sorry. And the ninth commandment talks about telling the truth, but this law goes a step further to remind people not to help those who are wicked by telling lies on the witness stand in a trial. Once again, God gave the children of Israel practical laws that would help them live in harmony with each other and God.

After receiving all the laws, the children of Israel said that they would do everything the Lord had said. Do you respond in the same way to God's laws? Think about it.

NEXT STOP: Danbury, Connecticut

Hello out there!

Green Prayer Warrior

Always be joyful. Never stop praying. Be thankful in all circumstances, for this is God's will for you who belong to Christ Jesus. **I Thessalonians 5:16-18, NLT.**

Danbury is located in the southwestern portion of Connecticut. In Danbury, along with cities throughout the state, you will find praying mantises, the state insect of Connecticut. This green or brown insect blends in with sticks and leaves and gets its name from the prayerlike posture it seems to continually be in.

Although it may look as if the praying mantis sits around "praying" all day, it is a hunter, eating mostly insects or other small prey that can be captured, such as birds, snakes, fish, frogs, lizards. I bet you didn't know that the cute praying mantis with the beady eyes that you let crawl on your hand is a predator and cannibal, meaning it will eat another praying mantis, especially during mating season.

But I prefer not to think about the praying mantises' eating habits. Instead, I've always enjoyed finding praying mantises because of what they remind me to do: to pray continually. But this insect that looks as if it is praying is not our only reminder to pray to God. Paul wrote today's text, and he told us how we as Christians should deal with life.

Here is my version of what Paul said in today's text, "Be joyful always, even when you lose your wallet, sprain your ankle playing soccer, or fail your math test. Because those situations are tough, pray to God. Talk to Him throughout the day, as you're studying or taking a test, as you're playing sports or talking with friends. Pray to Him whenever something good happens to you that you want to thank Him for, or when something bad happens and you need His help to make it through the day. God wants you to talk to Him. It is His will that you develop a relationship with Jesus and share everything with Him, your joys, your challenges, your hurts, your excitement, your times of thankfulness, and your times of sorrow."

You don't have to walk around like the praying mantis, with your hands folded and head bowed, but you can walk around with an attitude of prayer. That means you are constantly talking to God or sending prayers to heaven. Try it today. For example, tell God thank you when you open your lunch and find your favorite sandwich or ask Him to help you on your math test.

NEXT STOP: New Haven, Connecticut

Bringing in the Harvest

You take care of the earth and water it, making it rich and fertile. **Psalm 65:9, NLT.**

I'm guessing you've heard of Eli Whitney, the inventor of the cotton gin. However, what you might not know is that Eli went to school in Connecticut and operated a cotton gin factory in New Haven, Connecticut. If you are like me, you probably assumed that Eli was from Georgia, since that is where Eli introduced the machine.

After graduating from college, Eli accepted a position as a private tutor for a family in South Carolina. However, while traveling by ship to South Carolina, he met a family from Rhode Island who owned a plantation in Georgia, and they invited Eli to visit them. A number of New Englanders were settling in the South in hopes of becoming rich, and this family was no different.

Cotton was an important crop in the South, but it was a very time-consuming process to pick the cotton and separate the large black seeds from the cotton fibers that could be spun into thread and eventually turned into fabrics. With the introduction of a machine that could brush the cotton fibers off the seed mechanically, cotton suddenly became a cash crop!

Although God blessed Eli with a creative mind, without His blessing of the land and sending of the rain for the crops, nothing would have grown and the cotton gin would have been a waste of time and money. However, God does bless the land and provide for our needs by helping things to grow.

Read what King David wrote about his gratefulness for God's care for His people: "You take care of the earth and water it, making it rich and fertile. The river of God has plenty of water; it provides a bountiful harvest of grain, for you have ordered it so. You drench the plowed ground with rain, melting the clods and leveling the ridges. You soften the earth with showers and bless its abundant crops. You crown the year with a bountiful harvest; even the hard pathways overflow with abundance. The grasslands of the wilderness become a lush pasture, and the hillsides blossom with joy. The meadows are clothed with flocks of sheep, and the valleys are carpeted with grain. They all shout and sing for joy!" (Psalm 65:9-13, NLT).

Can you picture the farmland that David is describing? Read it again and name at least five things David is thanking God for. Now list at least five things that you are thankful for as you start another day.

NEXT STOP: Mystic, Connecticut

March 7

Hello out there!

Squeezed

Command the Israelites to bring you clear oil of pressed olives for the light so that the lamps may be kept burning. **Exodus 27:20.**

B. F. Clyde's Cider Mill is the oldest steam-powered cider mill in the United States, and it happens to be located in Mystic, Connecticut. All of the machinery is run by a steam engine that turns the necessary belts for the grinder and the press.

To make apple cider, they first dump a truckload of apples into a grinder. The ground apples are then pumped into a large frame that is covered by a large piece of cloth. When the frame is full, the workers fold up the corners of the cloth until the apple mixture is all covered. Then they remove the frame, place a wooden platform on top, and start the process over again. After they have three or four layers of apple-stuffed cloths, the squeezing begins. The stack is placed under a large press that is slowly lowered onto the stack. Because of all the pressure, the juice from the apples squeezes through the cloth and into a large container to be bottled into apple cider.

Apples aren't the only type of fruit that is squeezed to extract the juice. Olives are also squeezed, but instead of juice, olives produce oil. I'm sure you've tasted olive oil before because a lot of people cook with it, especially in Italian foods.

Olive oil can also be used as a fuel. We see in the Old Testament the command given to the Israelites to press their olives and bring the oil to the tent of meeting for use in the lamps. The sanctuary lampstand was located in the holy place, and as the only source of light in the sanctuary, it was important that oil be ready for use day and night. In fact, God commanded Aaron and his sons to keep the lamps burning before Him at all times.

You have to squeeze both apples and olives to extract another product. They are good by themselves, but they serve another purpose when they are squeezed. Sometimes that is like our Christian walk. You may be serving God and working for Him, but when He "squeezes" you and pushes you forward in a different direction, you discover that He has other plans for your life. You discover that you're really good at things you never imagined you could do. Don't be scared if God "squeezes" you; He's just getting more good stuff out!

NEXT STOP: Beacon Falls, Connecticut

Strike It

When all the people saw this, they fell prostrate and cried, "The Lord—he is God! The Lord—he is God!" I Kings 18:39.

I bet Thomas Sanford's mother never told her son not to play with matches, because Thomas invented a type of friction match in Beacon Falls in 1834. Obviously people lit fires before 1834, but they usually did so with flint and steel.

A friction match is a small wooden stick coated on one end with a chemical mixture that, when struck against another surface, bursts into a flame, allowing you time to light a candle or kindling for a fire before it burns the wooden stick and gets to your fingers.

Fire is a very important chemical reaction that gives us light and heat, but it can also be a very destructive force. When out of control, it can burn buildings, forests, and entire towns. Fires are powerful and dangerous, but all they need to start is one small spark.

God didn't use a match to start the fire He sent from heaven to demonstrate His power to the Israelites assembled on Mount Carmel, but He did make it clear to them who was the true God. Do you remember the story?

There had been a drought in the land for three years. God had hidden Elijah away for those three years, but now it was time for a showdown. Elijah appeared before King Ahab, and the king quickly blamed the drought on Elijah, who reminded the king that he and the country were facing the consequences of their choices not to follow God.

Grab your Bible and read 1 Kings 18:22-37. Elijah faced off against 450 prophets of Baal. In human terms he was outnumbered, but God was in control. (When God is on your side, you are never outnumbered.)

Elijah watched the prophets of Baal make fools of themselves all day, but nothing happened. Finally, it was his turn to offer a sacrifice to God. The people helped him prepare the altar, and then he prayed, "'Lord, the God of Abraham, Isaac and Israel, let it be known today that you are God in Israel. . . .' Then the fire of the Lord fell and burned up the sacrifice, the wood, the stones and the soil, and also licked up the water in the trench" (1 Kings 18:36-38). At that moment the people worshipped God and admitted they were wrong—all because of fire.

NEXT STOP: Hershey, Pennsylvania

March 9

Oh, So Good

When the dew was gone, thin flakes like frost on the ground appeared on the desert floor. **Exodus 16:14.**

Hershey, Pennsylvania, is considered to be the chocolate capital of the United States. It is nicknamed "Chocolatetown, USA" and "The Sweetest Place on Earth." If you hadn't guessed, the town is named after The Hershey Company, which is located there. The largest manufacturer of chocolate in North America, Hershey makes everything from chocolate bars and various candy bars to its famous Hershey's Kiss.

I want you to think about your favorite chocolate candy bar. What's inside it? Is it plain chocolate, or do you like nuts or caramel or crunchy cookie pieces in your chocolate bar? Now imagine eating it for 40 years! For every meal! Do you think you might get tired of it? (I know a few chocolate lovers who might tell me that they would never get tired of eating their favorite chocolate every day!)

As you know, the children of Israel spent years wandering in the desert, and they didn't have a grocery store around the corner, nor did they have gardens in which to grow food. But God took care of them. He sent them thin flakes that were like frost. Of course, the Israelites had no idea what it was.

"Moses said to them, 'It is the bread the Lord has given you to eat. This is what the Lord has commanded: "Everyone is to gather as much as they need. Take an omer for each person you have in your tent"'" (verses 15, 16).

So what was manna? Well, the Bible tells us that "manna was like coriander seed and looked like resin. The people went around gathering it, and then ground it in a hand mill or crushed it in a mortar. They cooked it in a pot or made it into loaves. And it tasted like something made with olive oil" (Numbers 11:7, 8).

Although the Israelites got tired of eating manna and whined and complained, God still provided for their needs. We don't often give God enough credit for what He does for us. Instead, we complain and beg for something different. But He still takes care of us even when we don't appreciate His blessings. Take time today to thank God for what He does for you.

NEXT STOP: Lancaster County, Pennsylvania

March 10

Living Off the Land

Don't let anyone capture you with empty philosophies and high-sounding nonsense that come from human thinking and from the spiritual powers of this world, rather than from Christ. **Colossians 2:8, NLT.**

We're entering Lancaster County, home of a large Old Order Amish community. If you've never heard of the Amish, they are a Christian group who choose to live a simple lifestyle. They dress in plain clothes, drive horses and buggies, grow much of their own food, wash their clothes by hand, and require that their children marry a baptized member of the Amish church. Many don't use electricity or telephones.

Although the Amish know and speak English, within their community they speak Pennsylvania German, also known as Pennsylvania Dutch. Church services are held every Sunday at a church member's farm (the meeting place rotates between the families in the community). Boys and men sit on one side and women and girls sit on the other. The service, which usually lasts for more than three hours, is conducted in German and consists of singing and listening to two sermons. (And you thought your church service went long on a Sabbath morning!)

The Amish people I have met, read about, or seen are very nice people who work hard and are dedicated to their families. They also seem to be God-fearing people who want to live a peaceful life with those around them. However, when you read about what they can and cannot do because of their religion—they aren't allowed to own or drive a car, for example, but they can ride in someone else's vehicle—it makes you wonder about traditions, ideas, or rules that have been passed from one generation to the next.

In Colossians 2:8 Paul warns the church about human traditions and worldly ideas, telling the members to make sure they aren't caught up in ideas that focus on everything but Christ. Sometimes human traditions become more important than Christ. The Pharisees had this problem. Their traditions, such as walking no more than a certain distance on Sabbath, were more important than Jesus who was with them. Don't ever let human traditions get in the way of Jesus. If a tradition doesn't follow what the Bible teaches, stop following it and ask Jesus what He wants you to do. Then you'll know you are on the right track.

NEXT STOP: Philadelphia, Pennsylvania

Hello out there!

Shout It!

Sing to the Lord, bless His name; proclaim good tidings of His salvation from day to day. **Psalm 96:2, NASB.**

If you've ever traveled to Philadelphia, you've probably stopped to look at the Liberty Bell. The bell, which originally hung in the steeple of the Pennsylvania State House, now called Independence Hall, is a symbol of America's fight for independence. Inscribed on the bell are the following words: "Proclaim liberty throughout all the land unto all the inhabitants thereof."

The bell was cast in London and shipped to Philadelphia, where it was hung in the state house. Unfortunately, it cracked the first time it was rung. It was recast twice in an effort to fix the crack, but it cracked again. Although the bell is no longer useful for ringing because of the large crack, it still serves a purpose. It has become a symbol of freedom and liberty and independence.

As Christians, how do we proclaim God throughout the land? The Liberty Bell was to "proclaim liberty throughout the land." Every time it rang, it was to serve as a reminder to the citizens of Philadelphia that liberty was an important thing. Of course, it turned into a national symbol that stands for liberty even today.

So how do we proclaim, or tell others about, God? We can tell them about all He has done for us. King David wrote: "Tell of His glory among the nations, His wonderful deeds among all the peoples. For great is the Lord and greatly to be praised; He is to be feared above all gods. For all the gods of the peoples are idols, but the Lord made the heavens" (Psalm 96:3-5, NASB).

We are to tell others about God's free gift of salvation. We are to tell others about the great things He does for us. We are to praise His name and talk about the things He created. He made everything around us, and we need to shout it from the mountaintops that we serve an awesome God.

You might feel shy or nervous about telling others about Jesus and the things He has done for you, but I would encourage you to be bold like David and proclaim God's goodness to those around you. The more you share, the more you will see how God is working in your life.

NEXT STOP: Philadelphia, Pennsylvania

Who's the King of the Jungle?

Then God said, "Let the earth produce every sort of animal, each producing offspring of the same kind—livestock, small animals that scurry along the ground, and wild animals." And that is what happened. God made all sorts of wild animals, livestock, and small animals, each able to produce offspring of the same kind. And God saw that it was good. **Genesis 1:24, 25, NLT.**

We're spending another day in Philadelphia! Today we are taking a trip to the Philadelphia Zoo, the first public zoo to open in the United States. It opened on July 1, 1874, with 1,000 animals, and the cost to get in was 25 cents for adults and 10 cents for children.

When you go to the zoo, what is your favorite animal to see? Do you like the elephants, giraffes, lions, tigers, hippopotamuses, monkeys?

I enjoy looking at the lions and tigers because I love cats, but my favorite animal would probably be the monkey. Not the gorillas or orangutans, but the chimpanzees or spider monkeys. I like watching them run and play, swinging from branch to branch, tackling each other, or playing games. They are so entertaining.

I wonder if God had a favorite animal when He created them. The sixth day was a busy day of Creation, because God made all of the living creatures that moved on the earth. That's a lot of animals! And then He made Adam and gave him the job of naming the animals. "So the Lord God formed from the ground all the wild animals and all the birds of the sky. He brought them to the man to see what he would call them, and the man chose a name for each one. He gave names to all the livestock, all the birds of the sky, and all the wild animals. But still there was no helper just right for him" (Genesis 2:19, 20, NLT).

Naming the creatures must have been a big job. I wonder if Adam got distracted as he petted a kitten or played with a kangaroo. We don't know how long it took Adam to name the animals, but I'm sure he and God had a good time looking at everything God had created and naming all of the creatures.

God created this world, and at the end of the sixth day, He said it was "very good" (Genesis 1:31, NLT). Even though this world has been stained by sin, many of the things God has made still reflect His love and goodness. And someday soon He is going to make a new earth for us to enjoy!

NEXT STOP: Valley Forge, Pennsylvania

Hello out there!

Winter Blues

Pray that your flight will not take place in winter or on the Sabbath. **Matthew 24:20.**

Valley Forge is located northwest of Philadelphia and is the site of the military camp of the American Continental Army at the beginning of the American Revolutionary War. It was almost winter when General George Washington decided to make camp at Valley Forge. It proved to be a good location for the Americans to prevent the British from advancing farther into Pennsylvania.

However, Washington and his men were in for a rough winter. They lacked food and supplies, including basic things such as shoes. In fact, of the 12,000 men in the army only about 4,000 had shoes. As they marched over the frozen ground, many of the men without shoes left bloody footprints on the ground.

The army constructed rough cabins and huts for the men to live in throughout the winter, but with the damp conditions of melting snow and freezing temperatures, many of the men became sick, and diseases spread in the close quarters. It didn't help matters that there was a short supply of blankets, and the men's clothes were very tattered and thin. Approximately 2,500 men died that winter because of these poor conditions. Humans were not the only ones who suffered, however, as hundreds of horses starved to death or died of exhaustion.

But the army didn't give up. They held their ground and kept the British from advancing. Six months later the Continental Army pursued the British as they moved toward New York, and five years later Washington and his men won the war.

What made the stay at Valley Forge difficult was the weather. The cold of winter made things much worse. But the men trusted Washington and listened to his commands.

Toward the end of Jesus' life He predicted the fall of Jerusalem, but He told His listeners to pray that they wouldn't have to flee on the Sabbath or in winter. Jesus knew the struggles of moving in winter, and He knew they wouldn't want to break the Sabbath. However, most of the Jews ignored Jesus and His prophecy about the future destruction of their city. They were more worried about living in their holy city than praying to the holy God of heaven for protection and guidance. What a sad mistake that cost hundreds of thousands of people their lives. Don't make the same mistake. Follow God's directions. He is the best general in the world.

NEXT STOP: Gettysburg, Pennsylvania

Second Is Better Than First

But many who are first will be last,
and many who are last will be first. **Matthew 19:30.**

The Battle of Gettysburg took place on July 1-3, 1863, and was the battle with the largest number of casualties in the Civil War. A total of more than 7,800 men were killed, more than 27,000 men were wounded, and more than 11,000 men were captured or reported missing. The battle was a turning point in the war that ended General Robert E. Lee's invasion of the North.

A little more than four months after the battle the Soldiers' National Cemetery was dedicated and a proper burial was provided for many of the Union soldiers who had died. The committee planning the dedication event asked Edward Everett, a politician and educator from Massachusetts, to give the main speech for the event. They also asked Abraham Lincoln to provide the dedicatory remarks.

As he traveled to Gettysburg, President Lincoln began feeling sick, but he proceeded to attend the ceremony and give his speech. After listening to Mr. Everett speak for more than two hours, Lincoln approached the podium and spoke for approximately two minutes. But in those two minutes he gave a moving speech that summed up the reasons behind the war and the fight for freedom for all people.

If you ask people who the men were who spoke at Gettysburg, most don't remember Mr. Everett, but they do remember Lincoln's address. Even though Lincoln wasn't the main speaker, his speech was more meaningful and has been named one of the most well-known speeches in American history.

Today's text reminds us that in God's eyes being number one is not what is important. The world tells us that if you want to be someone special, you need to be number one. Whether it is in your class, in sports, in band or choir, or in popularity, the world's standards say that being first is best. Nobody remembers who comes in second.

However, Jesus teaches a different way. He reminds all of us that He doesn't care what place we are in if we are following Him. There is no contest to get into heaven. So don't worry about being ahead of your friends. Just try your best and do everything for the glory of God. He will reward you; if not on earth, definitely in heaven.

NEXT STOP: Punxsutawney, Pennsylvania

Hello out there!

The Eternal Groundhog

"You are wearied with your many counsels; let now the astrologers,
those who prophesy by the stars, those who predict by the new moons,
stand up and save you from what will come upon you." **Isaiah 47:13, NASB.**

I know that today's location is a mouthful, but sound out each letter as it appears, and you'll get it: P-U-N-X-S-U-T-A-W-N-E-Y. What in the world is in Punxsutawney? A groundhog! And this is no ordinary groundhog that eats vegetables from your garden and digs holes in your yard. This is a special groundhog that can predict the weather.

On February 2 each year a celebration called Groundhog Day is held in the town, and Punxsutawney Phil, the groundhog, emerges from his hole in front of a large crowd of people. According to the legend, if Phil sees his shadow the country is in for six more weeks of winter weather. However, if he doesn't see his shadow, we will enjoy an early spring.

I was in Punxsutawney for a Pathfinder camporee, and Phil was brought out for the kids to see. As the two animal handlers were walking around showing off Phil, a little kid asked them how old Phil was. They told him that Phil was more than 120 years old. Talk about a big, fat lie! A groundhog's maximum life expectancy is 14 years in captivity. But Phil's fans and caretakers claim that they give him a mysterious medicine that helps him to magically live longer.

Although it sounds silly to you and me, there are many people who buy into the lie of Punxsutawney Phil or help keep the story going. It may seem like a harmless thing to do, but believing in superstitions to predict the weather or anything else in life is foolishness.

Isaiah writes about the fall of Babylon in chapter 47 of the Old Testament book that bears his name. He talks about where the people of Babylon are placing their trust—in astrologers and stargazers and people who predict the future. He challenges the Babylonian people, "stand up and save you from what will come upon you" (verse 13, NASB). But just as Elijah challenged the prophets of Baal to a showdown on Mount Caramel, Isaiah challenges the people of Babylon to stop and think about who and what they believe in.

God is the only one who deserves our trust. His predictions come true. Period. If you place your trust in anything or anyone other than God, you will be lost when Jesus comes. A groundhog can't save you, but Jesus can!

NEXT STOP: Atlantic City Boardwalk, New Jersey

True Friends

Wealth attracts many friends, but even the closest friend of the poor person deserts them. **Proverbs 19:4.**

It's time to leave Pennsylvania and travel east to the coastal state of New Jersey. We will be spending the next three days in Atlantic City, a seaside resort town known for its four-mile-long boardwalk that runs along the beach, separating the beach and the Atlantic Ocean from the shops, restaurants, hotels, and casinos that line the boardwalk.

Here's a trivia question for you. Do you know what board game is based on Atlantic City? If you guessed Monopoly, you are right. The properties on the board are based on locations in and near Atlantic City. If you've never played Monopoly, the whole point of the game is to buy as much property as you can, build houses and hotels on that property, and then collect rent when people land on your property. The goal is to get everyone to run out of money so that you are the only one with any money in your hand. At that time you have a monopoly, meaning you control everything, and you win the game.

Some people operate that way in life. They try to get as much money as they can from whomever they can until they are rich and everyone else is poor.

Now, I have a question for you. Do you think rich people have more friends than poor people? If you said yes, I would agree with you. But why do they have more friends? I tend to think rich people have more friends because the friends want the benefits that go with having rich friends, such as being invited to fancy parties and receiving nice presents from their friends. But what happens to those friends if their rich friend suddenly loses his or her wealth? That's right, they leave. They were friends with the person only because of the money.

King Solomon warns us about people's motives, the true reason behind what they do. Money attracts lots of friends, but once the money is gone and the person is poor, his or her friends disappear. This is a warning for those who are wealthy and those who are not.

Whether you have money or not, make sure you are a true friend. Don't become friends with someone because you hope they will invite you to their house to go swimming or play video games because you don't have a pool or video games. Become friends with people because you like them, not because you want to get something from them. Be a true friend!

NEXT STOP: Atlantic City Casinos, New Jersey

Hello out there!

Money! Money! Money!

Whoever loves money never has enough; whoever loves wealth is never satisfied with their income. This too is meaningless. **Ecclesiastes 5:10.**

Atlantic City is known as the gambling capital of the East Coast. In an effort to get more people to visit Atlantic City and spend their money in the city, New Jersey voters passed a law in 1976 that approved gambling. Two years later the first casino opened, offering visitors countless gambling games to spend their money on. The city is now home to 12 casinos, some with more than 2,000 rooms for rent.

Each year thousands of people travel to Atlantic City to bet money on card games and other games of chance in a quest to get rich quickly. They spend millions of dollars trying to win millions more, but most people walk away losers, wasting their money on dreams of getting rich and living a life without having to work or worry about money.

Yesterday we talked about true friends and how people act around others who have money. Today we are talking about how *you* act when you have money. As the richest man who ever lived, King Solomon has a lot of good advice on this subject. As he stated in Ecclesiastes 5:10, those who love money never have enough and are never satisfied.

When money is all that is important to you in life, you will never have enough. You are always going to want more. Many people who gamble have this problem. If they win $200 playing a card game, they turn around and spend that money on the next game, hoping they will win $400 the next round. They are never content with the money they have; they always want more. And if they lose $200, they tell themselves they can easily win it back if they gamble some more.

Are you consumed with wanting more money or more stuff? If so, stop and think about why you want more money and listen to King Solomon's advice. Once you get that extra $20 you want, you will want another $20 and another $20. Learn to be content with what you *have* and trust God to give you what you *need*. Life will go much more smoothly if you learn these lessons now.

NEXT STOP: Atlantic City, New Jersey

Beauty Pageant

Let the king appoint agents in each province to bring these beautiful young women into the royal harem at the fortress of Susa. . . . After that, the young woman who most pleases the king will be made queen instead of Vashti." This advice was very appealing to the king, so he put the plan into effect. **Esther 2:3, 4, NLT.**

Today is our last day in Atlantic City, which served as home of the Miss America pageant for 83 years from 1921 to 2004. What started out as a beauty contest is now a scholarship pageant to help young women attend the college or university of their choice. However, most people still see it as a beauty contest that combines good looks, talent, and brains.

The contest is now held each January, with women competing from each of the 50 states plus the District of Columbia, Puerto Rico, and the U.S. Virgin Islands. The prize in 2012 was a $50,000 scholarship and the privilege of serving as Miss America for one year, which includes traveling and speaking at special events around the country.

Regardless of what they call it, a beauty contest or a scholarship pageant, 53 women compete for one crown and the title of Miss America. Thousands of years ago in the land of Susa, Esther competed for a crown, but it wasn't for a one-year title. She and hundreds of other women were competing for the title of queen.

In Esther 2 the king's advisors recommend that he hold a beauty contest to select his next queen. Unlike the Miss America pageant, in which the contestants have to be well-educated young women, King Xerxes was worried only about his next queen's looks. It doesn't appear that he was worried about whether she was a nice person or was smart or funny; he just wanted her to look good.

So this is the situation Esther found herself in when she arrived at the palace. For one year she received beauty treatments of oils and spices on her skin and in her hair to make her prettier, and then she went before the king. Although she was pretty on the outside, I also believe she was beautiful on the inside, for she "was admired by everyone who saw her" (Esther 2:15, NLT). Girls who look good but treat people like scum make enemies, not friends. But Esther didn't do that. Her character shone through her beauty, making her that much prettier.

Make sure your good looks are not just skin deep. Make sure God shines through you.

NEXT STOP: Newark, New Jersey

March 19

Hello out there!

Stay in the Car

Laban said to Jacob, . . . "Why did you
steal my gods?" **Genesis 31:26-30.**

Today we are driving through Newark, New Jersey, but we are not getting out of the car. If we did get out, we might not have a car to drive away in. Why? Because Newark is known for auto theft. After general theft, auto theft is the next highest crime in Newark.

But why do people steal? Is it because they are tempted to have nicer things or more things? Is it because they are poor and don't have anything, so they steal what they need to get by? Is it because they get an adrenaline rush while trying to steal something and get away with it?

I don't know the answer to any of these questions because I've never stolen anything, but it's a temptation for some people, including a few Bible characters.

The story we are going to look at today is about Rachel. Jacob worked for Laban for seven years in order to marry Rachel, but Laban gave him her older sister, Leah. Jacob was really upset when he found out that Laban had tricked him into marrying Leah, since he loved Rachel, so Laban also gave him Rachel in exchange for another seven years of work.

Years later Jacob decided to leave Laban and return to the land of his father. But he was afraid that Laban would not let him leave, so he took his wives, children, servants, and livestock and fled. Of course, Laban pursued him, and when he caught him, he got after Jacob for leaving without saying goodbye. He then accused him of stealing his gods. Jacob didn't know that Rachel had stolen the idols, so he confidently told Laban to search the camp; if Laban were to find the gods, the person who had taken them would be put to death.

So Laban searched. And when he came to Rachel's tent, she lied in order to cover up her sin. "Rachel said to her father, 'Don't be angry, my lord, that I cannot stand up in your presence; I'm having my period.' So he searched but could not find the household gods" (Genesis 31:35).

One crime or sin usually leads to another one. To stay out of trouble and stay on God's path, do what He asks and follow His Word. It's your best bet against falling into temptation.

NEXT STOP: West Orange, New Jersey

No More Candles

You, Lord, keep my lamp burning;
my God turns my darkness into light.
With your help I can advance against a troop;
with my God I can scale a wall. **Psalm 18:28, 29.**

Thomas Edison is one of the most famous inventors in America. He held 1,093 United States patents, which gave him the right to make, use, or sell his inventions as he pleased. Thomas dropped out of school at an early age because his teacher thought he was "slow." His mother didn't believe he had any learning disabilities, so she taught him at home.

At age 19 Edison found himself working as a telegraph operator, but his real passion was experimenting, which got him fired when he spilled sulfuric acid on the floor and it dripped onto his boss's desk.

Although he had a rough start to his inventing career, Edison kept working on his experiments. People began to notice his talent for creating things when he developed a phonograph in 1877, which would be equivalent to today's CD players.

But what Thomas Edison is most known for is the invention of the first commercially practical lightbulb. He also patented a system for distribution of electricity, which brought electric lights to many homes, changing the way people lived and shaping how we live today.

If you imagine that you are a lightbulb, who flips your switch each morning? God! He wakes you up and gives you another day of life. He protects you and helps you make good decisions.

King David knew that God was the one who gave him life and kept him going each day. With God's help he could stand against any army in the world.

Do you have that kind of trust in God? Do you trust Him to help you with your schoolwork, special music performance, or problems with your sibling? God is your connection. He is the only one who has the power to keep you alive. Have you given your allegiance to God? If not, don't wait. He is your lifeline.

NEXT STOP: Dover, Delaware

March 21

 *Hello out there!*

Small Yet Strong

The Lord is my strength and my song; he has given me victory. This is my God, and I will praise him—my father's God, and I will exalt him. **Exodus 15:2.**

Dover is the capital of Delaware, the first state to ratify or sign the United States Constitution, thus accepting it as law of the land and agreeing to follow all that the document outlined. Delaware was one of the smallest colonies, along with Rhode Island. Many of the men who met to discuss whether to accept the Constitution were afraid that the larger colonies surrounding them would take advantage of Delaware because of its size. They felt protected by the laws outlined in the Constitution, and they did not hesitate to stand behind the document. Thus, Delaware is known as the First State.

We humans are pretty small in comparison to the universe and the great controversy that surrounds us. On our own we don't stand a chance against the devil and his army of evil angels. Like the representatives of Delaware who saw the benefit of the Constitution and the protection it offered their state, we need to recognize the benefits of following Christ and living as Christians. With God on our side we can stand up to Satan and his attacks.

In today's text Moses and the Israelites are singing praises to God after crossing the Red Sea and watching their enemies being washed away as the walls of water crashed down. Moses recognized that he was nothing without the Lord. He recognized that God was his strength. Without Him, Moses was weak and incapable of leading the Israelites, but with God, he was no longer small and insignificant. He didn't have to be afraid of the larger countries and people groups who surrounded the Israelites and threatened to overthrow them if they came onto their land. Why? Because God was their God. He was their strength and song.

Sometimes we feel pretty small, and we wonder how we are going to stand up to the giants that threaten us—giants such as bullies, bad grades, divorce, or annoying siblings. But we can stand tall when we team up with God and tap into divine strength!

NEXT STOP: Lewes, Delaware

How Far Can You See?

They said to all the people of Israel, "The land we traveled through and explored is a wonderful land! And if the Lord is pleased with us, he will bring us safely into that land and give it to us. It is a rich land flowing with milk and honey. Do not rebel against the Lord, and don't be afraid of the people of the land. They are only helpless prey to us! They have no protection, but the Lord is with us! Don't be afraid of them!" **Numbers 14:7-9, NLT.**

Imagine that you are an Israelite and that you are on the edge of the Promised Land. You have heard so much about this beautiful country that will be your new home. You are filled with excitement as you wait for the spies to return with their report. You scan the horizon to see if you can spot them coming up over a ridge that blocks your view of Canaan.

Finally, after many days and nights of waiting, Joshua and Caleb and the other 10 men return. You eagerly press toward the front of the crowd and strain to listen to Joshua and Caleb above the hum of the people whispering among themselves. You listen as they describe what sounds like a paradise with plenty of food and fertile ground. *Sounds good so far,* you think. Then they talk about the people you will have to fight with and overcome in order to take the land away from them. *Wait! We have to fight for this land? I don't want to fight. I don't want to get hurt. I don't want to die!*

In that moment fear takes over, and you forget all about God. From a human perspective, it *is* impossible, and the people of the land are giants compared to you. But you're forgetting that God just proved His ability to protect you and the Israelites. You're forgetting that He has promised to give you the land of Abraham, Isaac, and Jacob.

It is often difficult for us to let God protect us; we want to do things ourselves. In Lewes, Delaware, there is a park called Cape Henlopen State Park, where, right near the beach amid the rolling sand dunes and pine trees, there are 12 concrete observation towers that were constructed during World War II to protect the state's coastal towns from a German invasion. The U.S. Army wasn't taking any chances, and they prepared to protect the country against an attack.

Our country was founded on the idea that "in God we trust," but do we, or our country's leaders, live by that motto? Or do we take matters into our own hands and build towers around ourselves in hopes that no one will hurt us?

NEXT STOP: Delaware Bay, Delaware

Hello out there!

The Circle of Life

And God said, "Let the water teem with living creatures, and let birds fly above the earth across the vault of the sky." **Genesis 1:20.**

God created sea creatures and birds on the same day, and they were given charge over their respective environments. The sea creatures were to live and eat of things in the water, and the birds were to live in the air and eat of the things on the ground. In the Garden of Eden there was no need for the birds to eat the fish, but everything changed after sin entered the world. Now there are many birds that eat fish and other sea creatures in order to survive. The perfect harmony of Creation was destroyed when Satan succeeded in deceiving Eve.

The largest population of horseshoe crabs in the world lives in the Delaware Bay. Here in the waters off the coast of Delaware the crabs serve an important role in the ecosystem, because their eggs provide nutrients to birds migrating north each spring as they fly to their nesting ground in the Arctic. Unfortunately, the horseshoe crab population has declined over the past few years, going from 1.2 million spawning females to approximately 400,000. Scientists are concerned that the decrease of crabs will also affect the birds.

In order to protect the birds and the horseshoe crabs, scientists have had to find out what is causing the decline in crabs. The culprit? People, of course. The fishing industry uses the meat of the female horseshoe crab as bait to catch eels and whelks (a type of sea snail). Now scientists are working to develop an artificial bait that will work like the real thing. This will help save the horseshoe crabs and, in turn, the birds.

There are so many things in our world that are dependent on one another. God created this world to work in perfect harmony, but sin has messed up many things, and we humans mess things up even more. I'm so thankful that Jesus will soon return and restore the world to its original state of perfection. Then all animals and plants and people will live together in harmony.

NEXT STOP: Delaware River, Delaware

Don't Believe Everything You're Told

Then the Lord said to me, "The prophets are prophesying lies in my name.
I have not sent them or appointed them or spoken to them.
They are prophesying to you false visions, divinations, idolatries
and the delusions of their own minds." **Jeremiah 14:14.**

The Delaware River is located in Delaware—of course!—and is 301 miles long. It runs along the borders of New York, New Jersey, and Pennsylvania, and is the main water source in the Catskill Mountains in New York.

In the early 1700s the Delaware Indians lived throughout this area. In fact, they were one of the largest tribes in the East. They lived in grass- and bark-covered longhouses. Each village had a sweathouse for steam baths, a treatment they used for any illness in the village.

In the 1760s a native man known as the Delaware Prophet preached among the Delaware Indians a message of freedom from the advances of the White people. This religious leader told the Indians that if they wanted to be free, they needed to stop using guns and other European inventions. His ideas influenced Pontiac, an Ottawa Native American leader, to unite with the Delaware people and other Native Americans to drive out the White people. The resulting war, known as Pontiac's War, lasted from 1763 to 1766.

In 1818 the Delaware people surrendered their lands east of the Mississippi River to the United States government. Most of the Delaware people moved to Missouri and then to Kansas. In the 1860s they moved to Oklahoma.

Since Bible times many false prophets have existed. The Delaware Prophet was certainly not the first or last. As the end of the world approaches, we know that other false prophets will emerge, saying that they have seen Jesus or that they are Jesus. There will be others who will offer advice and say that you need to do certain things in order to be saved.

Above all, don't believe the teachings of false prophets! Read your Bible and rely on what God says. That is the only way to know truth from error.

NEXT STOP: Rehoboth and Bethany Beaches, Delaware

March 25

Hello out there!

The Longest Camping Trip

After leaving Marah, the Israelites traveled on to the oasis of Elim, where they found twelve springs and seventy palm trees. They camped there beside the water. **Exodus 15:27, NLT.**

Rehoboth Beach and Bethany Beach are popular resort destinations in Delaware. Many people come to the beach, especially during the summer, to play in the sand, swim in the ocean, stay in fancy hotels, or camp at nearby campgrounds. Interestingly, both of these beach resorts began as religious summer camps. Churches bought land along these beaches in the late 1800s and early 1900s and built summer camps for their church members to enjoy.

Small cottages were built to accommodate families who traveled to the remote location. With small three-burner oil stoves, the families bought their food from local farmers who traveled across the sand in wagons to deliver goods, since there weren't any roads.

These summer camps sound similar to car camping—although they had beds in a cottage instead of sleeping bags in a tent. And for anyone who enjoys camping with family during the summer, I'm sure this type of summer camp on the beach sounds wonderful.

But how would you like to camp for 40 years? Although I enjoy camping, I wouldn't want to live that way for more than a few weeks—certainly not for 40 years! But that's what the Israelites did. They camped for 40 years in tents in the desert.

Shortly after crossing the Red Sea, they entered the Desert of Shur. The Bible tells us that "they traveled in this desert for three days without finding any water. When they came to the oasis of Marah, the water was too bitter to drink. . . . Then the people complained and turned against Moses. 'What are we going to drink?' they demanded" (Exodus 15:22-24, NLT).

The Israelites had just witnessed a miracle from God in the parting of the Red Sea, but they seemed to quickly forget that and started grumbling about their thirst. But God was still watching over them, and He was prepared to provide for their needs. When Moses prayed, the Lord showed him a piece of wood and instructed him to throw it into the water. Once he did, "the water became fit to drink" (verse 25). Then Moses reminded the people that if they would place their trust in God, He would supply their every need. Shortly after that, the people came to Elim, where there were 12 springs and 70 palm trees to enjoy!

NEXT STOP: Annapolis, Maryland

Salute!

They replied, "Your servant our father is still alive and well." And they bowed down, prostrating themselves before him. **Genesis 43:28.**

The United States Naval Academy was founded in 1845 in Annapolis, Maryland, on 10 acres of old Fort Severn. Since then, the institution has trained hundreds of men and women to serve as officers in the Marine Corps and the Navy, first on steam-powered ships and now on high-tech nuclear-powered submarines, warships, and aircraft carriers, the most sophisticated floating airports in the world.

Students enrolled at the academy take academic courses and enroll in professional training programs that prepare them for their assignments after graduation. As with all of the military branches, honor plays an important role in shaping their identity. It is drilled into all students that they are training for a position of esteem and that it is their duty to live up to the respect that is given them.

There were many Bible characters who were respected for their leadership and given a place of honor, many times in the government. One such person was Joseph. Not only did the pharaoh treat him with respect and give him an important position as a ruler in Egypt, but his brothers also bowed to him and paid him honor. They recognized that Joseph was in a position of authority and could easily have them killed for how they had wronged him many years earlier in selling him to the caravan.

Joseph also recognized the respect and honor that had come to him because of his leadership role in Egypt, for he told his brothers, "Tell my father about all the honor accorded me in Egypt and about everything you have seen. And bring my father down here quickly" (Genesis 45:13). He was proud of what he had accomplished through God's leading, and he wanted to share his success with his father.

As children of the King, we hold a place of honor in God's kingdom. You may or may not be placed in a position of authority here on earth, but you will be honored in heaven when you receive the crown of life (see Revelation 2:10). Live up to your name! Hold your head high! Your Commanding Officer wants to remind you that you are made in His image. You are special!

NEXT STOP: College Park, Maryland

Hello out there!

Open Wide

The wicked plot against the righteous and gnash their teeth at them; but the Lord laughs at the wicked, for he knows their day is coming. **Psalm 37:12, 13.**

The University of Maryland's main campus is in College Park, Maryland, which is only about 15 minutes from Washington Adventist University, one of our Adventist colleges. An interesting fact about the University of Maryland is that the first dental college in the world, which was opened in 1840, is a part of its school system. The mission of the dental school and the dentists who graduated was to serve patients and offer them the best care possible. The instruments and equipment used to work on teeth are much more sophisticated now than they were back then, but the mission is still the same.

If you've ever been to a museum that has old medical equipment on display, you're probably glad you didn't grow up in the 1800s! I wouldn't have wanted to let a dentist shove a pair of pliers into my mouth to yank out a tooth. And since oral hygiene was somewhat lacking back then, I'm sure there were a lot of teeth that needed to be pulled.

Since we are on the topic of teeth, did you know that the Bible actually references teeth in a number of verses in both the Old and New Testaments? In a lot of the verses the phrase "gnash(ing) their teeth" is used. Do you know what it means to *gnash* your teeth?

According to the *New Oxford American Dictionary* the word *gnash* means to "grind (one's teeth) together, typically as a sign of anger."

Read today's text again. The wicked make evil plans against us, God's followers. They grind their teeth in anger at us. They want to destroy us. But we know that in the end the wicked will be the ones who are destroyed. In the end they will be gnashing their teeth in anger over their bad choices and the fact that they are lost. Check it out: "But he will reply, 'I don't know you or where you come from. Away from me, all you evildoers!' There will be weeping there, and gnashing of teeth, when you see Abraham, Isaac and Jacob and all the prophets in the kingdom of God, but you yourselves thrown out. People will come from east and west and north and south, and will take their places at the feast in the kingdom of God" (Luke 13:27-29).

Make sure you don't grind your teeth now in anger or later in sadness that you missed out on the best gift ever given.

NEXT STOP: Baltimore, Maryland

"Oh, Say, Can You See"—Part 1

Then everyone will see the Son of Man coming on the clouds with great power and glory. **Mark 13:26, NLT.**

Francis Scott Key was a young lawyer living in Georgetown, Maryland, when the War of 1812 broke out between the United States and Britain. The war was mostly fought in the Atlantic Ocean between the two countries' naval forces. A little more than two years after the start of the war, on August 19, 1814, the British entered the Chesapeake Bay, and by the evening of August 24 they had captured Washington, D.C. In an attempt to cripple the government, the British set fire to the Capitol and the White House. Fortunately, President James Madison, his wife, and the Cabinet had left Washington for a safer location when they learned of the invasion.

The residents of Baltimore, which is 40 miles northeast of Washington, D.C., heard about the attack and could see the flames of the burning buildings in Washington. Naturally, the residents of Baltimore were very afraid, and many quickly grabbed what they could carry or load on a cart or wagon and left town. Others huddled together in houses to wait and watch.

A week after the attack on Washington, Francis Scott Key found himself on a boat with Colonel John Skinner on a mission to request the release of Dr. William Beanes, a local physician who had been captured by the British and was being held a prisoner of war. In defense of Dr. Beanes, Francis Scott Key and Colonel Skinner had brought along letters from wounded British prisoners praising the American doctors who had treated them after a recent battle.

After listening to the young lawyer, the British agreed to release Dr. Beanes. However, because the three men had heard some of the plans for the attack on Baltimore, they were placed under guard and had to wait out the battle on a ship.

A few days later the British began shelling Fort McHenry, in Baltimore Harbor. The fighting lasted for 25 hours with the British firing 1,500 cannonballs at the fort. The fighting continued through the night and into the next morning. As the sun rose the next morning, Francis Scott Key, Colonel Skinner, and Dr. Beanes looked on in anxious anticipation, wondering if the American troops had survived the attack and held their ground.

They were looking for a sign, just as we are looking for a sign that this world will end.

NEXT STOP: Fort McHenry, Maryland

Hello out there!

March 29

"Oh, Say, Can You See"—Part 2

And he will send out his angels to gather his chosen ones from all over the world—from the farthest ends of the earth and heaven. **Mark 13:27, NLT.**

As I'm sure you know, the sign that Francis Scott Key and the other men were looking for was the large American flag that flew above the fort. One year before, Major George Armistead, the commander of Fort McHenry, had asked a local woman to make a flag for the fort. Working in her home, Mary Young Pickersgill and her 13-year-old daughter used 400 yards of fabric for the flag. They made 15 stars that were two feet from point to point and eight red stripes and seven white stripes that were two feet wide each. When it was finished, the flag measured 30 by 42 feet.

Major Armistead wanted the flag to be big enough that the British would be able to see it clearly from a distance. He wanted it to be a symbol of the strength of his troops and their determination to protect their country.

And it worked. The flag could be seen several miles from the fort and was what Francis Scott Key and the other two men looked for as the fog cleared on the morning of September 14. In spite of the bombs and rockets fired at the fort, the American soldiers had held their ground, and the flag was still flying.

Upon seeing the flag, Francis Scott Key wrote a poem in honor of this symbol of the United States of America. The poem contained four verses, and it immediately became a popular patriotic song. The first verse was later adopted as the national anthem on March 3, 1931.

Just as Francis Scott Key looked on in anticipation as the battle ended, hoping that the flag was still flying, we will be looking for Jesus in the clouds of glory as the world comes to a chaotic end. But unlike Francis Scott Key, we know the final outcome of the battle. He was not certain that the Americans had won; he was simply hopeful that they had survived the attack. We know with certainty that God's followers will win the battle against evil. We have His promise, right there in Mark 13:27, that when Jesus returns He will send His angels to gather up everyone who believes in Him and take them home to heaven.

Keep looking for the signs!

NEXT STOP: Assateague Island, Maryland

Just Plain Gritty

A stone is heavy and the sand weighty, but the provocation of a fool is heavier than both of them. **Proverbs 27:3, NASB.**

Have you ever been camping at the beach? My first time camping at the beach was on Assateague Island, home of the famous wild ponies. The island is home to two herds of horses totaling approximately 300 animals, and each herd has "divided themselves into bands of 2 to 12 animals," according to the National Park Service Web site.

Each year the herd on the Virginia side of the island is rounded up and the ponies swim from Assateague Island across the Assateague Channel to Chincoteague Island. Once across the channel, the foals are corralled and sold to help keep the population to a manageable size and to make sure there is enough food on the island to support the herd.

While camping on the island I got a glimpse of a few ponies munching on grasses in the marshy landscape near the beach. Of course, I tried to get some pictures of these beautiful animals, but my camera lens made horrible noises as it tried to open. I soon discovered that sand had gotten into the opening of the lens, and although I could take a picture, I wasn't sure how long the camera would last. Sure enough, it stopped working a few weeks later. All because of a few annoying pieces of sand that blew into my camera while I was sitting on the beach.

King Solomon talks about sand in today's text. He says that it is a burden. If you were to scoop a bunch of sand into a bag, it would be pretty heavy. Imagine carrying around a bag of sand in your backpack all day. Those tiny pieces of sand that can be so annoying if they get in your shoe, or in a camera, can be an even bigger burden if they are all lumped together. He also states that stones are heavy. Both of those statements make sense to me. But what does the last part of the verse mean?

Provocation is a big word meaning something that irritates, harasses, plagues, teases, torments, or insults. So what King Solomon is saying is that although stones are heavy and sand is a burden, teasing and tormenting other people is foolish, and people who act that way are trouble to those around them. Don't be foolish! Don't be annoying as sand or as heavy as a rock! Live your life for Jesus and make someone else smile today.

NEXT STOP: Glen Echo, Maryland

March 31

Hello out there!

Helping Others

Jesus was going throughout all Galilee, teaching in their synagogues
and proclaiming the gospel of the kingdom, and healing every kind of disease and
every kind of sickness among the people. **Matthew 4:23, NASB.**

At an early age Clara Barton had a gift for taking care of people. When she was
only 11 years old, her older brother David fell from the roof of a barn he was
fixing. The doctors did not give him long to live, but Clara would not give up on
him. She nursed him and took care of him until he was back on his feet. The doctors couldn't understand why he didn't die, but David realized that his sister had a
special gift of caring for sick people.

Although she was good at taking care of people, Clara did not enter the medical field. Instead she became a teacher and then worked for the U.S. government
as a clerk. Unfortunately, in each of her positions she ran into problems because
she wasn't a man. Although she was able to do the work, she, along with most of
the women back then, had a difficult time in what was considered a "man's world."

When the Civil War broke out, Clara got permission to ride in the army "ambulances" to nurse the injured soldiers. It took her awhile, but in 1862 she got permission to visit the front lines of the battle and bring her own supplies. Because she
was organized and provided excellent care to the soldiers, two years later Union
General Benjamin Butler appointed her "lady in charge" of the hospitals for a section of the Union Army.

It took her almost 20 years, but Clara worked to establish the American Red
Cross in an effort to help people in crisis, whether from war or natural disasters.
Today the American Red Cross provides food, water, clothing, blankets, emergency
first aid, and many other services to people who have lost their homes because of
tornadoes, floods, hurricanes, or wars.

Clara spent the last 15 years of her life living in Glen Echo, Maryland. Today
visitors can tour her home, which is a tribute to her years of service and the history of the American Red Cross. Clara's life was one of service to those around her.

How do you serve others? What things can you do to make someone's life a
little easier? Why not follow Jesus' example and show people God's love by talking
to them, listening to them, and taking care of their needs.

NEXT STOP: Sharpsburg, Maryland

Fighting for Your Life

Then I said to you, "Do not be terrified; do not be afraid of them. The Lord your God, who is going before you, will fight for you, as he did for you in Egypt, before your very eyes, and in the wilderness." **Deuteronomy 1:29-31.**

On the first Saturday night of every December, Antietam National Battlefield remembers the Union and Confederate soldiers who gave their lives fighting in the Civil War. The battle of Antietam was the bloodiest single-day battle in the Civil War; nearly 23,000 soldiers were either killed or wounded.

In honor of the men who fought, volunteers light 23,000 candles in brown paper bags that are arranged in neat rows in the open cornfields and pastures of the battlefield. As you drive your car on the roads that zigzag through the battlefield, it is hard to imagine 23,000 dead and wounded soldiers lying in the fields. The candles never seem to stop! Their lights flicker across the dark fields, dotting the landscape as you drive the five-mile course set out for the Memorial Illumination.

War is a horrible thing! As I thought about all of those men and the families who were affected by the loss of husbands, sons, brothers, uncles, I thought about the war we are fighting—the war against Satan and his evil angels. Don't be fooled. Just because Satan isn't pointing a gun at you doesn't mean that he can't hurt you. He is doing everything in his power to trick you and make you think that being a Christian is the worst thing you could do. He wants you to believe the lie that God doesn't love you. He wants you to believe that you can do things better on your own. He wants you to disobey, be rude and disrespectful, be mean, and get angry when things don't go your way. He wants you to act like him.

So how can we stand up against the devil and his tricks? How can we turn our back on temptation and make good choices? The children of Israel were also afraid. They were afraid of the real, live enemies they could see. But they were forgetting the most important weapon they possessed—God. He promised them that He would go before them and fight for them.

God is ready and able to fight for you, too. He wants to help you overcome temptation and the devil's tricks. Just ask and He'll be there.

NEXT STOP: Emmitsburg, Maryland

April 2

Hello out there!

Sainthood

Oh, the joys of those who trust the Lord, who have no confidence in the proud or in those who worship idols. **Psalm 40:4, NLT.**

Elizabeth Ann Bayley Seton had a rough start to life. Her mother died when she was only 3 years old, so her father remarried in order to provide a mother for Elizabeth and her sister. At first the little family was happy, and the couple had five more children. Unfortunately, her father and stepmother separated, and her stepmother rejected her. Elizabeth felt as if she had lost another mother.

At the early age of 19 she married and began having children. Nearly 10 years after she married William Magee Seton, he passed away, leaving Elizabeth to care for their children. About this time she was introduced to the Catholic Church, and she joined.

In order to provide for her children, she started a school for girls. However, when the parents found out she had joined the Catholic Church, they took their daughters out of the school and wouldn't send them back. A few years later she started a new Catholic school for girls in Emmitsburg, Maryland. The first free Catholic school in America, this one was successful. In addition to teaching she helped care for the poor children in the community. People in the town called her "Mother Seton."

She served her community for the rest of her life until she died of tuberculosis in 1821. She was only 46 years old.

In 1975, 154 years after her death, the Catholic Church named her a saint. In order to pronounce a deceased person a saint, the Catholic Church must be able to recognize at least three miracles that have taken place as a result of people having prayed to this specific person. In Mother Seton's case, three people claim to have been cured of diseases. As a result, she became the first native-born American to be honored as a saint.

But as we know from the Bible, God is the only one who can heal—dead people certainly cannot heal people. King David tells us that we will be blessed if we trust in God, not false gods. The saints of the Catholic Church are idols. People who worship them are worshipping false gods. Unfortunately, some people like to make fun of these people and tease them. Instead, we should pray for them and share the Bible with them, hoping they learn the truth.

NEXT STOP: Jamestown, Virginia

A Cash Crop

A wise youth harvests in the summer, but one who sleeps during harvest is a disgrace. **Proverbs 10:5, NLT.**

Jamestown was the first of the original 13 colonies that was founded in America. The colonists who sailed to the New World were sent by King James to establish a colony, grow crops, and send valuable resources back to their home country of England.

Sounds easy, right? Till the ground, plant some seeds, and harvest a big crop. Wrong! It was a lot of backbreaking work. They didn't own a John Deere tractor to plow the field; they didn't have a Home Depot down the street where they could buy seeds; and they didn't have an irrigation system to water the fields. But they weren't afraid of working hard, and when they discovered that tobacco grew really well, they planted plenty of it. It became a cash crop of the colony, which means it brought in a lot of money when it was sold. Now, don't get me wrong: tobacco is very bad for you (in some respects, it's too bad the colonists discovered that it grew well), but the point is that these early colonists didn't throw in the towel and say that farming was too hard. Nope! They stuck with it until they were successful.

King Solomon tells us that a wise person will gather their crops, but a foolish person will sleep and be lazy when they should be out working. Think about the picture of these two different people. Whom do you want to be like? Do you want to be like the wise son, who has food to eat because he picked the fruits and vegetables from his garden? Or do you want to be like the sleepy guy, who lets his food rot in the garden while his family goes hungry?

I understand that sometimes you just want to be lazy and sit on the couch and do nothing. Sometimes you want to give up when something doesn't work the first time. Sometimes you don't feel like doing your homework or making your bed or putting away your laundry. It's tempting to want to goof off when you should be working. But if you want to be wise, you have to fight against those temptations and work hard at whatever task you are given. You can do it!

NEXT STOP: Richmond, Virginia

April 4

Hello out there!

Huff, Puff

Or do you not know that your body is a temple of the Holy Spirit who is in you, whom you have from God, and that you are not your own? For you have been bought with a price: therefore glorify God in your body. **I Corinthians 6:19, 20, NASB.**

Richmond is the capital of the state of Virginia. Not only is it home to the government of Virginia, but it is also home to some of the largest tobacco manufacturers, which produce cigarettes, cigars, and chewing and pipe tobacco. The colonists at Jamestown who originally planted tobacco and discovered a cash crop taught their children how to plant and harvest tobacco. Because of its success, generation after generation has cultivated the land and planted and harvested tobacco.

Unfortunately, these people did not stop to think about the harmful effects of tobacco. And even after doctors discovered the truth about how tobacco causes cancer and other health issues, the tobacco companies have kept producing and selling it because it brings in a lot of money. Greed causes people to make really bad decisions.

The U.S. government finally stepped in and ruled that the tobacco industry had to put warning labels on cigarette packages stating the danger of smoking. Unfortunately, many people ignore the warnings because they are addicted and won't stop smoking.

Each year smokers die because of lung cancer and other diseases caused by tobacco, such as chronic obstructive pulmonary disease (COPD). COPD causes the airway into the lungs to narrow, which leaves people gasping for breath because they can't get enough oxygen into their lungs. They feel as if they are slowly being suffocated. It's a horrible way to die, but they refused to listen to the warnings about the dangers of tobacco.

In 1 Corinthians 6:19, 20, Paul tells us that our bodies are the temple of God and that we should honor God by treating our bodies with respect. That means that we need to be careful about what we put into our bodies. Would you take a can of orange spray paint and spray it on the walls of your church's sanctuary? No! Never! You would be damaging God's house. But people don't stop to think that they hurt God's "house" when they smoke, do drugs, eat too much sugar, don't get enough sleep, and so on. God gave you only one body. Make sure you treat it with respect.

NEXT STOP: Yorktown, Virginia

The White Flag

"Give us seven days to send messengers throughout Israel!" replied the elders of Jabesh. "If no one comes to save us, we will agree to your terms." **1 Samuel 11:3, NLT.**

George Washington pulled together a rag-tag group of farmers, shopkeepers, and gentlemen who were willing to fight for their freedom. Together they fought against the British Redcoats, who were trained soldiers. Although they were outnumbered, less equipped, and less prepared, the colonists had determination on their side. They so desperately wanted to be free that they kept fighting until they had reached their goal.

To the surprise of the British, General Cornwallis surrendered to Washington at Yorktown, Virginia, and the colonists were named the victors of the American Revolution. They had defeated their enemy and gained their independence.

Ever since Cain killed Abel, people have fought against each other, often mistreating those they do not like or even killing them. In 1 Samuel 11 we find a story of a town called Jabesh Gilead and a bully named Nahash the Ammonite. Nahash the Ammonite threatened to gouge out the right eye of everyone in Jabesh. The elders of Jabesh asked for seven days to send word to the other tribes in Israel asking for their help in fighting back against the Ammonites. Nahash agreed, and the message was sent.

When the messenger arrived at Gibeah where Saul lived, the people cried when they heard the news. Saul came in from the field and asked what the problem was. Upon finding out about the threat against the men of Jabesh Gilead, he "burned with anger" (1 Samuel 11:6). He then cut up a pair of oxen and sent the pieces throughout Israel with messengers who announced that the oxen of anyone who didn't follow Saul or Samuel would face the same outcome as the oxen who had been cut up. That made everyone very fearful, and the men of Israel came out in large numbers to help Saul defeat the Ammonites. It was after that event that Saul was crowned king of Israel.

History is filled with stories of two sides fighting over something, whether it was land, freedom, money, or religion. What do you think is worth fighting for?

NEXT STOP: Williamsburg, Virginia

Hello out there!

Warm? Hot? Cold?

But since you are like lukewarm water, neither hot nor cold,
I will spit you out of my mouth! **Revelation 3:16, NLT.**

Williamsburg, Virginia, became the capital of the colony after Jamestown burned to the ground. In addition to building a capitol building, houses, and shops, the people constructed the governor's palace as a focal point in the town. The structure was made out of brick and was very grand and impressive. Behind the palace was a series of gardens and paths for the governor and his guests to enjoy. In addition to flower gardens, the kitchen staff maintained a vegetable garden that helped supply their needs for dinners and parties.

With no automatic ice machine in their refrigerator—oh, wait, they didn't even have a refrigerator—the staff cut ice from the frozen ponds and used it to make ice cream or other cool treats. The ice was also used to keep things cold, such as drinks. However, what they really needed was ice during the summer when it was hot!

To solve their problem, someone came up with the idea of an ice house. So the staff got to work digging down into the earth underneath a large mound of dirt to where the temperature was cooler. Then they cut out large blocks of ice in the winter and stored them in the ice house with sawdust and straw to prevent it from melting. Sure enough, they were able to keep the ice cool enough to use in the summer for their cool treats. If the temperature of the ice house had been lukewarm or hot, the ice would have melted. It had to be cold in order to be useful.

Similarly, if we want to be useful to God, we can't be lukewarm. Lukewarm means that we really don't care about God and His mission; we are just going through the motions of attending church because we always have or because our parents make us. God says it is better to be cold or hot. He doesn't want us to be fake. He would rather have us be cold and admit that we don't want to follow Him than to pretend that we do. Of course, God ultimately wants us to be on fire for Him. He wants us hot so that no one will miss the fact that we love Him. Think about which temperature you are and what you can do to make sure you are "hot."

NEXT STOP: Stratford Hall, Virginia

Stand Firm

Be on guard. Stand firm in the faith.
Be courageous. Be strong. **I Corinthians 16:13, NLT.**

General Robert E. Lee served in the United States military for 32 years. Born in Stratford Hall, Virginia, Lee is best known for leading the Confederate troops in the Civil War. The interesting thing that you may not know is that Lee supported President Abraham Lincoln and the president's attempt to keep the Union together. However, when Virginia decided to split from the Union in April 1861, Lee chose to follow his home state. He couldn't bear the idea of fighting against the people he loved and cared about.

Have you ever been caught between two sides and forced to make a decision between what you knew was right and what you wanted to do? For example, let's say you overhear your best friend picking on the shy girl in your class and teasing her because she never says anything and doesn't have any friends. The right thing to do would be to stand up for the shy girl in your class and tell your best friend to leave her alone. But what you probably want to do is take the "easy" way out and say nothing.

Or maybe you see a kid in your class cheat on a math test. After the test your classmate comes to you and threatens you that if you tell, he will make you sorry for tattling. What should you do? The easy way out would be to keep your mouth shut so that you won't get hurt or make him angry. But the right thing to do is to tell your parents so they can talk to the teacher.

Every day we are forced to make choices. Every day we have to choose between right and wrong, good and evil. When writing to the church at Corinth, Paul told the church members to "stand firm in the faith." He reminded them to "be strong." He knew that life was hard and that the devil would try to trick them into doing things that would make God sad, so he reminded them to watch and be ready and stand tall for Jesus.

NEXT STOP: Monticello, Virginia

Hello out there!

April 8

The Word of God

Truly I tell you, until heaven and earth disappear, not the smallest letter, not the least stroke of a pen, will by any means disappear from the Law until everything is accomplished. **Matthew 5:18.**

Thomas Jefferson, the main author of the Declaration of Independence and third president of the United States, called Monticello, Virginia, home. It was here that he studied, farmed, wrote, and invented gadgets such as a book stand that could hold five books at once and spin around so the reader could pick which one to read.

Jefferson was a scholar. He loved to study and read. In fact, he founded the University of Virginia in Charlottesville, which is only a few miles from Monticello. In addition to studying history and science, he also studied the Bible.

Later on in his life he began a project that some people call the *Jefferson Bible*, but which Jefferson titled *The Life and Morals of Jesus of Nazareth*. The idea behind the project was to piece together the life and major teachings of Jesus as told in the Bible in the order they happened. To accomplish this, Jefferson used a razor to cut out portions of Scripture from Matthew, Mark, Luke, and John, which he then pasted into a new book to create one complete story. However, he chose to leave out any reference to the prophecy of Jesus' birth, including the angels who sang to the shepherds. He also left out Jesus' miracles and any mention of the Trinity or the fact that Jesus was God's Son.

Does that sound like a complete Bible? Does it make you wonder what Jefferson really believed about God? It makes me wonder!

Today's text reminds us that the Bible is God's letter to us and that it is not to be changed or altered in any way. God will preserve His Word so that people can discover the truth. It doesn't matter if religions or pastors or government officials try to change the Bible by publishing other books. They can write or print whatever they want, but the Word of God can never be changed.

NEXT STOP: Arlington, Virginia

On All Five Sides

> In the days of those kings the God of heaven will set up a kingdom which will never be destroyed, and that kingdom will not be left for another people; it will crush and put an end to all these kingdoms, but it will itself endure forever. Inasmuch as you saw that a stone was cut out of the mountain without hands and that it crushed the iron, the bronze, the clay, the silver and the gold, the great God has made known to the king what will take place in the future; so the dream is true and its interpretation is trustworthy. **Daniel 2:44, 45, NASB.**

Many people may assume that the Pentagon is located in Washington, D.C., since it is the military headquarters for the United States, but the Pentagon is located just outside of Washington, D.C., in Arlington, Virginia. The five-sided building is the largest office building in the world. Here are a few statistics about the building and its employees:

It has about 100,000 miles of internal telephone lines.

Approximately 28,000 military and civilian employees work there.

The building has five floors above ground and two floors below ground.

There is a five-acre outdoor courtyard in the middle of the Pentagon.

Construction began on September 11, 1941. Sixty years later the building was attacked on September 11, 2001, when hijackers flew a plane into the side of the Pentagon, killing 189 people.

The Pentagon serves as the central hub for everything dealing with security of the United States of America. From military operations overseas to protection of America's cities, the Pentagon is where major decisions are made that affect people and nations.

It's tempting to feel safe and secure when you hear about the strength of the Pentagon and the training of America's military forces, but we know that the Pentagon and all other strongholds made by the world's governments will vanish when Jesus comes again.

Nebuchadnezzar thought his kingdom was strong and secure. He thought he was safe. But God sent him a dream that showed the weakness of his kingdom and all the kingdoms that would come after him. God's kingdom is represented by a rock that will crush all the kingdoms of this earth. Don't place your trust in the things of this earth, because they are going to disappear when Christ comes again.

NEXT STOP: Arlington National Cemetery, Virginia

April 10

Hello out there!

Rest in Peace

Jesus said to her, "I am the resurrection and the life.
The one who believes in me will live, even though they die; and whoever lives
by believing in me will never die. Do you believe this?" **John 11:25, 26.**

Many people find Arlington National Cemetery a very sad place to visit because it is where more than 400,000 people who served our country are buried. The cemetery is divided into 70 different sections, and individuals are buried in each section based on their military rank, when they served their country, or in what capacity they served. For instance, there is a section for nurses who served in the military. There are also two presidents buried on the grounds of the cemetery. On average, 27 to 30 funerals are held each day, five days a week!

In addition to the straight rows of small white gravestones that stretch across rolling hills, there are some larger memorials and grave markers, including the Tomb of the Unknowns. This special monument marks the burial places of the remains of three unidentified soldiers from three different wars. To honor these soldiers who gave their lives, a memorial tomb was created, and a soldier has guarded the tomb 24 hours a day, seven days a week, since July 2, 1937.

Death is sad. But for those of us who believe in God, we have hope and a promise to hold on to. In today's text Jesus is comforting Martha, who is mourning the loss of her brother, Lazarus. And Jesus tells her that He is the resurrection. He is the one who gives life to people. He promises her that whoever believes in Him will live and never die.

Does that mean that we will live forever? Yes and no! Yes, we will live forever when Jesus comes and takes us home to heaven. But no, we will not live forever on this earth.

Although many Christians have died since Jesus' resurrection, they are just sleeping in the ground, waiting for His second coming. Once that trumpet blast pierces the air, signaling Jesus' return, those who have gone to sleep and are buried in the ground waiting for Jesus' return will be raised back to life and be taken up to meet Him in the air. It is going to be the most amazing sight to watch as people see Jesus for the first time and are reunited with their family and friends. We have nothing to fear about dying if we have Jesus in our hearts. Live in peace, because Jesus doesn't want you to be afraid of anything!

NEXT STOP: Mount Vernon, Virginia

Tooting Your Own Horn

Then we will be able to go and preach the Good News in other places far beyond you.... Then there will be no question of our boasting about work done in someone else's territory. As the Scriptures say, "If you want to boast, boast only about the Lord." When people commend themselves, it doesn't count for much. The important thing is for the Lord to commend them. **2 Corinthians 10:16-18, NLT.**

Mount Vernon was the home of our first president, George Washington, who was born and raised in Virginia. Located near the town of Alexandria, Mount Vernon is a sprawling plantation that overlooks the Potomac River. In addition to the home, there are numerous outbuildings on the grounds, including a washhouse, smokehouse, coach house, spinning room, blacksmith, and barns. Washington was a true farmer at heart, and he loved to garden and plant fruits and vegetables, trying different varieties and new ways to grow things.

It is interesting to note that after Washington, seven other political leaders who were born in Virginia became president of the United States—Thomas Jefferson, James Madison, James Monroe, William Harrison, John Tyler, Zachary Taylor, and Woodrow Wilson. In addition to that, six presidents' wives were born in Virginia—Martha Washington, Martha Jefferson, Rachel Jackson, Letitia Tyler, Ellen Arthur, and Edith Wilson.

Virginia can also boast about a lot of firsts. It was home to the very first president and first lady; the first permanent English settlement was established at Jamestown; the first peanuts grown in America were grown in Virginia; and some historians claim that the first Thanksgiving was held in Virginia.

But boasting can lead to trouble, especially when we place ourselves above others and think we are better than everyone else. Boasting is not a new problem; it has been around since the early Christian church. Check out Paul's instructions to the Corinthians. He warns them not to boast about the work they are doing in preaching the gospel. Instead, he tells them that they need to boast about Jesus. In other words, they need to sing the praises of God, toot the horn of the Bible, show off Jesus' love, and brag about God's goodness to those around them.

If you find yourself thinking you are better than everyone else in school or sports or music, stop! Instead of focusing on yourself, turn your attention to Jesus. When you do, you will boast about Someone much better than you will ever be.

NEXT STOP: Somerset Village, Bermuda

Hello out there!

You Can't Be Two People

With the tongue we praise our Lord and Father,
and with it we curse men, who have been made in God's likeness.
Out of the same mouth come praise and cursing. My brothers and sisters,
this should not be. Can both fresh water and salt water flow from the same
spring? My brothers and sisters, can a fig tree bear olives, or a grapevine bear figs?
Neither can a salt spring produce fresh water. James 3:9-12.

Welcome to the tropical island of Bermuda! Kick back, relax, and enjoy the warm breezes that blow from the Atlantic Ocean. Bermuda is a British territory that is located about 640 miles east-southeast of Cape Hatteras, North Carolina.

Since we are visiting Bermuda, guys, you have to wear the traditional Bermuda shorts, a dress shirt, blazer, tie, and knee socks. You may think this looks silly, but men on the island wear this type of outfit from April through November. Regardless of the activity, whether conducting business or having fun, men can be seen wearing Bermuda shorts in public.

Another interesting fact about Bermuda is that all of the homes have a tank under the house that collects rainwater from the roof. The water is then filtered and used by the family living in the home. Rain serves as Bermuda's only supply of fresh water, so these tanks and filtering systems are very important to the residents on the island. Although Bermuda is surrounded by water, residents cannot drink the ocean water because of its saltiness, and it is an expensive process to turn ocean water into drinking water.

As James said, a salt spring, or the ocean, cannot produce fresh water. And salt water and fresh water cannot come out of the ocean in the same bucket. Would you agree with his reasoning? OK, so now look at the beginning of the verse. Can a Christian praise God and put down a neighbor with their tongue in the same breath? H'mm. Interesting thought, isn't it?

Are there kids in your Sabbath school class who tease the new girl because she is wearing jeans instead of a dress and then they go into church and do the Scripture reading up front? If so, they need to become better friends with Jesus and take on His character. We are all learning and growing, but above all, we need to remember that everyone is made in the image of God, and all are special in His eyes.

NEXT STOP: Hamilton, Bermuda

Welcome!

Some, to be sure, are preaching Christ even from envy and strife,
but some also from good will; the latter do it out of love, knowing that
I am appointed for the defense of the gospel. **Philippians 1:15, 16, NASB.**

Bermuda is a popular tourist destination. The island features manicured golf courses and beautiful pink beaches. Yes, you read correctly. The sand is pink! The beaches are a girl's dream for building pink sand castles. All joking aside, the sand is pink because of small animals with a red shell. When these microscopic animals are crushed and washed up on shore, they tint the sand pink.

Tourists who visit the island are not only wowed by the beaches but also are impressed with Johnny Barnes. Now, Johnny is not some movie star or local politician. He is not a millionaire or a famous athlete. But he is a resident of Bermuda, and he loves his home and the people who visit it. That is why since 1986 Johnny has been greeting travelers going in and out of the town of Hamilton every weekday morning from 3:45 to 10:00. His smiling face and wave have brightened the day for thousands of people. In recognition of his contribution to the community as a goodwill ambassador of Bermuda, the town erected a statue in his honor.

What is our motive for sharing the good news of Jesus with others? Or what is our motive for acting like Christ? Is it so we stay out of trouble and make our parents think we are good so that we can get away with stuff when they aren't looking? Is it so we can look better than our classmates? We have to make sure we are not acting like Jesus out of rivalry, as Paul talks about in today's text. Instead, we should share God's love with others because we care about them and because we care about God.

Being a goodwill ambassador means that a person is friendly, helpful, kind, and cooperative. Think about how you can be a goodwill ambassador for Jesus today at home and at school. Like Johnny, if you are genuine in your actions people will notice that you are truly a follower of God, and hopefully they will want to be like you too.

NEXT STOP: Roanoke Island, North Carolina

April 14

Hello out there!

A Mystery

Daniel replied, "No wise man, enchanter, magician or diviner can explain to the king the mystery he has asked about, but there is a God in heaven who reveals mysteries. He has shown King Nebuchadnezzar what will happen in days to come." **Daniel 2:27, 28.**

On April 3 we talked about Jamestown, Virginia, being the first permanent English colony in America. But today we are visiting Roanoke Island, which was the first English colony in America. Huh? There is one word that separates these two firsts and makes them both unique: "permanent."

Roanoke Island was the first English colony in the New World. Founded by Walter Raleigh in 1587, the colony was made up of about 120 men, women, and children who braved the crossing of the Atlantic Ocean for the unknown wilderness of the New World. However, life was very hard, and the colonists sent Governor John White back to England for supplies later in the same year they arrived. However, because of war with Spain, Governor White was unable to return to the colony until 1590. When he arrived, the entire colony had vanished. The only thing left was the word "Croatoan" carved into a post. Talk about a mystery with no eyewitnesses!

Thus, the settlement has been nicknamed "The Lost Colony" because no one ever found the whereabouts of the colonists or clues as to what happened to them. Therefore, when Jamestown was settled, it became the first *permanent*, or lasting, settlement in the New World.

Mysteries beg to be solved. We look for clues, come up with theories of what may have happened, and talk to people who may have seen something. But some mysteries, like the disappearance of the Lost Colony, are never solved.

King Nebuchadnezzar dreamed a disturbing dream that was a mystery to him, and not knowing what it meant drove him crazy! He thought his magicians and wise men could tell him the answer and help him get some rest, but they couldn't. So Daniel was called. And notice what he did. First, he made it clear to the king that people can't explain dreams, but God can.

Always remember that there is no mystery or problem too big for God to handle. He knows the answer for everything, including the fate of the Lost Colony.

NEXT STOP: Kitty Hawk, North Carolina

Free as a Bird

Oh, that I had wings like a dove; then I would fly away and rest!
I would fly far away to the quiet of the wilderness. How quickly
I would escape—far from this wild storm of hatred. **Psalm 55:6-8, NLT.**

Orville and Wilbur Wright had a dream of creating a machine that could soar through the air like a bird. Other people had created gliders, but two early designers of hang gliders had crashed and died. The brothers felt that if flying was going to be successful and safe, there had to be a way for the pilot to control the glider. Once they felt that their glider was safe, they determined to add an engine to their craft so that it could be propelled forward.

After years of research and study of the angle of birds' wings in flight, Orville and Wilbur were ready to test their idea in a full-scale model. But they needed a good location that had enough wind, provided a soft landing, and had high points from which they could glide. Their home in Ohio did not fit that description. So they looked for a good location and settled on Kitty Hawk, North Carolina. There on the sand dunes near the Atlantic Ocean they launched their first glider in 1901 and a second model in 1902.

Then, on December 17, 1903, they launched the "world's first power-driven heavier-than-air machine in which man made free, controlled, and sustained flight." The above quote is inscribed on a plaque in memory of the airplane they flew, which is on display at the National Air and Space Museum in Washington, D.C.

If you could fly, would it be so you could run away from problems as King David wanted to do? Read today's text again. King David wished he had wings like a bird so he could fly away and get some rest from the storms of life.

You may not be able to run away from your problems by jumping on a plane and flying to another country, but there are ways you can deal with the hard times in life. Prayer is always first on the list. Talking to your parents or to another adult you trust or even to a close friend can help you deal with your problems. Another option is to find a special place you can go to that is quiet and peaceful. It might be your room, a tree in your yard, the porch, or another room in your house. Whatever the solution, "fly" to your spot and ask God to help you figure things out.

NEXT STOP: Asheville, North Carolina

Hello out there!

Is Bigger Better?

He lies down wealthy, but will do so no more; when he opens his eyes, all is gone. **Job 27:19.**

The Biltmore Estate in Asheville, North Carolina, is America's largest home. At 178,926 square feet (most homes today are 1,500 to 2,500 square feet), the Biltmore is a *huge* mansion. With 250 rooms, the mansion was built in the style of a European castle.

George Vanderbilt constructed the Biltmore Estate, which included its own village and church, between 1889 and 1895. The mansion amazed visitors with an indoor swimming pool, bowling alley, exercise room, library, dining rooms, bedrooms, parlors, a kitchen and pantry, and rooms for the servants. Outside, guests enjoyed the beautiful gardens and mountain views.

The mansion also featured an elevator, forced-air heating, and fire alarms, which were all new inventions that most people did not have in their homes, especially elevators. But with the massive size of the mansion, it was no wonder they installed an elevator. Talk about a fun house to play hide-and-seek in; you could hide for weeks and no one would find you!

Clearly George Vanderbilt was very wealthy. He had to be rich to construct such a large home and pay for servants to run the place.

Ask your parents to show you a picture of the Biltmore Estate. Now answer this question: Would you like to live there? My guess is that you probably said yes! Who wouldn't want to live in a mansion and be waited on by servants, right?

Being rich seems like an easy way to solve life's problems, but Job knew that money wasn't everything in life. Job was rich, and yet he lost all of his wealth and possessions in one day. He realized how fast it could disappear.

Life can change in an instant. Instead of seeking wealth so that you can buy gadgets and electronics and clothes that are newer and better, make sure you have a relationship with Christ that is firmly grounded in the Bible. That way, if life changes and you lose everything, you won't lose the only thing that matters in this world—Jesus.

NEXT STOP: Grandfather Mountain, North Carolina

Will You Stand?

And since we are his children, we are his heirs. In fact, together with Christ
we are heirs of God's glory. But if we are to share his glory,
we must also share his suffering. **Romans 8:17, NLT.**

If you are afraid of heights, be glad you are reading today's devotional and not actually visiting Grandfather Mountain and the Mile High Swinging Bridge in person. You see, the bridge stretches across an 80-foot chasm that is one mile above sea level. Then again, maybe you like heights and would love standing in the middle of the bridge, looking at the green mountains as their trees begin to bloom in the warm spring weather.

The views are wonderful from the bridge, but the bridge and the views would not be possible if it weren't for one man—Hugh Morton. He owned Grandfather Mountain, which is located in the Blue Ridge mountain range, for 54 years before he died.

Hugh obviously loved nature because he made sure the land he owned remained wild and available for everyone to enjoy. He worked hard to preserve the mountain's wilderness for outdoor enthusiasts to enjoy. After he died in 2006, the heirs to his estate sold part of the mountain to the state of North Carolina, and it is now a state park.

An heir is someone who is the beneficiary of their relative, meaning that the heir benefits from what the relative leaves them, which is usually money, houses, cars, land, or other things of value.

Now let's apply this to our text in Romans 8:17. If we are followers of Christ, we are heirs of God, and we will receive the same riches that Jesus received when He was raised to life and returned to heaven. But the text tells us that we must "share his suffering" if we are going to "share his glory" and the riches of heaven.

Hugh's heirs were willing to follow the instructions he left before he died. They were willing to protect the mountain as he wished. Are you willing to stand up for your heavenly Father and His Son? Are you willing to follow the instructions Jesus gave before He returned to heaven and share His love with the people around you? You are a prince or princess, but you need to protect the name of the King and spread the good news about Him. It won't always be easy, but the reward is beyond our imagination.

NEXT STOP: Tail of the Dragon, North Carolina

April 18

Hello out there!

Foolish Driving

A wise son makes a father glad,
But a foolish son is a grief to his mother. **Proverbs 10:1, NASB.**

Today we're going driving on the craziest road in North Carolina, and maybe in North America. Even its name makes it sound scary. Buckle up, because we are driving the Tail of the Dragon. This two-lane road stretches for 11 miles across the state line from North Carolina into Tennessee. So what's so scary about that? Eleven miles is nothing. Well, throw 318 curves into that 11-mile stretch, and now it's crazy.

Motorcycle riders and sports car enthusiasts travel to North Carolina for the pleasure of driving on a difficult road full of twists and turns. The speed limit on the Dragon is 30 miles per hour. Now, I want to ask you two questions. Why do you think the speed limit is set so slow? And do you think drivers obey the speed limit?

If you said that the speed limit is slow to protect drivers, you are correct. So if the speed limit is set to protect drivers, then everyone should be following it for their own safety and the safety of the other drivers on the road, right? *Wrong!* Year after year people, mostly motorcycle riders, die because they take the turns too quickly and fly off the road. The lucky ones walk away with broken bones or cuts and bruises from sliding across the pavement.

According to a July 29, 2007, article in the Knoxville *News Sentinel* about the Dragon, the average cost for treating a motorcycle rider's broken leg is $50,000! That includes the helicopter ride to the hospital's trauma/emergency center, treatment, and the hospital stay. If the person has more injuries, the bill goes even higher.

If riders know these things, why do they push their luck and go faster than they should? Because most people think they can get away with it without being caught or getting hurt.

Don't be foolish! When you are old enough to drive, follow the rules of the road. And follow the rules of your state and country. But more important, follow the rules that God has given us in the Bible. He gave us the Ten Commandments to keep us out of trouble and help us live the best life possible.

When you are wise, you make God and your family proud of you. But when you are foolish, you make a lot of people sad. Just think of all the moms who are sad because their sons or daughters drove too fast on the Dragon and died.

NEXT STOP: White Lake, North Carolina

Picture-perfect

In front of the throne was a shiny sea of glass, sparkling like crystal.
In the center and around the throne were four living beings,
each covered with eyes, front and back. **Revelation 4:6, NLT.**

Most kids love going to the beach. Digging in the sand, building sand castles, jumping waves, searching for shells, and swimming in the ocean are all exciting beach activities . . . for most people. I am not one of them. I love to swim, but I prefer seeing what is underneath the water, and you just can't do that in the ocean. That's why I like pools and clear lakes better.

Although I have never been to White Lake, it sounds perfect! It has a white sandy bottom, which is very unusual for a lake, and crystal-clear waters. Because of these great qualities, it has been labeled as the nation's safest beach. That's my kind of place!

The city of White Lake may advertise that their lake has crystal-clear water and is the safest beach to visit, but they are obviously speaking in earthly terms, because the most crystal-clear lake is the sea of glass in heaven. In heaven we will certainly be safe, so the sea of glass can also take that title away from White Lake.

There are many beautiful things on this earth that God has created that have not been completely spoiled by sin, but nothing will compare to the beauty of heaven and God's unspoiled creation.

Have you ever imagined what color the water in the sea of glass is? Is it blue or turquoise or clear? Whatever color it may be, the Bible and Ellen White give us a few more details about this special place, telling us that we will stand on the sea of glass and sing praises to God. Ellen White gives this description. As you read it, let your mind imagine each part of her vision. "Angels were all about us as we marched over the sea of glass to the gate of the city. Jesus raised His mighty, glorious arm, laid hold of the pearly gate, swung it back on its glittering hinges, and said to us, 'You have washed your robes in My blood, stood stiffly for My truth, enter in'" (*Early Writings*, p. 17).

Isn't that awesome? Jesus will swing open the pearly gate to the city and welcome us in because we have chosen to accept His free gift on the cross and we've stood up for the truth of the Bible. Let's all be ready so we can march across the sea of glass together.

NEXT STOP: Fayetteville, North Carolina

Hello out there!

The Best of the Best

Bring the best of the firstfruits of your soil
to the house of the Lord your God. **Exodus 23:19.**

Have you ever heard of Babe Ruth? No, not the candy bar! That's "Baby" Ruth. We're talking about Babe Ruth, a famous baseball player back in the early 1900s.

Babe Ruth was born and raised in Baltimore, Maryland, and began his baseball career playing for the Baltimore Orioles, who, although they are a major league team now, were a minor league team back then. The Orioles were holding their spring training in Fayetteville, North Carolina, in March 1914.

Babe Ruth had never left Baltimore before, so he was very fascinated by the sights and scenes in Fayetteville. The story is told that everything was so new to him that he rode the elevator in the hotel for fun and followed the team manager, Jack Dunn, around because he didn't know what to do in this new town. Some people say that a team member teased him and said, "There goes Dunn's new babe," and the nickname stuck.

Well, on March 7, 1914, he was playing in his first team game when he hit his first home run. It was the longest home run that any of the spectators had ever seen, which made the crowd go crazy.

Afterward Babe Ruth said, "I hit it as I hit all the others, by taking a good gander at the pitch as it came up to the plate, twisting my body into a backswing, and then hitting it as hard as I could swing." He did his best, and he became one of the best baseball players of all time.

God asks us to do our best in all we do. That includes homework, chores, volunteer jobs at church, Pathfinders, and all other activities we do each week. But that isn't the only "best" that God asks us to give Him. God told the children of Israel to bring Him the best of the firstfruits of their gardens, meaning the first produce to be harvested. This was how the children of Israel tithed.

Whether it is your tithe and offerings or your talents, make sure you give your best to God. Don't let Him down; instead, give Him all you've got!

NEXT STOP: Fort Sumter, South Carolina

Fighting Words

What is causing the quarrels and fights among you?
Don't they come from the evil desires at war within you? James 4:1, NLT.

Charleston is a charming Southern town full of old plantation-style homes, small shops and restaurants, quiet side streets, and towering old trees that spread out their limbs under a canopy of Spanish moss that hangs down and provides shade from the sun.

While visiting Charleston, be sure to see one of the historical highlights of the area, Fort Sumter, which is located just offshore in Charleston Harbor. It was at this fort that the first shots were fired that started the Civil War. You see, U.S. soldiers were stationed at the fort when South Carolina seceded, or left, the Union. Upon making this declaration, the state demanded that the U.S. Army leave the fort and return to Washington, D.C. However, the commanding officer of the army refused to do so. A standoff took place, and the newly formed Confederate forces laid siege to the fort, shooting at ships that tried to get near the fort to bring the U.S. soldiers much-needed food and other supplies.

Then, on April 12, 1861, the Confederate forces blasted the fort with artillery fire from on the shore. The U.S. soldiers returned fire, but they were significantly outnumbered. After 34 hours of fighting, the U.S. forces surrendered and agreed to leave the fort. But there was no turning back. The Civil War had begun; sides had been drawn.

Do you ever fight with your brother or sister or friends? If you are honest with yourself, I'm guessing your answer will be yes. But why do we fight? Why do we pick sides? As with the Civil War, fighting can get us into a lot of trouble and cause a lot of pain and problems in life. So what does James say about the reason we fight? Right after he asks the first question, he asks another one: Don't you fight because you are selfish and you want your way and those desires push to the surface?

It can be really hard to listen to God when we want things our way, but that is the advice James gives us. He wrote, "So humble yourselves before God. Resist the devil, and he will flee from you. Come close to God, and God will come close to you. Wash your hands, you sinners; purify your hearts, for your loyalty is divided between God and the world" (James 4:7, 8, NLT). The key to stop fighting with others is to be like Christ. It's your choice! Choose wisely!

NEXT STOP: Charleston, South Carolina

Hello out there!

Cool Breezes

I will refresh the weary and satisfy the faint. **Jeremiah 31:25.**

If you live in the South or anywhere else where it gets really hot in the summer, you know how good air-conditioning feels. I lived in Florida for 10 years, and whenever I opened the front door during the summer, it often felt as if I had just opened the oven door. I didn't want to leave the air-conditioned house unless I was going swimming, because it was just so hot.

I've wondered how people survived without air-conditioning in the South. Then when I visited Charleston, I learned how at least one town found some relief from the sweltering heat. Because Charleston is located on the Atlantic Ocean, cool breezes blow off the water and offer a refreshing break from the summer heat. In order to take advantage of these breezes, the citizens of the town built their houses with large porches and front doors that faced the ocean so that the breeze would blow through the open door and cool the downstairs. Their houses also had porches upstairs that also featured a door and windows that opened toward the ocean. These openings helped to cool the rooms and served as air-conditioning way before it was invented.

Being out in the sun too long can make you cranky, and sometimes you even feel sick after standing in the blazing sun. But a cool breeze can give you energy to keep going. It can renew you and make you happy again.

In the same way, Jesus longs to refresh us and help us to handle the problems of life. If your brother or sister is annoying you, God cares and wants to help you. That doesn't always mean He is going to get rid of your problem. I don't think He will cause your little brother or sister to vanish so that you don't have to deal with them coming into your room and wanting to borrow your stuff, but He can give you patience and a loving attitude to deal with your frustration. Or He may help your mom to recognize the problem and offer to take you on a special outing without your sibling. But however God chooses to handle the situation, you can trust that He will refresh you like a cool breeze on a hot summer day.

NEXT STOP: Mount Pleasant, South Carolina

Moses' Basket Boat

But when she could hide him no longer, she got him a wicker basket and covered it over with tar and pitch. Then she put the child into it and set it among the reeds by the bank of the Nile. **Exodus 2:3, NASB.**

South Carolina was home to many plantations that were worked by slaves from Africa. Far from their homeland, the African slaves tried to adapt to their new surroundings. Part of adapting meant making things the way they did in Africa. One such thing was baskets.

Sweetgrass is a type of grass that grows along the coastal dunes of the Carolinas, and the African slaves used it to make the tightly woven coiled baskets that they were used to creating in Africa. The basket-making tradition and techniques have been passed down from generation to generation, with a large number of basket weavers living and working in Mount Pleasant. Today sweetgrass baskets are made and sold to tourists as a form of income for local basket weavers.

Speaking about baskets, today's Bible text talks about the basket that Moses' mother made, which was for the very practical reason of saving Moses. If you have ever tried to keep a baby quiet all day, you know it is impossible. They squeal, squeak, coo, cry, giggle, grunt, yell, and jabber. I don't know how Moses' family kept him quiet as long as they did, but obviously he began to make so much noise that they worried about the soldiers finding him. So Jochebed, Moses' mother, came up with a plan and got to work weaving a basket and coating it with tar and pitch so that it would float and keep her baby dry.

After the basket boat was finished, she did something very brave. She placed Moses in the basket, put it among the reeds along the bank of the Nile, and left Miriam in charge of watching out for her brother. I'm sure that Jochebed prayed for baby Moses as she walked home along the dusty path that led away from the Nile. I think she must have prayed that God would keep him safe and watch over him, since she couldn't. But no matter what, it took faith for Jochebed to leave Moses in a basket on the Nile River.

Do you trust God with the things that are most important to you? Do you trust that He knows what is best? Be like Jochebed and "float" your troubles out on the water, then wait to see what "royal" solution God sends your way.

NEXT STOP: Bomb Island, South Carolina

April 24

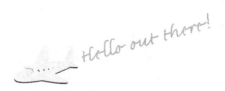
Hello out there!

Bombs Away!

But no one says, "Where is God my Maker, who gives songs in the night, who teaches us more than he teaches the beasts of the earth and makes us wiser than the birds in the sky?" Job 35:10, 11.

Although Bomb Island originally got its name during World War II when pilots used it for bombing practice, now the island has other "bombs" dropped on it. In late July of every year, hundreds of thousands of purple martins, a member of the swallow family of birds, return to the island to build their nests and roost for the summer. All those birds obviously drop "bombs" of bird poop all over the island.

But why do they return year after year? Who tells them to fly to Bomb Island in North Carolina instead of going to Disney World in Orlando, Florida? The Creator of the universe designed the birds and animals with instincts—they know what to do and where to go. God has programmed them with a certain amount of knowledge so that they know how to live.

But we are different. God created us with the ability to think and make decisions. Job recognized that God teaches us more than the animals and makes us wiser than the birds. But with the increased brainpower, we have the freedom to make choices and decide whom we are going to follow.

God didn't make us to be robots that automatically do everything He has programmed us to do. No, He made us with powerful brains. But with that power comes responsibility. Are you up for the challenge? How are you going to use your brain? Will you make wise choices that will honor God? Or will you act like a bird or animal and follow the rest of the "flock" or "herd," even if that means trespassing on someone else's property, taking something that doesn't belong to you, or lying to your parents about finishing your homework when you never did it?

It's your choice. God has given you the power to choose your path. Which way are you headed?

NEXT STOP: Stumphouse Mountain Tunnel, Walhalla, South Carolina

April 25

Smelly Cheese

I pray that your love will overflow more and more,
and that you will keep on growing in knowledge and understanding.
For I want you to understand what really matters, so that you may live pure
and blameless lives until the day of Christ's return. **Philippians 1:9, 10, NLT.**

In the 1800s America invested in building railroads as a means to transport goods and people from one place to another, thus speeding up travel and making it easier to get from town to town. Of course the landscape didn't always cooperate with their plans. There were mountains to cross or blast through and forests to cut down and clear.

The Stumphouse Mountain Tunnel was started in 1856, but the project was halted in 1859 after the state of South Carolina had spent more than 1 million dollars on the tunnel and refused to waste any more money on it. I can't say that I blame them—only 1,617 feet of the intended 5,863-foot-long tunnel had been excavated by then because the blue granite rock was so hard.

After the Civil War work on the tunnel was never resumed. Almost 100 years later Clemson University found a use for the abandoned tunnel. Because the temperature stays a constant 50 degrees Fahrenheit with humidity at 85 percent, the university decided that it was the perfect environment in which to make blue cheese, which it successfully did!

You may like cheddar cheese, but blue cheese is a whole different story. Blue cheese has a very strong taste, and it smells bad. Why? Because it has mold growing in it! Most blue cheese is made by adding the cultures of the mold *Penicillium* to the cheese and letting it sit, or age, in a temperature-controlled environment. This allows the mold to grow, which contributes to the unique flavor. Doesn't that sound yummy?

If you looked at a block of blue cheese and compared it to mozzarella, which one, would you say, is pure? The mozzarella, right? It hasn't had anything added to it to change it.

In order for us to make good choices, we need to keep our minds pure. If we add "mold" to our minds through bad music, TV shows, movies, or books, we are letting Satan pollute us. Keep God's love in your heart, and let Him help you stay pure and blameless in His sight.

NEXT STOP: Georgia

123

April 26

Good Food

Food gained by fraud tastes sweet,
but one ends up with a mouth full of gravel. **Proverbs 20:17.**

If you are allergic to nuts, be careful as you read today's entry, because there are nuts on this page! Georgia is the largest producer of peanuts, pecans, and peaches in the United States. These three "P" foods are each tasty in their own way.

Peanuts can be eaten plain or used to make trail mix or peanut butter. With peanut butter, you can make peanut butter and jelly sandwiches, cookies, peanut butter cup candies, and many other treats. With pecans you can make pecan pie or put the nuts in cookies or casseroles. And peaches, of course, are wonderful eaten fresh off the tree or in a pie or fruit cobbler. Sweet, juicy peaches are wonderfully sticky and extremely tasty, even if you get messy eating them.

Since we are talking about food today, I wanted to look at a text that talks about eating, and this one is a good one! It made me smile when I read it and imagined the word picture that came to my mind. Let's look at it more closely.

Fraud is another word for tricking someone to get what you want. So food gained by tricking someone may taste sweet at first, during the first bite. People may devour a fresh peach and enjoy the juice dripping down their chin. But their enjoyment won't last long.

King Solomon warns us that people who trick others to get what they want (in this case, food) will be sorry in the end. Because in the end they will end up with a mouth full of gravel instead of a juicy peach! Eating gravel sure doesn't sound good!

His point is that when you do something wrong, you may think you are going to get away with it and may enjoy the rewards of your trick for a short time, but King Solomon reminds us that in the end our sin will catch up with us. And the consequences of that bad choice will be as uncomfortable as eating gravel. Yuck!

NEXT STOP: Atlanta, Georgia

"Magical" Soda

And a woman who had been suffering from a hemorrhage for twelve years, came up behind Him and touched the fringe of His cloak; for she was saying to herself, "If I only touch His garment, I will get well." **Matthew 9:20, 21, NASB.**

D r. John S. Pemberton invented Coca-Cola in May 1886 in Atlanta, Georgia. Does anything in that sentence seem strange to you? If you caught the fact that a doctor created a type of soda, you've found the unique point about Coca-Cola. The fact of the matter is that Coca-Cola was invented as a patent medicine, not a soda.

Patent medicine was popular in the 1800s and early 1900s and referred to the "medicines" that people created. Unlike today, the medicine did not have to be approved by any committee of doctors or researchers. Someone could mix a few liquids, herbs, and even chemicals together and sell it to people as a "magical" medicine that would cure all their illnesses. Many people in search of relief from whatever illness was bothering them would buy the "medicine" from peddlers, people whose livelihood depended on selling these products.

There was one woman in the Bible who tried the medicines and "magical" potions the doctors gave her, but she didn't get better. She spent a lot of money seeing different doctors and trying their remedies, but nothing stopped the bleeding. Then she heard about Jesus and His power to completely and truly heal people. It was worth a shot; she had to try. She believed that if she could just touch His robe, she would be healed.

When Jesus passed through her town, she joined the crowd and pushed her way toward Jesus. At last she got close enough to touch His outer coat. At that instant she was healed! What true power and love!

Amazingly, Jesus felt her touch His coat, even though all those other people were brushing against Him and walking all around Him. "But Jesus turning and seeing her said, 'Daughter, take courage; your faith has made you well.' At once the woman was made well" (Matthew 9:22, NASB).

There are some drug companies that claim that their medicine will make you well, but the only true restorer of your health is Jesus.

NEXT STOP: Macon, Georgia

Hello out there!

April 28

A Special Place

This is a record of the ancestors of Jesus the Messiah, a descendant of David and of Abraham. **Matthew 1:1, NLT.**

Wesleyan College in Macon, Georgia, was the first college in the world chartered to grant degrees to women, making it the world's oldest women's college. Today the college still offers young women a variety of four-year degrees on a small campus that is just for women.

Although this may not seem special to you now, back in 1836 when the college was founded, women were not granted the opportunity to get a higher education. It was difficult for women to study and train for a career, because that was considered a man's place.

Back in Bible times the place of women in society was even lower. Women were considered property, the same as a house or a donkey or a plow. A woman was "owned" by her husband, and she didn't have many, if any, rights of her own.

But in a very significant way, Jesus showed us the value He places on women. Check out the genealogy of Jesus in Matthew 1. A genealogy is a family tree, showing a person's parents, grandparents, great-grandparents, great-great-grandparents, and so on. In those days the family tree was naturally based on the men in the family, but the Holy Spirit inspired Matthew to add women to Jesus' family tree to show how important women are to God.

There are five women listed in Jesus' family tree: Tamar, Rahab, Ruth, Uriah's wife, and Mary. The other interesting thing about this list is that some of these women were not born into the house of Israel. Rahab lived in Jericho and was saved by the Israelite spies; Ruth was from Moab, but she returned with Naomi, her mother-in-law, to Bethlehem, where she eventually married Boaz.

Once again God is showing us in His Word that it doesn't matter where we come from or who we are, because we are all special in His sight. Your classmates may ignore you and act like you don't exist. Your friends may go behind your back and say mean things about you. Your parents may punish you even when you didn't do anything wrong. But no matter how other people treat you, always know that God is on your side. He has your back. You are definitely special in His eyes!

NEXT STOP: Trail of Tears, Georgia

Forced Out

Love must be sincere. Hate what is evil;
cling to what is good. Be devoted to one another in love.
Honor one another above yourselves. **Romans 12:9, 10.**

Today we are not visiting a specific town or place. Instead, we are traveling along the Trail of Tears, which includes various points across Georgia and heads west. The Trail of Tears is the name given to the forced removal and relocation of a number of Native American nations from the southeastern states—Georgia, Florida, North Carolina, Alabama, and Mississippi.

President Martin Van Buren assigned the military the duty of removing the Native Americans from their homeland and moving them out West as part of the Indian Removal Act of 1830. As the Native American nations made their way westward, many died along the route because of starvation, disease, and exposure to the weather.

Hence, the route the Native Americans followed was named the Trail of Tears in recognition of the pain and suffering they experienced in being kicked out of their homeland and forced to walk thousands of miles to the barren and unsettled West.

The sad thing about the Trail of Tears is that the White people viewed the Native Americans as inferior, or of less importance. They viewed them as objects to be moved about and told what to do. The White people felt that they were better than the Native Americans, that they should be able to take the Native Americans' land and send them somewhere else. The White people were selfish and treated the Native Americans poorly.

Although they were establishing a nation founded on the equal rights of all people, the White people seemed to apply this freedom and right to themselves and no one else. And somehow, although America claims it was created as a Christian nation, they failed to act as Paul instructed the early church to behave. The White people failed to love and honor the Native Americans, and in that way, they failed to honor God.

Is there anyone in your life whom you find hard to love and wish would just move away so you don't have to deal with them? It can be hard to treat others the way you want to be treated, but God asks us to do just that. Ask Him to help you accept others for who they are. Ask Him to help you love others as He loves them.

NEXT STOP: Montgomery Lake, Georgia

Hello out there!

April 30

The Big One That Didn't Get Away

Simon Peter climbed back into the boat and dragged the net ashore. It was full of large fish, 153, but even with so many the net was not torn. **John 21:11.**

It's time to take a break from all our driving and go swimming. But we'll have to be careful to stay away from where the fishermen are fishing. I don't think they would be too happy if we scared the fish away.

The official state fish of Georgia is the largemouth bass, and the largest bass caught in the United States was caught in Montgomery Lake in 1932 by a 19-year-old man named George Perry. He had taken the day off from working on the farm and had gone fishing. That day he caught a bass weighing 22 pounds and 4 ounces; he held the world record for 77 years until it was tied in 2009 by a fisherman in Japan who caught a fish weighing the same as George's catch.

When George caught the fish, he knew he had a big one! So he took it into town to be officially weighed and measured. The fish was 32.5 inches long. The height and weight of the fish is comparable to the average height and weight of a 2-year-old child. Imagine catching a 2-year-old kid on a fishing line!

Like George, Peter had his own fishing stories to tell. And I'm guessing that one of his favorite stories was the last fishing experience he had before he dedicated his life to teaching others about Jesus. Do you remember the story? Jesus had been raised from the dead after the Crucifixion and had appeared to the disciples. Now Peter and six other disciples were out fishing on the Sea of Tiberias. They had been out all night and hadn't caught anything. I'm sure they were tired, hungry, and maybe discouraged, because they had wasted a whole night and not earned any money.

Then a man called from the shore and asked if they had caught anything. When they responded that they hadn't, the man said, "Throw your net on the right side of the boat and you will find some" (John 21:6). Then they couldn't even get the net into the boat because it was so full. Talk about a good catch! At that point Peter figured out that Jesus was on the shore, so he jumped overboard and swam to meet the Savior, leaving his friends to drag the nets in. Miraculously, the nets didn't tear. When they counted their catch, they had 153 large fish in all. When we listen to God, we will be amazed at the results!

NEXT STOP: Stone Mountain, Georgia

A Firm Foundation

I also say to you that you are Peter, and upon this rock I will build My church; and the gates of Hades will not overpower it. **Matthew 16:18, NASB.**

Stone Mountain is a must-see location outside of Atlanta, Georgia. The mountain, which is a solid piece of granite, suddenly rises up out of the grassy fields around it, stretching 825 feet above the surrounding area. But what is more impressive is how deep the mass of rock goes. At its deepest point the rock extends nine miles underground!

The mountain has long been named the largest exposed piece of granite in the world. The funny thing is that although the mountain is often called a pink granite dome, it is actually made up of quartz with some granite running throughout the rock. But whether it is quartz or granite, one thing is certain: it isn't going anywhere! That massive rock would provide a firm foundation for any building that people could build on it.

From the summit, hikers can see the skyline of downtown Atlanta, Kennesaw Mountain, and even, if it is a really clear day, the Appalachian Mountain range. All along the summit, small rock pools are formed from rainwater that collects where there are dips in the bare rock, allowing small shrimp and other creatures to grow until the end of the rainy season when the pools dry up and the creatures die.

Standing on top of such a massive amount of rock made me think about the foundation beneath my feet stretching deep into the earth. In Matthew 16:18 Jesus told Peter that the Christian church would be built on the foundation that Christ was laying and that death would not overcome Him. No matter how many people try to change the Bible to say what they want it to say, no matter how many individuals dismiss the Bible as a set of outdated guidelines we no longer need to follow, no matter how many times Satan tries to destroy Christians and God's church, they will not succeed.

Just as Stone Mountain stands firm, so does God's church. Jesus will not let His church be destroyed. So when you see people leaving the church or others saying they don't believe in God anymore, hold on tight and make sure your feet are planted on the Rock. If they are, you will stand firm and will not be moved!

NEXT STOP: St. Augustine, Florida

Hello out there!

The Best Water

Jesus replied, "Anyone who drinks this water will soon become thirsty again.
But those who drink the water I give will never be thirsty again. It becomes a fresh,
bubbling spring within them, giving them eternal life." John 4:13, 14, NLT.

Welcome to the Sunshine State! Florida is a favorite destination for vacationers who love beaches, sunshine, warm weather, and amusement parks. Today we are visiting St. Augustine, the oldest continuously occupied European settlement in the United States. The city was settled in 1565 by a Spanish explorer named Pedro Menéndez de Avilés.

St. Augustine changed hands a few times. It began as a Spanish colony, came under British rule in 1763, and was returned to Spain in 1783. Then in 1819 Florida was given to the United States, and Spain lost all control of the colony.

In St. Augustine the Spanish culture and architecture are still very visible. You can see red tile roofs atop white stucco buildings and visit the Castillo de San Marcos, the oldest masonry fort in the United States. Another favorite attraction is the Fountain of Youth Archaeological Park.

When Spanish explorers arrived, they were in search of a legendary spring in the area that supposedly restored health and youth to anyone who drank the water. Of course, many people sought to drink from the water near St. Augustine in hopes of finding a better life.

Those first Spanish settlers were not the only ones seeking a better life through a quick fix such as a drink of water. The Samaritan woman at the well asked Jesus for a drink of water after He told her that the water He had would cause her to never thirst again. "Please, sir," the woman said, "give me this water! Then I'll never be thirsty again, and I won't have to come here to get water" (John 4:15, NLT). She, like those who looked for the fountain of youth, wanted a temporary fix. She thought that if she never got thirsty, she wouldn't have to walk to the well or carry water back to her home in heavy jugs.

But Jesus was talking about the Water of Life. He was talking about Himself. When we ask Jesus into our life, we have eternal life, which is way better than any temporary happiness on this earth. Don't waste your time looking for things that will make you happy on this earth; money and things only disappear in the end. Instead, look to Jesus for life eternal.

NEXT STOP: Plant City, Florida

A Festival to Celebrate

Three times a year you are to celebrate a festival to me. **Exodus 23:14.**

Plant City is known as the winter strawberry capital of the world. Strawberry fields stretch in all directions and provide some of the first early strawberries to grocery stores across the country.

In late February or early March the town hosts the annual Florida Strawberry Festival, which attracts people from across Florida and all over the United States. The festival lasts for 11 days and features crafts, food, entertainment, concerts, a beauty pageant, and delicious strawberry shortcake. In fact, on February 19, 1999, the festival claimed the Guinness record for the world's largest strawberry shortcake, measuring 827 square feet and weighing 6,000 pounds.

Festivals are fun events to attend, and there seems to be an abundance of them around the world—there are seasonal festivals, religious festivals, music festivals, flower festivals, film festivals, craft festivals, fine art festivals, and food festivals.

But did you know that God talked about festivals in the Bible? God instructed the Israelites to celebrate three festivals each year: the Festival of Unleavened Bread, the Feast of Harvest, and the Feast of Ingathering. Each had a specific purpose. The Feast of Unleavened Bread was to remind the Israelites of when God brought them out of Egypt. The Feast of Harvest was to be celebrated when the first of their crops were picked, and the Feast of Ingathering was to be celebrated at the end of the growing season when they gathered in the last of their crops.

Each festival was a time of celebration and a time to remember what God had done for them, whether it was remembering how He had led them out of Egypt or how He was providing for their needs with good food to eat.

Christians no longer celebrate these festivals, but maybe we should celebrate the principle behind the festivals. For example, can you think of a time God really helped you out of a difficult situation? If so, take a minute to remember God's goodness, as the Israelites did during the Feast of Unleavened Bread. Now name five things the Lord has blessed you and your family with; this is similar to the Israelites celebrating the Feasts of Harvest and Ingathering. Just remember, you don't need a special holiday to remember God's blessings. Do it every day!

NEXT STOP: Disney World, Orlando, Florida

May 4

Hello out there!

The Happiest Place

Now I saw a new heaven and a new earth, for the first heaven
and the first earth had passed away. Also there was no more sea.
Then I, John, saw the holy city, New Jerusalem, coming down out of heaven
from God, prepared as a bride adorned for her husband. **Revelation 21:1, 2, NKJV.**

Walt Disney was a talented artist and animator in the early 1900s, but what brought him fame and fortune was the introduction of Mickey Mouse in 1928. The cartoons he created were silent pictures featuring Mickey doing silly things while music played in the background. I know it is hard to believe, but the cartoons were in black and white, and they were an immediate hit. Walt had hit the jackpot.

But Walt had other ideas up his sleeve. His next idea was to build an amusement park where kids and parents could spend time together playing and having fun. In 1955 Disneyland opened in California to the delight of visitors who traveled from near and far to visit this unique park with rides and shows and shops. After the success of Disneyland, Walt made plans to build a larger theme park near Orlando, Florida, called Disney World, which opened in 1971. In 2011 approximately 17 million visitors came to the park to see Cinderella's castle and ride the rides in Adventureland, Frontierland, Fantasyland, and Tomorrowland.

Some people call Disney World the happiest place on earth, but we know that the happiest place on earth will be the New Jerusalem when it descends from heaven and the former earth will be no more. We will be so happy because God "will wipe away every tear from [our] eyes; there shall be no more death, nor sorrow, nor crying. There shall be no more pain, for the former things have passed away" (Revelation 21:4, NKJV).

God promises to make everything new. With sin erased from this earth, we can finally be truly happy. We won't have to worry about Satan's temptations. Instead, we will be able to focus on loving God and enjoying all that He has prepared for us.

There are a lot of places we may enjoy visiting on this earth, but nothing compares to heaven. Make sure you never lose sight of the happiest place on earth, which is yet to come—the New Jerusalem.

NEXT STOP: Sea World, Orlando, Florida

The Wolves of the Sea

The wolf will live with the lamb, the leopard will lie down with the goat, the calf and the lion and the yearling together; and a little child will lead them. Isaiah 11:6.

I have always enjoyed SeaWorld. Growing up in Florida, I was able to go a number of times as a child, and I've been back to visit as an adult. Dolphins are one of my favorite animals, so I love watching the dolphin show. And the last time I was there, I had the chance to feed the dolphins and touch them. That was awesome! They are such smart animals, and their gentle personality makes them fun to watch as they flip, dive, and jump.

The killer whales also fascinate me. They are such powerful creatures, and yet they can do so many amazing tricks. I have always admired the trainers who get into the pool with them, because I would be scared to swim with such massive creatures. And after learning more about their behavior in the wild, I definitely would not get in the water with them.

In the wild, killer whales are known as the wolves of the sea because they hunt in packs. When they find a seal floating on a small patch of ice, they swim under the ice in unison and flick their tails under the water. This causes the ice to break up and a wave to flow over the ice, knocking the startled seal into the water. Killer whales also hunt other whales, surrounding them and taking turns biting their victim or hitting it until it gets too tired and weak to fight back. Then they drag it under water and drown it before feasting on the animal.

In the years since SeaWorld opened and brought killer whales into captivity to train, a handful of trainers have been killed. In recent years SeaWorld has changed their killer whale shows so that trainers give all their commands from the edge of the pool so that they are no longer swimming with the whales.

No matter how much we tame wild animals in captivity and teach them awesome tricks, the fact of the matter is that they are still wild. They won't be completely tame until heaven, when the wolf will live with the lamb and not eat it for lunch!

I look forward to the day when we can really play with the animals God has created and not be worried about whether or not they will attack us or bite us. That's just one more thing to look forward to in heaven.

NEXT STOP: Kennedy Space Center, Merritt Island, Florida

May 6

Hello out there!

Bright Night

Be on the alert then, for you do not know the day nor the hour. **Matthew 25:13, NASB.**

The John F. Kennedy Space Center opened on July 1, 1962, and is located on Merritt Island, a small stretch of land that juts out into the Atlantic Ocean between Miami and Jacksonville.

Since opening, countless missions have been launched, from deploying satellites to sending astronauts into orbit. But regardless of the mission, one thing is needed to launch the rocket or shuttle—fuel, and plenty of it. And when that fuel burns, it creates an extremely bright tail of fire behind the spacecraft, pushing it higher and higher into the sky.

When the Space Shuttle program was still in operation, people would travel from across Florida and other states to watch the shuttle launch, especially if it was at night, as those launches made for a spectacular view as the fiery orange flame lit up the night.

My grandparents lived approximately five miles from the Kennedy Space Center, but I had never seen a launch—until the night the shuttle was launched while I was playing outside with my cousins. We were outside goofing off on my grandparents' dock near the canal when suddenly we heard a thundering sound, and a few seconds later the sky looked as if it was on fire! The whole sky lit up, making it easy to see the shocked looks on our faces. We all took off running for the house as fast as we could go. We didn't stop to think about what it was because we were so startled and scared.

If we had known the shuttle was launching, we would have been in for a real treat, but the unexpected event caused us more fear than excitement. The same will be true of Jesus' return. Those who are ready and waiting will be excited. But those who are not ready will be taken by surprise. And their surprise will quickly turn to fear and trembling.

Please don't be caught off guard. God has given us plenty of signs and instructions to follow so that we will be ready. But it's your choice if you want to follow Him and embrace the plan He has for your life.

NEXT STOP: Homestead, Florida

Blown Away

Before very long, a wind of hurricane force,
called the "Northeaster," swept down from the island. **Acts 27:14.**

Wind is a very powerful force of nature that can easily destroy homes and trees and vehicles in its path. Tornadoes and hurricanes produce some of the most destructive winds on the planet, flattening whole towns in minutes.

I was 15 years old when Hurricane Andrew hit Homestead, Florida, and made its way across the state toward the Gulf of Mexico. Our family was living on the west coast of Florida at the time, and although we were not in the direct path of the storm, our town experienced torrential rain and some flooding as the hurricane traveled from east to west.

Sadly, whole neighborhoods in Homestead were completely demolished, leaving the streets covered with upside down vehicles, uprooted palm trees, roof tiles, walls, and furniture. The highest recorded wind gusts for Hurricane Andrew topped out at 177 miles per hour.

The Bible records a couple of big storms. One is in Acts 27 when Paul is sailing as a prisoner to Rome. After leaving the shore of Crete, a hurricane caught the ship off guard (verse 14). In the days that followed, the sailors did everything in their power to keep the ship from breaking apart. They even "passed ropes under the ship itself to hold it together" (verse 17). Finally, they decided to throw their cargo overboard to lighten the load of the ship. After fighting against the storm for a number of days, many gave up hope of being saved.

The "winds" of life can seem as if they will blow us over sometimes. Our problems seem way too big to deal with some days. But God is with us as He was with Paul. And just as He saved Paul from death, He will save you from whatever problem you are dealing with.

Check out what Paul told the sailors: "But now I urge you to keep up your courage, because not one of you will be lost; only the ship will be destroyed. Last night an angel of the God to whom I belong and whom I serve stood beside me and said, 'Do not be afraid, Paul. You must stand trial before Caesar; and God has graciously given you the lives of all who sail with you.' So keep up your courage, men, for I have faith in God that it will happen just as he told me" (verses 22-25).

NEXT STOP: "Cuban Miami," Florida

Hello out there!

Searching for More

All the believers were united in heart and mind. And they felt that what they owned was not their own, so they shared everything they had. **Acts 4:32, NLT.**

Cuba is an island located approximately 140 miles south of the mainland of Florida. Since Fidel Castro, a member of the Communist Party, became the prime minister in 1959, hundreds of thousands of Cubans have fled to America for protection and freedom, many of them settling in Miami, Florida. Miami has become the largest city in the United States with a significant Cuban-American population.

Communists feel that everything should be equal—there should not be a wealthy, middle-ranking, and low-income class. Sounds great, right? Although this sounds good on paper, Communist countries control their citizens and often won't let them visit other countries for fear they will never come back. Communist governments also tell people what jobs they will have, and they provide limited money to people to live on because everyone must contribute to the cost of treating people at the doctor's office, constructing new buildings, maintaining the roads, and paying for teachers who will teach what the Communist Party wants them to teach.

Communist leaders throughout history have ruled their countries with an iron fist, meaning whatever they say is the law and no one can go against their ideas. The idea that everyone is equal and that all property is owned by the public doesn't work when you have a ruler with absolute power running the country. This is why so many Cubans have fled their country and made new lives for themselves in Miami and elsewhere.

Similar to Communism's ideal of sharing things with all members of society, the early Christian church shared all of their property with one another. The big difference is that God was their ruler. They were not following a human being who was hungry for power and authority. God was their leader, and with Him in charge, there was harmony and unity. The early Christians worked together for a common goal of spreading the message of Christ's death and resurrection with everyone they met. They were a team fighting for a good cause. Make sure you are on that team!

NEXT STOP: Everglades National Park, Florida

King of the Swamp

They will wage war against the Lamb, but the Lamb will triumph over them because he is Lord of lords and King of kings—and with him will be his called, chosen and faithful followers. **Revelation 17:14.**

Have you ever sung the song "Who's the King of the Jungle?" If not, there is a verse that asks who the king of the swamp is, and the motions mimic the snapping of a crocodile's mouth when you sing "chomp." The song is correct about crocodiles and alligators being king of the swamp, but there isn't anything fun about meeting one of these creatures in person.

I am very afraid of alligators and crocodiles. They can eat small dogs, typically grow up to 15 feet in length, and have very sharp teeth, a powerful jaw, and beady eyes. And not only can they swim fast, but they can run up to 11 miles per hour on land!

Needless to say, growing up in Florida, I stuck to swimming in a pool, where I could see what was under the water. In my mind it did not seem safe to swim in the canals or lakes or ponds, because I wasn't sure what was lurking under the water. I wasn't about to be a snack for some hungry alligator or crocodile.

Well, come to find out, the American crocodile is listed as a "threatened" animal because there are only approximately 1,400 to 2,000 crocodiles currently living in Florida, many of them in the Everglades and Biscayne national parks.

This got me thinking. Are Christians a "threatened" or "endangered" species? Are true Christians who follow the principles God set forth in the Bible, who study His Word, and who act like Jesus a dying breed? Sure, a lot of people say they are a Christian, but do their actions match their words? Do your actions match your claim to be a follower of Christ?

Please make sure you are a faithful follower so that you will be on God's side when the final war between Satan and God takes place. You don't want to be on the wrong side!

NEXT STOP: Montgomery, Alabama

May 10

Hello out there!

Sit Tight

> Be strong and courageous, do not be afraid or tremble at them,
> for the Lord your God is the one who goes with you.
> He will not fail you or forsake you." **Deuteronomy 31:6, NASB.**

Rosa Parks was an African-American who grew up in Alabama during a time when White people did not accept Black people. It's hard to imagine, but although slavery had been done away with almost 90 years before, many White people often treated Black people as though they were second-class citizens and not as important as White people.

Especially in the South, Black people experienced this hatred through segregation, meaning that they were separated from White people. They had separate public bathrooms, separate entrances for restaurants and stores, and separate seating on buses and other public transportation. But on December 1, 1955, Rosa decided to take a stand. While riding on a bus in Montgomery, Alabama, the bus driver told her that she needed to move and make room for a White passenger, but Rosa refused to give up her seat, so she was thrown in jail for disobeying the bus driver's orders.

It took a lot of courage for Rosa to stay true to what she believed in, which was that she was just as important as any White person and that she and the other Blacks in her community and across the country should be treated with respect.

It can be scary standing up for what you believe or what God asks you to do. But God promises to be with you when you are doing His will. Today's text was spoken by Moses as he was preparing to turn over the leadership of the children of Israel to Joshua.

The Israelites had been wandering in the wilderness for 40 years, and now they were ready to enter the Promised Land. But they were still scared. There were so many unknowns in Canaan. There were giants and walled cities and warriors. It was for these reasons that Moses wanted to encourage the Israelites to put their trust in God. He reminded them to be strong and courageous. He told them to not be afraid. He reminded them that God would be with them and go before them.

When you are faced with a tough decision, take it to God. And then have courage to do what He asks you to do.

NEXT STOP: Selma, Alabama

The Same—But Different

Just as a body, though one, has many parts, but all its parts form one body, so it is with Christ. For we were all baptized by one Spirit so as to form one body—whether Jews or Gentiles, slave or free. **1 Corinthians 12:12, 13.**

Rosa Parks's refusal to give up her seat on the bus started the Montgomery Bus Boycott, in which nearly all Black people in the city refused to ride the buses. Since most of the people who rode the buses were Black, the transportation system suddenly lost a lot of money. And they continued to lose money because the boycott lasted for a little over a year. During that time, a separate case was filed by four other Black women who had had disputes with the bus system in Montgomery that year. The United States Supreme Court ruled that the bus segregation laws were unconstitutional, meaning those laws went against the rights of the Blacks who, just like the White people in their town, were American citizens.

Rosa's action was a key event in the civil rights movement, which was a nonviolent movement that sought freedom and equal rights for all people, regardless of race, color, religion, or place of birth. A few years after the Montgomery bus boycott, a group of Black leaders who cared about the rights of their people organized three marches in March 1965 from Selma, Alabama, to Montgomery, Alabama. The purpose of the marches was to make people aware of the need for equal rights, including voting rights, for Blacks in America.

Paul talked about "equal rights" in 1 Corinthians 12 when he said that we, the church, are all one body. We are each just as necessary to the body as the next person. He points out that when you become a member of the family of God, it doesn't matter if you are Black or White, slave or free, rich or poor, Canadian or American. It doesn't matter if you wear hand-me-downs or live in a smaller house than those of your friends.

What matters is that we are all God's children—He loves each one of us! And He asks us to love one another as He loves us. Remember, we are all equal in His sight. The world might try to segregate us and keep certain groups of people away from each other, but God calls us together under the title of "Christians."

Take a minute and think about these questions. Are there any individuals whom you treat differently because of how they look or act? Do you treat them as equal to you, or do you look at them as being lower and less important than you are? Think about how Jesus wants you to act.

NEXT STOP: Magnolia Springs, Alabama

May 12

You've Got Mail

Then I saw another angel flying in midair,
and he had the eternal gospel to proclaim to those who live on the earth—
to every nation, tribe, language and people. **Revelation 14:6.**

Although the United States Postal Service does not have an official slogan, the following quotation is inscribed on the James Farley Post Office in New York City, and many people, therefore, say that it applies to America's mail delivery system: "Neither snow nor rain nor heat nor gloom of night stays these couriers from the swift completion of their appointed rounds."

If this quotation were to be used for the postal service in Magnolia Springs, Alabama, it would need to read as follows: "Neither rain nor floods nor waves nor heat nor gloom of night stays these couriers from the swift completion of their appointed rounds." You see, Magnolia Springs has a river route in which the mail carrier delivers the mail by boat. The mailboxes are located in boathouses or on docks along the riverbank!

The mail carrier travels up and down the Magnolia River to deliver letters, packages, and postcards to the town's residents who live along the river. No matter what, these mail carriers are committed to delivering the mail.

Similarly, the first angel in Revelation has a message. It is the "eternal gospel," and it must be proclaimed to everyone living on the earth—everyone! That's where we come in. Each one of us is to tell others about Jesus and His soon return. We are God's messengers, like mail carriers. It's just that instead of letters from family and friends we are delivering the good news of God's love and the free gift of salvation, which is a much more important job and message.

So, if we had to come up with a slogan for our job as Christian mail carriers, what would it be? How about this: "Neither persecution nor hardships nor trials nor teasing nor the end of the world keeps God's couriers from the swift completion of spreading the gospel to the whole world." It might feel impossible to take the gospel to the whole world, but remember, a mail carrier has a set route. If the approximately 17 million Adventists in the world each took a "route" in their community and shared God's love with those around them, the job would be done. Who is on your route?

NEXT STOP: Enterprise, Alabama

Munching Beetles

And we know that in all things God works for the good of those who love him, who have been called according to his purpose. **Romans 8:28.**

Have you ever heard of a boll weevil? It is a type of beetle that is native to Central America but showed up in Alabama in 1915. The boll weevils thought they had landed in paradise, because they eat cotton buds and flowers, and there were plenty of cotton crops in Alabama. Just three years after the insects arrived, they were destroying whole cotton crops, and farmers were faced with a big problem—how were they going to earn enough money to care for their families if the beetles ate all of their crops? But one man had an idea. He convinced a farmer in the area to plant peanuts instead of cotton. The farmer did, and with the first crop the two men were able to pay off their debts. Fortunately, the boll weevil did not bother the peanut crops.

In 1919 a local businessman in Enterprise, Alabama, paid for the construction of a monument to the boll weevil. It is the only monument in the world to be dedicated to an agricultural pest. But the message on the monument goes along with our text for today. It reads: "In profound appreciation of the Boll Weevil and what it has done as the Herald of Prosperity this monument was erected . . ." The people of Enterprise realized that although it was hard when the beetles killed their crops, if the beetles hadn't come they wouldn't have thought to plant peanuts. They chose to look on the bright side of things and see how a bad situation worked out for the best.

Paul tells us to do the same thing in Romans 8:28. Bad things are going to happen. We live on a sinful earth—life is not always going to be perfect. But God promises us that in the end good will come out of the situation. For example, our family once took a wrong exit while traveling home from visiting my grandparents, adding 20 minutes to our time in the car. After driving for four hours, we finally turned onto our street, but we were startled to find fire trucks with their lights flashing and to learn that a tornado had gone down our street 20 minutes earlier, damaging the house across the street from us. We quickly realized that had we not gotten lost, we would have been on our street when the tornado hit.

All things work together for good for those who love God, even frustrating distractions like getting lost. He takes care of us in mysterious ways. Look for ways He is taking care of you.

NEXT STOP: Tuskegee, Alabama

May 14

Hello out there!

Honored Airmen

So the last shall be first, and the first last. **Matthew 20:16, NASB.**

A few days ago I told you the story of Rosa Parks and the challenges she and other Blacks faced living in America. Many American states had laws intended to segregate or keep the Black people separated from the White people. During World War II the segregation laws were in effect, yet the United States needed men who would fight, so they signed up Black soldiers and trained them for combat. But in order to uphold the segregation laws, they kept the Black soldiers separate from the White soldiers.

In the midst of this unjust treatment the Tuskegee Airmen, the first African-American military pilots, trained and prepared for battle. It was their job to protect their country, a country that treated them as if they didn't belong. But they worked hard and trained to the best of their ability, and they served their country with all their might. After the war they returned home—10 years later Rosa Parks made her stand in Montgomery, Alabama.

But that was not the end of the story for the Tuskegee Airmen. On March 29, 2007, the Tuskegee Airmen were awarded the Congressional Medal of Honor in recognition for their service. This is the highest award given by the U.S. Congress to individuals who make a positive impact on their country. The Tuskegee Airmen were last in the eyes of some people because of the color of their skin, but in the end they became first and were praised for their dedication and service to their country.

On this earth you may feel as if you are last. You may be picked on and teased because you choose not to watch certain movies or listen to music that you feel doesn't honor God. You may not be invited to sleepovers by friends because they know you won't approve of what they watch or how they talk. But stand firm. Don't give in to peer pressure. If you feel as if what they are doing goes against what God teaches in the Bible, stick to your beliefs.

It's hard now because you want to feel accepted and be part of the group, but in the end you won't be the one left out. If you stay faithful and true to God, in the end you will be first because you will be in heaven with Jesus, living in a mansion that He has built just for you. Stay focused on the final prize. With that in mind, you are guaranteed to come in first!

NEXT STOP: Sharkey County, Mississippi

Stuffed Teddy Bears

They will have no fear of bad news; their hearts are steadfast, trusting in the Lord. Their hearts are secure, they will have no fear; in the end they will look in triumph on their foes. **Psalm 112:7, 8.**

Theodore Roosevelt was president of the United States from 1901 to 1909. His nickname was Teddy, which was short for Theodore. Roosevelt loved the outdoors and exploring new areas and learning about the animals and plants in different parts of the country and world. He also liked to hunt.

In November 1902 while hunting in Sharkey County, Mississippi, Roosevelt was faced with an interesting situation. His hunting assistants were scouting out animals to alert him to when they came across an American black bear. The assistants got close enough to hit the bear with their clubs. They then tied the bear to a tree and called Roosevelt to come shoot the animal. But he refused to shoot the bear because he felt it was unsportsmanlike. However, he told someone else to put it out of its misery since his assistants had injured it.

When Roosevelt got back from his trip, a cartoon was featured in the Washington *Post* teasing him for not killing the bear. Morris Michtom saw the cartoon and decided to create a stuffed toy that looked like the bear in the cartoon. He created a stuffed bear cub and sent it to the president, asking permission to use his name to market the product "Teddy's bear." Roosevelt gave him permission, and Morris put it in his store window with a sign that read "Teddy's bear." The toy became an immediate success.

Today there are teddy bears in every toy store, and they are often a child's favorite stuffed animal. I don't know if you had a favorite animal that you slept with as a little kid, but many children have a favorite teddy bear that makes them feel secure and safe. Did you ever lose your favorite stuffed animal when you were younger and cried because you didn't want to go to sleep without it? I'm guessing you might have said a prayer with your mom or dad and asked Jesus to help you find your favorite stuffed animal.

Although things such as stuffed animals can make us feel better, there is no substitute for God. When we place our trust in Him, He will help us feel secure in His love and protection. We don't have to fear when God is our "teddy bear."

NEXT STOP: Tupelo, Mississippi

May 16

Living It

I know that the Lord has given you land and that a great fear
of you has fallen on us, so that all who live in this country
are melting in fear because of you. **Joshua 2:9.**

Elvis Presley was born in Tupelo, Mississippi, on January 8, 1935. When he was 13 his family moved to Memphis, Tennessee, and by age 19 he had launched his career as a musician. Within two years he released a number one hit and immediately became a rock-and-roll star and one of the most famous people in the world. He went on to star in Hollywood movies, record 23 studio albums, perform live in front of sold-out crowds, and release 33 number-one singles.

But all of this fame and fortune didn't bring Elvis happiness. In fact, he was a very sad man who used drugs to cope with life. On August 16, 1977, he died suddenly at the age of 42. Although reports vary regarding the cause of death, whether it was from an overdose or a heart attack, it can't be denied that he didn't take care of his body. Trying to determine what caused Elvis' death, medical examiners discovered 11 drugs in his body and learned that Elvis' doctor had prescribed him more than 10,000 doses of different medications in 1977!

Although Elvis was rich and famous, although he had fans who hung on his every word and screamed for him at concerts, Elvis was a broken man because he lived his life without God. He grew up attending an Assembly of God church with his parents, and he recorded gospel songs on some of his records, but that did not mean that he had a relationship with Jesus.

People can go through the motions of being Christian and say that they believe in God, but that doesn't mean that they *live* for God. Believing in God and living for God are two totally different things. When the spies stayed at Rahab's house, she told them that she knew the Lord had given the land to the Israelites. She believed that there was a God who protected the children of Israel. But she chose to go beyond just believing and decided to live for God. Thus, she and her family were saved and lived among the Israelites after the fall of Jericho.

Do you just believe that there is a God, or do you believe in Him *and* live for Him? There is a big difference, and it will shape your life. I hope you are living for Him. Nothing on this earth matters more than having a relationship with God.

NEXT STOP: Mississippi River Delta, Mississippi

The Importance of Water

This is what the Lord says: By this you will know that I am the Lord:
With the staff that is in my hand I will strike the water of the Nile,
and it will be changed into blood. **Exodus 7:17.**

The Mississippi River system is the longest river in North America. It serves as the border of or cuts through 10 states, flowing 2,530 miles from Minnesota to the Gulf of Mexico. The Mississippi River has been an important part of United States history since the country was founded. The Native Americans were the first to live along the river. They used it as a source of drinking water, hunting grounds, and irrigation for their crops. Once the European settlers arrived, they used the river as a form of transportation as they explored the New World.

Once America became a nation, people moved from the colonies toward the Mississippi. They were drawn to the area because of the good soil that existed along the river, which made for good crops. As large cities began to grow up along the river, the early 1900s featured the building of levees, locks, and dams to control the flow of the river and better utilize it for transportation. Today the Mississippi River is a major transportation highway for barges and large ships.

Just as the Mississippi River is important to America, the Nile River is important to northern Africa. The Nile is the longest river in the world, traveling 4,130 miles through 11 countries. The Bible mentions the importance of the Nile to the Egyptians. They used the water for drinking, bathing, washing clothes in, and growing crops in the rich soil left along the banks after the river flooded. So when God told Moses to strike the Nile River and it turned to blood, it was an attack not only on the Egyptians' way of life but also on their god. It was bad enough that they couldn't drink the water and all the fish died, but God was trying to show Pharaoh that the god he worshipped was a false god. Hapi didn't have any magical powers. He couldn't defend himself against the God of heaven, because Hapi was a false god—a god the Egyptians had made up. But Pharaoh was a stubborn man who hardened his heart to the messages of God, and he paid the ultimate sacrifice of eternal death.

Don't ever harden your heart against God. Listen to Him, and He will direct your path.

NEXT STOP: Greenwood, Mississippi

Hello out there!

White Gold

*The law of Your mouth is better to me
Than thousands of gold and silver pieces.* **Psalm 119:72, NASB.**

In the little town of Greenwood, Mississippi, home to about 16,000 people, the term *white gold* is mentioned when talking about cotton. Greenwood has long prospered as the "Cotton Capital of the World." Its location along the Yazoo River has made it a major shipping point for cotton. Today the city is home to the second-largest U.S. cotton exchange, with large warehouses storing the cotton for shipment elsewhere.

Think about how many things in your house are made from cotton—T-shirts, socks, towels, sheets, curtains, blankets, etc. I'm sure you could think of a few other items, but it goes to show that cotton is a valuable resource that is used in a lot of the things we buy. This means it is a cash crop and brings in a lot of money for the farmers and shipping companies that sell it to manufacturers. Hence, it is called white gold because of its value as a moneymaking crop.

King David knew the value of money. He had little of it as a shepherd boy and while running from King Saul, but he had plenty of it once he became king and lived in palaces full of food and jewels and fine clothes. Despite being surrounded by riches, he knew that those riches did not bring him happiness. King David knew that true happiness came from following God. He knew that he was at peace when he followed God's law. In fact, as he stated in today's text, he placed more value on God's law than on silver or gold.

As you read the text, do you agree with King David's statement? If you had a bar of gold, would you trade it for a Bible? That's a tough question, but you have to think about what value you place in your Bible. Is it just another book with good stories and good advice in it, or is it a letter from your Best Friend, who wants to spend eternity with you?

Without the Word of God we would not know about the plan of salvation, and we would be lost forever. If you don't do this already, take a little time each day to read your Bible. You may choose to read a few verses or a whole chapter. It doesn't matter how much you read; what matters is that you take time to learn what your Best Friend wants to tell you.

NEXT STOP: Lorman, Mississippi

The Battle of Slavery

This message came to Jeremiah from the Lord after King Zedekiah made a covenant with the people, proclaiming freedom for the slaves. **Jeremiah 34:8, NLT.**

Captain Isaac Ross moved his household, including his slaves, from South Carolina to Mississippi in 1808. He settled in the town of Lorman and set to work establishing Prospect Hill Plantation, which his slaves built. As Captain Ross aged he drafted a will, which informed the court and his relatives of his final wishes. But after he died in 1836, his relatives became angry because his will freed all of his slaves and instructed the court to sell the plantation and use the money to pay for the slaves to return to Africa on a ship. His grandson was especially angered by his grandfather's last wishes, and he fought it in the court system. Sadly, the case was tried in courtroom after courtroom until it finally reached the Supreme Court. Twelve years after Captain Ross's death, the Supreme Court ruled that the will had to be upheld and the slaves were free to go to Africa.

Because of the cost of the court battle, a large portion of Captain Ross's fortune was spent on legal fees, and it took more than a year to raise enough money to pay for the slaves to return to Africa. In total 90 slaves reached their destination.

We often think of slavery as just a problem in early American history, but slavery was an issue in Bible times as well. And surprisingly, it was an issue with the Israelites, the very people whose ancestors had been slaves in Egypt. Grab your Bible and read Jeremiah 34:8-22 to get the full picture of the issue of slavery. The Hebrew people made a promise to King Zedekiah that they would release their slaves and set them free. "But later they changed their minds. They took back the men and women they had freed, forcing them to be slaves again" (verse 11, NLT). God gave a message to Jeremiah to tell to the people. "Therefore, this is what the Lord says: Since you have not obeyed me by setting your countrymen free, I will set you free to be destroyed by war, disease, and famine. You will be an object of horror to all the nations of the earth" (verse 17, NLT).

Because of their disobedience, God told the Hebrews that He would remove His protection from them and they would be "free" to die by the "sword, plague and famine." I don't think I would want to be "free" under those terms.

NEXT STOP: Tennessee

Hello out there!

May 20

Volunteering

All these were fighting men who volunteered to serve in the ranks. They came to Hebron fully determined to make David king over all Israel. All the rest of the Israelites were also of one mind to make David king. **1 Chronicles 12:38.**

Welcome to the Volunteer State. Tennessee received this nickname during the War of 1812 against the British. The war had been going on for more than two and a half years when the British Army attacked New Orleans with the intent of capturing the city and taking over the territory the Americans had bought in the Louisiana Purchase. However, the British Army's plans failed, thanks in part to Major General Andrew Jackson and the volunteer soldiers from Tennessee, and the British retreated. Because of their courage and determination to push the British back, the state of Tennessee was nicknamed in recognition of the men who had voluntarily put their lives on the line in defending their country.

In a similar show of support, more than 340,000 men left their families and came to Hebron in Israel to show their dedication to David. They left their families and homes to fight alongside David and his men. They believed in David and the Lord's appointment of him as ruler over Israel. Because of this belief, they didn't hesitate to give their all for something or—in this case—someone they believed in.

Do you volunteer at your church or in your community? If so, is it because you are passionate about what you are doing, or do you feel as if you have to? It doesn't feel like work or volunteering when you enjoy what you are doing. Growing up, I went Ingathering to collect money for people in need. But it was more of a chore than something I loved to do. As I grew older, I felt guilty if I didn't help with that type of witnessing. But then I discovered something I love to do. I love working with kids and helping to plan Vacation Bible School programs. I love leading out in song services and doing skits and helping kids with crafts and talking to them about Jesus.

My point is that you need to figure out what you are good at and what you enjoy doing and then see how that fits into the church and serving God. When you do, you will be begging your parents to take you to church to help out with activities and events. Find something you enjoy, and then volunteer and give your talents and interests to God. You won't be sorry you did.

NEXT STOP: Great Smoky Mountains National Park, Tennessee

May 21

Bears!

> Elisha turned around and looked at them, and he cursed
> them in the name of the Lord. Then two bears came out
> of the woods and mauled forty-two of them. **2 Kings 2:24, NLT.**

The Great Smoky Mountains got its name from the smokelike haze that often hangs over the mountain range. Similar to a light fog, the haze makes the mountains appear to be on fire, hence their name. The Great Smoky Mountains National Park is the most visited national park in the United States. With more than 850 miles of trails, there are plenty of outdoor recreation opportunities in the park. The park is home to more than 200 species of birds, 50 species of fish, and 66 species of mammals, including approximately 1,500 black bears.

Although I have been to this park many times, I will never forget the year I visited with my family when I was 11 and my brother was 9. We had hiked on some trails and were in the process of driving around Cades Cove, an 11-mile loop in the park that features log cabins and churches built by settlers in the area. The Cades Cove loop takes you through beautiful open meadows with purple wildflowers and forested areas with towering trees.

While driving, we noticed a number of cars had pulled over to the side of the road. People were standing beside their cars, cameras in hand, pointing across the road. We stopped, too, and hopped out of the car to see what was going on. It was then that we noticed a black bear sitting among the trees. I was so excited! As we stood there snapping pictures, my brother picked up a rock, looked at it, and then tossed it over his shoulder into the woods. Within a split second the bear ran across the road toward my brother! We held our breath, but the bear wasn't interested in eating my brother for lunch. He ran straight past him into the woods beyond our car.

Bears are mentioned in the Bible, but not in a cuddly kind of way. The bear story takes place shortly after Elijah was taken to heaven, leaving Elisha in charge of continuing the work as God's prophet in Israel. Elisha was walking toward Bethel when a group of teenagers came out of the town and began teasing him, saying "Go away, baldy!" (2 Kings 2:23, NLT). Elisha thought the boys needed punishing. Two bears then appeared from the woods and mauled 42 of the teenagers. The moral of the story: Always treat people with respect!

NEXT STOP: Ocoee River, Tennessee

149

Hello out there!

May 22

Drowning

The currents swirled about me; all your waves and breakers swept over me.... The engulfing waters threatened me, the deep surrounded me; seaweed was wrapped around my head. **Jonah 2:3-5.**

I'll give you one guess who prayed the prayer in today's text—of course, the book of the Bible is a dead giveaway! From the belly of the great fish Jonah prayed to God. He remembered the awful feeling of almost drowning, of being tossed about by the waves, of being covered with seaweed. But then God sent the fish to swallow Jonah, and although it had to have been the most disgusting place on earth, Jonah was grateful that he had survived and was alive.

Jonah finished his prayer with the following words: "But I, with a song of thanksgiving, will sacrifice to you. What I have vowed I will make good. Salvation comes from the Lord" (Jonah 2:9). Jonah turned his life over to God, and God honored his allegiance to Him by commanding the fish to spit Jonah out onto dry land.

I have always been a strong swimmer and have never experienced a near-drowning incident, but after visiting the Ocoee River in southeastern Tennessee, I can only imagine how terrifying it is to almost drown and how scared Jonah must have been. The Ocoee River is rated among the top whitewater rivers in the nation, and it was the site for the 1996 Summer Olympics whitewater canoe/kayak competition. The one-mile Olympic whitewater course is fed by the release of water from a dam that was originally constructed in 1940 to generate electricity for the Tennessee Valley. Now the dam serves to feed a world-class whitewater course that is usually dry or has very little water in it but can quickly fill with water when the dam is released. Before the water is released, an alarm is sounded to alert swimmers and those playing in the river that the dam is being opened. Soon water floods the area and creates currents that will sweep you off your feet in a split second. The power of the water is amazing—and scary.

Life can sometimes seem as deadly as a whitewater river, tossing us around and trying to drown us with worry. But God is in the business of rescuing people! When you feel as if you are drowning in your problems, lift up your hand and let God pull you out of the water.

NEXT STOP: Reelfoot Lake, Tennessee

Changing Tides

For nation will rise against nation, and kingdom against kingdom, and in various places there will be famines and earthquakes. **Matthew 24:7, NASB.**

We often think of California as the state that has the most earthquakes, but there have been major earthquakes in the East as well. It doesn't happen often, but in late 1811 and early 1812 the most powerful earthquakes to hit the East Coast occurred. A series of four earthquakes took place between December 16, 1811, and February 7, 1812, that caused the Mississippi River to actually reverse direction and flow backward. The water followed the path of least resistance and filled the area that is now known as Reelfoot Lake. Today Reelfoot Lake is home to bald cypress trees, which grow in wet, swampy areas, and a number of bald eagles that nest in the trees around the lake.

Since 1811 thousands of earthquakes have occurred around the world. In fact, the United States Geological Survey estimates that about 500,000 detectable earthquakes happen worldwide each year, and about 100,000 of them can be felt. That's a lot of shaking!

Toward the end of His life on earth, Jesus tried to prepare His disciples for the future by telling them what signs would occur before He appeared in the clouds of glory. In addition to wars and famines, the Bible records that earthquakes will occur in various places, and we are clearly seeing that take place. So what should we do? Should we curl up in our beds and wait for the end of the world? Should we run and hide in fear that an earthquake may destroy our homes?

Neither of those options are good. Instead of living in fear, we must continue to trust that God will watch over us during the good times and the bad times. No matter what happens, God will give us the strength to make it through the storm. As we see the signs pointing to Jesus' soon return, we need to make sure we are right with God, and then we should share what we know with our friends and family who don't believe in God.

Jesus does not want us to be caught by surprise, so He told us what to expect before His second coming. May we live in peace knowing that someday soon we will be in heaven where we will never have to worry about earthquakes!

NEXT STOP: Memphis, Tennessee

Hello out there!

May 24

Worshipping the Wrong Things

They worshiped idols, though the Lord had said,
"You shall not do this." **2 Kings 17:12.**

When we were visiting Mississippi, we stopped in Tupelo, which is where Elvis Presley, the famous rock-and-roll singer, was born. After reaching celebrity status, Elvis bought a house in Memphis, Tennessee, but the neighbors began to get annoyed at the constant noise from fans and reporters who camped out in his yard. Because of this problem, Elvis gave his parents a budget to buy him a new home. After shopping around, they purchased Graceland, a large mansion on 13.8 acres in Memphis. The street was soon renamed after Elvis—the home is located at 3764 Elvis Presley Boulevard. Elvis lived in the home for 20 years before dying on the floor of his bathroom.

The home is now a tourist attraction and museum. Amazingly, Graceland is the most visited private house in the country. People come from all over the world to peek into the life of Elvis Presley. For many visitors it takes on a semireligious atmosphere as they visit the home of the "King of Rock and Roll," as he has been nicknamed. In the garden many people stop at Elvis' grave and pray or sing one of Elvis' favorite hymns, which made me wonder, Are these people worshipping Elvis?

In addition, there is a stone wall that surrounds the grounds of the mansion. The wall is covered with graffiti. But it isn't graffiti by gangs or people who hate Elvis. Instead, the graffiti has been created by people who admire the singer. Some people even ask for favors from the dead singer. Does this sound like worship to you?

The children of Israel struggled with this concept. They were drawn to idols and gods they could "see." They tried to fit in with the other nations and adopt their cultures. They became even more corrupt under the poor leadership of many of their kings. It was because of all these sins and more that the Lord allowed the Israelites' enemies to destroy them and take them into captivity. Take a few minutes to read 2 Kings 17:7-23. The passage outlines the things the Israelites were doing that took them away from God. The Lord had told them not to worship idols, but they didn't listen, and they paid the price.

When you are tempted to worship someone or something other than God, think about the consequences of making that choice. The earthly consequences may not be unpleasant, but the eternal consequences will be devastating.

NEXT STOP: Nashville, Tennessee

All Kinds of Music

David and all Israel were celebrating
with all their might before the Lord, with castanets, harps,
lyres, timbrels, sistrums and cymbals. **2 Samuel 6:5.**

Nashville, Tennessee, has earned the nickname "Music City" because of the high population of musicians and recording studios in the area. Nashville is the home of country music and a large number of contemporary Christian recording artists. The city is also home to the Grand Ole Opry, a weekly country music concert that started as a radio broadcast in 1925.

For as many people who are die-hard country music fans, you can find just as many who hate that style of music. And that is true with all types of music. I listen only to contemporary Christian music, but some of my friends prefer classical. Is there a right or wrong style of music? Does one type of music glorify God more than another style?

If you read the Bible in search of texts that talk about music, you will find plenty that mention music. Today's verse talks about King David and the people celebrating the return of the ark of the covenant to Jerusalem. It was a big celebration with singing and accompaniment with harps; lyres, another type of stringed instrument; timbrels; sistrums, a type of percussion instrument; and cymbals, a very loud and commanding instrument. I would love to hear what the instruments sounded like together and what types of songs the people sang.

Now that you have read a verse that features some of the musical instruments used in Bible times, let's return to my original question. What makes one style of music better than another? Any ideas? I would like to propose that the words are what matters. Does the message make you think about God's love and goodness and His plan for your life? Or does the message leave you thinking about alcohol, sadness, loneliness, girls, boys, riches, etc.?

As you grow older, if you are not already doing so, you will have to choose what music you listen to. Just remember that whatever you put in your brain is there to stay. Make sure you are filling it with godly messages of love and hope instead of worldly messages of despair and temporary pleasure. Music is a vital part of our lives, which is a wonderful blessing.

NEXT STOP: Lexington, Kentucky

Hello out there!

Ride Like the Wind

> And soon the sky was black with clouds. A heavy wind brought
> a terrific rainstorm, and Ahab left quickly for Jezreel. Then the Lord gave
> special strength to Elijah. He tucked his cloak into his belt and ran ahead of Ahab's
> chariot all the way to the entrance of Jezreel. I Kings 18:45, 46, NLT.

All you horse lovers should be excited about today's destination. Grab your boots and a cowboy hat, because we are visiting the Kentucky Horse Park, a working horse farm in the town of Lexington. The park features rolling hills with white fences sectioning off large pastures in which sleek horses munch on the greenest grass. The park is also home to a large arena where equestrian events, such as jumping and riding competitions, are held.

Visitors to the park can see some of the world's greatest horse champions who are retired and being cared for at the park. One of the fastest horses we saw was Cigar, a dark-brown horse with white "socks" on three of his legs. This amazing horse with strong muscles and a shiny coat ran one of his races, a one-mile track, in 1 minute and 35 seconds!

Horses are powerful creatures that can run like the wind when they have someplace to go. That's what makes the story of Elijah running in front of Ahab's chariot so miraculous. Elijah had just challenged the prophets of Baal on Mount Carmel to prove to the children of Israel who the true God was. After God sent fire from heaven to devour the sacrifice and the altar, the people fell down on the ground with their faces in the dirt and cried out, "The Lord—he is God! Yes, the Lord is God!" (1 Kings 18:39, NLT).

After the victory, "Elijah climbed to the top of Carmel, bent down to the ground and put his face between his knees" (verse 42), praying that God would send the rain. He then sent his servant to go see if a cloud was in the sky. Elijah did this seven times, and on the seventh time the servant returned to tell him that a cloud was rising from the sea. Immediately he told his servant to tell Ahab to hitch up his chariot and get off the mountain as fast as possible before the rain came. But the rain moved in quickly, and Ahab was caught in the storm. It was then that the Lord gave Elijah extra power and strength to run faster than the horses and help safely escort Ahab off the mountain. Now, that's fast!

NEXT STOP: Mammoth Cave, Kentucky

Flashlights Needed

I am the light of the world. Whoever follows me will never walk in darkness, but will have the light of life. **John 8:12.**

Yesterday I told you to wear your boots and hat, but today you need to wear something you don't mind getting dirty, and you have to bring a flashlight with you. Today we are visiting Mammoth Cave, the longest known cave system in the world. As you enter the cave, you are faced with a choice. You can choose to go on a lighted tour that follows a set path into large rooms and corridors in the cave, or you can choose to join a tour that requires you to crawl through muddy and dusty tunnels and less traveled sections. So which tour would you like to join? How adventurous are you?

I have been on both types of caving expeditions, but I prefer the guided tour that follows a designated path. Actually, the caving expedition I went on that did not follow a marked path was with a group of friends when I was in college. To enter the cave, we had to get down on our hands and knees and crawl 300 feet before the cave widened and we could stand. One of the guys in my group had gone caving there before, so we followed him. We turned this way and that way, and with each turn I wondered if we were ever going to find our way out again. Then, deep inside the cave, the leader of our group suggested that we all turn off our lights and sing a song. It was so dark I couldn't even see the person standing next to me, but as we sang together, a sense of peace came to me in spite of my uneasiness about turning off all our lights.

After singing, we flicked our lights back on. What a relief! Without our lights we would have been lost forever. Similarly, Jesus told the people that He is the light of the world. Those who follow Him won't ever get lost (John 8:12). With Jesus as the light in your life, you will always be able to see where you are going, which is very reassuring.

The next time you go camping, try walking along a path in the dark without a flashlight. Or try this in your backyard. Then walk the same path with a flashlight. Walking around with a flashlight is better than walking around without one. Remember this example when you think about your life without Jesus. Always keep the Light with you!

NEXT STOP: Louisville, Kentucky

May 28

Happy Birthday!

*Suddenly, the angel was joined by a vast host of others—
the armies of heaven—praising God and saying, "Glory to God in highest heaven,
and peace on earth to those with whom God is pleased." **Luke 2:13, 14, NLT.***

Louisville, Kentucky, is home to two sisters who wrote the melody of the song "Happy Birthday," although their tune is now far more popular than they are. Patty Hill was a kindergarten principal at the Louisville Experimental Kindergarten School. Her sister, Mildred, was a teacher there and a pianist and composer, so when Patty wanted to develop a song that would be easy for the younger children to learn, Mildred got busy writing a piece. The end result was a song titled "Good Morning to All."

Apparently the Kindergarten children enjoyed the song so much that they began singing it at birthday parties by simply changing the words to "happy birthday" in place of "good morning." And it stuck!

According to the 1998 *Guinness Book of World Records*, the "Happy Birthday" song "is the most recognized song in the English language." No birthday party seems complete without it; it's a traditional song people sing to a person once a year on the day that marks that person's birth.

Of course, no song can top the one the angels sang when Baby Jesus was born. And they announced Jesus' birth not only by singing a song but also by lighting up the sky in an angelic fireworks celebration. Heaven knows how to celebrate special occasions. I can't wait to see the announcement of Christ's arrival the second time! I'm sure it will be much more spectacular than His first advent.

The next time you sing "Happy Birthday" for someone's birthday, think about how special that person is to Christ. And then imagine all the birthdays you are going to celebrate in heaven. I wonder what those celebrations will be like and whether or not we will sing a special song. There are so many things to look forward to in heaven and so many things to learn.

Enjoy each birthday God gives you and continue to live your life for Him so that He can mold you and shape you into the person He wants you to be. Happy birthday!

NEXT STOP: Fort Knox, Kentucky

156

Pure Gold

How much better to get wisdom than gold,
and good judgment than silver! **Proverbs 16:16, NLT.**

Fort Knox is home to the United States' second-largest supply of official gold reserves. Although it would be awesome to see 4,578 metric tons of gold worth more than $100 billion, I can guarantee you that we aren't getting anywhere close to that much shiny, yellow gold until we get to heaven! But here's the story behind Fort Knox.

In 1933 President Franklin D. Roosevelt issued an executive order that made it illegal for any American citizen to own gold coins; gold bullion, meaning bars or ingots of gold; or gold certificates, documents stating that someone owns gold held at a bank. The order required all citizens to sell their gold to the U.S. government. Because of this order, the U.S. government suddenly had a lot of gold reserves, so it began building Fort Knox in 1936 in order to store the gold in a secure location.

Talk about ultimate security—the walls of the gold vault are made out of granite, and the vault is protected by a blastproof door that weighs 22 tons. And as you can imagine, the United States Mint Police don't take any chances with intruders. Submachine guns are positioned at the corners of the building, and it is rumored that a minefield, laser beams, and other sensing devices are used to detect movement and wound or kill anyone who trespasses on the property.

Although you might care less about how much gold the United States has, some people in the government live and breathe money and acquiring more of it for the country. Is that a good or bad thing? Well, King Solomon, the wisest and richest man who ever lived, had a lot to say about wealth. In Proverbs he mentions gold 11 times, often reminding readers that wisdom is better than gold.

Now look at Ecclesiastes 2:8-11: "I amassed silver and gold for myself, and the treasure of kings and provinces. . . . I became greater by far than anyone in Jerusalem before me. . . . Yet when I surveyed all that my hands had done and what I had toiled to achieve, everything was meaningless, a chasing after the wind." King Solomon realized that his wealth was worth absolutely nothing without a relationship with God. Make sure you stay focused on heaven instead of earthly riches.

NEXT STOP: Martinsburg, West Virginia

May 30

Hello out there!

The GIANT Plane

The bridegroom was a long time in coming, and they all became drowsy and feel asleep. At midnight the cry rang out: "Here's the bridegroom! Come out to meet him!" **Matthew 25:5, 6.**

I used to live 45 minutes away from the 167th Airlift Wing, West Virginia Air National Guard base in Martinsburg, West Virginia. The planes that are assigned to the base are cargo transport planes, officially known as the C-5 Galaxy. When I tell you that the planes are massive, I'm not joking! The height from the ground to the top of the tail is equal to the height of a six-story building!

Because it transports cargo, the plane has nose and rear doors that open and drop ramps for easy loading and unloading. When the door at the nose is open and the ramp is down, it looks like a huge great white shark with its mouth open.

To give you an idea of how mammoth these planes are, they can transport six school buses at one time! But actually they transport military supplies such as Humvees, helicopters, small submarines, tanks, food, and other supplies to airbases around the world.

I was lucky enough to visit the base one day and tour the C-5 and the base's fire station. It was at the fire station that I learned a few interesting things. First of all, the firefighters work for 24 hours straight, and then they have 48 hours off. On their shift, they check all of the firefighting equipment: the hoses, the trucks, their clothes, and air tanks—everything. They practice drills and learn about different fires and new chemicals and equipment and methods to help extinguish fires composed of burning metal and aircraft fuel. Fighting a fire on a plane is very different than fighting a house fire.

And yet, when we asked a soldier if he had ever been called to fight a fire on one of the planes, he said no. But he told us, "You never know if someday it will happen. We have to be ready, and we have to imagine that today is the day we will have to use our skills and training to save lives."

Similarly, we are preparing for Christ's second coming every single day of our lives, but we don't know the day or the hour He will return. We may be tempted to give up or think that Jesus won't come, but we have to be like that soldier. We have to be ready, because Jesus *is* coming back!

NEXT STOP: Harpers Ferry, West Virginia

158

Floodwaters

When you pass through the waters, I will be with you; and when you pass through the rivers, they will not sweep over you. When you walk through the fire, you will not be burned; the flames will not set you ablaze. **Isaiah 43:2.**

Harpers Ferry is a historic town in West Virginia that is located right where the Shenandoah and Potomac rivers merge. The town is bordered on two sides by these two rivers. It is a beautiful location, with trees, cliffs, and water. In fact, after visiting Harpers Ferry in 1783, Thomas Jefferson wrote that the area was one of the prettiest scenes in nature he had seen.

In the late 1700s and early 1800s the town was an important military armory, where firearms were manufactured and stored. Harpers Ferry supplied weapons and supplies that Lewis and Clark needed for their expedition out west. Harpers Ferry also played an important role in the Civil War.

Although the town has played a part in early American history, Harpers Ferry has a problem. Can you guess what it is? The clue lies in the first two sentences of today's entry—the town is bordered by two rivers. And what happens to rivers when too much rain falls? They flood. And we aren't talking about one foot of extra water—we are talking about major flooding.

The worst flood was recorded on October 16, 1942, when floodwaters reached 33.8 feet, thus covering most buildings in the lower portion of the town. But in 1996 the town got hit twice in one year. On January 20 rain and snowmelt caused the rivers to rise to 29.4 feet in the lower section of town, and then on September 8, rain from Hurricane Fran fell in the area, causing the rivers to rise to 29.8 feet. I can't imagine how the business owners and residents of the town felt when they had to clean up their shops and homes twice in one year from all the mud, debris, and river water that had swamped their town.

Sometimes school might cause you to feel as if you are drowning in a flood that is sweeping you off your feet. Or sometimes you may have problems at home or with friends. But during those times, remember that Jesus promises to be with you. I encourage you to memorize today's text. It is Jesus' promise to you that He will not let you be swept away by life's problems. When the "water" is swirling around you, Jesus is right beside you. Remember that!

NEXT STOP: Berkeley Springs, West Virginia

June 1

Hello out there!

Spa Resort

They must wash their clothes and bathe themselves with water, and they will be clean. **Leviticus 14:9.**

What should you do if you've been playing soccer and you're all sweaty? Take a shower! What should you do if you've been caving and you have dirt in your hair and on your clothes and all over your body? Take a shower! What should you do if you've been backpacking for three days and haven't bathed? Take a shower, of course!

Some of you may not like to take showers, but I think showers are great! Especially when you are hot, sweaty, and dirty, a cool shower feels super refreshing.

Nowadays we don't even think about taking a bath or shower; we just jump in and turn the knobs, and warm water comes pouring out of the faucet. However, bathing was not so common hundreds of years ago. So much more work had to go into bathing. You had to heat the water over the fire and pour it into a small free-standing tub. Then the whole family bathed in the same water, one after another.

Not surprisingly, things were slightly different for the elite class. In Berkeley Springs, West Virginia, which was originally named Bath, the natural warm springs of the area made for a lovely place to bathe. In the late eighteenth century many high-society people and government officials, including George Washington, took advantage of the bathhouses and spas that were established in the town to pamper the rich and famous.

But these wealthy people bathed more for pleasure rather than for cleanliness. At that time people did not understand that disease and skin problems were connected to being dirty and not bathing. The Israelites had the same problem. But God, in instructing them to bathe, taught the people how to take care of their bodies and keep diseases from spreading throughout the camp. The book of Leviticus talks about bathing quite a bit. God wanted to make sure the people understood how best to care for themselves and their families.

God cares about every aspect of our lives. If this were not true, He wouldn't have given the children of Israel instructions on how to pitch their tents, when to take a bath, where to get their food, and how to govern themselves. He gave them guidance in all aspects of life, and He will do the same for you if you read His Word.

NEXT STOP: New River Gorge Bridge, West Virginia

Making Good Decisions

Show me the right path, O Lord; point out the road for me to follow. Lead me by your truth and teach me, for you are the God who saves me. All day long I put my hope in you. **Psalm 25:4, 5, NLT.**

Near the town of Fayetteville, West Virginia, is the New River Gorge Bridge, which is the third-highest vehicular bridge in America. The bridge is 3,030 feet long and stands 876 feet above the river. The bridge connects two mountain ridges and provides breathtaking views for those who don't have a fear of heights.

Not only does the bridge get cars from point A to point B, but the bridge serves as a source of adventure every October on Bridge Day. On that day the bridge is shut down to vehicle traffic, and tens of thousands of people walk out on the bridge to . . .

Watch a parade? Nope.

Take pictures? No.

Look at the fall leaves changing color? No way!

Jump off? Yes!

Are you kidding? No!

Approximately 400 BASE jumpers take the plunge off the bridge each year, deploying their parachutes just seconds before they hit the ground. The difference between BASE jumping and skydiving is the amount of time in the air. BASE jumpers jump from low-altitude, fixed objects. This gives them less time in a free fall before they have to open their chute and land.

Statistics from a study of BASE jumps from a mountain in Norway show that about one in every 2,300 jumps resulted in death. Although it may seem that chances are pretty good that you will be safe, what if you are the "2,300th" person to jump?

When you make decisions, you have to think about the risks involved in the activity and decide whether you will take the risk. Are there risks in rock climbing? Sure. But are your risks minimal if you use the proper equipment, go with an experienced climber, and wear appropriate safety gear? Yes!

We often don't take the time to think about the risks or consequences of life, but we need to. And we need to consult our Guide, because He wants to help us make good decisions that will keep us safe. Ask God to guide your path today and protect you along the way.

NEXT STOP: Sago, West Virginia

June 3

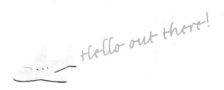

Hello out there!

Failed Hope

"Did I ask you for a son, my lord?" she said.
"Didn't I tell you, 'Don't raise my hopes'?" **2 Kings 4:28.**

On January 2, 2006, right after New Year's Day, a group of miners reported to work and rode the mining cart deep into the mine. At approximately 6:30 a.m. an explosion occurred, ripping through the mine and causing the ceiling to collapse, trapping 13 men.

After the blast, rescuers were called to begin the process of locating the trapped miners and safely removing them from the mine. But the rescue process was anything but easy. The air in the Sago Mine was filled with high levels of methane and carbon monoxide gases. The rescue crews drilled holes from the surface down into the mine to try and locate the miners with video cameras lowered on cables through the hole. But they found no signs of life. When rescuers finally reached the miners, they found that only one of the 13 miners had survived. All of the other men were dead.

Unfortunately, miscommunication sparked a rumor that spread quickly to the media and to the families of the trapped miners, namely, that 12 miners were safe and only one man was dead. This was the complete opposite! But the families were so hopeful that the miners were safe that they believed it with all their hearts. When the deaths were confirmed, the owners of the mining company had to tell the families the terrible truth.

Hope is an interesting thing. We can hope and pray that things turn out for the best in our lives, but that doesn't always happen. In today's Bible story the Shunammite woman didn't have any children, but after she showed kindness to Elisha, the prophet told her she would become pregnant and have a son, and it happened exactly as he said. But when the boy was young, he collapsed in the field and was brought to his mother, and he died in her arms.

That's when the Shunammite woman went to Elisha and told him what had happened. When she arrived at Elisha's home she pleaded with him to do something. She asked him, "Why did you raise my hopes and make me happy by having God give me a son only for him to die and be taken away forever?" Elisha immediately returned with the woman, and after he prayed to God, the boy was raised back to life.

Regardless of whether good or bad things happen in this life, we have hope that one day God will make all things new and perfect!

NEXT STOP: Akron, Ohio

Being Flexible

Moses did as the Lord commanded him. He took Joshua and had him stand before Eleazar the priest and the whole assembly. Then he laid his hands on him and commissioned him, as the Lord instructed through Moses. **Numbers 27:22, 23.**

Akron, Ohio, is nicknamed the Rubber Capital of the World because four large tire companies built their headquarters in the city in the late 1800s and early 1900s. We know that tires are made of rubber, but can you think of anything else around your house that is made of rubber? What about flip-flops, swings, balls, and the soles of your shoes? I'm sure you can think of some other items.

So what do all of those items have in common, other than the fact that they are made from rubber? If you said that they are all flexible, you are correct. Rubber is a very stretchy, flexible material. If your shoes were made of wood, would it be easy or hard to play basketball? It would be difficult, wouldn't it? You need shoes that will bend and flex with your foot as you run so that you can move as easily as possible.

Tires are the same way. Rubber tires flex and bend as the vehicle goes over bumps in the road. This was a huge improvement to wooden wagon wheels, which jolted and jostled the rider and often broke on rough roads.

When God called Joshua to take Moses' place and lead the children of Israel into the Promised Land, he had to make a choice. Was he going to be flexible like rubber and trust God to show him how to conquer the land, or was he going to be like wood and remain rigid and unmoving? As we know from the Bible, Joshua trusted God and decided that life was better bending and following God's plan rather than holding stubbornly to his own ideas.

Are you like rubber or wood? When your parents promise to treat you to ice cream but it gets too late and you can't go, are you flexible and understanding, or do you pout and throw a fit? When your teacher switches your part in the school play and gives you a smaller part, do you smile and do your best, or do you complain and talk bad about your teacher when he or she isn't around? It isn't always easy to be like rubber, but God wants us to be flexible so that He can mold and shape us into the person He wants us to be!

NEXT STOP: Newark, Ohio

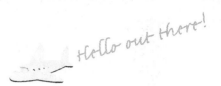

Hello out there!

The Biggest Picnic

They all ate as much as they wanted, and afterward, the disciples
picked up twelve baskets of leftovers. **Matthew 14:20, NLT.**

Today we are driving through Newark, Ohio, in search of the world's largest basket. That's right! We are looking for a HUGE tan-colored basket with two handles on top. Keep your eyes open. You should be able to see it from a long way off. Yep, there is it! It is an office building in the shape of a basket!

The Longaberger Company makes and sells baskets, and their main office is located in a building made to look like their most popular basket, a rectangular basket with two handles on top, called the Medium Market Basket.

The company makes a wide variety of baskets, from small ones to hold your keys to large ones that can hold big bags of dog food. The company also makes baskets large enough to carry a picnic lunch in, which reminds me of the biggest picnic in the history of the Bible.

Jesus had been healing the sick and preaching to a large gathering of men, women, and children, but everyone's stomachs were growling. The disciples wanted to send the people away, but Jesus told them, "That isn't necessary—you feed them" (Matthew 14:16, NLT). I'm sure the disciples looked at one another funny, as if to say, *Is He joking? All we have are five loaves of bread and two fish from some little kid.* Jesus told them to bring Him the little boy's food. He then asked the people to sit on the grass.

After that He prayed to His Father in heaven and then started breaking the loaves and fish into smaller pieces and handing them to the disciples to distribute. Jesus kept breaking bread until all the people were fed, which was way more than 5,000, since the number recorded in the Bible only counts the men, not the women and children. And if that weren't enough, there were 12 basketfuls of leftovers! Talk about a big picnic!

When I read these stories in the Bible, I am grateful that we serve such an amazing and powerful God. Aren't you?

NEXT STOP: Cincinnati, Ohio

First Responders

Come quickly to help me, O Lord my savior. **Psalm 38:22, NLT.**

If you are in a car accident, and glass is shattered all over your seat, you have cuts on your arms, and your shoulder feels as if it is broken, who is going to take you to the hospital? That kind of accident would get you a quick ride to the hospital in an ambulance.

But what if your wagon tipped over in 1865, pinning you under the back wheel and breaking your leg? If you lived in Cincinnati, Ohio, you still would have gotten a ride in an ambulance. But the ambulance didn't have flashing lights, and it couldn't go 65 miles per hour, because it was pulled by a horse. In 1865 Commercial Hospital in Cincinnati began the first hospital-based ambulance service in the United States. The service was very successful, and in the next few years more cities around the world began providing emergency medical services to its residents.

In his lifetime King David didn't have the pleasure of emergency medical services on the battlefield. There were no ambulances to rush in and rescue the wounded and dying. But David had God, and he placed his trust in his heavenly Father.

In Psalm 38 David cries out to God. He tells God that he feels guilty for all the sins he has committed. He confesses his sins and asks God to forgive him and stay close by his side. Then he ends the psalm with today's text: "Come quickly to help me, O Lord my savior" (verse 22, NLT).

God is a great ambulance driver! He is always ready to come to our rescue, but we have to "call" Him first. An ambulance will not arrive at an accident unless someone calls 9-1-1. Similarly, God will not come to your aid if you don't ask Him for help. He will not force Himself into your life—you have to invite Him. Jesus wants to save you, but you have to *want* to be saved. If you haven't given your life to Jesus, what are you waiting for? And if you have, give it to Him again today and make sure you have confessed your sins and are right with God.

NEXT STOP: Cambridge, Ohio

Hello out there!

Old Versus Young

One day when Moses was forty years old, he decided to visit his relatives, the people of Israel.... Forty years later, in the desert near Mount Sinai, an angel appeared to Moses in the flame of a burning bush. **Acts 7:23-30, NLT.**

A retired U.S. Marine Corps pilot, astronaut, and U.S. senator, John Glenn was born in Cambridge, Ohio. Among his list of accomplishments, his most notable is being the first American to orbit the Earth. On February 20, 1962, he was pilot of the Mercury spacecraft, which orbited the earth three times in just less than five hours.

Three years later he retired from the military and the National Aeronautics and Space Administration (NASA) and ran for political office. In 1974 he was elected as a senator of Ohio, and for the next 25 years he held that position and served in the United States Senate.

On October 29, 1998, one year before retiring from the Senate, John Glenn flew on *Discovery* and, at age 77, became the oldest person to fly in space. His age didn't stop him from doing the things he loved.

Unfortunately, some people feel that once a person reaches a certain age, he or she should stop being active and simply sit around and do nothing. On the flip side, some people feel that young people your age should not get involved in church or school until they are older. They think you should wait a few years to grow taller and wiser before you get involved in church. I don't know about you, but I'm glad that God doesn't work this way. He uses young and old people—and those in the middle. He has a job for anyone who wants to serve Him.

Moses is a perfect example of someone who was used by God throughout his life. We don't know what kind of influence he had in the palace as a boy, but I'm sure he was a good example. At age 40 he made a mistake and killed an Egyptian and ran away. God spent the next 40 years teaching Moses His ways. When Moses was 80, God spoke to him through a burning bush and asked him to lead the Israelites to the Promised Land, a job he did for the next 40 years until he died, at age 120. God had work for Moses to do throughout his life.

Can God use your talents at age 11 just as much as he can use them when you are 22, 44, or 99? Absolutely!

NEXT STOP: Canton, Ohio

Important Women

Adam named his wife Eve, because she would become the mother of all the living. **Genesis 3:20.**

Canton, Ohio, is home to the National First Ladies' Library. "Big deal," you say. "The first lady doesn't run the country. The president is the one who should be honored and have buildings named after him and exhibits set up to visit."

Think again! The first lady plays a very important role in the success of her husband's presidency. Her role goes beyond pretty dresses and perfect makeup and dinner parties. Many first ladies have developed national programs that address issues they are passionate about. Michelle Obama, wife to the forty-fourth president of the United States, has worked to educate the nation about childhood obesity and the health risks that kids face when they are overweight.

Eleanor Roosevelt, wife of Franklin D. Roosevelt, donated money she earned from speaking engagements to help poor and disadvantaged people. Her heart went out to these people, so she did her best to help them.

When the British marched toward Washington in 1814, Dolley Madison acted quickly and packed important government paperwork and silverware and dishes from the White House dining room. She also made sure that a large portrait of George Washington hanging on a wall in the White House was safely removed and hidden from the British. With these treasured possessions she fled before the British set fire to the White House and burned it to the ground. Her quick thinking saved important pieces of American history.

Each first lady leaves her own unique lasting impression on the country. And each first lady helps her husband in a different way as he serves the American people.

As you know, God created Eve to be Adam's partner. He created her to help Adam in his job of caring for the Garden of Eden. God created Eve to be Adam's friend and companion. Wives have a very important job of working with their husbands, supporting them, and helping them succeed at whatever they do. God created the husband-wife relationship and gave women the job of being a help-mate to their husbands, which is a very important job!

NEXT STOP: Dayton, Ohio

Hello out there!

Hardworking Brothers

Lazy hands make for poverty, but diligent hands bring wealth. **Proverbs 10:4.**

Orville and Wilbur Wright successfully launched their glider on December 17, 1903, in North Carolina. But that wasn't the end of their story. The two brothers were from Dayton, Ohio, where they had opened a bicycle shop in 1892.

After gliding to a world-class accomplishment, the brothers returned home and continued working on perfecting their flying machine. During 1904 and 1905 they tested new designs and modifications in a nearby cow pasture, and by 1905 they had built the world's first practical plane.

With the success of their airplane, the brothers opened the Wright Company and manufactured airplanes for five years from 1910 to 1915.

Orville and Wilbur could have easily given up or stopped working after their successful flight at Kitty Hawk. They had reached their goal! They had figured out how to glide through the air and safely come to a stop. Why go further? They had succeeded!

Fortunately, these two brothers were diligent and committed to their work, and they continued experimenting until they could go no further. They kept trying new techniques and building additional models until their flying machine was the best they could make it. They worked hard and didn't slack off after achieving their goal.

When you have a project at school, do you do just enough to get by and get an average grade? Or do you work hard and learn all you can on the subject so that you get the best grade possible? King Solomon wrote today's text. People who are lazy are often poor because they don't want to work. And if you don't work, you don't get paid. On the flip side, "diligent hands bring wealth" (Proverbs 10:4). People who work hard earn a living and, if they use their money wisely, can become wealthy.

When you are faced with a task, do it to the best of your ability. Give it your all! The rewards for working hard will follow you into adulthood.

NEXT STOP: Detroit, Michigan

June 10

Lightning Speeds

The king told his chariot driver, "Wheel around and get me out of the fighting. I've been wounded." I **Kings 22:34.**

Welcome to Detroit, Michigan, the car capital of the world. Detroit is home to the three largest automobile makers in the United States and Canada: Ford, General Motors, and Chrysler.

I bet some of you are getting excited thinking about your favorite car and how cool it would be to tour a car factory. On the other hand, for those of us who aren't car enthusiasts, we are just glad to have access to a car that runs and gets us places. But there are those who live, breathe, and dream about cars, especially when it comes to going fast.

In 2012 Ford produced 50 Mustang Cobra Jets that can hit 100 miles per hour in just a little more than three seconds! That's crazy fast! But these cars are not street legal, so their owners can't drive them to the grocery store and back home. This means that the owners can drive them only on closed-course tracks built for cars that are not street legal. And at a price tag of $104,000 for the fully loaded model, select car enthusiasts and those who have a need for speed pay a high price for a car they can drive only at select locations.

Some people clearly like to drive fast just to drive fast. I would drive fast only in an emergency, such as rushing one of my kids to the hospital. Today's scripture talks about an emergency in which King Ahab was wounded in battle. I'm sure the chariot driver who was driving spun the horses around and headed for safety as quickly as he could.

The Bible says that King Ahab disguised himself before going into battle. In fact, he asked the king of Judah to dress in his royal robes to try to trick the enemy. It worked for a short time, but the chariot commanders for the enemy realized the trick and withdrew. Remarkably, someone shot an arrow at the king of Israel by chance, and it hit King Ahab between the sections of his armor. It was then that he gave the command to his driver to get out of there as quickly as possible. But it was too late. He bled to death while sitting in his chariot. King Ahab tried to run from God, but in the end it didn't matter how fast he was traveling—his wickedness caught up with him, and he died.

NEXT STOP: Mackinac Island

June 11

Hello out there!

Forced Exercise

Dear friend, I pray that you may enjoy good health and that all may go well with you, even as your soul is getting along well. **3 John 2.**

Today we are boarding a boat that will take us from the mainland of Michigan to Mackinac Island, a resort town that is only 3.8 square miles or 8 miles in circumference if you were to travel around the whole island. But I must warn you, you need to wear sneakers or other comfortable shoes, because once we get to the island, we have to walk or ride bikes everywhere we go. In 1898 the island banned motorized vehicles for personal use, limiting travel to foot, bicycle, horse-drawn carriages, or roller skates.

No matter where you want to go on the island or how far it is, you can't just jump in a car and quickly drive to the store. Nope, you have to use your own power (unless you use a horse as transportation) to get you where you want to go.

Some people may not like having to "exercise" to get to where they want to go, but can you imagine how much healthier people would be if they had to walk or ride a bike a couple of times a week to go where they wanted to go?

What keeps us healthy? Well, it's a package deal. You need to eat healthy foods, such as vegetables, fruits, and grains. And you need fresh water, sunshine, and sleep. But what about exercise? All of the other things I mentioned are important, but so is exercise. It's what keeps your heart healthy. It's what helps your muscles become stronger.

We all hope to enjoy good health. It's not fun to be sick. It's miserable to be coughing or have a runny nose, sore throat, headache, or fever. So what are you doing to stay as healthy as possible? Think about what you eat and about what you enjoy doing that is active and gets your heart pumping. Do you like playing soccer or baseball or football? What about basketball or riding your bike or hiking? Find what you like to do, and then do it! Be active, and enjoy good health. If you form good habits now, it will be easier to continue those habits when you are an adult. Go exercise!

NEXT STOP: Battle Creek, Michigan

It's Time for Breakfast

Jesus said to them, "Come and have breakfast." **John 21:12, NASB.**

What is your favorite breakfast food? Pancakes, waffles, toast, eggs, oatmeal, cereal? If you asked that question in my house, both of my kids (and my husband) would say cereal. They love cereal—all kinds! Just give them a bowl and spoon, milk, and a box of cereal, and they are happy campers. I, on the other hand, could take it or leave it.

You may be wondering what this has to do with Battle Creek, Michigan, and I'm getting to that part. Dr. John Harvey Kellogg was a Seventh-day Adventist doctor in Battle Creek who helped found the Battle Creek Sanitarium, a health-care facility that treated people for all sorts of ailments and taught them how to live healthier lifestyles. Dr. Kellogg and the staff at the sanitarium served patients vegetarian meals in an effort to improve their health.

One day Dr. Kellogg and his brother, Will, were cooking when they had to handle a pressing matter in the sanitarium. In their rush to leave, they left some cooked wheat sitting out. When they returned, the wheat was stale. Because they were on a tight budget, they did not want to throw out the food. So they sent the wheat through a roller, and it came out as flakes, which they then toasted. Thus, flaked cereal was created. The cereal was very popular with the patients, and 10 years later Will decided to produce the cereal for mass distribution to more than just the sanitarium patients. This resulted in the Kellogg brand cereal products you buy at the store today.

Now that you know a little bit of the history behind the cereals you eat, what do you think Jesus was offering the disciples for breakfast in today's text? I'll give you a clue: it wasn't cereal!

This was the third time Jesus appeared to His disciples after His resurrection, and it involved the miraculous catch of fish that Peter, Thomas, Nathanael, James, John, and two other disciples pulled in after Jesus told them to throw the net on the other side of the boat. Then, after they rowed to shore, they noticed that Jesus had made breakfast for them, consisting of bread and fish, staple foods of that day. To me, the awesome part of this story is that Jesus cared about not only their job (catching fish) but also their everyday needs. He knew they would be hungry after working all night, so Jesus made breakfast. What an awesome God!

NEXT STOP: Battle Creek, Michigan

June 13

Fire! Fire!

So fire blazed forth from the Lord's presence and burned them up,
and they died there before the Lord. **Leviticus 10:2, NLT.**

Battle Creek was home not only to the sanitarium but also to the Review and Herald Publishing Company, an Adventist orphanage, and a large church. Ellen White had warned the church members that they needed to spread out and populate other cities instead of building larger and larger institutions in Battle Creek, but the church leaders did not listen to her counsel. Instead, they tried to glorify themselves and their own efforts to build up the church.

Ellen White received visions from God that depicted the coming disasters that would strike Battle Creek if they continued to ignore God's commands. She recalled that one time she saw an angel with a sword of fire stretched over Battle Creek, with disaster upon disaster happening as the angel pointed the sword from one location to another.

True to God's message as sent to Ellen White, the sanitarium burned to the ground on February 18, 1902. The Review and Herald Publishing Association caught fire on December 30, 1902, and was also completely destroyed. These sad circumstances were the result of people following their own plans instead of listening to God.

Aaron's two sons Nadab and Abihu also did not listen to God. They chose to disregard His instructions and offer their own fire and incense before the Lord in their censers. They disobeyed, and they paid the ultimate price for their sins—immediate death.

It is so tempting to disobey our parents or God's Word, but don't do it! Throughout the Bible and history, people who disobey God reap the horrible consequences of separating themselves from God. Fire might not come down from heaven and strike you dead as it did Nadab and Abihu, but life will not go as smoothly for you if you choose your own path and disregard the wise counsel that God has given you. Please save yourself a lot of pain and obey your parents and God. It really is worth it!

NEXT STOP: Indian River, Michigan

The Cross of Christ

Fixing our eyes on Jesus, the pioneer and perfecter of faith.
For the joy set before him he endured the cross, scorning its shame,
and sat down at the right hand of the throne of God. **Hebrews 12:2.**

The Cross in the Woods is the largest crucifix in the world, measuring 31 feet high. The cross is a Catholic shrine in Indian River, Michigan, that attracts 275,000 to 325,000 visitors each year. The crucifix, which features a sculpture of Jesus on a wooden cross, is the centerpiece of the Cross in the Woods, which has indoor and outdoor churches on site. At these churches the Catholic Church holds Mass every day of the year.

Visitors from all over North America and around the world travel to see the large crucifix and worship in one of the churches on the premises. When it opened, people would pray and worship at the foot of the cross only in good weather. But in 1997 the congregation built a new church that can hold 1,000 people and has large glass windows that face the cross. In addition to the large cross, there are five other shrines on the property honoring different people revered by those of the Catholic faith.

Now that you know about the Cross in the Woods, I have a few questions. Do you think the Cross in the Woods is a holier location to worship God than your local church? Do you think visitors who pray at the foot of the cross receive a special blessing for having visited the crucifix? I hope you answered no to these two questions.

Paul reminded the early Christians that they were to look to Jesus and fix their eyes on Him. Jesus gave His life for us on the cross. He offered the ultimate sacrifice for us. He is the only one we should be looking at. We shouldn't look to statues or shrines or so-called holy places to find Christ. We find Jesus in the Bible, and we can pray to Him directly.

If we keep our eyes on Him, we won't get distracted by the things of this world that Satan wants to trick us with, which even includes statues of Christ. Make sure you are worshipping Christ. Focus on Him and His sacrifice, as Paul says, and you will be on the right track.

NEXT STOP: Upper Peninsula, Michigan

June 15

Hello out there!

The Great Unknown

As they traveled from town to town, they delivered the decisions reached by the apostles and elders in Jerusalem for the people to obey. So the churches were strengthened in the faith and grew daily in numbers. **Acts 16:4, 5.**

The Upper Peninsula, or UP, is the upper portion of Michigan that is separated from the lower portion by the place where Lake Michigan and Lake Huron join. To the north of the UP is Lake Superior. Lake Erie and Lake Ontario are the only Great Lakes that don't touch the UP.

The area is sparsely populated because of the colder climate and rugged countryside. The population in the Upper Peninsula is very small—almost 300,000. The UP has approximately 1,700 miles of uninterrupted shoreline along the Great Lakes. In addition to the water from the Great Lakes, the area has 4,300 inland lakes and 12,000 miles of streams! That's a lot of water. Because of its remote location and the abundance of forests and lakes, the UP has a wide variety of wildlife that thrive in that type of environment, such as moose, black bears, coyotes, foxes, wolves, river otters, raccoons, snowshoe hares, bobcats, white-tailed deer, and bald eagles, just to name a few.

Now that you know a little about the UP, how would you like to move there and become a Yooper (the nickname for people who live in the Upper Peninsula)? Do you think you could just pack up and move to the remote regions of the UP and share the good news of God's love with the people there?

Timothy was a young man when Paul visited Lystra. After the church members spoke well of Timothy, Paul asked him to travel with him from town to town preaching the gospel. Timothy struggled with homesickness early on in his ministry, but God had called him so he kept developing his relationship with Jesus until he was a strong minister in the early church.

No matter how scary the unknown can be if God is asking you to do something, He will give you the strength to do it. And just remember, He gives each of us different jobs. He didn't call every follower in the Bible to pack up their family and move to a land that He would show them. That was what God had planned for Abram. But remember, if God's plan is for you to become a Yooper, He'll give you what you need to make it happen.

NEXT STOP: Indianapolis, Indiana

"The Greatest Spectacle in Racing"

Do you not know that those who run in a race all run, but only one receives the prize? Run in such a way that you may win. **I Corinthians 9:24, NASB.**

If you have a parent who likes cars, you've probably heard about the Indianapolis 500, but if not, we're going to learn about what some call "The Greatest Spectacle in Racing."

Carl Fisher was a businessman who decided to embark on a new business venture of building a 2.5-mile racetrack that would test the skills of drivers and vehicles in a race to the finish. He began construction on the track in March 1909 and held the first automobile race on August 19, 1909. Fifteen teams participated in the race, but it was a disaster! It was a gravel-and-tar track, and during the race some of the potholes and ruts that formed were dangerous to drive over. In fact, halfway through the race a stone shattered the race leader's goggles and temporarily blinded him. To make matters worse, the rear axle of one of the cars broke, and the car flipped and hit a fence post, killing the driver and the mechanic riding with him.

On the third day of racing, a tire blew on one of the cars, and the car drove over the fence posts, killing two spectators and the driver's mechanic. Needless to say, the race was halted and further races canceled until improvements could be made to make the track safer for the drivers and spectators. Two years later the first long-distance race was held on May 30, 1911. The race distance was 500 miles, and the first-place prize was $14,000. The average speed of the winning driver was 74.5 miles per hour. It was after that race that the sport of automobile racing in the United States was born. Today the average speed of the Indianapolis 500 is more than 167 miles per hour, and the winning prize is more than $2.5 million.

As Paul said in 1 Corinthians 9:24, we are all racing—toward heaven. Fortunately, there isn't going to be only one winner who gets into heaven. We can all go to heaven. But if you want to go to heaven, you have to sign up for the race and agree to be on Jesus' team. You can't stay on the sidelines and think you can win the race. A racecar driver can't possibly win the race if he or she doesn't register, practice, and show up for the race. Driving around the parking lot outside the track won't help. The driver has to participate in the race in order to win. The same goes for us. We have to get into the "race" to make it to heaven.

NEXT STOP: Santa Claus, Indiana

June 17

 *Hello out there!*

Merry Christmas!

But the angel reassured them. "Don't be afraid!" he said. "I bring you good news that will bring great joy to all people. The Savior—yes, the Messiah, the Lord—has been born today in Bethlehem, the city of David!" **Luke 2:10, 11, NLT.**

OK, I know it's the beginning of summer and Christmas is about six months away, but we're in Santa Claus, Indiana, so we have to talk about Christmas! Santa Claus is a legendary character who is said to bring gifts to good children each year on Christmas Eve, so take a wild guess as to what the post office in Santa Claus, Indiana, receives each December. Letters to Santa Claus! Thousands of children write letters to Santa Claus hoping he will give them the gifts they want.

I want you to look around this next holiday season (which seems to start in October in the stores!) and see what kind of decorations are in the stores and what people place in their yards. Since you might forget to do this assignment, I'll tell you what I remember from last year. Driving through my neighborhood, I saw houses with Santa Claus statues and plastic Nativity sets. I saw lights and candy canes and Baby Jesus in the manger. It seems that Santa Claus and Baby Jesus go hand in hand now for most people, but is that how it should be? Should the Savior of the world be a lawn decoration alongside Santa Claus and his reindeer?

A lot of people seem to treat Baby Jesus as another decoration for the holiday season instead of a real person who came to this earth, lived among us, and died for our sins.

After the shepherds heard the good news, they ran to Bethlehem where they worshipped the newborn King. Then, in their excitement, "after seeing him, the shepherds told everyone what had happened and what the angel had said to them about this child. All who heard the shepherds' story were astonished" (Luke 2:17, 18, NLT).

When Christmas rolls around again in a few months, think about what your priority is for the season. Are you going to get caught up in the list making and excitement of more things, or will you find a way to tell others about Jesus and remind them that we can celebrate His birth during the Christmas season and throughout the year.

NEXT STOP: Terre Haute, Indiana

176

Roadside Assistance

As Jesus was approaching Jericho,
a blind man was sitting by the road begging. **Luke 18:35, NASB.**

A crossroads is an intersection where two roads meet. When you come to a crossroads, you have to choose which direction you will go. You could go straight ahead and continue on the road you were traveling, or you could turn left or right.

Some people use the expression that they are at a crossroads when they are faced with a difficult decision and multiple options to choose from.

Indiana is known as the crossroads of America because a number of major interstate highways go through the state. Fourteen major interstates cross through Indiana, not including all the major highways that service the state.

Terre Haute, Indiana, is unique because two major highways cross there: U.S. Highway 40, which runs coast to coast from Maryland to California, and U.S. Highway 41, a north–south route that runs from Michigan to Florida.

Today's Bible story is about the road to Jericho, which Jesus and His disciples were walking along. Sitting by the roadside was a blind man who was probably begging for money or food. The Bible tells us that when he heard the commotion of the crowd, he asked what was going on. When someone told him that Jesus was passing by, he immediately called out, "Jesus, Son of David, have mercy on me!" (Luke 18:38, NASB). People told him to be quiet, but he didn't give up. He knew that Jesus was his only hope. He called again, "Son of David, have mercy on me!" (verse 39, NASB).

At this point Jesus stopped and spoke to the man: "What do you want Me to do for you?"

The man replied, "Lord, I want to regain my sight!" (verse 41, NASB).

Jesus then said, "Receive your sight; your faith has made you well" (verse 42, NASB). The man had faith; he believed Jesus could heal him, and He did.

Do you believe that Jesus can help you? Do you believe He loves you enough to take care of you? Do you believe He is coming back to take you home with Him?

There are many "roads" in this life that will lead you toward God or away from Him. Make sure you pick the "roads" that make you stronger in Christ. Pick the "road" to Sabbath school and church. That is a good start. Pick the "road" to a good Christian friend's house. Pick the "roads" that will help you move closer to God and heaven!

NEXT STOP: Fountain City, Indiana

Hello out there!

Escape Route

Whatever you do, do it all for the glory of God. **I Corinthians 10:31.**

Fountain City is a farming community in Indiana. In the 1800s a home in this town was nicknamed the "Grand Central Station of the Underground Railroad." Levi Coffin's home got this nickname after he moved to the area and discovered that runaway slaves would hide in the nearby woods and surrounding community but were getting caught and returned to their masters. Levi decided to help the slaves, so he contacted members of the Black community and told them that he would be happy to hide any runaway slaves in his home, since Fountain City was located along the Underground Railroad.

The Underground Railroad was a network of houses and buildings that provided safety for runaway slaves who were trying to gain their freedom by escaping from their masters. The route was maintained by supporters who wanted to see slavery abolished. These people were willing to risk their lives to hide the slaves as they traveled north.

Levi was one of the supporters of the slaves, and he did everything in his power to hide the slaves who stopped at his house seeking protection. Slave hunters often threatened his life, but he stuck by his belief that the slaves should be free. It is estimated that Levi and his wife helped approximately 100 runaway slaves each year escape to freedom.

Freedom is a precious thing. Freedom allows you to decide what you want to be when you grow up. Freedom allows you to travel from one town to the next. Freedom allows you to worship God on Sabbath. Freedom allows you to choose whether you will follow God or Satan.

Paul reminded the Galatians of their freedom from sin because of Christ's death on the cross. He reminded them that "Christ . . . set us free" when He paid for our sins with His blood (Galatians 5:1).

Just as many of the slaves who escaped with Levi's help owed him their lives, we owe our lives to Jesus. He set us free. So we should do everything for the glory of God (1 Corinthians 10:31). He deserves our praise, our obedience, and our devotion!

NEXT STOP: Chicago, Illinois

Wild Weather

Then the Lord said to Moses, "Go to Pharaoh, for I have hardened his heart and the hearts of his officials so that I may perform these signs of mine among them that you may tell your children and grandchildren how I dealt harshly with the Egyptians and how I performed my signs among them, and that you may know that I am the Lord." **Exodus 10:1, 2.**

Welcome to the Windy City! Chicago, Illinois, received the nickname in 1858 when the name appeared in an article in the Chicago *Tribune* newspaper. Some people say that the city got its nickname from a rivalry with Cincinnati, Ohio. The two cities were enemies when it came to which city had the larger meatpacking operation and which city had the better baseball team. The nickname was used by a Cincinnati newspaper to imply that people who lived in Chicago were full of hot air and couldn't live up to their claims of living in the better city.

On the other hand, many feel that the nickname came about because of the natural breeze that blows off the shores of Lake Michigan. With the tall buildings in Chicago, the wind blows down the streets and swirls around corners in the city—thus earning the nickname the Windy City.

Chicago is also known for how cold it gets in the winter and the heat waves that can hit the city during the summer. The city is also prone to severe winter storms with lots of snow and ice, and thunderstorms in the spring and summer.

You may be reading this and be glad you don't live in Chicago. Or you may live in Chicago and be saying, "It isn't that bad!"

All this talk about weather reminds me of the crazy weather the Egyptians endured when the plagues fell on Egypt. Talk about weather that was wild and out of control! They experienced hail and thunder, locusts that were brought in by strong winds, and total darkness. Those were all forces of nature. And with a word, God stopped each plague. He had all power and control over nature back then, and He still does today. But because Pharaoh chose to ignore God and not recognize His power, he and his people suffered the consequences of their choices. Make sure you know the One who controls all nature. He is the only God we should worship and follow.

NEXT STOP: Chicago, Illinois

June 21

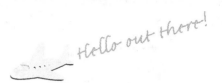

Hello out there!

People Power

And they said to each other, "We should choose a leader and go back to Egypt." **Numbers 14:4.**

We are spending a few days in Chicago because there is so much to see and do and talk about in the largest city in Illinois. Today we will be visiting the location of the first skyscraper. Although today's skyscrapers are much taller (the tallest building in the world has 163 floors and is located in the city of Dubai in the United Arab Emirates), when the Home Insurance Building was built in 1884, it was quite an achievement. The building was the first of its kind to be framed with structural steel, and at 10 stories tall, it was considered an architectural accomplishment.

Throughout history, men and women have achieved many things with and without God. Look at the Tower of Babel, the pyramids, and today's skyscrapers. Consider all of the things that people have created in the last 200 years, such as cars, electricity, phones, computers, cell phones, and iPads. There is no question that God made us to be smart and creative. He gave us the power to think and build. It is our choice, though, whether we use the talents He has given us for His glory or for ourselves so that we can become rich and famous.

The Bible is full of examples of people making good choices for God and others deciding to do their own thing. The Israelites made countless choices to follow their own plans instead of God's. After the spies got back from Canaan, the people panicked and decided that the land was too dangerous to enter because of the giants and warriors living there. Instead of trusting God's plan, they decided to make their own plans and appoint a leader and go back to Egypt. They let their fear of the unknown override their trust and faith in God. Instead of moving forward with God, they somehow thought it would be better to try and find their way back to Egypt. You may think they are crazy, but are we any different?

Is there anything in your life right now that you are trying to do on your own instead of letting God work out the situation for you? If so, stop trying to do it on your own. Stop trying to "build your own skyscraper." Let God help you! He will show you the way!

NEXT STOP: Chicago, Illinois

Sweet Tooth

He replied, "Out of the eater, something to eat; out of the strong, something sweet." **Judges 14:14.**

I have a riddle for you to figure out. What kind of sandwich is sweet in your mouth but turns your fingers black? Any guesses? Once you read the next paragraph, you will quickly figure it out. If you can't think of anything, keep reading.

Today is our last day in Chicago, and we are visiting the world's largest bakery. Approximately 1,500 employees work at the Nabiscol factory, which produces about 320 million pounds of snack foods each year. One of its top-selling cookies is the Oreo. The company makes and sells billions of Oreo cookies each year!

Some people like to dunk their cookies in milk and eat them soggy. Some like to split their cookies apart and lick out the crème filling and then eat the chocolate cookie. Some people try to stick the whole cookie in their mouth and eat it all at once. But no matter how you eat the cookie, you are going to enjoy the sweet taste of chocolate and crème.

Samson told a riddle to a number of men at his wedding that involved something sweet. The story began when Samson was traveling with his father and mother to Timnah to arrange for his marriage to a Philistine woman he had met. As Samson approached the town, a lion tried to attack him, but the Lord gave Samson power to protect himself, and "he tore the lion apart with his bare hands" (Judges 14:6).

The two families agreed upon the marriage proposal, and the wedding was set. On the appointed day, Samson traveled to Timnah for the wedding. As he passed the place where he had killed the lion, he saw the decaying carcass with a "swarm of bees and some honey" in it (verse 8). He then proceeded to the wedding feast, where he told a riddle to a number of men at the party. He made a deal with them that if they couldn't tell him the answer, they would have to give him "thirty linen garments and thirty sets of clothes" (verse 13). His plan to gain some new clothes for himself backfired when he told his new wife the answer to the riddle, and she told the men. Samson tried to trick the men, but in the end he was the one who was tricked. Take note: trickery never pays off!

NEXT STOP: New Salem, Illinois

June 23

Hello out there!

Honest Abe

Have nothing to do with a false charge and do not put an innocent or honest person to death, for I will not acquit the guilty. **Exodus 23:7.**

At age 23 Abraham Lincoln and another man in the town of New Salem bought a small general store. Unfortunately, the business did very poorly, leaving Abraham and his business partner in debt. Not long afterward, the business partner died, and Abraham became responsible for additional debts from the business failure. Although it took him 13 years, he slowly paid off the debt instead of walking away and trying to get out of the situation. This is one of the reasons he earned the reputation of being an honest man, resulting in his nickname: Honest Abe.

His honesty and reputation helped him get elected during his second campaign for a seat on the state legislature. Two years after the election he moved to Springfield, Illinois, where he began his career as a lawyer. He had a successful law practice and was known for his strong cross-examinations and closing arguments during a trial. He served four terms in a row in the Illinois House of Representatives before running for Congress and then for the presidency of the United States of America.

In all the political offices that Abraham Lincoln held, he was known for his honesty, which is a very noble trait to have. God told Moses a long time ago to be honest when dealing with legal situations. He warned the people that they should never listen to false charges and put an honest person to death. If they did, they would be guilty and be punished for their dishonesty.

What does honesty mean to you? Does it mean admitting to your teacher that you didn't do your homework because you didn't feel like it, not because you forgot or your dog ate it? Does it mean making things right with your friend and admitting that you talked about her behind her back and said you didn't like her new dress when, to her face, you told her you did? Honesty doesn't just involve telling the truth in a courtroom. It applies to all aspects of life. And it has a powerful effect on the people around you. Think about it. Which friends do you trust? The ones who are always honest with you, or the ones you know lie to their parents and teachers and try to get away with things? Be honest! Be trustworthy! Be like Jesus!

NEXT STOP: Springfield, Illinois

You Are Special

Are not two sparrows sold for a penny? Yet not one of them will fall to the ground outside your Father's care. And even the very hairs of your head are all numbered. So don't be afraid; you are worth more than many sparrows. **Matthew 10:29-31.**

With main offices in Springfield and Chicago, the Vehicle Services Department of the Illinois Secretary of State registers about 9 million vehicles every year. Apparently, the people of Illinois like to personalize their cars and show that they are different from everyone else, because their state has the highest number of personalized license plates. Here are a few license plates for you to try to decode and figure out:

- 10SNE1
- 1MOTOY
- 2CUTE4U
- 2FAST4U
- BADHBT
- DOG8IT
- FNY BNY
- LV2FLY

Any luck figuring these out? Some of them are easier than others. Here are the answers: *Tennis Anyone?; One More Toy; Too Cute For You; Too Fast For You; Bad Habit; Dog Ate It; Funny Bunny; Love To Fly.*

So many people in today's society want to stand out and show that they are different from everyone else. Why do you think people get tattoos or body piercings? So many people are trying to be their own person and stand out from the crowd, but often they go about it the wrong way. Many people try to be their own person apart from Jesus.

We are already special and unique in God's eyes without trying to make a name for ourselves. The Bible tells us that God knows the number of hairs on our head. We are worth far more than the birds of the air.

Instead of trying to make yourself stand out from the crowd by being different in a crazy way, stand out by being a follower of Jesus. Let Him make you different from the inside out. You are already special in His eyes! Let Jesus turn you into the person He wants you to be.

NEXT STOP: Monroe, Wisconsin

June 25

 *Hello out there!*

Cheese Country

Now Jesse said to his son David, "Take this ephah of roasted grain
and these ten loaves of bread for your brothers and hurry to their camp.
Take along these ten cheeses to the commander of their unit. See how your
brothers are and bring back some assurance from them." I Samuel 17:17, 18.

Wisconsin is known for its cheese. In fact, if you live in Wisconsin, people may call you a "cheesehead." Although the nickname started out as a negative term used by Illinois football and baseball fans to tease Wisconsin sports fans, the people of Wisconsin decided they liked the name. Nowadays Wisconsin sports fans often wear a cheesehead hat to sports games in support of their team.

The town of Monroe, Wisconsin, is the swiss cheese capital of the United States and home of the Chalet Cheese Factory and host of Cheese Days, a biannual celebration of the area's dairy and cheese heritage. If you attend the festival, you may end up with a stomachache after being stuffed full of cheesy samples!

Cheese has been around for a long time. In fact, cheese is mentioned in a few different verses in the Bible. One of them is the story of David and Goliath. Jesse, David's father, asked David to check on his brothers at the battlefield. But he didn't send him empty-handed. Jesse sent David with roasted grain, bread, and cheese. The grain and bread were for his brothers, while the cheese was for the commander of the unit. Jesse was looking out for his sons and providing for their needs by sending them food.

What are some ways that God looks out for you? Can you identify some specific ways that God has provided for you in the last week? See if you can think about something other than food, clothes, and a place to live. Think hard and come up with a blessing the Lord has given you that shows He cares about your everyday needs.

NEXT STOP: Spring Green, Wisconsin

House on the Rock

Therefore everyone who hears these words of mine and puts them into practice is like a wise man who built his house on the rock. **Matthew 7:24.**

In Spring Green, Wisconsin, there is a house built on a large rock. The structure is actually called the House on the Rock. The house is a unique architectural structure that was completed in 1959 on top of Deer Shelter Rock. The house is situated on a 60-foot rock column and has 14 rooms, many of which are themed.

With 3,264 windows for walls, the Infinity Room provides panoramic views of the valley. Another room features the world's largest carousel, boasting more than 20,000 lights and 269 handcrafted animals. The dollhouse room has more than 200 dollhouses on display. Visit the Spirit of Aviation room, and you'll see a collection of model airplanes.

The House on the Rock is not the first "house on the rock." The Bible tells us of the first "house on a rock" in Jesus' story of the wise man who built his house on a rock. And what do we know about that rock? When a storm came and the wind and rain pounded the house, "it did not fall, because it had its foundation on the rock" (Matthew 7:25). Jesus then cut to the main point He was trying to make. He told the people listening to Him, "But everyone who hears these words of mine and does not put them into practice is like a foolish man who built his house on sand" (verse 26).

If you read the Bible and listen to God's Word but don't do what it says, you are like a foolish person who builds on sand. As you know, sand is not a stable foundation. It shifts and moves and does not stand firm. Those who say they are Christians but choose to disregard the Bible and do their own thing are foolish and will reap the consequences of their choices.

Build on the Rock! Don't just pretend to be built on the Rock. You can't be built partly on the Rock and partly on the sand. It is all or nothing. Center your life on God and commit to following His commands. If you do, you will not fall when the wind blows!

NEXT STOP: Oshkosh, Wisconsin

June 27

Hello out there!

Calling All Pathfinders

They devoted themselves to the apostles' teaching and to the fellowship, to the breaking of bread and to prayer. **Acts 2:42.**

The International Pathfinder Camporee is held every five years, and since 1999 it has been held in Oshkosh, Wisconsin. Tens of thousands of Pathfinders from the North American Division and around the world gather to camp, complete honors, and sing and worship together. It is an awesome experience to be with that many other Adventist youth!

The first year that the camporee was held in Oshkosh a major storm began to brew, and tornadoes and other destructive forces were headed toward the thousands of Pathfinders who were camping. Immediately everyone prayed and asked God for safety. Everyone continued to pray as they sought shelter from the storm. But by God's grace the storm split and went around the campground, completely missing the Pathfinders and reminding everyone of God's protection and care for His children.

If you are involved in Pathfinders, what do you enjoy most about your club? If you aren't involved in Pathfinders, what do you enjoy most about your Sabbath school class? There is something similar between your Pathfinder club and your Sabbath school class. Have you figured out what it is? It's called fellowship! Do you know what *fellowship* means? It means getting together with people who believe as you believe or who have the same kinds of interests as you do. That's why it is so important whom you choose as your friends.

Acts 2:42 tells us that the first Christians devoted themselves to learning all they could about the Bible and encouraging one another through prayer and eating together. Is it easier to choose a good movie to watch if you are with someone who believes as you do and only wants to watch things that are pure? Or is it easier if you are with someone who is opposite of you and likes to watch violent movies?

It is important to surround ourselves with friends who have the same goal we do: being a disciple of Christ and preparing for heaven. Then, with their support, we can stand up for what is right and reach out to others who don't know Jesus. Make sure you are fellowshipping with Christian friends.

NEXT STOP: Eagle River, Wisconsin

Snowmobile Racing

As you know, we count as blessed those who have persevered. You have heard of Job's perseverance and have seen what the Lord finally brought about. The Lord is full of compassion and mercy. James 5:11.

With more than 500 miles of incredible snowmobile trails, Eagle River is considered the Snowmobile Capital of the World. Eagle River also hosts the World Championship Snowmobile Derby. The first snowmobile race in the town took place in 1964. It was founded by a local innkeeper, his wife, and a friend of theirs. They each owned a snowmobile, and they knew that many of the other townspeople owned snowmobiles, so they figured it would be fun to hold a race on and around Dollar Lake.

It is unclear how many people entered the race, but it is interesting to note that out of all the participants, the winner was an eighth-grade student. Many of the snowmobiles had a hard time climbing a small hill, but not Stan Hayes's snowmobile. He managed to navigate up and over the hill and race to the finish to win the competition.

He persevered. He didn't give up. He could have easily thought, *I'm just a kid. There are so many older teenagers and adults who are racing. I'll never win.* But I'm guessing he didn't let this thought enter his mind, because he ended up winning the race!

Again and again in the Bible, the apostles remind us to persevere, to never give up. In this text James is reminding us that Job persevered. In spite of all the bad things that happened to Job, he didn't give up on God or on life. He didn't quit talking to God and asking Him tough questions. And in the end we know that God, who, James reminds us, is "full of compassion and mercy," rewarded Job for staying true to Him, and God blessed Job in ways beyond what He had done before.

Are you currently in a situation in which you need to do your best not to give up? Do you need to persevere in a certain area? Maybe it's school in general. Or maybe it's just one subject, like math or English. Maybe you need to persevere when you have to run a mile at school. Whatever the case may be, don't give up. Ask God to help you and then keep plowing forward until you have accomplished what you need to finish. You can do it with God's help!

NEXT STOP: Willow, Wisconsin

June 29

Hello out there!

Fake Beauty

Your beauty should not come from outward adornment. . . . Rather, it should be that of your inner self, the unfading beauty of a gentle and quiet spirit, which is of great worth in God's sight. **I Peter 3:3, 4.**

Willow is the name of a real town in Wisconsin, and Willows is the fictional (imaginary) town in Wisconsin that Barbie is from. Here's the whole story. Ruth Handler had a daughter named Barbara who liked to play with paper dolls and baby dolls. One day Ruth noticed that her daughter enjoyed pretending that her dolls were adults. Ruth began to wonder if an adult-looking doll should be made that little girls could dress and play with. She shared the idea with her husband, who cofounded Mattel, a large toy company, but he didn't like the idea.

A little while after this encounter, Ruth and her two children were in Europe on vacation, and Ruth found a German-made adult-figured doll that looked like what she had thought of creating in America. She bought a doll for her daughter and two others to take back to Mattel. Back in the States, she shared the doll with a toy engineer, who then slightly redesigned it, and she named it Barbie, after her daughter. The first doll was sold wearing a black-and-white-striped bathing suit, and it was an instant success. In addition to the doll, a series of books were written based in the fictional town of Willows, Wisconsin.

In spite of Barbie's success, many people don't like the doll because they feel that all she promotes is good looks and a perfect body. From makeup to hair to clothes, the doll presents the image of fake beauty.

The Bible talks about beauty, and it urges girls not to worry about fancy hair, jewelry, and the best clothes. Instead, Peter tells us that girls should be worried about what is on the inside, such as a gentle and loving character. This is what is of great worth to God. But that doesn't mean girls should walk around with uncombed hair and dirty clothes. The important thing to remember is to focus on character more than on looks.

Guys would be smart to do the same. This principle applies to all of us. We should all be more worried about what God thinks and how we look to Him than how we appear to each other.

NEXT STOP: Boundary Waters Canoe Area Wilderness, Minnesota

Let's Go Canoeing!

Once again, the kingdom of heaven is like a net that was let down into the lake and caught all kinds of fish. When it was full, the fishermen pulled it up on the shore. Then they sat down and collected the good fish in baskets, but threw the bad away. **Matthew 13:47, 48.**

Minnesota is known for the boundary waters that separate the United States from Canada and provide endless miles of canoeing and fishing in crystal-clear rivers and lakes that are bordered by towering trees. The Boundary Waters Canoe Area Wilderness features more than 1 million acres that are maintained by the U.S. Forest Service and is a premium vacation location for outdoor adventure enthusiasts.

Canoes or other nonmotorized boats are the only watercrafts allowed in the majority of the lakes and rivers, which provide more than 1,000 miles of routes to travel. The lakes and rivers are connected by portage trails that require boaters to carry their gear and canoes to the next lake or river, where they can once again paddle.

In addition to paddling, many people fish along the way, catching different types of bass, perch, and trout for supper or just for fun.

We have already talked about a few fishing stories in the Bible, but there is another fishing story in Matthew 13 that is actually a parable. It is not one of the more popular parables, such as the lost coin, lost sheep, or prodigal son, but it is another example that Jesus used to tell the people about heaven and what the future holds.

Jesus compares the separation of "the wicked from the righteous" (verse 49), to that of fishermen separating the good fish from the bad fish. All of the fish are scooped up in the net, but only the good ones are kept. Likewise, only the righteous will be taken to heaven. The wicked people, represented by the bad fish, will be thrown into the lake of fire, where they will be lost forever.

When Jesus returns and casts His "net" upon the earth, make sure you are caught and not thrown away. I know I want to be in heaven with the greatest Fisherman to ever walk this earth!

NEXT STOP: Bloomington, Minnesota

Shopping Spree

If anyone has material possessions and sees his brother in need but has no pity on them, how can the love of God be in that person? **I John 3:17.**

Welcome to Bloomington, Minnesota, and the Mall of America. Talk about shopping till you drop! The mall could fit seven Yankee Stadiums inside of it, which is equivalent to 4.2 million square feet! The mall is rectangular in shape and is four stories tall. More than 520 stores are arranged along the first three floors, with the fourth floor reserved for restaurants and special events and meetings. The center of the mall is completely open and features an amusement park complete with roller coasters and carnival-type rides.

One Christmas my husband and I were flying to Canada to visit his family when we got stuck in the Minneapolis airport for 12 hours. With nothing to do, we decided to catch a bus from the airport to the Mall of America. Since we had the time, we thought it would be fun to walk the *whole* mall from bottom to top. We went past every store and stopped at a number of them, including the LEGO store (my favorite) and a store that sold only hot sauce and hot peppers. We finally took a break and ate in the food court. By the end of the day we were exhausted and ready to board our flight so that we could sit and do nothing!

It is fun to go shopping, but we have to be careful not to get caught up in the excitement of spending and wanting more than we need or can afford. Go open your closet. Do you have a different outfit to wear every day? Do you have sports equipment? Do you have books on your bookshelf to read? We have so much to be thankful for. But because you have material possessions—clothes, sports equipment, books, etc.—you have a responsibility to help others. Did you know that?

Read today's text, 1 John 3:17, again. Ouch! John doesn't mess around; he tells it like it is. If we see people who are in need but we don't help them, then do we really have Jesus in our hearts? If we have Jesus in our hearts, we will want to help others instead of selfishly trying to get more and more things for ourselves.

NEXT STOP: Minneapolis, Minnesota

Walking in the Clouds

*As they were walking along the road, a man said to him [Jesus],
"I will follow you wherever you go."* **Luke 9:57.**

Minneapolis, Minnesota, is the largest city in the state, and it is home to the famous Skyway System. The Skyway System is a series of walkways that link buildings together above the city streets, sparing city residents from having to venture out into the freezing Minnesota winters. The walkways are usually one or two stories above the street, and they are climate-controlled, so they stay cool in the summer and warm in the winter. Windows along both sides of the walkway allow pedestrians to see the street below and the surrounding city.

The Skyway System links 69 full city blocks that total more than seven miles of walkways. The city's Skyway System makes most of downtown accessible to residents through these connecting walkways. People can live, eat, work, and shop without going outside. But they have to walk, which for some people is a hassle. Some people would rather bundle up, face the cold, and drive a few blocks than walk.

We have it easy now that we can drive almost anywhere we want to go, but back in Jesus' day He and the disciples had to walk to get to wherever they wanted to go. Jesus spread the gospel throughout the region by walking from place to place. And it was while He walked that He was able to talk and visit with people along the way. He healed many people along the road while walking between towns.

In today's verse Jesus was walking along the road when a man approached Him and told Him that he would follow Him wherever He went. Jesus clearly wanted to make sure the man knew what he was agreeing to, because Jesus said, "Foxes have dens and birds have nests, but the Son of Man has no place to lay his head" (verse 58). Jesus wanted the man to know that it wouldn't always be easy following Him. The rewards would be amazing—serving others, spreading the gospel, and watching miracles unfold before his eyes—but he had to be willing to commit to following Jesus when he didn't have a place to call home and life wasn't comfortable.

Are you willing to follow Jesus no matter what? Make a commitment before it's too late.

NEXT STOP: Rochester, Minnesota

July 3

Hello out there!

The Heart of the Matter

The Lord regretted that he had made human beings on the earth, and his heart was deeply troubled. **Genesis 6:6.**

You don't have to be a doctor to know that you will die if your heart stops working. Your heart is the key organ that keeps every other organ functioning. Without your heart pumping blood throughout your body, you will cease to live and breathe. Because the heart is so vital to our existence, doctors have studied the heart for years trying to figure out how to help people who have a bad or weak heart.

The Mayo Clinic is a huge teaching hospital in Rochester, Minnesota, that excels in research and specializes in new treatments in pursuit of advancing the medical profession. One such advancement occurred on September 2, 1952, when doctors performed the first open-heart surgery in which they cooled the patient's body and lowered her core temperature so they could work on her heart.

After I read this story, I came across today's text, which talks about God's heart being filled with pain. Have you ever thought about God's heart hurting? In this text God was looking down on His creation and the wickedness that was spreading throughout the land. Here were the people He had made. He loved them, and that's why His heart hurt. He didn't want to see them suffer and die, but their choices were leading them down a path of destruction. So God talked to Noah, and the rest is history. Noah began building the ark and warning the people of the coming flood, but in the end Noah and his family were the only ones to listen to God's message.

Is there anything you do that hurts God? Do you think He is sad when you talk back to your parents or hit your brother or sister? So what do you do when you hurt God and make Him sad? The Bible tells us to confess our sins and ask God for forgiveness. He freely gives us grace and forgives us and forgets the pain we have caused Him!

You are human. You are bound to cause God pain, but the goal for each of us is to live our lives for God and to make His heart happy instead of sad. Keep doing your best to live for God. He is the only thing worth living for. No person on this earth will love you as God does. His heart longs for you to love Him in return.

NEXT STOP: Forest City, Iowa

Freedom

When hard pressed I cried to the Lord;
he brought me into a spacious place. **Psalm 118:5.**

It's the Fourth of July, and we are traveling to Forest City, Iowa, the home of Winnebago Industries, a manufacturer of motor homes. This might not be your idea of an Independence Day celebration, but many families enjoy camping over this holiday weekend.

I've done a lot of tent camping, but I've never stayed in a motor home. I think it would be fun to camp in a motor home, though—they look really cool! The new motor homes have refrigerators, stoves, washers, dryers, showers, toilets, cabinet space, stereos, TVs, etc. If you have enough money, you can buy a motor home with all kinds of gadgets. These homes on wheels are a great way to take your house with you all over the country.

No matter where you lay your head this Fourth of July, remember that our independence started when Jesus died on the cross for our sins. Sure, our independence in the United States was the result of many men and women fighting for our freedom, but our true freedom comes from a relationship with God. The same can be said for Canadians, who celebrate Canada Day and their freedom on July 1. No matter what country you live in, true freedom comes from God.

Are there things in your life that are pulling you down? Do you want to be free from bad habits or harmful friendships? If so, cry out as David did. Pray to God and ask Him to help you to be free from whatever is causing you pain and heartache in your life. He is more than able to free you as He did David. But when you pray, you also have to let go and let God handle the situation. As He frees you from a bad relationship, don't try to snatch it back and fix it. Let go and let God show you a better way.

When you allow God to be in charge of your life, you will experience true freedom!

NEXT STOP: Burr Oak, Iowa

July 5

Hello out there!

Life on the Prairie

Even the sparrow has found a home,
and the swallow a nest for herself, . . . Blessed are those who dwell
in your house; they are ever praising you. **Psalm 84:3, 4.**

If you have read any of the *Little House on the Prairie* books or watched the television series, you know about Laura Ingalls Wilder. If not, let me tell you a little bit about this American author. During her childhood, Laura and her family moved around a lot, living in Wisconsin, Iowa, Minnesota, and Kansas. While living in Iowa, Laura's father managed a hotel in Burr Oak, and the family had nice accommodations. But the family also lived in Walnut Grove, Minnesota, for two years, where they lived in a dugout home that was carved into the banks of Plum Creek. Their dirt home was covered with a grass sod roof.

How would you like to live in a dirt house with no private bedroom or bathroom? Could you handle sleeping on a blanket on a dirt floor with your parents and sibling(s) in the same room? Could you eat, live, and sleep in a one-room home?

Laura and many pioneer families lived very simple lives in small homes as they tried to make a living growing their own food or working in a trade as a carpenter, blacksmith, shopkeeper, or doctor. Are you happy in your home, or do you wish for bigger rooms, nicer furniture, more windows, or a larger yard?

God wants us to be content with what He has given us. He wants us to trust Him for all of our needs. We know that God provides a home for the sparrows and other animals, so we need to believe that He will do the same for us and that whatever He has given us is just right for our family. If we are focused on God, we won't be so focused on the things of this world.

King David reminds us that we are blessed when we live in God's house (Psalm 84:4). Is King David talking about living in a church? He could be, but we know that God lives in our hearts when we invite Him in, so if we focus on God, we will praise Him and worship Him no matter where we are. This will help us keep our eyes on the final prize and not the earthly possessions that tempt us and try to take our attention away from Jesus.

It doesn't matter if our home on this earth is a mansion or a shack. What matters is if Jesus is our best friend.

NEXT STOP: Indianola, Iowa

Up, Up, and Away

After that, we who are still alive and are left will be caught up together with them in the clouds to meet the Lord in the air. And so we will be with the Lord forever. **I Thessalonians 4:17.**

During Vacation Bible School one year our church rented a hot-air balloon, and each child who wanted to could take a ride in it. The balloon was tethered to the ground by ropes, so you got to go only about 40 feet up in the air, but it was still an awesome ride. As I floated up in the basket with the operator, I got a bird's eye view of the church parking lot and our school's baseball field.

The thing I like most about hot-air balloons is the wide variety of colors they come in. There are all different patterns and designs, and some balloons even have pictures or other images printed on them.

In Indianola, Iowa, the National Balloon Museum features exhibits that trace the past 200 years of ballooning. Many people ask why the museum is located in the middle of Iowa, and it is because the weather and flat terrain make for good flying conditions. Each year the town hosts ballooning events and competitions where people from all over the country come to fly their balloons.

If you have ever seen a number of hot-air balloons up in the sky, whether in pictures or real life, it is a spectacular sight. But a much more stunning scene will take place when Jesus returns to take us home to heaven. Paul describes what will happen when Jesus returns. He tells us that those who are still alive "will be caught up in the clouds to meet the Lord in the air" (1 Thessalonians. 4:17, NLT). We will be able to fly without a balloon! That will be such an amazing feeling as we join angels and loved ones and friends in the clouds to greet Jesus upon His "cloud" throne.

Whether or not you get the privilege to ride in a hot-air balloon on this earth, I can guarantee that you don't want to miss out on the ultimate flying experience. Ask God to help you to be ready for His soon return.

NEXT STOP: Cedar Rapids, Iowa

Hello out there!

It's Breakfastime!

At the end of the ten days they looked healthier and better nourished than any of the young men who ate the royal food. **Daniel 1:15.**

What is your favorite cold cereal? If you remember, I'm not a cereal lover, but if I have to choose, I do like Crispix, Special K Red Berries, and Quaker Oatmeal Squares. What about hot cereal? Do you like oatmeal with fruit or brown sugar?

Cedar Rapids is home to the largest cereal mill in the world, Quaker Oats. The Quaker Oats Company makes cold cereal, oatmeal, snack bars, and rice snacks, and promotes their products as being healthy for your heart and an important start to your day.

In fact, in 2009 Bob Harper, one of the trainers on *The Biggest Loser* TV show, became a spokesperson for Quaker oatmeal. As someone who helps contestants on *The Biggest Loser* exercise and make healthy food choices so they can lose weight and keep it off, Bob takes health seriously, and he knows the importance of eating the right food.

Daniel also knew the importance of eating good food. But he knew something more than Bob Harper. Daniel knew that the food he ate would not only keep him healthy but help him think more clearly, which would help him in his relationship with God. It was important for Daniel to hear God's voice and be open to listening to Him. Another reason Daniel refused to eat of the king's food was that some of the king's food was unclean and went against what God had instructed His children to eat.

You only have one body here on this earth. What are you doing to take care of your body? Do you exercise? Do you drink plenty of water and eat lots of fruits and vegetables? There are more and more medical studies proving that many of the diseases plaguing our society today could be prevented if we would eat nutritious foods. The consequences of eating foods high in sugar and fats are sickness and disease.

God promises to watch over us, but we have to do our part to take care of our bodies. Eating foods that are full of vitamins and minerals will help us maintain good health and live life to the fullest. Follow God's diet of fruits, grains, vegetables, and nuts, and you will be healthier and happier.

NEXT STOP: Iowa Farmland

Rich Crops

Isaac planted crops in that land and the same year reaped a hundredfold, because the Lord blessed him. **Genesis 26:12.**

Iowa is part of the fertile farmland of the Midwest. If you drive through Iowa, you will see field after field of corn, soybeans, and oats. There are also large tracts of land dedicated to raising beef cattle and hogs. It was estimated that, on average, one Iowa farm grows enough food to feed about 155 people.

Today we often take our food for granted. We just expect that when we go to the grocery store, there will be plenty of produce, bread, and canned goods. But what if there was a serious famine and drought that affected a large portion of the world? What would happen to our food supply then?

In Isaac's day there was a famine in the land, which meant that there probably wasn't much to eat since they had to grow all their own food. But God told Isaac to stay where he was, in Gerar, so he did. Now, Gerar was in Philistine territory, and Isaac was afraid the men in the town would kill him if they found out Rebekah was his wife, so he told them that she was his sister. Does that sound familiar? That's right. His dad, Abraham, had fallen into the same trap.

But Abimelech, the king of the Philistines, found out about the trick, and he called Isaac to the palace and asked him to tell the truth. Then the king ordered all the people to leave Isaac and Rebekah alone and not to harm either of them.

It was after this incident that Isaac planted crops in the land, and he "harvested a hundred times more grain than he planted, for the Lord blessed him" (Genesis 26:12, NLT). Did he reap a good crop because he picked the perfect field and carefully tended the plants? I'm sure he took care of his crops, but he reaped such a good harvest because the Lord blessed him. Whether the famine was over or not, the Bible doesn't say. But in either case, God made sure that Isaac and his family had food to eat.

Always remember that all good things come from God. Even when we make mistakes, if we turn back to God, He will bless us.

NEXT STOP: West Branch, Iowa

July 9

Hello out there!

From Orphan to President

> Mordecai had a cousin named Hadassah, whom he had brought up because she had neither father nor mother. This young woman, who was also known as Esther, had a lovely figure and was beautiful. Mordecai had taken her as his own daughter when her father and mother died. **Esther 2:7.**

Herbert Hoover, the thirty-first president of the United States, was born in West Branch, Iowa, to Jessie and Hulda Hoover. His father was a blacksmith in the town and also owned a store that sold farm equipment. Sadly, when Herbert was 6 years old, his father died. And then, three years later, his mother passed away, leaving him an orphan at the age of 9.

He lived with one of his grandmothers and then an uncle in Iowa before moving to live with another uncle in Oregon, where he stayed until he went to college. Herbert never attended high school; instead, he took some night classes and then moved on to college, where he obtained a degree in geology and became a mining engineer.

In 1897 Herbert obtained a job with a London-based mining company and moved to Australia. From there he moved up the ladder until he was managing and exploring gold mines in Australia and, later, around the world. By 1914, just 17 years after beginning his career, Herbert Hoover was worth an estimated $4 million! Fourteen years later, in 1928, he was elected president of the United States.

The Bible records a similar story of an orphan who went on to obtain an important position in the government of that day. Esther lost both of her parents at an early age. Fortunately, her cousin took her in and raised her as his own. As you know, she went on to be chosen as queen in the biggest beauty pageant of all time.

A character trait that both Herbert and Esther seem to have in common is that they did not give up when presented with tragedy. Both could have decided to give up on life when they lost their parents, but both went on to become great people. Herbert's parents had raised him to know about God, and if Esther did not learn about God from her parents, she did from Mordecai. A relationship with God makes all the difference when we are faced with tragedy.

I don't know what you are facing today, but remember that no matter what happens today, you are not alone. God is by your side!

NEXT STOP: Missouri

198

Show Me!

Then he said to Thomas, "Put your finger here; see my hands. Reach out your hand and put it into my side. Stop doubting and believe." John 20:27.

Welcome to Missouri, the Show Me State. In the late 1890s the nickname came about, and it stuck. It even appears on the state's license plates. But the story behind the nickname varies. There are four different stories as to how the name came about, but in three of the stories the nickname has to do with the idea of proving something.

Do you ever ask your parents or teachers to show you the answer or prove that something is the way it is? I've done it. When someone tells me something I find hard to believe, I want proof! If you told me that the oldest cat on record was named Creme Puff, and she died three days after turning 38 years old, I would want to research that fact. (That actually is a fact, by the way!)

It isn't bad to ask questions and not believe everything you hear. Making sure people are telling you the truth will keep you from believing lies. Do you remember the character in the Bible who demanded proof for things and wanted people to "show" him? He is often called "Doubting Thomas," but I prefer to look at him as someone who wanted to make sure he didn't fall for something that wasn't the truth.

The disciples told Thomas that they had seen Jesus, but he said, "Unless I see the nail marks in his hands and put my finger where the nails were, and put my hand into his side, I will not believe" (John 20:25). Jesus did not have to appear to Thomas. He could have said, "The disciples told him; he has to learn to trust and believe." But one week later Jesus appeared before the disciples again, and this time Thomas was present. It was then that Jesus invited Thomas to touch Him and feel where the nails had been. He then told Thomas to stop doubting.

Did Jesus tell Thomas he was stupid for not having faith? No! He knew what Thomas needed to believe in the resurrection, and He was patient with Thomas. If you have a hard time believing something in the Bible, tell God about it. He will be patient with you and will show you the truth, just as He did for Thomas.

NEXT STOP: St. Louis, Missouri

Hello out there!

July 11

Gateway to the West

But I [God] said to you, "You will possess their land; I will give it to you as an inheritance, a land flowing with milk and honey." I am the Lord your God, who has set you apart from the nations. **Leviticus 20:24.**

The Gateway Arch in St. Louis, Missouri, is the tallest human-made monument in the United States. At 630 feet tall, the arch is a popular tourist attraction, allowing visitors to travel by elevator to the top of the arch, where they can look out over the city and the Mississippi River.

Underneath the arch is the visitors' center, which includes the Museum of Westward Expansion, a museum dedicated to telling the story of the United States' push to expand westward into the unknown territory acquired in the Louisiana Purchase. In the 1800s anything west of St. Louis and the Mississippi River was considered the wilderness, and plenty of adventure-seeking individuals moved westward in hopes of discovering riches or fame.

Similarly, the children of Israel were looking for a more comfortable life away from the imprisonment of slavery. However, when God set them free, they complained and worried and basically threw temper tantrums at times because life wasn't perfect and they still had bad days.

Yet God promised them He would lead them to a land flowing with milk and honey. God promised them they would own the land and raise their families in the beautiful countryside. God promised them they were His special people.

But many of them chose not to trust. Many of them chose to look at the negative side of life and believe that God had led them out of Egypt to die in the wilderness. They chose not to believe in a loving God who had their best interests in mind.

Do you believe God loves you? Do you believe He will work things out in your life in the way He knows is best? I know it can be hard sometimes to trust, but remember the Israelites and the pain they would have avoided if they had just trusted in God. Avoid their mistakes and trust in your heavenly Father.

NEXT STOP: St. Charles, Missouri

On the Move

Abram traveled through the land. **Genesis 12:6.**

About 24 miles northwest of St. Louis is the town of St. Charles. On May 14, 1804, Meriwether Lewis and William Clark, along with 31 other people, set out on the adventure of a lifetime. The party included Sacagawea, a Shoshone woman who accompanied her husband on the journey to the Pacific Ocean and helped to translate when the group met other Native American tribes.

Thomas Jefferson commissioned the expedition in an effort to explore and document the land west of the Mississippi River that had been obtained in the Louisiana Purchase. In addition to surveying the land and creating maps of the territory, Jefferson requested that Lewis and Clark make it known to the Native American tribes in the territory that the land was owned by the United States.

For two years the expedition traveled over the unfamiliar terrain of the Plains and the Rocky Mountains in pursuit of their final goal, the Pacific Ocean. It was a dangerous journey filled with wild animals, unknown tribes, and extreme weather. But the group did not give up. They pushed forward until they accomplished their goal of mapping the territory between the Mississippi River and the Pacific Ocean and claiming the land for the United States. Their expedition provided a wealth of information to the government about the territory and the plants and animals in the region, and it opened the way for westward expansion.

Abram could be considered an early explorer or world traveler, whichever way you look at it. God told Abram where to go, and he went. When we are introduced to Abram in Genesis 12 we read that God told Abram to leave his country and go to a land that God would show him, so he did. He left Haran and traveled as far as Shechem. From there he went to Bethel and then to Egypt. Genesis 13 tells us that Abram traveled from Egypt to the Negev (south) and then back to Bethel and finally to Hebron. That's a lot of moving! Especially since he had to pack his whole household on the backs of donkeys and haul it to the next spot. But Abram, who was later named Abraham, was a man of God, and he wanted to follow God's instructions no matter how tired he was or how frustrated he felt about moving again.

Are you ready to go on an expedition for God? You never know what He might want you to do. As long as you are willing, He will use you!

NEXT STOP: St. Joseph, Missouri

Hello out there!

July 13

Express Mail

Very well, I will grant this request too; I will not overthrow the town you speak of. But flee there quickly, because I cannot do anything until you reach it. **Genesis 19:21, 22.**

As people moved west, they were somewhat cut off from the world they knew. They didn't have e-mail or cell phones or texting. There was no easy way to stay in touch with family or friends who still lived in the East. The only way to communicate was through good, old-fashioned letters. But there was another problem with this form of communication. The mail didn't always reach its intended destination, and sometimes it took months for the letter to arrive. Thus the news in the letter was often quite old by the time the recipient received the letter.

In an effort to speed up mail delivery and make it easier for people to communicate when thousands of miles separated them, the Pony Express was established. Although it operated only for a year and a half, the Pony Express cut down mail delivery to 10 days in the summer from St. Joseph, Missouri, to Sacramento, California.

Here's how it worked. A rider would jump on a horse with a satchel of mail and ride to a designated station about 10 miles away, where he would mount a fresh horse and race to the next station. Each rider covered an average of 75 miles per day. The faster they rode, the faster the mail was delivered.

Although the Pony Express delivered the mail quickly, it was a tiring and dangerous job. Attacks were common, which explains why the ad for riders said they preferred orphans, since they wouldn't leave a family behind if they were killed on the trail.

The lasting memory of the Pony Express is the speed with which the mail was delivered. Sometimes speed is very important. In the case of Lot and his family, speed was crucial to saving their lives. The angels told them to flee quickly to the mountains, but Lot begged them to let them go to a nearby town. The angels agreed, saying that they could not destroy Sodom and Gomorrah until Lot and his family were safe in the nearby town. But as we know, Lot's wife didn't listen to the angels' instruction not to look back. Sadly, her disobedience resulted in her death.

When God asks you to obey, do it quickly. You may not get another chance to do it right.

NEXT STOP: Independence, Missouri

Long Trail West

*Enter through the narrow gate. For wide is the gate and broad
is the road that leads to destruction, and many enter through it.
But small is the gate and narrow the road that leads to life,
and only a few find it.* **Matthew 7:13, 14.**

Missouri is home to a number of cities that were crucial to westward expansion. Independence is one such city. After Lewis and Clark's expedition, fur trappers and traders began to travel west in search of more hunting grounds. As they moved west, they began to establish a path that was accessible by foot or horseback. Then in 1836 the first wagon train left Independence and made its way to Fort Hall, Idaho, along a wagon trail that had been cleared.

Additional wagon trails were cleared until the path led from Missouri to Oregon. Thus the trail was named the Oregon Trail. From the mid-1830s to 1869, when the Transcontinental Railroad was opened, approximately 400,000 people made the journey along the Oregon Trail as they moved west.

Although the trail was cleared for wagon travel, it was anything but a luxurious trip. Wild animals, conflict with Native American tribes, unexpected weather, disease, broken wagons, and injured animals were just a few of the problems the settlers experienced as they traveled to Oregon.

Similarly, we know that the path that leads to heaven is not always an easy one. Jesus told us that the road is narrow and few walk down it, but the reward is better than we can imagine. Eternal life is ours if we ask Jesus to come into our lives. As His children, ours is the duty to follow Him and walk in the path He calls us to walk in. The path is narrow, and you may face "dangerous" situations in the form of teasing when you choose not to swear, cheat on a test, or be mean to the unpopular kid in class.

When these and other situations happen, be brave and strong. Stand up for what is right and keep walking along the narrow path. You may feel as though you are alone, but Jesus promises to never leave you. He is right beside you. The narrow path may seem hard now, but in the end you will reap its rewards. Keep walking along the narrow path; the prize is worth it!

NEXT STOP: Fayetteville, Arkansas

Hello out there!

Watch Out Below!

From the sky huge hailstones, each weighing about a hundred pounds, fell on people. And they cursed God on account of the plague of hail, because the plague was so terrible. **Revelation 16:21.**

Do you know what a meteor is? According to the *New Oxford American Dictionary*, it is "a small body of matter from outer space that enters the earth's atmosphere" and burns up, thus creating a "streak of light."

Fayetteville, Arkansas, is one of 15 locations in the state where meteorites have fallen. Six of the meteorites were witnessed by individuals and then recovered, while nine of the meteorites were found by residents of the state. The meteorites are heavy in iron, and they rust in the state's wetlands. But they are a valuable source in the study of outer space, so it is important to locate and preserve them.

The meteorites that have fallen in Arkansas weigh a couple of pounds or more, but can you imagine a stone falling from the sky that weighs 100 pounds? That kind of meteorite or hailstone would crush a car, break windows, squash bushes and trees, and make big craters in the ground. Sounds crazy, right? Read today's text again, and you will see that this is not an imaginary event.

John the revelator records in Revelation that hailstones weighing about 100 pounds each will plummet from the sky during the last plagues to fall on this earth. But do we need to fear this event? No. Why not? A study of Revelation tells us that the last plagues will fall on the wicked and not those whose allegiance is to God.

The last seven plagues are similar to the plagues that fell on the Egyptians. If you remember, there were 10 plagues that fell in Egypt. The first three impacted the Egyptians and the Israelites, but the last seven affected only the Egyptians. The children of Israel were spared.

The same will happen at the end of the world when the last plagues fall. But God will protect His children. We don't have to fear the end of the world as long as we are on God's side. Have you made the choice to follow Him? I hope so!

NEXT STOP: Rogers, Arkansas

Your Name

A good name is more desirable than great riches;
to be esteemed is better than silver or gold. **Proverbs 22:1.**

Have you ever heard of Sam Walton? Probably not. Have you heard of Walmart? Probably yes. Sam Walton opened the first Walmart store on July 2, 1962, in Rogers, Arkansas. Its actual name was Wal-Mart Discount City, and it sold a wide variety of household items, clothing, toys, and beauty products. When it first opened, it did not sell groceries, as most of the stores do today.

The company has grown like crazy since it began in 1962. In 2012 Walmart was operating more than 10,000 stores in the United States, Canada, and 25 other countries around the world, and the number of employees had reached 2.2 million.

If you've ever heard adults talking about Walmart, I'm sure you have heard mixed comments. Some people dislike the store because it is so big and rich and puts smaller stores out of business, and others like it because it offers lower prices and has so many options of things to buy. But regardless of how people feel about the store, most people should agree on one thing—Sam Walton didn't let all of his riches and wealth go to his head.

For 30 years Sam Walton played a big role in running Walmart, but in all those years Sam chose to live modestly and not extravagantly, as some rich people do. He lived in a comfortable home that, until it was struck by lightning and had to be rebuilt, didn't have air-conditioning. Also, Sam drove around the same old pickup he had owned for years, and he wore clothes from Walmart, not some designer store that sold expensive suits.

Sam died on April 5, 1992, from blood cancer. And although he built one of the richest companies in the world, many people remember him for his name. He was a man who didn't let wealth go to his head and change who he was. He also chose to live a simple and humble life.

King Solomon wrote that a good name is better than riches. You might want to disagree with him, but having friends and people who trust you is way better than being a lonely rich person. Take King Solomon's word for it!

NEXT STOP: Murfreesboro, Arkansas

Hello out there!

Diamond Hunting

The Lord their God will save his people on that day as a shepherd saves his flock. They will sparkle in his land like jewels in a crown. **Zechariah 9:16.**

We are hunting for diamonds today! Just outside of the town of Murfreesboro is Crater of Diamonds State Park. The first diamond was found in the area in 1906 by John Huddleston. A few years later a diamond rush erupted, and thousands of people flocked to Murfreesboro to mine for diamonds in hopes of getting rich.

Over the years the land changed hands between different owners, until it finally became a part of the state park system in 1972. At that time the park was opened to the public. Now people can pay a small fee and dig for diamonds in a 37.5-acre plowed field.

Thousands of people visit the park each year, and only a few find any gems. But those who do get to take home whatever they find. The gems and minerals found at the park include diamonds, amethyst, garnet, jasper, agate, and quartz. More than 29,000 diamonds have been found since it became a state park.

Can you imagine walking through a plowed field and seeing something sparkling in the dirt? That would be amazing! You would be ecstatic! You would probably be bouncing off the walls with excitement over the treasure you found.

Now read Zechariah 9:16, today's verse, while still thinking about how excited you would be if you found a diamond. God compares us to jewels. We are His children, and we are as precious to Him as jewels.

As Christians, we should attract the attention of others, but not in a bad way, as a diamond on the ground would. We should attract people by our good deeds, words, actions, and behavior. We should attract people by our love for those around us. When we act as Christ acted, we will stand out like diamonds in a field full of dirt!

NEXT STOP: Ouachita National Forest, Arkansas

Copycat, Copycat

Dear friend, do not imitate what is evil but what is good.
Anyone who does what is good is from God.
Anyone who does what is evil has not seen God. **3 John 11.**

Welcome to Ouachita National Forest. Today we are stretching our legs and going on a hike through the forest. It's a beautiful summer day. The sun is shining in a clear blue sky. We've got a backpack with a picnic lunch in it and water bottles for our hike.

As we walk along the trail away from the parking lot, we hear fewer people and more of the sounds of nature. We hear bees buzzing as they fly from wild-flower to wildflower and birds calling to each other. Wait! That sounds like a swallow. No, it's a dove. Nope, maybe it's a cardinal. Then you see a bird perched on a branch a few feet off the trail.

The bird is gray all over, with a slightly lighter colored chest. Its tail feathers look really long. You jump as a frog startles you and leaps onto the path. *Ribbit. Ribbit.* The frog makes his presence known, but all of a sudden you hear the same sound coming from the bird! What? That doesn't make sense. How can a bird sound like a frog? Because it is a mockingbird! After it hears a sound, it can imitate it, making the same bird call or insect sound as what it just heard.

So the state bird of Arkansas, the northern mockingbird, really is a copycat! I'm sure most of you would agree that you dislike people who copy you. Try holding a conversation with a copycat. It doesn't work because they repeat everything you say. It isn't much fun.

When siblings or friends copy us, it is annoying, but is there ever a time to be a copycat? What about when we copy Jesus and act as He acted and talk as He talked? Isn't that like being a copycat? Yes, but when we copy Jesus, we show the rest of the world whom we follow. John wrote in his third book that we are "not to imitate [or copy] what is evil." We don't want to copy Satan, because that will leave us in a heap of trouble. But we do need to copy what is good. We are human; we are made to copy. But we get to choose whom we copy or follow—God or Satan. Pick wisely so that you are copying the King of kings and Lord of lords.

NEXT STOP: Pine Bluff, Arkansas

Hello out there!

Bull's-eye!

Saul tried to pin him to the wall with his spear,
but David eluded him as Saul drove the spear into the wall.
That night David made good his escape. I Samuel 19:10.

Ben Pearson was an archer who lived in Pine Bluff, Arkansas, when he decided to start a company to make archery equipment. It was the first company in the United States to mass-produce archery equipment.

Ben made his first bow after reading and reviewing Boy Scout articles. Then in 1926 at the age of 38 he entered the state championship in archery using his own equipment. He came in next to last, but he learned a lot and decided to take his knowledge and improve upon his design. One year later he entered the same competition with his new equipment, and he became the Arkansas state champion. Obviously his aim and his equipment were right on!

Aiming well is half of the equation when it comes to archery. The other portion of the equation is obviously the equipment, but you still have to aim to be successful.

Fortunately for David, Saul couldn't aim. He had the equipment, but the king could not aim, thanks to David's angels! On more than one occasion Saul threw a spear at David as the young man played his harp for the king in a quest to calm his spirit and make him less crazy. But it didn't always work. Sometimes King Saul would be so worked up and consumed with the idea that David was going to steal his throne that he tried to kill David.

It was after the event in 1 Samuel 19:10 that David came up with a plan to know whether King Saul was trying to kill him. David asked Jonathan to test King Saul to see if he wanted to kill David. While Jonathan investigated the situation at the palace, David hid in a field in the area. As a secret signal, Jonathan agreed to shoot three arrows. If Jonathan told the boy accompanying him to find the arrows "on this side of you" (1 Samuel 20:21), then David would know that it was safe. But if he said, "the arrows are beyond you" (verse 22), then David would know that King Saul was indeed trying to kill him and he needed to run for his life.

That night David said goodbye to his best friend, Jonathan, and fled. But God was with him and blessed him during the difficult years he was hiding from Saul.

NEXT STOP: New Orleans, Louisiana

Partying Gone Wild

While Belshazzar was drinking his wine, he gave orders to bring in the gold and silver goblets that Nebuchadnezzar his father had taken from the temple in Jerusalem, so that the king and his nobles, his wives and his concubines might drink from them. **Daniel 5:2.**

New Orleans is a major city in Louisiana located near the mouth of the Mississippi River. The city is known for its food, jazz music, and yearly festivals and celebrations. Mardi Gras is one such celebration. The huge carnival-style party features a parade and lots of dancing, music, food, alcohol, and costumes.

The interesting thing about Mardi Gras is that it has roots in a Catholic holiday. It is celebrated right before Lent, a six-week time period leading up to Easter during which people are supposed to spend time in prayer repenting for their sins and denying themselves the luxuries of life, including rich food.

Does this "holiday" seem strange to you? It does to me! First, you can party and drink and act as crazy as you want, and then a few days later you are supposed to spend the next six weeks repenting of your sins and denying yourself the pleasures of this world. People can't have it both ways! Are they following God or their own desires?

Look at Belshazzar, for example. He was partying with a bunch of his officials when he decided to drink from the gold and silver goblets from the Temple. Talk about a bad choice! As they drank from the goblets, they praised their gods (see Daniel 5:4). Yet another bad choice.

"Suddenly the fingers of a human hand appeared and wrote on the plaster of the wall, near the lampstand in the royal palace. The king watched the hand as it wrote. His face turned pale and he was so frightened that his legs became weak and his knees were knocking" (Daniel 5:5, 6). Daniel was called before the king to interpret the writing on the wall, and he told the king, "You, Belshazzar, . . . have not humbled yourself, though you knew all this. Instead, you have set yourself up against the Lord of heaven. . . . But you did not honor the God who holds in his hand your life and all your ways" (verses 22, 23).

Belshazzar knew the truth! But he chose to disregard it and do his own thing, and he paid the price for his sins. That very night he was killed by the Medes and Persians.

NEXT STOP: New Orleans, Louisiana

July 21

Football Fanatics

I will give thanks to the Lord according to His righteousness
and will sing the praise to the name of the Lord Most High. **Psalm 7:17, NASB.**

We are spending another day in New Orleans. Today we are visiting the Superdome, a huge sports stadium and exhibit center that happens to be the largest fixed domed structure in the world and is located in the business section of the city.

The Superdome was damaged when Hurricane Katrina hit New Orleans in 2005. Thousands of people flocked to the Superdome and took shelter as the floodwaters rose, but part of the roof was damaged, and people were exposed to the wind and rain they were trying to escape.

Of course, the Superdome is home to the New Orleans Saints and is known for being a great stadium to play football in. In addition to hosting home games for the Saints, a number of football tournaments and special games are played throughout the year, the most famous of which is the Sugar Bowl. The Sugar Bowl takes place on or around New Year's Day and has been played in the Superdome since 1975. The only year the game was played somewhere else since then was in 2006, when the Superdome was being repaired after Hurricane Katrina.

The Sugar Bowl attracts tens of thousands of football fans who come to New Orleans and spend hundreds, if not thousands, of dollars on tickets, lodging, food, and souvenirs. They paint their faces, wave banners or flags in support of their team, and yell at the top of their lungs for their favorite player. In the excitement of the moment, fans post pictures on Facebook or tweet about their experience at one of the most recognized football games in the country.

Wouldn't it be awesome if Christians were as excited about Jesus and working for Him as football fans are about attending a national game? Do you "give thanks to the Lord" and "sing praise" to His name as King David did? Football fans are quick to tell you their favorite team. Are you quick to tell others you are on God's team? Make sure God is your "favorite player"!

NEXT STOP: Morgan City, Louisiana

Swampy

For we are God's handiwork, created in Christ Jesus to do good works, which God prepared in advance for us to do. **Ephesians 2:10.**

Welcome to bayou (pronounced *BY-you*) country! Louisiana is known for its bayous, which are low-lying, swampy, marshy areas. The water in the bayou is brackish, a slightly salty mix of seawater and fresh water, and is home to a wide variety of critters, including crawfish, catfish, frogs, alligators, crocodiles, and shrimp.

Needless to say, you won't find me jumping into any swamps. The dark water is far from welcoming with all the hidden creatures swimming in it. But for those people who live and work in the swamp, it's another day at the office! I watched one TV show about a man who was a logger in the bayou. He spent the day in his boat traveling throughout the bayou in search of sunken logs. When he found a prize log, he would jump in the water, hook a chain around it, and pull it back to shore. But what surprised me was the fact that he had no fear of the water. He didn't even blink when he jumped in, even though the video camera showed alligators in the area. I wasn't sure whether he was brave or crazy!

But that got me to thinking. Things aren't scary when we do them on a regular basis. For instance, I would be afraid to jump into the bayou, but, possibly, that logger would start sweating if someone asked him to write a 500-word article about logging! Why? Because it is out of his comfort zone—it's not his normal routine. Hypothetically, he wouldn't know where to start in writing an article, but he knows exactly what to do to find a prize log and bring it back to his dock to sell.

I believe this same idea applies to our Christian walk. I remember the first time I played the piano for song service at my church. I was so nervous my hands were shaking! But I made it through that first Sabbath, and I tried it again a few weeks later. Each week I played I was a little less nervous than the previous week. And over time it became a natural part of who I am. Working for God and using the talents He gave me isn't as scary now as it was when I first started serving in church.

Although it might be scary at first, jump in and work for Christ. He will prepare you for the job He has given you to do. And in time it will become second nature to you!

NEXT STOP: Rayne, Louisiana

Hello out there!

Froggy Capital

If you refuse to let them go, I will send a plague of frogs on you.
The Nile will teem with frogs. They will come up into your palace
and your bedroom and onto your bed, into the houses of your officials
and on your people, and into your ovens and kneading troughs. **Exodus 8:2, 3.**

Rayne is considered the frog capital of the world because of its annual Rayne Frog Festival, which takes place each November. It's kind of a funny thing to be known for, but the annual frog racing and jumping contests held at the festival are apparently the talk of the town. At the first annual contest in 1975 more than 50 people from across the United States entered their frogs in the competition.

Today people can rent a frog or bring their own, thus giving everyone a chance to get in on the action. As I was reading about the festival, I laughed when I came across the rules for the contest. See if you think they are funny too:

1. The frogs have to be at least four inches long from nose to tail so that no one will step on them.
2. All frogs must have a name.
3. You cannot feed your frog any type of hot sauce to make it jump farther.
4. You cannot touch your frog during the race to make it go faster, but you can blow on it, shout at it, or jump up and down.

The people of Rayne like frogs because they attract tourists and bring in money for their town. Similarly, the Egyptians liked frogs because they were a symbol of life. Each year millions of frogs would emerge from the Nile River after the annual flood that watered the barren land and enabled them to grow crops. The frog was a god to them, but the God of heaven changed all that with the plague of frogs. Frogs were everywhere! They invaded their homes, including their beds and kitchens. I'm sure they were stepped on, sat on, lain on, and generally squished.

Unfortunately, Pharaoh did not learn his lesson. He did not choose to see that God was stronger than Heqet, the Egyptian frog god. Instead, he continued to place his trust in false gods, which ultimately led to his destruction.

Make sure you are following the true God and banishing all false gods from your life!

NEXT STOP: Iota, Louisiana

Cajun Music

Then Miriam the prophet, Aaron's sister, took a timbrel in her hand,
and all the women followed her, with timbrel and dancing. Miriam sang to them:
"Sing to the Lord, for he is highly exalted. Both horse and driver
he has hurled into the sea." **Exodus 15:20, 21.**

Louisiana is often referred to as Cajun country because of the high population of Cajuns living in the southern portion of the state. People of this ethnic group are descendants of French-speaking Acadians who lived in Canada but were forced to leave their homes during the French and Indian War. (The term *Cajun* actually developed from a way of pronouncing *Acadian*—try pronouncing *Acadian* really fast!) After settling in Louisiana, the Cajuns developed their own French dialect. They also developed a distinct spicy cuisine and style of music.

Their lively music features the Cajun accordion and often a fiddle, steel guitar, triangle, and bass guitar. But the main instrument that carries the melody is the accordion. Cajun accordions are constructed in small shops throughout Cajun country, such as in Larry Miller's Bon Cajun shop in Iota, Louisiana.

Music has a big impact on who we are as a people. Different cultures have different styles of music, and different events often call for a specific genre of music—there is such a wide variety of music. You wouldn't play "Happy Birthday" at a funeral or "Home, Home on the Range" at a wedding! Music is used to set the tone for events. Think about the role that music plays at church. It should help you focus on Christ and prepare you to worship God.

Look at Miriam, for instance. After the children of Israel safely crossed the Red Sea, they held a celebration and thanked God for His protection. They were obviously really excited about the miracle they had just witnessed, so they praised God with singing and dancing. Miriam played a tambourine, and all the women joined her in singing the simple song found in Exodus 15:21, part of today's text.

If you are musically talented, ask God to use you to praise His name by getting involved in worship at home or school or church. If that isn't your talent, ask God how you can still participate and praise Him in song without leading out.

NEXT STOP: Texas

July 25

Hello out there!

Fighting for Control

Of the greatness of his government and peace there will be no end. He will reign on David's throne and over his kingdom, establishing and upholding it with justice and righteousness from that time on and forever. **Isaiah 9:7.**

Welcome to Texas, where everything is larger than life! We have a lot of places to visit, but today and tomorrow we aren't going to a specific city. We are just talking about some fun facts about Texas in general.

Did you know that Texas was an independent nation from 1836 to 1845? It was its own country, like Spain, England, Canada, or Peru! Strange, huh? But before it became its own nation and before it later joined the United States of America as a state, Spain, France, and Mexico controlled some or all of the territory at one time or another. You've heard of "six flags over Texas"? No, not the amusement park—"six flags over Texas" refers to the six nations that have ruled some or all of Texas. Spain first set up colonies in Texas; then France established a short-lived colony, Fort Saint Louis. The Spanish were worried about competition from France, so they stepped up their colonizing efforts. For more than 100 years Spanish colonies existed in Texas. But in 1821 the Mexicans revolted against the Spanish and won. Mexico governed Texas for 15 years before Texas gained its independence and became its own nation from 1836 to 1845. In 1845 Texas decided to become a part of the United States; then Texas seceded in 1861 and joined the Confederate States of America during the Civil War. After the Civil War ended, Texas once again joined the United States of America.

What a rocky history of power and control for the second largest state in America. But isn't that how it goes with governments on this earth? They come and go. Throughout history the countries of this world have fought huge battles over land and ultimate power of a region.

I don't know about you, but I will be glad when Isaiah's prophecy is completely fulfilled. The first part has already happened; Jesus was born as a baby to save us. But I look forward to the fulfillment of the last two sentences of today's texts, when there will be no end to the peace of God's government, and His justice and righteousness will go on forever. When Jesus comes, we will no longer have to worry about wars and rumors of wars. All will be at peace forever!

NEXT STOP: Texas

Suit Up

Put on the full armor of God, so that you will be able to stand firm against the schemes of the devil. **Ephesians 6:11, NASB.**

Have you ever seen an armadillo or a picture of one? If not, ask your parents to show you a picture of this unique (some might say ugly) creature. The nine-banded armadillo is the official state small mammal of Texas, which is why we are featuring it.

A nine-banded armadillo is about the size of a cat, although it is certainly not cuddly. It has short legs, clawed feet, a long tail, a pointy snout, and a hard shell that looks like the armor a knight would wear. Its tough armor even covers the top of its head and tail. When running away from its enemies, it can hide in thorny bushes because its armor protects it from getting poked. If it wants to swim across a small stream, it swallows air to inflate its intestines, which makes the armadillo float and allows it to swim. Otherwise, the animal sinks because of the density of its armor and walks across under the water—it can hold its breath for up to six minutes under water.

Another species of armadillo can even roll up in a ball when attacked, thus completely protecting the animal and presenting a fully armored exterior to its predator.

The Bible teaches us that we need to put on the armor of God in order to fight against the devil. We are fighting in a war for our lives, and we can't win by ourselves. If you don't believe me, think about what is at stake: eternal life or eternal death. A real battle is being fought for your life, and you can't avoid the war. You have to engage. You have to fight.

How did Jesus fight against Satan in the wilderness? He quoted Scripture and relied on the Word of God to protect Him. We have to do the same thing. The Bible is our most important weapon. The other vital weapon we have in our arsenal is prayer. When we pray we are connected with God, and He gives us power to overcome Satan.

As you finish your devotions today, think about a temptation or sin you are struggling with. Then ask your parents to help you find a Bible text that talks about overcoming sin or about God's power in your life. Memorize it this week, and pray that God will help you put on His armor so that you can stand against Satan's attacks.

NEXT STOP: San Antonio, Texas

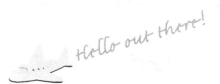

Hello out there!

The Terrible Nature of War

So while Joab had the city under siege, he put Uriah at a place where he knew
the strongest defenders were. When the men of the city came out
and fought against Joab, some of the men in David's army fell; moreover,
Uriah the Hittite died. **2 Samuel 11:16, 17.**

Remember the Alamo!" was the battle cry of the Texans as they fought against General Santa Anna and the Mexican Army. You see, the Mexican Army had laid siege to the Alamo for 13 days before launching a fierce attack. A siege is a military strategy in which an army surrounds a city and cuts off all supplies and communication to the people inside. The hope is that those inside will surrender or be weakened because of the lack of resources.

The Texan soldiers inside the Alamo fired through holes made in the walls so as to stay protected from enemy fire, but they were no match for the cannons the Mexicans unleashed on the Alamo. One by one the Texan soldiers were killed, until none remained alive. General Santa Anna then ordered that all of the Texan soldiers' bodies be stacked together and burned.

The rest of the Texan soldiers were outraged at how barbaric the Mexicans had been. So when they faced the Mexican Army in the Battle of San Jacinto, the cry was "Remember the Alamo!" This spurred the Texas army on until they had gained the victory, captured General Santa Anna, and forced the Mexicans out of Texas.

In today's text we read about a siege that Joab, the chief commander of David's army, was involved in. But there was more going on in this story than a siege on a city. David had slept with Bathsheba, Uriah's wife, and now she was pregnant. David tried to cover up his sin by bringing Uriah home from the battle so he could sleep with Bathsheba. But David's plan didn't work, and Uriah would not go home to his wife. So David sent Uriah back to the front line with a message to Joab instructing the commander to put Uriah at the front of the battle and pull back when the enemy attacked so that Uriah would be killed.

David's initial sin, sleeping with another man's wife, led to other sins: lying and murder. And he paid the consequences for his actions in the deaths of four of his sons, including the child Bathsheba was pregnant with, and years of guilt and turmoil in his kingdom. Today's lesson: If you sin, don't try to cover it up with another sin. Ask for forgiveness and move on. You will suffer far less consequences if you do.

NEXT STOP: Irving, Texas

Happy Trails to You

As for God, his way is perfect: The Lord's word is flawless; he shields all who take refuge in him. **Psalm 18:30.**

Irving, Texas, is home to the National Scouting Museum. For more than 100 years the Boy Scouts of America have been working with boys ages 7 to 21. With more than 130 merit badges or awards, the Boy Scouts focus on teaching boys through outdoor activities and educational programs. Scouts learn wilderness survival skills, leadership skills, teamwork, and how to be good citizens in their communities.

If you have been in Pathfinders, does Scouting sound a lot like a Pathfinder club? So what are the main differences between the Boy Scouts and Pathfinders? Well, Boy Scouts is only for boys (Girl Scouts is a completely separate club), whereas Pathfinders accept both boys and girls into the same club. The other difference is the focus on Christ. The Pathfinder pledge sums up the purpose of Pathfinders and sets it apart. The pledge says, "By the grace of God, I will be pure and kind and true. I will keep the Pathfinder Law. I will be a servant of God and a friend to man."

As Christians we should always focus on following God and serving others. And Pathfinders seeks to do that. The first club was started in Anaheim, California, in the late 1920s. From that point forward other clubs began, and a national structure was put into place to outline the classwork and honors for each grade level.

You may or may not be a Pathfinder, but the whole idea of the program is to help you strengthen your relationship with God. Are you a part of a group that encourages you to be best friends with Jesus? It may be a youth group or your school choir or your Sabbath school class. It may be you and a few friends getting together to study the Bible or your parents and siblings reading during family worship. It doesn't matter who it is or how many people are in your group, but it is important to surround yourself with others who will remind you that God is perfect, and His Word is flawless (Psalm 18:30).

If you involve yourself in such a group, it will give you strength to stand up for what is right when you are surrounded by people who believe differently than you do.

NEXT STOP: Alvin, Texas

July 29

Hello out there!

Downpour

The rain fell on the earth for forty days and forty nights. **Genesis 7:12, NASB.**

Tropical storms and hurricanes can drop a lot of rain. I should know. I grew up in Florida, and we experienced a number of tropical storms and hurricanes. But the most rain we ever got was probably a little more than a foot. Our pool would fill up to the brim, but we never experienced any flooding.

As does Florida, Texas experiences quite a number of tropical storms and hurricanes, which travel up through the Gulf of Mexico. One year a tropical storm set the record for the most rainfall in a 24-hour period. In July 1979 Tropical Storm Claudette hit Alvin, Texas, and dropped 42 inches of rain, causing more than $400 million in damages. That is three and a half feet of water! If you have eight-foot ceilings in your house, which is standard, the water would have been nearly halfway up the wall. Although you may wish you had a swimming pool at your house, I don't think you would want one in your bedroom!

That is a lot of rain and flooding, but it doesn't even come close to the rain that fell on the earth after God closed the door of the ark. The Bible tells us that it rained for 40 days and 40 nights. I can't even imagine that much water, but we know it happened because the Bible documents this event in the book of Genesis.

The flood cleansed the earth and eliminated all the people who refused to obey God and wanted to do things their way, but it did not eliminate evil from this world. Yes, Noah and his family were righteous, but as people began to multiply upon the face of the earth, many chose not to follow God, and once again evil reigned as men and women rebelled against God.

Not until Jesus returns to take us home will the earth be cleansed of evil. After we spend 1,000 years in heaven, we will return to this earth, and the wicked will be raised to life. Satan will rally his troops and convince them that they can capture the New Jerusalem and destroy us. This time the earth will not be cleansed by water. Instead, fire will rain down from heaven and destroy all the wicked, and the earth will be purified once and for all (see Revelation 20).

NEXT STOP: King Ranch, Texas

Where's the Beef?

Listen, my people, and I will speak; I will testify against you, Israel: I am God, your God. I bring no charges against you concerning your sacrifices or concerning your burnt offerings, which are ever before me. I have no need of a bull from your stall or of goats from your pens, for every animal of the forest is mine, and the cattle on a thousand hills. I know every bird in the mountains, and the insects in the fields are mine. If I were hungry I would not tell you, for the world is mine, and all that is in it. **Psalm 50:7-12.**

As I mentioned when we arrived in Texas, everything is bigger in this state. For example, the King Ranch is bigger than the state of Rhode Island! One ranch! The state's cattle population is estimated to be near 14 million. Compare that to the population of people in Texas, which is about 26 million. That's just about one cow for every two people in the state!

There is a lot of land in Texas, and there are a lot of farms and ranches. There is plenty of land to spread out on and raise cattle, driving them across the open plains that you read about in the history of the American West. It is a very lucrative business, and many ranch owners are very wealthy. But is it really their money? Did they become rich on their own?

That may seem like a trick question, but think about it for a minute. Where do your parents get their money? Where do you get your money?

Read what King David wrote about God. "For all the animals of the forest are mine, and I own the cattle on a thousand hills" (Psalm 50:10, NLT). "If I were hungry, I would not tell you, for all the world is mine and everything in it" (verse 12, NLT). Everything belongs to the Lord.

The money your parents earn from their jobs comes from God, which means that the money your parents give you comes from God. The food you eat comes from God. He sent the sun and rain to water the farmers' crops, which we purchase in various forms at the grocery store. God owns the universe and everything in it. Think about that the next time you find it difficult to share with someone else, because what you are sharing is really not yours; it's God's.

NEXT STOP: Edwards Plateau, Texas

July 31

Hello out there!

Woolly Sheep

I am the good shepherd. The good shepherd lays down
his life for the sheep. John 10:11.

Edwards Plateau is located in west central Texas. This region of the state is not suitable for farming, because of the shallow soil. However, the soil is rich and produces plenty of good grass, making this area an ideal place to raise sheep.

There are not as many sheep ranches as cattle ranches in Texas, but sheep are an important animal because of their wool. Sheep were very important in Bible times as well, which is why Jesus mentioned them frequently in His illustrations and parables. In order to help people understand His teachings, Jesus used everyday examples—by telling stories and drawing on real-life scenarios—people could relate to.

I'm sure you have heard the parable of the lost sheep, so I want to examine another sheep/shepherd parable. Jesus starts off by saying He is the Good Shepherd who protects His sheep. Hired hands run away when they see a wolf, because they really don't care about the sheep. Applying that parable to our experience, we learn, for example, that you can place your trust in a teacher or pastor or friend, but they are human, and they might run away when danger strikes. But Jesus will never leave you. He is the Good Shepherd, and He will always protect you.

In this parable Jesus goes on to say that as the Good Shepherd He knows His sheep, and His sheep know Him. He also points out that He will lay down His life for His sheep (see John 10:15). Then Jesus says something very interesting: "I have other sheep that are not of this sheep pen. I must bring them also. They too will listen to my voice, and there shall be one flock and one shepherd" (verses 16, 17). Any idea what He is talking about here?

The Jews were in the "sheep pen," but Jesus came to save all people. After His death He told the disciples to share the good news of God's love with everyone, even those outside the Jewish faith. Jesus was telling this parable to Jews and saying that He came to call everyone into one flock or church.

I'm glad Jesus came to save everyone who follows His voice! Whether you can trace your heritage back to Abraham or not, it doesn't matter as long as you love Jesus and ask Him to come into your heart. He wants to save all those who love Him.

NEXT STOP: Tyler, Texas

Watch Out for the Thorns

You can identify them by their fruit, that is, by the way they act. Can you pick grapes from thornbushes, or figs from thistles? A good tree produces good fruit, and a bad tree produces bad fruit. A good tree can't produce bad fruit, and a bad tree can't produce good fruit. **Matthew 7:16-18, NLT.**

The city of Tyler is home to the Tyler Municipal Rose Garden, a 14-acre park that is the largest rose garden in the United States. The park is free and open to the public. Being surrounded by at least 600 different varieties and 38,000 rose bushes, your nose might be a bit overwhelmed. Some of the bushes are grafted rose trees, while others are miniature roses no bigger than a dime.

I love how roses smell, but I hate the thorns. The thorns aren't a big deal on the bouquets that my husband buys me, but if you try to grow a rosebush, the trimming you are required to do can be dangerous. Even with gardening gloves on, I've been stabbed multiple times trying to trim the rosebush in my garden. After I moved, I decided I would never try to grow roses again. For me, they are too much work, and the thorns are too much of a hassle.

Jesus uses an interesting illustration in today's Bible verse. He warns us about false prophets and tells us that we have to test people based on "their fruit" (Matthew 7:16, NLT). Then He asks a question in the same verse. "Do people pick grapes from thornbushes . . . ?" In other words, a person's life reveals whom they are following, Jesus or Satan. For example, someone who claims to have a message from God but is cheating on his wife and going to the bar every night to drink alcohol with his buddies isn't really connected to God.

Jesus goes on to say that good trees bear good fruit, and bad trees bear bad fruit. True prophets will only tell the truth and their lives will reflect the fact that they are connected with God. But a good tree cannot bear bad fruit. People who are connected to God will not go against God's principles. Thus, Jesus tells us that we can identify His followers based on "their fruit."

As you finish today's devotional, think about what kind of fruit you are producing. Can people tell by your fruit that you are a follower of God?

NEXT STOP: Oklahoma

Hello out there!

You're Too Soon!

He also said, "This is what the kingdom of God is like. A man scatters seed on the ground. Night and day, whether he sleeps or gets up, the seed sprouts and grows, though he does not know how. All by itself the soil produces grain— first the stalk, then the head, then the full kernel in the head. As soon as the grain is ripe, he puts the sickle to it, because the harvest has come." **Mark 4:26-29.**

The majority of Oklahoma was Indian Territory, but in 1889 it was opened to settlers, and there was a big land rush. Who doesn't want something for free, especially land! In March 1889 it was announced that on a set date and time settlers could enter the territory and lay claim to a plot of land, and if they lived on the land and improved it, they could receive the title for free.

Well, 50,000 people lined up on April 22, 1889, to get in on the action and race to claim a portion of the 2 million acres up for grabs. However, there were a few people who jumped the gun and entered the territory before the noon starting time. These cheaters were called "Sooners," a nickname that stuck for the whole state.

The settlers were impatient. They didn't want to wait. They wanted to do it their way and in their time. Do you ever get impatient? I'm sure you do! We all do. There are times we just don't want to wait—we want things now.

But God wants us to learn patience and total dependence on Him. He wants us to learn that His timing is perfect. Read the above parable of the growing seed. Now read the last sentence again. "As soon as the grain is ready, the farmer comes and harvests it with a sickle, for the harvest time has come" (Mark 4:29, NLT).

If a farmer tried to harvest the grain before it was ready, would it be any good? No! The farmer has to patiently wait for the crop to be ready. Similarly, can you rush God into answering your prayers because you want an answer? No! God will answer your prayers in His perfect time. As soon as the timing is right, the answer will come because the harvest will be ready. It is hard to be patient, but it is a very important character trait to learn.

NEXT STOP: Indian Territory, Oklahoma

No Home

In the third year of the reign of Jehoiakim king of Judah, Nebuchadnezzar king of Babylon came to Jerusalem and besieged it. The Lord gave Jehoiakim king of Judah into his hand, along with some of the vessels of the house of God; and he brought them to the land of Shinar, to the house of his god, and he brought the vessels into the treasury of his god. **Daniel 1:1, 2, NASB.**

By the 1890s, 67 different Native American tribes had been forced to relocate to Indian Territory in what is now Oklahoma. When Oklahoma became a state in 1907, Indian Territory and Oklahoma Territory were joined together in one state. Of course, over time the land given to the Native Americans shrank as the white settlers moved into the area and as the government took more and more land despite promises that the tribes would be able to live on the land.

Today Oklahoma is home to more than 400,000 Native Americans, many of whom are descendants of the tribes living in Indian Territory when Oklahoma became a state. Currently more than 30 tribes operate their headquarters in Oklahoma.

The Native Americans were forced off their land, while Daniel was forcefully taken from his city, but in both instances they lost their homes and their sense of security. Daniel and his friends were captives of the Babylonians. They couldn't do as they pleased or go where they wanted to go. They had to answer to the Babylonians and do as they were told.

Similarly, the Native Americans were told where they could live. They were no longer free to decide what was best for their tribe and were required to follow the decrees of the United States government.

But there is a big difference between these two stories. Daniel and his friends had God to rely on, whereas different Native American tribes believe in multiple gods, and not one of those gods can offer them the comfort and protection that God can. But Daniel considered the Most High God his friend. Through all the ups and downs, he trusted that God was with him. He believed that in the end everything would work out for His glory. And Daniel took every opportunity he had to tell others about God and let his light shine. May we all be like Daniel and stand up for God no matter what happens.

NEXT STOP: Okmulgee, Oklahoma

223

August 4

Hello out there!

Bigger Is Better

This is how you are to build it: The ark is to be three hundred cubits [about 450 feet] long, fifty cubits [75 feet] wide and thirty cubits [45 feet] high. Make a roof for it, leaving below the roof an opening one cubit [about 18 inches] high all around. Put a door in the side of the ark and make lower, middle and upper decks. **Genesis 6:15, 16.**

In 1988 the Okmulgee Pecan Festival served up the world's largest pecan pie, which made the *Guinness Book of World Records*. The pie was 40 feet in diameter and weighed more than 16 tons. It took a lot of people to accomplish the task of making and baking such an enormous pie.

Two years later the city decided to make a pecan cookie instead of a pie. The cookie was 32 feet in diameter and weighed 7,500 pounds. That was also a big project. So the next year, they decided to throw a "smaller" event and celebrated the "World's Largest Pecan Cookie and Ice Cream Party." But this still required them to bake 15,000 cookies and hand out 5,000 helpings of vanilla ice cream.

If someone asked you to make a chocolate cake that was 40 feet long and could feed 6,000 people, what would you say? Would you panic? Would you think the person was crazy? Or would you tackle the project?

The events in the town of Okmulgee would not have taken place were it not for a bunch of people coming together and working as a team. Their teamwork enabled them to accomplish a big task.

Although it seems impossible, you could come up with a plan to make a 40-foot cake if you assembled the right team of bakers, cake decorators, and chefs who had experience cooking for large crowds of people.

When I think about Noah's task of building the ark, I wouldn't have blamed him for feeling overwhelmed. A 450-foot boat that was 75 feet wide and 45 feet high was unheard-of in those days. That's a big boat in *today's* standards, let alone back then, when it would have had to be built without power tools! But Noah accomplished the task because God was on his side and he gathered a group of people who helped him build it. Just remember, anything is possible with God and a little help from your friends.

NEXT STOP: Ponca City, Oklahoma

Tornado Alley

But let all who take refuge in you rejoice;
let them sing joyful praises forever. Spread your protection over them,
that all who love your name may be filled with joy. **Psalm 5:11, NLT.**

Oklahoma is known for its tornadoes. There is something about the Plains States that sets up the perfect weather for tornados. Often the sky turns a slightly green, eerie color before the funnel drops out of the dark clouds above and spins across the ground, destroying everything in its path. That's why the safest place to be during a tornado is underground, away from the flying debris and dangerous winds.

Of course, in order for people to seek shelter from an approaching tornado, they have to know about it. And until 1948 no one knew how to predict when a tornado would hit. Then on March 25, 1948, that all changed. A few hours before a tornado hit Tinker Air Force Base Captain Robert C. Miller and Major Ernest J. Fawbush correctly predicted that the conditions of the atmosphere were ripe for a tornado. Their prediction was instrumental in helping the nation develop accurate forecasting instruments, thus saving many lives each year.

But even with warning sirens and early predictions, some people still get caught in the wake of a tornado. And miraculously, some walk away from the ordeal. One such couple was a man and his wife who lived in Ponca City, Oklahoma. Their house was hit by a tornado and was actually picked up off its foundation and carried through the air. The scary thing was that the couple was in the house! The walls and roof blew off, but the floor stayed together until it glided to the ground with the couple still sitting on the floor.

Some people would say they were lucky, but I believe their angels were huddled around them, shielding them from the flying debris and guiding their "houseplane" safely to the ground.

We are safe when we are in God's care. He spreads His protection over us, as Psalm 5:11 says. And we can rejoice and sing praises to His name because of the shelter He provides for us.

NEXT STOP: Oklahoma City, Oklahoma

225

August 6

Hello out there!

Giddy Up!

The Lord is my light and my salvation—whom shall I fear?
The Lord is the stronghold of my life—of whom shall I be afraid? **Psalm 27:1.**

Today we are visiting the National Cowboy and Western Heritage Museum in Oklahoma City. Grab some boots and a hat so that you'll blend in, and let's go check it out. The museum is home to a large collection of Western and Native American artwork and artifacts, including barbed wire, saddles, American rodeo photography, and rodeo trophies. The barbed wire may seem to be a strange thing to put on exhibit, but it became an important part of the American West when cattle ranchers used it to contain their own cattle and keep other cattle and cowboys off their property.

Cowboys were typically strong men who could spend days on a horse riding around the open countryside herding cattle. They were a tough breed who slept on the ground and worked in all kinds of weather from blazing heat to blizzards. Always on the move, the life of a cowboy in the early days of the American West was rugged and hard.

As I thought about which Bible character reminded me of a cowboy, I immediately thought of David. Although he didn't wear a cowboy hat and boots, he was constantly on the move when he was running from King Saul. Regardless of the weather, he had to keep moving for fear that King Saul would catch him and kill him. Life certainly was not comfortable sleeping on the ground and moving camp every few days.

But in spite of the hardships that David endured, he still trusted in God. He was confident that God would take care of him. Read the words he wrote about his trust in God: "When the wicked advance against me . . . [they] will stumble and fall. Though an army besiege me, . . . even then will I be confident. . . . For in the day of trouble he will keep me safe in his dwelling; he will hide me in the shelter of his sacred tent and set me high upon a rock" (Psalm 27:2-5).

Then he ends the psalm with these two sentences: "I remain confident of this: I will see the goodness of the Lord in the land of the living. Wait for the Lord; be strong and take heart and wait for the Lord" (verses 13, 14). In other readings we have talked about how hard it is to wait sometimes, but follow David's advice: trust in God, wait on Him, and watch Him deliver you from your problems!

NEXT STOP: Cawker City, Kansas

Ball of Twine

Go therefore and make disciples of all the nations, baptizing them in the name of the Father and the Son and the Holy Spirit, **Matthew 28:19, NASB.**

Cawker City is home to the largest and heaviest ball of sisal twine constructed by a community, although there is a heavier ball of twine in Wisconsin that was created by only one person. Cawker City's ball is made of sisal twine, a fiber from the agave plant that is used for ropes.

The twine ball was started by Frank Stoeber, and by the time he died in 1974, he had wrapped 1.6 million feet of twine onto the ball, which was 11 feet in diameter. Cawker City built a gazebo for the ball of twine, and each August they host an event where they invite townspeople to add more twine to the ball. In 2006 the ball was made up of 7.8 million feet of twine and weighed 17,886 pounds.

Have you ever heard someone compare the Trinity to a piece of rope? Let me explain. The Trinity, or Godhead, is made up of three beings: God the Father, God the Son (Jesus), and the Holy Spirit. The Bible teaches us that these three beings are God. So how can three individuals be one God? Here is where the rope example comes into play. Take three strands of twine or yarn and weave them together. When separated, they are all independent, but when combined, they form one rope. The three strands are strong when they are apart, but they are stronger when they are together.

God the Father, Jesus, and the Holy Spirit are so connected in Their ministry that They act as one. Yet They each have Their own special job. God is our heavenly Father, who teaches us and disciplines us as a loving earthly father would. Jesus is our Savior, who gave up His life for us. He is our best friend and judge. The Holy Spirit is our comforter and guide here on earth. He helps us throughout the day by giving us ideas and helping us fight against Satan and temptations that come our way. Each individual of the Godhead plays an important role in our lives.

The Trinity can be a complicated mystery to understand, but hopefully this illustration gives you a better idea of how God can be three beings in one.

NEXT STOP: Argonia and Atchison, Kansas

August 8

Hello out there!

A Special Job

After the Sabbath, at dawn on the first day of the week, Mary Magdalene and the other Mary went to look at the tomb. **Matthew 28:1.**

Today we are visiting two cities that are significant because of the women who lived in them. First we are stopping in Argonia, where Susanna Madora Salter became the first woman elected to serve as mayor of a town in the United States. She also holds the title of first woman elected to any political office in the United States. She was elected in 1887, and, as you can imagine, this caused quite a stir, since women were not even allowed to vote in national elections yet!

Susanna served as mayor for one year and then declined seeking reelection. She was paid one dollar for her service as mayor. A few years later her family moved to Oklahoma, where she lived until her death at 101 years of age. She was buried in Argonia.

Next, we are traveling about 240 miles northeast to Atchison, where Amelia Earhart, the first woman to fly solo across the Atlantic Ocean, was born. At the age of 23 Amelia began taking flying lessons. Soon afterward she bought her own plane and began setting records, including being the first woman to reach an altitude of 14,000 feet. Unfortunately, at age 39 Amelia disappeared while trying to fly around the world. Her plane went missing somewhere over the Pacific Ocean.

These two women were pioneers in their own ways. What women Bible characters can you think of who were pioneers? Of course, there are Sarah, Rahab, Esther, Deborah, Ruth, Mary the mother of Jesus, Mary Magdalene, and Lydia. Those are just a few of the women to whom God gave special jobs. But I want to look at Mary Magdalene. What special role did God give her? Let's read Matthew 28:5-7 to find the answer.

"The angel said to the women, 'Do not be afraid, for I know that you are looking for Jesus, who was crucified. He is not here; he has risen, just as he said. Come and see the place where he lay. Then go quickly and tell his disciples: "He has risen from the dead and is going ahead of you into Galilee. There you will see him." Now I have told you.'"

Talk about an important job! Mary Magdalene was one of the first people to hear the good news that Jesus was alive, and she was given the job of sharing the news with the disciples and the world. God had a plan for her life, and He has a plan for yours.

NEXT STOP: Lyons, Kansas

Laying Down Your Life

And Stephen, full of grace and power, was performing great wonders and signs among the people. **Acts 6:8, NASB.**

During the 200 years before the United States became an independent country, a number of adventurous men landed on the North American continent and explored the land. One such individual was Francisco Vásquez de Coronado, a Spanish soldier, explorer, and adventurer who explored a large portion of the southwestern United States.

Coronado was searching for the mythical Seven Cities of Gold, which he obviously never found. But it is believed that he and his men were the first Europeans to see the Grand Canyon. Traveling with Coronado was Father Juan de Padilla, a Spanish Roman Catholic missionary. While Coronado was seeking gold, Padilla was seeking to convert people to the Catholic faith.

The group traveled as far as Kansas, but after they didn't find any cities of gold, they returned to Mexico. One year later Padilla left the exploration party and returned to Kansas, where he established the first Christian mission in what is today the United States. His goal was to preach to the Wichita Indians. Unfortunately, the Native Americans killed him in 1542, making him the first Christian martyr in the United States.

Stephen was also martyred for his faith. In fact, he was the first Christian martyr. After the Holy Spirit gave the disciples power to preach in Jesus' name, thousands of people joined the church. The disciples soon realized that it was necessary to appoint other people to help them care for the needs of fellow Christians. So they prayed about it, and God gave them wisdom to select seven men who could help with the work. One of those men was Stephen.

The Bible tells us that Stephen was "full of God's grace and power" (Acts 6:8, NLT). In fact, he performed miracles and wonders in God's name. Of course, this stirred up the anger of the Jewish leaders, and they arrested him and brought him before the Sanhedrin and accused him of speaking against God. Just as they had done to Jesus, they brought false accusations against him and fake witnesses to testify against him. Then they sentenced him to death by stoning.

Stephen died for the cause of Christ, but his reward is in heaven, and someday soon he will be raised to life and see Jesus face to face!

NEXT STOP: Wellington, Kansas

August 10

Hello out there!

Fresh Bread

I am the bread of life. **John 6:48.** I am the living bread that came down from heaven. Whoever eats this bread will live forever. This bread is my flesh, which I will give for the life of the world. **Verse 51.**

Wellington is located in southern Kansas and is known as the wheat capital of the World. In 1997 Kansas produced a record 506 million bushels of wheat. If all of that wheat had been made into bread, it would have produced nearly 37 billion loaves of white bread, which would have supplied every person on earth with more than five loaves of bread!

Wheat is in a *lot* of products—bagels, pasta, cereal, crackers, pancakes, pastries, doughnuts, cakes, cookies, muffins—but we most commonly think of it as being in bread. I don't know about your home, but bread is a main source of food in my house. We usually eat bread for at least one meal a day. It might be toast for breakfast, sandwiches for lunch, or garlic bread for supper. And if it is fresh homemade bread, we can devour almost an entire loaf in one meal. It's good stuff!

Have you ever heard someone say that they could live on bread and water if they had to? I've heard of missionaries who have been arrested, and prisoners of war in foreign countries who survived on bread and water for weeks, months, and years. With bread to eat and water to drink, you can survive and keep going.

Isn't it interesting that thousands of years before people began saying they could live on bread and water, Jesus compared Himself to bread and water? In John 6 Jesus repeatedly referred to Himself as the Bread of Life. Elsewhere in the Bible, He also said that He was the Water of Life.

Can you survive without Jesus any more than you can survive without at least bread to eat and water to drink? No! Without any food or water, you would probably die within three or four days. Without Jesus you will die, not within a few days, but at the end of the world.

Just like you need to eat and drink every day, you need to spend time with Jesus every day, and I don't mean just in Bible class at school or at Sabbath school in church. Although that is good, taking time to read and talk to Jesus by yourself will make you stronger. So make sure the Bread of Life is on the menu every day!

NEXT STOP: Hutchinson, Kansas

Never Give Up

But as for you, be strong and do not give up,
for your work will be rewarded. **2 Chronicles 15:7.**

I have never experienced a plague involving insects, but I can only imagine how gross it is. Can you imagine grasshoppers invading your town to the point that every time you take a step you kill a grasshopper? Think of all the crunching and squishing that would happen during a grasshopper plague. Of course, hundreds of the insects would try to avoid being stepped on by hopping on you, houses, cars, restaurants, churches, etc. An invasion by little green grasshoppers doesn't sound so great, does it?

In 1874 the First United Methodist Church was being built in Hutchinson, Kansas, when a grasshopper plague hit. The church was just pouring the foundation when the grasshoppers showed up and began hopping around the town. The pastor didn't want a few grasshoppers to stop the building project, so he told the workers to keep going. As they poured the foundation, grasshoppers got stuck in the wet concrete. Instead of picking them out, the workers smoothed out the surface and let it dry. As a result, thousands of grasshoppers are still stuck in the foundation of this church! The important thing to remember from this story is that the pastor didn't let something get in the way of the church's goal. No matter how annoyed, they didn't stop the work because of the grasshoppers.

King Asa didn't give up either when he faced challenging times. The new leader of Judah had his work cut out for him. The people had turned from God and were worshipping idols. They were headed down the wrong path, and God was not pleased with them. But King Asa was determined to make a change for the better in Judah. So he assembled the people together at Jerusalem and asked God to forgive them. King Asa commanded that 700 cattle and 7,000 sheep and goats be sacrificed to God. Then he asked the people to promise to follow God. So they took an oath, a solemn promise, in allegiance to God.

If you feel you don't have a good relationship with God, don't stress out and give up. Be like King Asa and make things right with God. He is right there waiting for you to be His friend. Turn to Him, and He will gladly turn to you!

NEXT STOP: Nebraska

Hello out there!

Land of Corn and Water

You prepare a table before me in the presence of my enemies. You anoint my head with oil; my cup overflows. Surely your goodness and love will follow me all the days of my life, and I will dwell in the house of the Lord forever. **Psalm 23:5, 6.**

Welcome to Nebraska, nicknamed the Cornhusker State because of the cornfields that stretch for miles across the flat landscape. Driving across Nebraska is pretty, but some people find it somewhat boring because mile after mile the scenery is the same.

Corn is the number one crop in Nebraska. It grows well because about 75 percent of the rain that falls in the state occurs between April and September, which is the growing season. Also, the state is home to the United States' largest aquifer, which is an underground lake or water supply.

The Ogallala Aquifer was tapped in 1911 to irrigate fields. Of course, the farmers were excited to have a ready water supply, since Nebraska is in the Great Plains and is hot and dry. Farmers dug wells and pumped water from below the earth's surface to water their crops. They thought they had an endless supply of water from this magical underground lake.

However, as the years went by, the farmers began to realize that they have to conserve the water or they will risk using up the underground water reserves. The United States Geological Survey has studied the aquifer and discovered that the total water storage of the aquifer was 2.9 billion acre feet in 2005, which is about 253 million acre feet less than the total water storage in the 1950s, when irrigation became extremely popular.

On this earth we have to be careful that we don't use up the resources God has given us. We have to be careful with our forests, our lakes, and our fields. But there is one thing we never have to worry about using up, and that's God's love! His love for us overflows and pours down upon us in so many ways. God's goodness is sure. We can count on Him to give us food and shelter and protection in this crazy world.

NEXT STOP: Nebraska City, Nebraska

Planted Deeply

But blessed is the one who trusts in the Lord, whose confidence is in him. They will be like a tree planted by the water that sends out its roots by the stream. It does not fear when heat comes; its leaves are always green. It has no worries in a year of drought and never fails to bear fruit. Jeremiah 17:7, 8.

J. Sterling Morton moved to Nebraska City in 1854 to stake his claim in the West. Soon after arriving, he began working as the editor of the Nebraska City *News*. Later he served in the territorial government of Nebraska, including serving as acting governor of Nebraska for a short period of time.

Morton did pretty well for himself, and he earned enough money to construct a 52-room mansion in Nebraska City that looks like the White House in Washington, D.C. After he finished building the mansion, Morton turned his attention to the grounds. He had always been fascinated with trees, so this was his opportunity to plant a wide variety in the gardens around the estate.

His love for trees led him to found Arbor Day, a holiday in which people plant and care for trees. The first Arbor Day took place on April 10, 1872, and historians estimate that 1 million trees were planted! Today a similar holiday is celebrated in many countries around the world. In the United States the national holiday takes place on the last Friday in April.

Trees give us food. Trees give us shelter and provide shade from the heat. Trees clean our air. Trees give us wood. Morton knew the value of trees for our existence, and he was determined to remind people to take care of the trees we have and plant more each year.

Have you ever thought about how we are like trees? Think about it, and read our text again. Jeremiah compares a person who is trusting in God to a tree with roots that plunge deep into the ground near a stream. If we are firmly "planted" in God, meaning that Jesus is our best friend, then we won't be shaken. If you have a bad day at school and your friends won't talk to you or if you fail a test, you won't give up and you won't blame God. Why? Because you will keep trusting in God and believing that He will take care of you. Just as a tree planted by a stream with deep roots isn't bothered by hot weather or lack of rain, you won't fear the bad things of life if you have God beside you.

NEXT STOP: Omaha, Nebraska

August 14

Hello out there!

Life Insurance

But these are written that you may believe that Jesus is the Messiah, the Son of God, and that by believing you may have life in his name. **John 20:31.**

Mutual of Omaha is a large insurance company headquartered in Omaha, Nebraska. The company was founded in 1909 and is known for selling life insurance. If you have never heard of life insurance, it is something adults purchase to make sure that their families have money to live on if they die.

Not everyone purchases life insurance, but many people do, especially the parent who earns the most money in the family. The idea is that if a person dies early in life, his or her spouse and their kids will still have money because the insurance company will give them the face value of the policy, which, depending on the policy purchased, is usually more than $100,000.

But why would someone pay between $50 and $100 a month for life insurance when he or she will probably never use it? Good question. But that's why it's called insurance. That person is preparing for something that *might* happen.

Let's look at a different type of insurance. The majority of drivers have car insurance. Each month the driver pays a set amount of money, and if the car is involved in an accident, the insurance company helps pay for the damage to the vehicle. But once again, this is for those "just in case" moments. I have car insurance, and I have needed it a handful of times throughout my life, but I don't need it every month, even though I pay for it every month.

That's the thing about insurance: it is for the unexpected things in life. You can't predict *when* bad things are going to happen, so you prepare yourself by having insurance.

Did you know that you can get life insurance that's free? But although it is free, many people still don't accept the offer. They either think it is too good to be true or they would rather pay money each month and live life for themselves. So what is this free insurance? It's called salvation! When you accept Jesus' free gift of salvation, you are given eternal life. Sure, bad stuff will happen during our lives, but we have the "assurance," not insurance, that we can leave this world behind when Jesus returns!

NEXT STOP: Hebron, Nebraska

Bigger Is Better!

Watch out! Be on your guard against all kinds of greed; life does not consist in an abundance of possessions. **Luke 12:15.**

Welcome to Hebron, home of the largest porch swing in the United States. The swing is located in the city park and is 32 feet long! The swing is like your typical porch swing with a wooden seat and back. Such a large swing needs serious support, so it hangs from a section of center pivot, the irrigation equipment that farmers use in their fields.

Now think about this, the swing can hold 18 adults, 24 children, or 128 babies! I guess you wouldn't have to fight over who got to swing first, since you and 23 of your friends could pile onto the swing together. Of course, it would probably require all of your parents to push at the same time. I'm sure it would be hard for one mom to push that many kids.

Often we are attracted to things that are big. I'm guessing you're drawn to the biggest set of LEGOs in the store or the largest slice of pizza or cake. What about the biggest present under the Christmas tree? Do you secretly hope that the biggest one has your name on it?

Our world teaches us that things that are bigger are better. But Jesus warned us against falling into the trap of greed. In Luke 12 He tells a crowd of listeners about the parable of the rich fool. You see, there was this rich man who had such a good crop that he decided to tear down his barns and build bigger ones in which to store all his grain and goods. Then the man decided to take life easy and eat and drink and be merry (see verses 18, 19).

But God called him a fool for thinking only about riches and wealth and the biggest and best. Then Jesus said, "This is how it will be with whoever stores up things for themselves but is not rich toward God" (verse 21).

Remember, the best pair of Nikes will wear out, the biggest slice of pizza will be eaten, the best electronic device will break or one day become quite useless, the biggest balloon will pop, and the most popular toy or clothing item will be considered boring in a year. Nothing on this earth lasts forever. Don't be a fool! Make sure you are storing up your treasure in heaven instead of on this earth.

NEXT STOP: Cozad and Kearney, Nebraska

August 16

Hello out there!

Stuck in the Middle

When all Israel heard the verdict the king had given, they held the king in awe, because they saw that he had wisdom from God to administer justice. **I Kings 3:28.**

We are passing through two cities today as we drive east to Lincoln, the capital of the state. These two cities are both the center of something. We are starting in Cozad, which is located on the 100th meridian, where the humid East meets the arid West, and driving to Kearney, which is located exactly between Boston and San Francisco. The cities are only about 50 miles apart, but they both mark the middle of something.

I know these two cities could care less that they are in the middle of the country marking two different things, but it isn't the same for people. Have you ever been caught in the middle between two people? I have, and it isn't fun! For example, Olivia comes to you and says that Emily borrowed a DVD from her but won't return it, and she wants you to go talk to Emily, since she has tried but Emily won't listen. You want to help your friend, so you go to Emily and ask her for the DVD. Emily then tells you that Olivia is lying and trying to accuse her of keeping the DVD when in reality Olivia lost her own DVD, but because she is mad that she lost it, Olivia is blaming Emily for losing it and wants her to pay for the DVD.

Sounds confusing, doesn't it? Especially when you are stuck in the middle and it isn't even your problem. What should you do? The best advice I can give you is to pray for wisdom and ask your parents or a teacher for help if you are ever caught between friends or family members. That is what Solomon did, and he was the wisest man who ever lived.

Do you remember the story of Solomon and the two women who had each given birth to a baby boy but one of the two babies had died? The mother whose baby had died switched her dead baby for the other mother's live baby in the middle of the night. In the morning, the mother of the live baby discovered what had happened and accused the other mother of switching the babies. Of course, the dishonest mother claimed the live baby was hers, so they took their case to King Solomon for him to judge. He wisely saw what was happening, and after testing the women with an order to cut the baby in two, he discovered who the real mother was. Then he ruled in her favor.

When in doubt, pray about it! Prayer always helps you out of sticky situations.

NEXT STOP: Lincoln, Nebraska

Paying in Advance

Why aren't you repairing the damage done to the temple? Take no more money from your treasurers, but hand it over for repairing the temple. **2 Kings 12:7.**

The Nebraska state capitol in Lincoln is the second-tallest statehouse in the United States and is the heaviest state capitol in North America. But the thing that impresses me the most about this building is that the construction job came in under budget and the building was paid for in full by the time the 10-year construction project was completed.

And when you realize that the building cost a little more than $9.8 million, I think you will agree with me that that is pretty impressive. Rarely are building projects, especially large ones like a capitol building, paid for by the time construction is finished. That's because our society is used to paying for things on credit.

Credit cards can be convenient and easy to use, but they can also trap people into spending more than they have in the bank. An average American has eight credit cards and owes $8,000 in debt. Instead of paying for everything, they have purchased each month using a credit card, they pay only part of that amount. Less than half of American credit card holders pay the full amount they owe each month.

It seems simple, but a lot of people have a hard time with this idea. If you have money, you can buy things. If you don't have money, you shouldn't buy things. God calls us to be good stewards of the money He gives us. And part of being a good steward—someone who looks after something—is using money wisely to buy what is needed and to save for the future for emergencies or more expensive things that are desired.

There was a building project in the Bible that the king and the workers used God's money wisely to do His work. In 2 Kings 12 we read the story of King Joash, the young king who repaired the Temple. The priests collected money for the repairs, and when they had enough, they hired carpenters and masons and stonecutters to fix the Temple in Jerusalem.

This story is not only a lesson in saving your money until you are able to pay for something but also a lesson in honesty. Check this out. The priests "did not require an accounting from those to whom they gave the money to pay the workers, because they acted with complete honesty" (verse 15). When you are honest with God's money, you will be rewarded.

NEXT STOP: Mitchell, South Dakota

237

August 18

Hello out there!

Decorating With Corncobs

Since God has made all this known to you, there is no one so discerning and wise as you. You shall be in charge of my palace, and all my people are to submit to your orders. Only with respect to the throne will I be greater than you. **Genesis 41:39, 40.**

Mitchell, South Dakota, is home to the Corn Palace, a large building that looks like a castle and features corn murals on the outside. Each year the Corn Palace features a different theme. Work on the new murals begins in late May or early June each year and is finished by the beginning of October. The 2013 theme was "We Celebrate" and featured various celebrations and holidays such as Valentine's Day, Mother's Day, Veterans Day, Thanksgiving, Christmas, and New Year's Day, to name a few.

The designers who create the murals use different types of dried corn, including traditional yellow corn, reddish Indian corn, and other varieties. They also use rye, seeds, and other grains and native grasses to create the frames and fill in the pictures. Although you might not typically think of using ears of corn as artwork, the finished pieces are amazing.

Since 1892 the exterior of the Corn Palace has been decorated in corn, except for 2007, when severe drought forced the creators of the murals to leave the design from 2006.

As I was thinking about my visit to the Corn Palace a few years ago, I thought about Joseph and when he was put in charge of the entire land of Egypt in preparation for the famine. Because Joseph correctly interpreted Pharaoh's dream, thanks to God, Pharaoh put Joseph in charge of the whole kingdom. He also gave him the sole responsibility of collecting and storing the grain needed to sustain the kingdom during the seven years of famine.

Had I been Joseph, I would have been overwhelmed with the task of storing enough food to feed thousands of people for seven years! But God was with Joseph, and He directed and blessed him. In fact, "Joseph stored up huge quantities of grain, like the sand of the sea; it was so much that he stopped keeping records because it was beyond measure" (Genesis 41:49).

NEXT STOP: Philip, South Dakota

August 19

A Guide for All to See

There he [Jacob] built an altar, and he called the place El Bethel,
because it was there that God revealed himself to him when he
was fleeing from his brother. **Genesis 35:7.**

Eight miles west of Philip, South Dakota, stands a 14-foot tall monument called the Silent Guide Monument. It was built in the late 1800s or early 1900s by a sheepherder in the area to mark a waterhole that never went dry. The monument was made of flat stones stacked one on top of another. Because it was so tall, it could be seen as far as 35 miles away.

As more people moved into the area, arguments often arose between cowhands and sheepherders as to who had access to the land for grazing their herds. More than once the monument was destroyed by the cowhands, only to be rebuilt by the sheepherders. In 1924 the stones were actually cemented together so that the historical monument would last forever.

In this case the monument was practical and served as a guide for the sheepherders to know where to get water. In other cases monuments are erected to pay honor to someone or something. In today's text we read about Jacob, who built an altar or monument, to God at El Bethel, which means "house of God," because that is where God talked with Jacob and gave him the new name of Israel. The monument Jacob built for the Lord was a testimony of his relationship with God. It was a reminder to others who heard Jacob's story and saw the altar in Bethel that Jacob served a living God.

On the other hand, check out the type of monument Absalom built. "During his lifetime Absalom had taken a pillar and erected it in the King's Valley as a monument to himself, for he thought, 'I have no son to carry on the memory of my name.' He named the pillar after himself, and it is called Absalom's Monument to this day" (2 Samuel 18:18). Absalom's monument had nothing to do with God and everything to do with himself. It was all for show and display. It was all about impressing people and making a name for himself.

If you were to build a monument, would you create something that reminded others about God or about yourself? Do you want to be like Jacob or Absalom?

NEXT STOP: Badlands National Park, South Dakota

239

August 20

Hello out there!

A Bad Place

I will set my face against anyone who turns to mediums and spiritists to prostitute themselves by following them, and I will cut them off from their people. **Leviticus 20:6.**

The Badlands National Park is an area of South Dakota that looks very barren and desolate. Approximately 244,000 acres are inside the park, which features eroded buttes and mixed grass prairie. A butte (pronounced with a long "U" sound, as in "you") is a hill with steep sides and a flat top.

Before American settlers moved west into South Dakota, the area was home to the Lakota Native American tribe. As more and more settlers demanded that they be given the best land, the Native Americans were mistreated and killed. They were desperate for hope and security, so when Wovoka, an Indian prophet, said that he had had a vision directing the natives to dance the Ghost Dance and wear ghost shirts, the people believed him.

The Ghost Dance was a group dance that was supposed to bring back the spirits of the dead and create peace and unity for the natives still living in the region. The natives were also supposed to wear a ghost shirt, which was supposed to protect the person wearing it from being struck by a bullet. The shirt was said to have sacred and magical powers.

One of the last known Ghost Dances was held about 45 miles south of Badlands National Park. After the ceremony the natives left the area, but they were pursued by the U.S. Army and were finally overtaken at Wounded Knee Creek. The soldiers ordered that everyone camp there overnight, but when they attempted to take away the Native Americans' weapons, gunfire erupted, and it is estimated that between 150 to 300 Native Americans and approximately 30 soldiers were killed. The event was named the Wounded Knee massacre, and it was the last official battle of the American Indian wars.

Anytime we mess with Satan and the spirit world, we are in for trouble. God instructed the children of Israel that He would turn His face against anyone who went to a medium or spiritist for counsel. Satan wants to lead us down a path of destruction, like the Native Americans who were killed at Wounded Knee, while making it appear that his way is the best way. Don't fall for his lies and tricks. Stay on the straight and narrow path.

NEXT STOP: Keystone, South Dakota

Water From Where?

But the people were thirsty for water there, and they grumbled against Moses.
They said, "Why did you bring us up out of Egypt to make us
and our children and livestock die of thirst?" **Exodus 17:3**.

Mount Rushmore National Memorial is located near Keystone, South Dakota, and is home to four famous faces that are carved into the side of the granite mountain. The 60-foot sculptures feature presidents George Washington, Thomas Jefferson, Theodore Roosevelt, and Abraham Lincoln.

Sculptor Gutzon Borglum was hired to facilitate the project, which began in 1927 and took 14 years to complete. In order to carve the granite, large sections of the stone first had to be blasted off by dynamite. Workers would climb over the mountainside with ropes and sit on small wooden swings as they inserted dynamite and blasted sections before using chisels, hammers, and a type of jackhammer to carve the granite to resemble the faces of the presidents. It was a very dangerous job without any of the safety equipment we would use today when rock climbing or working thousands of feet above ground, but amazingly, no one died while working on the project.

Each year workers have to seal cracks and monitor the sculptures to make sure they remain intact. Over the years hairline cracks have grown because of water entering the crevices and freezing and thawing. This process expands the crack. Thus, careful monitoring and sealing efforts are put into place to preserve the monument.

As I think about how the workers carved Mount Rushmore, they used explosives, not sticks, to break off chunks of rock. Furthermore, water did not gush out of the rock when they blasted a section off. Do you know what Bible story I'm thinking of? That's right, when God brought water from the rock.

God heard the cries of the children of Israel. They were thirsty and grumpy and tired. And even though they didn't ask politely, God took care of them. He told Moses to take his staff and strike the rock at Horeb. And when he did, water poured from the rock so that all the people could drink. Just as God was good to the Israelites even when they didn't deserve it, He is good to us, too!

NEXT STOP: Custer State Park, South Dakota

Hello out there!

Be Careful!

So be careful to do what the Lord your God has commanded you;
do not turn aside to the right or to the left. Walk in obedience to all that the Lord
your God has commanded you, so that you may live and prosper and prolong
your days in the land that you will possess. **Deuteronomy 5:32, 33.**

Years ago when the Native Americans lived in South Dakota, bison or buffalo roamed freely across the land. *Tatanka*, the Lakota name for bison, were a major resource for the Native Americans. The Lakota used them for food, clothing, and shelter. Today these 2,000-pound animals still roam certain areas of South Dakota, but they are especially prominent in Custer State Park, which is home to a herd of 1,500 free-roaming bison.

Our family was very excited when we entered the wildlife loop at the state park. All eyes were glued to the windows in search of bison. Finally we rounded a corner, and there they were! Hundreds of them were in the fields on both sides of the road, and at least 50 others stood in the middle of the road. We were officially stuck in a bison jam! The bison were in no hurry to move, so we slowly inched forward, weaving in between the bison as they stood on the road chewing their cud. We came within just a few feet of these massive creatures.

But what amazed me as we sat in the bison jam were the people on motorcycles who were a few feet away from the bison and were revving their engines and trying to get them to move. Any one of the male bison could have taken a biker out in one charge.

Then we heard the story of a park ranger who tried to rescue a woman who was hit by a bison. The woman had gotten out of her car to take an up-close picture of the bison. Although there are plenty of signs reminding you to stay in your car and give the bison space because they are wild animals, she didn't follow directions, and a bison charged her from behind and slammed into her. The ranger saw what happened, jumped in her car, drove between the woman and the bison, and pulled her into the back seat of the car. Sadly, the woman died of her injuries.

Rules are there for a reason—they exist to protect you from danger. God gives us laws to live by in order to protect us. Moses was constantly reminding the children of Israel to follow God's laws, and his words in Deuteronomy 5:32, 33 still apply to us today.

NEXT STOP: Needles Highway, South Dakota

Squeeze Through

The disciples were amazed at his words. But Jesus said again, "Children, how hard it is to enter the kingdom of God! It is easier for a camel to go through the eye of a needle than for someone who is rich to enter the kingdom of God." **Mark 10:24, 25**.

The Needles Highway is a narrow roadway that leads through the Black Hills of South Dakota. The highway features sharp turns and low tunnels, but the beautiful scenery is well worth the drive. Towering granite spires that look like needles sticking up out of the forest floor reach to the sky and seem to touch the clouds.

The Needles Eye Tunnel leads you to the Eye of the Needle, a rock formation that is 30 feet tall with a three-foot-wide slit near the top of the rock that makes it look like a sewing needle. When a bus drives through the Needles Tunnel, it looks like a thread going through the eye of a needle. With only a few inches to spare on all sides, most people hold their breath as they watch the buses slowly inch their way through the tunnel. Can you picture a tour bus with only inches to spare in a granite tunnel?

OK, now try to picture a camel squeezing through the eye of a sewing needle. Impossible, right? Isn't it interesting that Jesus used this illustration to describe how difficult it is for a rich person to go to heaven? So why do you think it is hard for a rich person to go to heaven? Is it because they have to do more? Are there other rules that apply to them?

No, of course not. Rich people have access to the same gift of eternal life as poor people. All they have to do is confess their sins and ask Jesus to save them. They don't have to do anything different than anyone else who enters a saving relationship with God.

So why would Jesus make this statement? The truth is that a lot of people who are rich don't see their need of a Savior. They feel as if they have everything they need. They can go anywhere they want, do anything they please, and buy anything they wish.

Although I don't think I would change if I had a lot of money, I trust that God knows best, and He gives me what I need. And if I had to choose, I would rather be a poor person who clings to the promise of eternal life than a rich person who squanders that gift.

NEXT STOP: Grenora, North Dakota

Hello out there!

August 24

Angry Birds

The Lord is slow to anger, abounding in love and forgiving sin and rebellion. Yet he does not leave the guilty unpunished; he punishes the children for the sin of the parents to the third and fourth generation. **Numbers 14:18**.

I'm sure most of you have heard about or played Angry Birds, but the game was not the original "angry bird." At Writing Rock State Historical Site near Grenora, North Dakota, there are two large granite boulders that have petroglyphs, or rock engravings, carved in them by Plains Indian tribes. The two boulders feature thunderbirds, mythical creatures with huge wings and teeth within their beaks that were said to bring storms in their wake.

All of the early tales about this creature suggest that anyone who comes in contact with a thunderbird should be very careful because they are extremely angry birds that control rainfall and weather. One story suggested that the thunderbird was a servant of the "Great Spirit." Another story suggested that thunderbirds could become humans by tilting their beaks back like a mask and removing their feathers like a feather-covered blanket.

I hope you read this and say, "What? That doesn't make sense! The Bible tells us that there is only one God in heaven, and an animal cannot become a person or the other way around." But people who don't have the Bible or don't believe what it says live in the shadow of Satan and his lies.

Instead of living in peace by following a loving God who is slow to anger and forgives sins, people who believe Satan and his lies can live in fear of evil spirits and creatures that will attack them if they don't chant the right prayer or leave the right animal sacrifice on their doorstep.

The only way people can be freed from Satan and his lies is through the Bible and the promises of God. If you sometimes feel that God is an angry God who punishes those who don't follow His rules, read today's verse. God is *slow* to anger, and He *forgives* sin and rebellion. And if that were not enough, He *loves* us unconditionally with a love that never ends. When bad things happens, remember who is to blame—and it isn't God.

NEXT STOP: Devils Lake, North Dakota

They Just Didn't Get It

But the Pharisees said, "It is by the prince of demons that he drives out demons." **Matthew 9:34.**

Devils Lake is the largest natural body of water in North Dakota, and it was named by the Lakota Indians. In their language, the lake was pronounced *mni wak'áŋ chante*. This translates as follows: *mni* (water), *wak'áŋ* (spirit), and *chante* (bad).

The White settlers translated *mni wak'áŋ chante* into "Bad Spirit Lake" or "Devils Lake," thus the name it has to this day. The White settlers didn't stop to think that the Native Americans do not have a "devil" in their religious beliefs, so that word doesn't exist in their vocabulary. They believed what they wanted to believe, fueling the fires of legends about warriors drowning in the lake and lake monsters appearing from the depths of the waters. What the Lakota really meant by naming it *mni wak'áŋ chante* was that you couldn't drink the water because it was salty. The White settlers twisted the Lakotas' name and meaning to fit their own ideas about the lake.

The Pharisees, like the superstitious and illogical settlers, changed Jesus' teachings to fit their own understanding of how things should be. Jesus presented the truth from heaven, but the Pharisees either closed their ears to His messages or twisted them to mean something completely different.

Today's text is part of a story of a demon-possessed man whom Jesus healed. The man could not speak, but after Jesus drove the demon out, the man could talk. The Pharisees witnessed the miracle, but they accused Jesus of driving the demon out in the name of Satan.

Yes, you read that correctly. They accused Jesus of working with Satan. Now, why would Satan cast one of his own demons out of a man under his control? It doesn't make sense, does it? The Pharisees hated Jesus so much that they made up accusations that didn't even sound logical. But that's what happens when people are blinded by Satan. They make up things to fit their own ideas, which usually don't make sense.

When Jesus is our friend and we spend time with Him as with our earthly friends, we won't get mixed up with our own ideas and fall into the trap of the Pharisees who didn't take the time to get to know Jesus and, thus, didn't understand His teachings.

NEXT STOP: Fargo, North Dakota

August 26

Hello out there!

Follow the Son

The crowds that went ahead of him and those that followed shouted, "Hosanna to the Son of David!" "Blessed is he who comes in the name of the Lord!" "Hosanna in the highest heaven!" **Matthew 21:9.**

Summer is slowly slipping away, but we can still enjoy the sights of summer as we drive past sunflower fields in North Dakota. The large golden heads all face the same direction and sway in the breeze, a picture of cheery warmth against a brilliant deep blue sky. Growing anywhere from five to 12 feet, the sunflowers reach to the sky as if drinking up the last rays of the summer sun.

Many flowers grow in all different directions, but sunflowers seem to line up and turn their beautiful faces in the same direction, which makes for amazing photographs. Here are a few things I thought about when comparing sunflowers to Christians:

Sunflowers all face in the same direction with the purpose of growing until they produce their seeds and are ready for harvest. If we as God's followers all faced in the same direction as a church and moved forward together as one group, we would be so much more powerful and would produce the fruit of the Spirit. Does that mean we all have to do the same thing? No. We can each use our talents and minister in special ways, but we all need to move together as one group with the sole mission of telling others about Jesus. We may each have a different way of doing that, but we should all be working toward that goal.

Also, the sunflower needs light from the sun to grow. Without sun, the sunflower would wither and die. Likewise, spending time with Jesus in prayer and reading the Bible is like allowing light to shine on us in order for us to grow. People who have never heard of Jesus will die the eternal death if the light of His truth doesn't shine on them.

See if you can think of any other ways we are like sunflowers. Think about their roots, their seeds, their leaves, and so on, and think about other spiritual lessons and things that remind you about Jesus and your relationship with Him.

NEXT STOP: Steele and Parshall, North Dakota

Extremes

As long as the earth endures, seedtime and harvest, cold and heat, summer and winter, day and night will never cease. **Genesis 8:22.**

My husband was born in North Dakota, and lived there for a number of years while growing up. He tells stories about the brutal cold that would take your breath away the minute you stepped outside during the winter. He also tells about listening to the meteorologists warning people to stay inside because it was so cold that frostbite could set in immediately if you ventured out with even your nose uncovered. But I didn't realize how hot it could get. Of course, since most of North Dakota is open plains, the land bakes under the summer sun.

So as you can see, North Dakota has its extremes. Visit in the summer and you might fry; visit in the winter and you might freeze. Well, in 1936 people did both, because the highest and lowest temperatures were set that same year, just in different cities. In February the lowest temperature recorded in the state occurred in Parshall, with the thermometer reading minus 60 degrees Fahrenheit. Then five months later, in July, the highest temperature ever recorded in North Dakota was 121 degrees Fahrenheit in Steele. That's quite the swing in temperatures!

Today's text talks about heat and cold, summer and winter. But do you know what story this comes from? I didn't either until I stumbled across this verse. I've read the story of Noah countless times, but this verse never stuck in my mind.

After Noah and his family and all the animals exited the ark, Noah built an altar and offered sacrifices to the Lord. The Bible tells us that "the Lord smelled the pleasing aroma" (Genesis 8:21), and He promised Noah, and us, that "as long as the earth remains, there will be planting and harvest, cold and heat, summer and winter, day and night" (verse 22, NLT). God made this promise before He sent the rainbow. We know that until the world ends at Jesus' second coming, life will continue. The sun will come up and go down. The seasons will change as usual, bringing heat and cold in turn. And the plants will continue to bloom and produce food. God will keep this world functioning until the appointed time when He will return.

I don't know about you, but I'm glad He is in charge of everything. It's a very comforting feeling to know that God ultimately controls this world!

NEXT STOP: Rutland, North Dakota

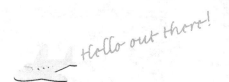

Hello out there!

August 28

Let's Eat

The rabble with them began to crave other food, and again the Israelites started wailing and said, "If only we had meat to eat! We remember the fish we ate in Egypt at no cost—also the cucumbers, melons, leeks, onions and garlic. But now we have lost our appetite; we never see anything but this manna!" **Numbers 11:4-6**.

In 1982 the people of Rutland, North Dakota, attempted to enter the *Guinness Book of World Records* for grilling and eating the world's largest hamburger. And they did it! Can you guess how many people they fed? Between 8,000 and 10,000 people sampled the 3,591-pound burger.

Then in 1999 Loran Green and a group of friends in Montana claimed the title for the world's largest hamburger when they cooked a 6,040-pound burger that measured 24 feet in diameter.

Regardless of who holds the title of the largest hamburger, that amount of meat is hard to even imagine. Think about it, that size hamburger is probably larger than your family room and kitchen put together!

Some of the Israelites craved meat and complained about the manna God was giving them. So God granted their desires and sent a wind from the sea that blew a bunch of quail into the camp. There were so many quail that they stacked up three feet above the ground and covered an area "as far as a day's walk in any direction" (Numbers 11:31). The people then gathered the quail, collecting approximately 60 bushels per person.

The people were so excited to have meat that they immediately began to devour the quail. The Bible tells us that "while the meat was still between their teeth" (verse 33) the people were struck with a plague and many of the complainers died. Their greed and their desire for food other than what the Lord wanted them to eat was their downfall.

Sometimes we desire something so strongly that we tell God we want it no matter what. We think we know what is best, but we are definitely not smarter than God. When we follow our own ways, we suffer the consequences. When we follow God's ways, we reap the rewards.

NEXT STOP: International Peace Garden, North Dakota

Blessed Peace

The Lord bless you and keep you; the Lord make his face shine on you and be gracious to you; the Lord turn his face toward you and give you peace. **Numbers 6:24-26.**

Today we are leaving the United States and traveling back into Canada. Our last destination in North Dakota is the International Peace Garden, which also shares land with the province of Manitoba.

The park was built in 1932 and featured a monument with the inscription "To God in His Glory," with the American flag flying on one side and the Canadian flag on the other. The border for the two countries runs right down the middle of the monument. The park is also home to the Peace Tower, four 120-foot towers that straddle the border with two columns in North Dakota and two in Manitoba. A chapel near the base of the towers features on its walls famous statements about peace.

After the September 11, 2001, attacks on New York City, steel girders from the World Trade Center were sent to the International Peace Garden to display as a reminder of the horrors of hatred and evil in this world.

We all long for peace. Peace from studying. Peace from annoying siblings. Peace from arguments at school. Peace from parents who disagree. Peace from wars. Peace from natural disasters. Peace from the troubles of this world.

As you start your day, I would like to offer this prayer over you. Aaron and his sons blessed the Israelites with these words, and may you also be blessed today.

"May the Lord bless you and take care of you;
   may the Lord be kind and gracious to you;
   may the Lord look on you with favor
   and give you peace" (Numbers 6:24-26, TEV).

NEXT STOP: Manitoba

Hello out there!

August 30

Trading Up

By your great skill in trading you have increased your wealth, and because of your wealth your heart has grown proud. **Ezekiel 28:5.**

Directly above North Dakota and the Plains States in America, Manitoba offers a wide variety of scenery. From fields of planted crops to rolling hills, tree-covered mountains to beaches and lakes, the landscape is beautiful. If you want even more variety in one province, you can travel to the northernmost region where polar bears are seen in the winter and beluga whales can be spotted in the summer.

Early European settlers of Manitoba ventured into the region in search of beavers. Beavers were hunted in the nineteenth century for their thick furs. Skinned and dried, the pelts were sold and made into moccasins, coats, blankets, and hats. Because their thick fur repels water, the pelts were a good source of warmth against the cold northern winters in the United States and Canada.

As the trappers explored the area in search of beavers, many stayed and settled. The beaver served as a good source of income to the point that the trappers and traders killed off nearly all the beavers in the province by the early 1900s. Through protection efforts, the beaver went from being endangered to being overpopulated. Today there are approximately 5 million beavers in the province.

The near extinction of beavers in Manitoba was the result of a desire for wealth. As we've talked about before, having lots of money can lead to problems. In the case of the king of Tyre, trading and wealth definitely got him into trouble.

God sent a message to the prophet Ezekiel to tell the king of Tyre that he had a problem. The king had trade routes established with Greece, Tarshish, Aram, Judah, Israel, Damascus, Arabia, and Sheba, to name a few. The king was clearly powerful and prosperous, based on the long line of merchants that are listed in Ezekiel 27. But he was also proud, and in his heart he claimed to be a god.

Big mistake! The king of Tyre followed the same path as did Lucifer when he said in his heart that he was wiser than God. Remember, no one is wiser than God.

NEXT STOP: Winnipeg, Manitoba

Getting in Trouble for Honey

> The entire army entered the woods, and there was honey on the ground. When they went into the woods, they saw the honey oozing out; yet no one put his hand to his mouth, because they feared the oath. I Samuel 14:25, 26.

Lieutenant Harry Colebourn was a Canadian officer in the military during World War I. Before shipping out to England, where he was from, to fight in the war, Leutenant Colebourn purchased an orphaned bear cub from a trapper for $20. He wanted the bear to be a mascot for his troops, so he took the cub to England with his men and named it Winnie, after his adopted hometown of Winnipeg. A few months later, when he and his men left for France, he left Winnie at the London Zoo.

One day a young boy named Christopher visited the zoo with his father. Christopher fell in love with Winnie and nicknamed the bear "Winnie the Pooh." Christopher's father, A. A. Milne, decided to write stories featuring Winnie the Pooh and his forest friends.

If you have ever read Winnie the Pooh stories, you know that Pooh Bear *loves* honey! In fact, the crazy bear gets himself stuck in holes because he has eaten too much and can't get out, or he gets his hand stuck in jars of honey while trying to eat the sticky, gooey, sweet liquid. It seems that Pooh Bear is always hungry when it comes to honey, even if he has just eaten.

Of course, you would be hungry if you had been working hard all day and hadn't eaten anything. That's what happened to Saul's troops one day when they were fighting the Philistines, their archenemy. But Saul had made his troops take an oath saying they would not eat anything until their enemies were dead. But then the ultimate temptation happened. They entered the woods, and honey was oozing out of honeycomb lying on the ground. Although the troops were exhausted and hungry, they obeyed Saul's orders, but Jonathan hadn't heard about the oath, so he dipped his staff into the honeycomb and ate it. Then one of the soldiers told him about the order.

Jonathan then said, "My father has made trouble for the country" (1 Samuel 14:29). Why? Because the troops were weak from lack of food. If they had been able to eat, they could have fought better. It's a big responsibility to be in charge and make good decisions. But when you ask God for help, He will give you wisdom. At this time in his life Saul was not following God, and it showed in the poor decisions he made.

Hello out there!

Avoid the Trash

Finally, brothers and sisters, whatever is true, whatever is noble, whatever is right, whatever is pure, whatever is lovely, whatever is admirable—if anything is excellent or praiseworthy—think about such things. **Philippians 4:8.**

Harlequin Enterprises is a romance novel publisher that was founded in 1949 in Winnipeg, Manitoba. The company began publishing books by British writers that were geared toward women and featured a female hero who would fall madly in love with a handsome man. Generally, the hero would do anything to keep the man within her grasp, even if it meant lying to him or fighting over him with other women, including his wife. Sounds ridiculous, doesn't it?

The company also published medical romance stories, and now it has moved on to publishing books of a genre called psychological thrillers; the plot will usually feature deception between characters who try to ruin one another's lives by messing with their minds. The company is now located in Toronto, Ontario, and publishes approximately 120 new titles each month! A few years ago the company sold 131 million books in one year. That's a lot of trashy books filling the bookshelves in people's homes.

When Paul wrote to the church in Philippi, he warned them to think only about things that were true, noble, right, pure, lovely, and admirable. He said that if something deserved to be praised, then it was good enough to think about. This same warning applies to us.

I want you to think about the books you read. Do they meet the criteria in this verse? What about the TV shows you watch? Are they true, right, and pure? Now think about the music you listen to. Are the lyrics praiseworthy?

A lot of people, both kids and adults, don't want to think about this verse when it comes to entertainment. They just want to chill and watch TV or a movie. "It's just for fun," they say. "I'm not going to act that way. I know it's wrong to kill people and steal and lie."

Sure, we know those things are wrong, but when we let those things into our minds, we let a piece of Satan and his kingdom into our thoughts. You can't ever erase those images and ideas; they stay planted in your mind forever. Please follow Paul's advice and be careful what you put into your mind!

NEXT STOP: Narcisse, Manitoba

Snake Dens

The Lord said to Moses, "Make a snake and put it up on a pole; anyone who is bitten can look at it and live." **Numbers 21:8.**

I plan to stay in the car at this next stop, but you are more than welcome to get out and look around. Today we are in Narcisse, Manitoba, the home of the Snake Dens. I bet you can imagine why I'm staying in the car.

Each year when the snow melts in late April or early May (yes, they still have snow on the ground when it is springtime in most of the United States), tens of thousands of red-sided garter snakes emerge from their dens in the ground and mate in big piles of slithering reptiles. Then they slide off into the marshes for the summer before returning to their dens in the fall.

As I looked at a picture of a *huge* heap of these snakes, I thought about the snakes that invaded the Israelites' camp. But unlike the garter snake, which is not poisonous, the snakes that entered the camp were very poisonous. And many Israelites were bitten and died.

But why did the snakes enter the camp in the first place? Well, the Israelites spoke against God and Moses. They complained about the food God was sending them and how they were going to die in the desert. They failed to trust God and His plan for them. They were impatient and grumpy.

The invasion of the snakes was a result of their sins and complaining. As people began dying from the snakebites, "the people came to Moses and said, 'We sinned when we spoke against the Lord and against you. Pray that the Lord will take the snakes away from us'" (Numbers 21:7). They realized their mistake and repented. Then the Lord told Moses to form a bronze snake and place it on a pole for everyone to see. Those who were bitten and looked at the snake lived.

Like the Israelites, we often complain and make bad choices that result in unpleasant consequences. But if we repent and look to Jesus, we will be forgiven. It's important to remember both of those things. The Israelites repented, but if they didn't look at the snake on the pole, they still would have died. We must repent *and* look to Jesus on the cross for the forgiveness of our sins and for the strength to make better choices the next time.

NEXT STOP: Churchill, Manitoba

Hello out there!

Arctic Bears

Nothing in all creation is hidden from God's sight. Everything is uncovered and laid bare before the eyes of him to whom we must give account. **Hebrews 4:13.**

I am very excited about visiting Churchill, Manitoba, for the next two days. Since we have to fly to this remote town, which does not have any roads connecting it to the rest of the province, we are going to stay an extra day and enjoy the amazing animals that call Churchill home.

Churchill, which is located on the Hudson Bay, is called the polar bear capital of the world because it is right in the migration route of the bears that come toward the shore in the summer months after the ice cap has melted. Occasionally a polar bear wanders into town and has to be tranquilized and placed into the "polar bear jail" until the Hudson Bay freezes in the fall and it can be released to continue its journey into the frozen wilderness.

I love the beginning of today's Bible verse—"Nothing in all creation is hidden from God's sight." That means you and I, but that also means the polar bears that God made during Creation. He formed them to withstand the freezing temperatures that they would endure in the Arctic. God did not leave out any detail when He created them. In fact, He made them with up to four inches of fat all over their bodies so they can keep warm in their chilly environment. God also made their fur oily so that it repels water.

If God put that much thought into making the polar bear and ensuring that it could survive in its environment, how much more time did He spend making Adam and Eve? We know that we are more precious to Him than anything in this world because we are made in His image. We are His!

God cares about every human being who has ever lived, but this verse also means that we can't hide any of our actions or decisions from God. You may or may not like that idea, but I would rather have a loving God see all that I do and be willing to help me along the way as I do my best to obey His commands than be left to the fate I will receive if I follow Satan and his destructive path.

NEXT STOP: Churchill, Manitoba

Canaries of the Sea

"Look! I am creating new heavens and a new earth,
and no one will even think about the old ones anymore. Isaiah 65:17, NLT.

One other animal that calls Churchill home is the beluga whale. If you have never seen a beluga whale, they are solid white, have a rounded head, and their faces look like a dolphin whose nose has been pushed in and is flat against its head.

Beluga whales are the only whale that can turn its head and watch you, and because of their facial features, they often look as if they are smiling at you. Their nickname is sea canary, because they are the most vocal of all whales, making high-pitched chirping sounds and whistles and clicking noises as they communicate with one another.

Approximately 3,000 beluga whales live near Churchill in the Hudson Bay each summer. Tourists can enjoy whale watching tours, while some even swim with the belugas. Wearing wet suits complete with gloves, boots, hood, and mask and snorkel, swimmers prepare for the icy waters of the bay. Even though it is summer, the warmest the water temperature gets is about 48 degrees Fahrenheit. But those who go snorkeling say it is well worth jumping into the cold water with these amazing creatures.

You may never swim with beluga whales or dolphins, go on a safari in Africa to see lions and elephants in their natural habitat, or search for exotic birds in the Amazon rain forest here on earth. When we get to heaven, though, we will be able to interact with all the animals we only dreamed of seeing and playing with on this earth.

What animal do you want to see when you get to heaven? Ask each member of your family what animal they want to see and why. It's fun to dream about heaven. And the more you talk about it, the more you are reminded that this world is not our home. God has given us wonderful things on this earth, but nothing compares to the glories of heaven!

NEXT STOP: Iqaluit, Nunavut

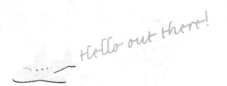
Hello out there!

September 5

What Does Your Name Mean?

Joseph, a Levite from Cyprus, whom the apostles called Barnabas (which means "son of encouragement"), sold a field he owned and brought the money and put it at the apostles' feet. **Acts 4:36, 37.**

Today we are visiting Iqaluit, the capital city of the territory of Nunavut, which is the largest Canadian territory in terms of land size but the least populated. Approximately 32,000 people call Nunavut home, with about 6,700 living in Iqaluit. The majority of the territory is in the Arctic Circle, which is why there aren't many people living in the region.

Because of the sparse population, there are no roads linking one town to another town in the territory. The only roads are within towns, and the only paved road is in Iqaluit. All travel between towns is done by boat or plane.

Iqaluit also has the only hospital in the territory. Most towns have a community health center for basic medical needs, but if an emergency arises and they need to go to the hospital, they have to fly to Iqaluit for treatment.

The city is located on Frobisher Bay, and its name means "place of many fish" in the native Inuit language, which obviously indicates that the bay is a good location for fishing.

In certain cultures names are chosen for their meanings. This was often the case in Bible times. After Jacob dreamed of a ladder ascending to heaven, he named the place Bethel, which means "house of God." When Gabriel came to Mary, he told her she would name her baby Jesus, which means "Savior."

In Acts 4:36 we read about a man named Joseph, "whom the apostles nicknamed Barnabas" (NLT). His new name meant "Son of Encouragement" (NLT). That's a pretty cool nickname! People must have loved being around Barnabas because he was always encouraging others, believing in them, and pointing them to Christ.

What does your name mean? If you don't know the origin, you can have your parents look it up. Then I want you to think about what you *want* your name to mean. What do you want your parents, friends, and teachers to think about you when they hear your name? Are you a son or daughter of encouragement and sunshine, or are you a son or daughter of sadness and gloom?

NEXT STOP: Iqaluit, Nunavut

Bad Habits

Besides, they get into the habit of being idle and going about from house to house. And not only do they become idlers, but also who talk nonsense and busybodies, saying things they ought not to. **I Timothy 5:13.**

We are spending another day in Iqaluit, but we aren't looking at the animals in the area or at the rugged landscape. Today we're here to observe some of the litter found in this community—cigarette butts.

More than half of the people who live in Nunavut smoke! Based on a survey in 2010, the total number of smokers in the territory was 61 percent. That's a lot! Especially when compared to the national average of smokers in Canada, which is 21 percent. In the United States 19 percent of adults 18 years of age or older are smokers, according to 2011 statistics.

Would you consider smoking a bad habit? A habit is something you do on a regular basis that is hard to give up. I think smoking qualifies as a habit that is hard to break, especially when approximately 69 percent of smokers say they wish they could quit completely but can't seem to give up their cigarettes. Sadly, tobacco use is projected to cause more than 8 million deaths each year by 2030.

What are some other bad habits that people struggle with? What bad habit do you struggle with and would like to break?

In 1 Timothy 5:13 Paul wrote to Timothy and warned him of a bad habit that a number of the young widows were getting into. These women whose husbands had died were getting into the bad habit of being idle, and instead of working or helping with the activities of the church, they spent their day going from house to house visiting. And they weren't visiting and giving Bible studies. They were visiting so that they could gossip and talk about others in the church and the community.

Have you ever thought about gossiping as a bad habit? We are often quick to tell juicy news to our best friend, such as "Did you hear that Michelle's parents are getting a divorce?" or "I heard our teacher was fired because he is such a bad teacher" or "Someone told me that Jason can't read because he's dumb."

Don't spread stories or rumors about others. And don't share other people's news. If Michelle wants to tell kids in her class that her parents are getting a divorce, that is her choice. It isn't your job to share for her. Don't fall into this bad habit, because once you start, it, like other bad habits, is hard to break.

NEXT STOP: Baker Lake, Nunavut

September 7

Hello out there!

All Tongues

And this gospel of the kingdom will be preached in the whole world as a testimony to all nations, and then the end will come. **Matthew 24:14.**

Baker Lake, Nunavut, is a hamlet, or small settlement, that is the only inland community in the Canadian Arctic. In the Inuktitut language, the name of this hamlet means "big lake joined by a river at both ends."

The Inuktitut language is spoken by the Inuit people, and is supposedly one of the most difficult languages to learn. The Inuit people, sometimes called Eskimos by Americans, are an ethnic group who live in the arctic regions of Greenland, Russia, Canada, and the United States. In addition to speaking Inuktitut, many residents also speak English, French, Danish, and Russian, or various combinations of those languages.

So what would you do if you were called to be a missionary to the Inuit people living in Nunavut? God clearly calls us to preach the gospel to the whole world. But how can we do that if we don't speak the language? How are we possibly going to tell the world about Jesus' return if we can't speak their languages?

When we look at a problem from a human perspective, it seems impossible. There is no way *I* could learn Inuktitut! But through God all things are possible. If He really wanted me to be a missionary to the Inuit people, He would help me learn the language. He would send me a native who spoke English and would be willing to help me learn how to communicate with the native speakers. Or maybe He would send someone who was already a Christian who would be willing to translate for me from English into Inuktitut so that I could share God with the people in the area. Or maybe God would miraculously give me the gift of tongues so that I could immediately speak their language and understand what they were saying.

The point is that if God wants you to do something, He will provide a way. He will not leave you stranded if He has called you to speak, sing, teach, or serve others. When God impresses you to do something, don't run away from the challenge. No matter how impossible or hard it may seem to you, God has a plan to help you!

NEXT STOP: Pond Inlet, Nunavut

Wasted or Worth It?

Then Mary took about a pint of pure nard, an expensive perfume; she poured it on Jesus' feet and wiped his feet with her hair. And the house was filled with the fragrance of the perfume. John 12:3.

Today we are visiting the hamlet of Pond Inlet on the Baffin Bay, but we need to pack our own lunch because I'm not sure we can afford to purchase groceries in the little settlement. Four liters of milk, which is about one gallon in the United States, costs about $13! Compare that to the cost of milk in the majority of Canada and the United States, which ranges from $3.50 to $8, depending on whether you buy whole milk, organic milk, soy milk, or almond milk.

Of course, milk is not the only expensive item in the grocery store here. Why the high prices? Remember, there are no roads for trucks to bring in supplies. Everything has to be shipped in by boat or plane, which is much more expensive. For families who can afford it, some will order their dry food products (such as beans, flour, cornmeal, rice, pasta, etc.) for a whole year and then wait for a large cargo ship to arrive once the ice breaks apart in the summer. When the sealift arrives, the families fill their cabinets with the goods. I guess you would be pretty careful how much you ate, since whatever was in the cabinets had to last an entire year!

Food may cost a lot more in Nunavut, but is it too expensive seeing that it is a necessity and the people can't live without it? That's a tough question, isn't it?

Let's now turn to John 12 and the story of Mary anointing Jesus' feet in Bethany. Judas felt that she had spent way too much money on the perfume she poured over Jesus' feet, saying that it was worth a year's wages and that the money should have been given to the poor. The funny thing is that he didn't care about the poor; he just wanted more money in his own pockets. But Jesus put Judas in his place and thanked Mary for honoring Him before His death.

In fact, in Mark 14:9 Jesus said, "Truly I tell you, wherever the gospel is preached throughout the world, what she has done will also be told, in memory of her."

People may criticize you for your actions or how you serve God, but even Mary was criticized, and yet Jesus thanked her. If you are doing what Jesus asks you to do, it doesn't matter what others say. You are on the right track!

NEXT STOP: Cape Dorset, Nunavut

Harvesttime

All Scripture is inspired by God and is useful to teach us what is true and to make us realize what is wrong in our lives. It corrects us when we are wrong and teaches us to do what is right. God uses it to prepare and equip his people to do every good work. **2 Timothy 3:16, 17, NLT.**

Cape Dorset, Nunavut, is known as the capital of Inuit art and has been a center for drawing, printmaking, and carving since the 1950s. As you can imagine, each type of art form requires the use of a unique set of tools and skills.

Tools help us get a job done faster. Just look around the next time you are in a store that sells tools. Whether your mom or dad needs to fix the car or something in the house, there are all kinds of tools that can help make the job easier.

An ulu is a special knife used by Inuit women for a wide variety of jobs. The ulu features a half circle blade with a handle at the top. If you were to put the blade on a cutting board and hold the handle at the top, you could rock it back and forth on the curved blade. An ulu is used to skin and clean animals that have been killed for food. It is also used to cut food.

Although this next tool is not used in Nunavut because they don't plant grain crops that need harvesting, it is an older tool that was used before modern farm machinery was invented. A sickle was used in Bible times to harvest grain crops. The sickle featured a short handle and a curved blade in the shape of a C.

Would an Inuit woman try to use a sickle to clean the fish her husband brought home after a day of fishing on the bay? Would a carpenter use a saw to pound in a nail? Would a mechanic use a drill to change the oil? No! Each of these people needs the right tool for the job. With the right tool, the job is easy.

The same can be said about our lives. What is the right "tool" we need to guide us through life? You're right: the Bible. God's Word is given to us by God as Paul says in 2 Timothy 3:16, 17. And it is useful for a lot of things. It is the right "tool" for a bunch of jobs. We can use the Bible for teaching people about God, correcting people who are headed in the wrong direction, and training people who want to follow Christ; most important, it will continually reveal to us what parts of our character could use some improvement. The Bible is our guide. Make sure you have the right "tools" in your tool belt so that you can be successful in all that you do.

NEXT STOP: Yellowknife, Northwest Territories

In Need of a BIG Fire

> Because it was cold, the household servants and the guards
> had made a charcoal fire. They stood around it, warming themselves,
> and Peter stood with them, warming himself. **John 18:18, NLT.**

Welcome to Yellowknife, the capital of the Northwest Territories. We are still in the Far North, where the cold wind blows and snow is on the ground from October to April. In fact, Yellowknife is the coldest city in Canada with average low temperatures ranging from minus 9.9 degrees Fahrenheit to minus 23.6 degrees Fahrenheit from December through March.

The lowest temperature ever recorded in the city was minus 60 degrees Fahrenheit on January 31, 1947. Those temperatures will turn you into a block of ice if you step outside!

In this extremely cold climate, wood burning stoves keep houses toasty warm. These units are not just fireplaces that heat up the family room. No, most wood-burning stoves that are installed in the Far North are hooked into the house's overall ventilation system. That way, warm air from the fire blows throughout the house and provides much needed warmth to each room. Throw a couple of logs on the fire before bedtime, and everyone stays nice and warm until the next morning.

A fire is a very welcome sight when you are cold. If you have ever been camping in late fall or winter, you know what I mean. So it isn't hard to understand why Peter ventured into the courtyard and warmed himself by the fire the night Jesus was arrested. He was not only cold, but also wanted to see what was happening to his Friend and Master. Obviously, the chill that night wasn't nearly as cold as the temperatures in Yellowknife, but it was still cold, and the fire was a welcome relief.

If Peter thought he felt cold when he entered the courtyard, I think he felt even colder when he denied Jesus three times and heard the rooster crow and met Jesus' eyes. I can only imagine how much he shivered as he realized he had done the very thing he promised Jesus he would not do—deny Him.

I'm so glad Peter's story doesn't end there. Cold swept over him when he denied his Lord, but Jesus' love warmed him back up and turned him into a great preacher and teacher in the early church.

NEXT STOP: Inuvik, Northwest Territories

September 11

Hello out there!

Thin Ice

On the first day of the week we came together to break bread.
Paul spoke to the people and, because he intended to leave the next day,
kept on talking until midnight. **Acts 20:7.**

With temperatures well below freezing on a daily basis, the rivers and lakes freeze pretty quickly. But the people of the Northwest Territories don't get excited just because they can ice skate on the frozen lakes; they get excited because they can *drive* on the ice. Towns that are only accessible by boat or plane during the summer are suddenly easy to get to if you are brave enough to drive a 4,000-pound car across a sheet of ice that is a little more than three feet thick.

From late December to late April cars, trucks, snowmobiles, and dogsleds can travel between Inuvik and Tuktoyaktuk on a frozen road that crosses the Mackenzie River delta and tundra before reaching Kugmallit Bay.

Ice roads are also constructed and maintained for hauling heavy equipment. Instead of transporting things by barge in the summer, it is easier to transport construction equipment and other large items over the ice roads so that the machinery is ready to be used once the ice melts. The world's longest ice road begins at Tibbitt Lake, about 43 miles east of Yellowknife, and extends 360 miles to Contwoyto Lake on the western edge of Nunavut.

Obviously, the depth of the ice is closely monitored because a crack would spell disaster for the drivers, equipment, and cargo. No one wants to be caught driving on thin ice!

Likewise, people should make sure they are not standing on thin ice when it comes to the Bible. God asks us to follow His Word, but we have to study it for ourselves to know what it says and to make sure we are following the Bible and not human ideas. Take a look at today's text. Some people use this verse to try and prove that we should go to church on Sunday, since Paul and a group of people had a meeting on the first day of the week. However, this idea is like standing on thin ice. Instead of looking at all the verses that talk about the seventh day being the Sabbath, including the fourth commandment in Exodus 20:8-11, people take one verse and make big assumptions about God's laws.

People who stand on one verse of the Bible are standing on thin ice. Make sure you have a solid footing and are standing on the whole Word of God!

NEXT STOP: Inuvik, Northwest Territories

Obeying God or Humans

Love the Lord your God and keep his requirements, his decrees, his laws and his commands always. **Deuteronomy 11:1.**

Today we are visiting the Igloo church. The actual name of it is Our Lady of Victory, but it looks like an igloo, so it got the nickname Igloo church. The church was designed by a Catholic missionary and built by volunteers. The construction process took two years to complete, partly because wood and materials had to be transported approximately 870 miles in to the building site. The church holds services on a weekly basis and is open to visitors in the summer months. It is the most photographed building in town.

The Our Lady of Victory (or Igloo) church is part of the worldwide Catholic Church, which relates to yesterday's reading about standing on the truth of the Bible and the whole Word of God instead of what human beings interpret the Bible to say or mean. You see, the Catholic Church admits to having changed the day of worship from Saturday to Sunday. James Cardinal Gibbons of the Catholic Church wrote the following in a letter: "Is Saturday the seventh day according to the Bible and the Ten Commandments? I answer yes. Is Sunday the first day of the week and did the church change the seventh day—Saturday—for Sunday, the first day? I answer *yes.* Did Christ change the day? I answer *no!*" He also wrote this in *The Catholic Mirror:* "The Catholic Church, . . . by virtue of her divine mission, changed the day from Saturday to Sunday."

I was surprised when I read these statements. Gibbons didn't even attempt to use Bible verses (such as the one from yesterday or the one that talks about Jesus being raised to life on the first day of the week) to try to prove his point for worship on Sunday. He just said the Catholic Church chose to change it. Sadly, many Catholics and Christians who observe Sunday as holy are blindly following the opinion of human beings who think they have the authority to change the sacredness of the Sabbath and thus disregard God's law.

Do you see why you can't just take somebody's word for why we believe what we believe? You have to study for yourself, or Satan can trick you into believing a lie because you won't know it's a lie. God calls us to obey His commands and laws so that we'll be safe from Satan's attacks. By studying God's Word every day, He will protect us and keep us on the right path.

NEXT STOP: Inuvik, Northwest Territories

September 13

Hello out there!

Hunting Fun

"I am an old man now," Isaac said, "and I don't know when I may die. Take your bow and a quiver full of arrows, and go out into the open country to hunt some wild game for me. Prepare my favorite dish, and bring it here for me to eat. Then I will pronounce the blessing that belongs to you, my firstborn son, before I die." **Genesis 27:2-4, NLT.**

On our final day in Inuvik we're going to observe an ancient ritual. The blanket toss is probably a cousin to the trampoline, but unlike a trampoline that you can bounce on for hours by yourself, the blanket toss requires the gathering of a whole community. The blanket toss is a game that is often enjoyed at Inuit celebrations, but it began as a means to assist the hunters in the village find their prey.

This hunting ritual required someone with good eyesight to be the one tossed up into the air. Strong men would surround and hold the blanket, which was made of walrus or seal hide. They would then toss the person in the middle of the blanket up in the air. Some reports say that the person in the middle could reach heights of up to 20 feet! The key is to not bend your knees if you are the one flying; otherwise, when you land, you could break your legs. In addition to keeping their legs straight so as not to break them, the person's job was to look for game across the land or in the water or on the ice flows. Working as a team, the Inuit would use this fun hunting technique to locate game and spend time bonding as a community.

Jacob and Esau could have worked as a team, but they were definitely on opposite sides. Instead of hunting together, they worked against each other. Of course, Esau didn't have a clue as to his mother's schemes. So when Isaac asked him to go hunting and prepare his favorite meal before receiving his blessing, Esau did as he was told. But Rebekah quickly put her plan into action to steal the birthright away from Esau and give it to Jacob. As you know, the lying and deception that took place between husband and wife and the two brothers split this family and caused years of pain and suffering.

God designed families to be a team and a safe place to live and grow, but we often turn our families into war zones with our angry words and disrespectful actions. You can't change everyone in your family, but you can change yourself. Make sure you are being respectful and treating your parents and sibling(s) as you would want to be treated.

NEXT STOP: Ekati Diamond Mine, Northwest Territories

September 14

Lying to God

But a man named Ananias, with his wife Sapphira, sold a piece of property, and kept back some of the price for himself, with his wife's full knowledge, and bringing a portion of it, he laid it at the apostles' feet. **Acts 5:1, 2, NASB.**

The Ekati Diamond Mine opened in 1998, and over the next 11 years it produced 40 million carats of diamonds. That is a total of 17,637 pounds of diamonds! It is difficult to put a price tag on this amount of diamonds because diamonds are priced based on their carat, or weight. Depending on quality, a one-carat diamond can be worth between $850 and $10,000. Larger diamonds are rarer, so a three-carat diamond could be worth *nine times* as much as a one-carat diamond of equal quality. So, as you can see, 40 million carats is worth a fortune!

What would you do if you had $1 million worth of diamonds? Take a minute to dream about what you would do with that much money . . .

OK, now snap back to reality. What kind of plans did you make? Did your plans involve helping your parents, giving money to friends, assisting an organization such as ADRA take care of people around the world? Or did your plans center on things you wanted to buy?

I want to look at a story in the New Testament about a husband and wife who sold a piece of property and gave some of the money to the church. Sounds good, right? It would have been good, but Ananias kept part of the money while saying he had brought all of the money to the Lord. He lied about what he was giving, and he fell over dead in front of Peter. About three hours later Sapphira, Ananias' wife, came to Peter. She too lied when Peter asked her if the money Ananias had donated was the total sale price of the land. And she too fell over dead!

Jump back to imaging that you own $1 million worth of diamonds. Would you die if you didn't give all of that money to the church? No! But what about if you went to church and told your pastor that you wanted to give all of the money from the diamonds to the church but then only gave part of it? You would probably not fall over dead for lying, but lying is a sin, and the wages of sin is death (see Romans 6:23). Fortunately, if we ask Jesus into our lives, He covers everything with His blood! Don't be foolish like Ananias and Sapphira and think you can trick the Holy Spirit. Be honest, and reap the rewards of a good relationship with God.

NEXT STOP: Last Mountain Lake, Saskatchewan

Hello out there!

Good and Bad Instincts

No one who is born of God will continue to sin, because God's seed remains in them; they cannot go on sinning, because they have been born of God. **I John 3:9.**

We are finally leaving the Arctic Circle and heading toward Saskatchewan. Try to say Saskatchewan 10 times fast, and your tongue will end up in a knot! Today we are visiting the Last Mountain Lake, the location of the oldest bird sanctuary in North America. The sanctuary was established in 1887, and hundreds of thousands of birds stop there as they migrate north in the summer and south in the winter.

Throughout the years more than 280 species of birds have been spotted in the wildlife area, including a handful of endangered birds, such as the peregrine falcon, the burrowing owl, the piping plover, and the whooping crane. During the fall, as the birds prepare to fly south for the winter, visitors to the wildlife area can see up to 50,000 sandhill cranes, 450,000 geese, and hundreds of thousands of ducks! That's a lot of birds. I'm sure the noise is deafening!

What makes all those birds stop at the wildlife area year after year? What makes them fly north in the summer and south in the winter? Instinct! God designed them with built-in instincts that tell them how to act.

For us as humans, our instinct is to sin. We are born into a sinful world to sinful parents. Our built-in instinct is to mess up, but we can change our instinct to follow Jesus. When we are born again and become one of Jesus' disciples, we will start thinking and acting like Jesus. At first it will be hard to train our brains to think like Jesus instead of thinking like the world, but over time it gets easier. Then when temptations come, like cheating on a spelling test, our instinct will help us to "fly" away from that which is wrong.

NEXT STOP: Little Manitou Lake, Saskatchewan

Let's Go Floating—I Mean Swimming!

Salt is good for seasoning. But if it loses its flavor,
how do you make it salty again? You must have the qualities of salt
among yourselves and live in peace with each other. **Mark 9:50, NLT.**

We are visiting another lake today—Little Manitou Lake. It isn't a very big lake, only 14 miles long and about one mile wide, but it has something else that makes it unique. If you jump into this lake, you are going to float instead of sink. In fact, you can sit and read a book without a pool float or other raft. And you don't have to tread water. Just sit down in the water, and you will rise to the top and be able to sit there as if you were sitting in a chair.

I'm sure you're thinking, *What's the catch?* The secret is in the amount of salt in the water. The lake is five times saltier than the ocean, which makes you more buoyant than the water, causing you to float and not sink in the dense water.

In the early 1900s the lake was a favorite resort during the summer months for people who lived on the prairies. Many people believed that the lake had healing properties, and salt does help your body. A salt bath can relax stiff muscles and help prevent the growth of certain bacteria. Thus, people traveled to visit the lake and immerse themselves in the "healing" waters, which they thought were magical.

So, what if the lake lost all of its saltiness and turned into a regular freshwater lake? Would it be special? Would people want to visit it? I doubt that as many people would come.

Jesus compared true Christians to salt. As salt is added to food to bring out its flavor or preserve it, so we, as followers of Christ, are called to touch other people's lives and help them become better people. By letting Jesus' love shine through us, we will help lead people to Christ. But in Matthew 5:13 Jesus says that salt that is no longer salty is not good for anything. So similarly, Christians who do not share Christ with others are missing their purpose. Apart from Christ we are nothing, but as sons or daughters of Christ, we are everything!

So what if you have lost your saltiness? What if you aren't following Jesus as you should be? Can you become salty again? Yes, you can. Take the time right now to ask Jesus to help you be salt in this tasteless world.

NEXT STOP: Moose Jaw, Saskatchewan

September 17

Hello out there!

Underground Escape

That very night Belshazzar, the Babylonian king, was killed. And Darius the Mede took over the kingdom at the age of sixty-two. **Daniel 5:30, 31, NLT.**

Moose Jaw is located in southern Saskatchewan and is an important stop for the Canadian Pacific Railway. In the late 1800s and early 1900s the town built a maze of tunnels underneath the shops on the street to connect them and avoid having to walk outside in the cold of winter. Workers could move from one building to another to keep the furnaces going in the winter without having to freeze outside.

However, when Canada prohibited the sale and purchase of alcohol, the tunnels became a hiding place for bootleggers, people who ignored the laws and still produced and sold alcohol. It has also been alleged that gangsters used the tunnels as a hideout.

Tunnels are usually built with a specific purpose in mind. Most people don't just dig a tunnel because they like to dig and have a bunch of free time on their hands. For Moose Jaw, the tunnels were initially used to make it easier to work. Tunnels that go through mountains are created to make it easier for a driver to get from one side of the mountain to the other.

The Persian army used an underground passage, basically a tunnel, to invade Babylon and defeat Belshazzar. Although this tunnel was not made by humans, it still served as a passageway under the city walls, allowing the whole army to march directly into the city without any resistance. The Persian army dug a canal and diverted the Euphrates River so that it flowed away from the city. Once the water level dropped, the army marched along the riverbed, which ran under the exterior city wall. Once inside the first city wall, they discovered that the city gate to the interior wall was left wide open because Belshazzar and all his officials were partying. Thus, they entered and killed Belshazzar and conquered the city, as God had predicted.

NEXT STOP: Calgary, Alberta

September 18

Watch Out Below!

So they came out and went into the pigs, and the whole herd rushed down the steep bank into the lake and died in the water. **Matthew 8:32.**

The Calgary Stampede is a 10-day event that features good old Western entertainment and hospitality each July. More than 1 million people attend the stampede each year to watch roping contests, bull riding, horse races, chuck wagon races, and fireworks. In addition to all the fun at Stampede Park, free pancake breakfasts are offered at different locations throughout the city. It is estimated that 200,000 pancakes are served during the event!

The Calgary Stampede was first held in 1912 and is one of the largest rodeos in the world today. In fact, it claims to be the Greatest Outdoor Show on Earth. The rodeo events and chuck wagon races are even broadcast on TV across Canada. It has turned into a huge event for the city.

Although it is called the Calgary Stampede, there are no stampeding animals. An actual stampede is extremely scary. When animals suddenly panic or are spooked over a loud noise, they often run as a mass group in whatever direction they are facing. Animals don't think about where they are going. They just run as fast as they can to get away from whatever startled them. As you can imagine, stampedes are a serious matter. If you are standing in the way of these crazed animals, you will be trampled. They don't care what is in front of them. They are just running for their lives.

Do you remember a stampede that took place in the Bible? Here's a hint: It was not a stampede of cattle or horses; it was a stampede of pigs! Jesus was near Gadarenes when two demon-possessed men came out of some caves in the area and said, "What do you want with us, Son of God?" (Matthew 8:29). The demons then begged Jesus, "If you drive us out, send us into the herd of pigs" (verse 31). So Jesus sent the demons into the pigs, and the whole herd rushed over a cliff into the water and drowned.

Jesus is omnipotent, meaning He has all power over nature and Satan. Nothing is beyond His control.

NEXT STOP: Calgary, Alberta

Hello out there!

Top Speed

My righteousness draws near speedily, my salvation is on the way,
and my arm will bring justice to the nations. **Isaiah 51:5.**

Millions of people visit the Calgary Stampede each summer, and many of them also visit Canada Olympic Park, where the Winter Olympic Games were held in 1988. But only a handful of brave people take a trip down the bobsled track in the winter. Yes, you can actually ride down the Olympic bobsled track, but this outing is not for the weak!

The track currently serves as a practice arena for Olympic hopefuls, and competitions are also held at the track. After paying for your ticket on this high-speed ride, you are assigned a professional driver and brake person. Then you hop into the bobsled and begin your terrifying— I mean, amazing— ride down the track. You reach speeds of up to 74 miles per hour as you hurtle around corners and blast down straightaways. Because of the speed, you experience 4.5 to 5 g forces, which is the gravitational pull you feel on your body as you accelerate and hurtle down the track. These g forces are higher than what astronauts feel!

For those who do not like speed, this ride would be miserable. For those who like riding on roller coasts, this type of rush would be exhilarating.

Have you ever thought about God as acting fast? As we sit here waiting for His return, it seems that things are moving along slowly, not quickly. But remember, our human perspective is so different from God's. What seems to us to take a long time is but a blink of an eye to God.

Today's text talks about God's righteousness drawing near "speedily." The text also says that His "salvation is on the way" and He "will bring justice to the nations" (Isaiah 51:5). Although to us it may appear to be taking a long time, Jesus is coming again, and He will return in His perfect timing.

NEXT STOP: Pincher Creek, Alberta

A Big Change

Two other men, both criminals,
were also led out with him to be executed. **Luke 23:32.**

On January 27, 1962, a Chinook wind blew through Pincher Creek, Alberta, and caused a 40-degree change in temperature! People's thermometers went from minus 2 degrees Fahrenheit to 38 degrees Fahrenheit in one hour! Obviously it was still cold, but talk about a drastic change.

A Chinook wind is a warm wind that blows inland from the ocean. In this case it blew from the Pacific Ocean over the Rocky Mountains and down into the plains of Alberta. Named after the Chinook people who lived in the Pacific Northwest, where this type of wind is most common, a strong Chinook wind can actually melt one foot of snow in a single day.

A lot of changes take place over a period of time. If you're building a house, change will occur over a series of weeks and months. If you paint your bedroom, the change will happen within a day or two. If you cut your hair and get a new style, the transformation will happen within an hour. In the case of a Chinook wind, change comes quickly.

In the case of the two thieves on the cross, a change occurred for one of them in a matter of seconds when he acknowledged Jesus as Savior and King. His buddy taunted Jesus and said, "Aren't you the Messiah? Save yourself and us!" (Luke 23:39). But the other thief shot back, "'We are punished justly, for we are getting what our deeds deserve. But this man has done nothing wrong.' Then he said, 'Jesus, remember me when you come into your kingdom'" (verses 41, 42).

The thief made a change for the better. Within moments he went from being a lost sinner to being an heir of the kingdom. Right then and there, as they hung on their crosses, Jesus promised him a place in heaven.

It only takes a moment to change your life and live for Jesus. But just as the thieves on the crosses next to Jesus had to make a choice, you do too. Are you going to live for Jesus or live for yourself?

NEXT STOP: Evansburg, Alberta

September 21

Grumble, Grumble

Do everything without grumbling or arguing, so that you may become blameless and pure, "children of God without fault in a warped and crooked generation." Then you will shine among them like stars in the sky as you hold firmly to the word of life. **Philippians 2:14-16.**

I don't know about you, but if I were to ever win a title, I would want to be named the best mom or the person with the best smile or the most positive attitude. I certainly wouldn't want the title "Town Grouch." How horrible!

The event started after John Lauer, a sign artist, painted a welcome sign for the town of Evansburg, Alberta, that included the following information: "603 people, 29 dogs, 41 cats, and 1 grouch." After painting the number of people and dogs and cats, John had extra room, so he added the information about the grouch. Of course, it brought a lot of attention to the town, so it stuck.

Since 1979 the town has elected a new Town Grouch each year. In order to become the Town Grouch, you have to be very annoying. You have to criticize the town and complain and grumble about everything. You also have to harass your neighbors, family, and friends until they give you money, because the person who raises the most money by bothering people wins the title. And that's the only good thing about this contest—the money raised benefits a local festival. Otherwise, I don't see any good in going about complaining about life.

Paul seems to agree with me about complaining. In Philippians 2:14 he reminds the church members in Philippi to do everything without complaining or arguing. As God's children we are representing Him to the world around us.

For example, let's say your Sabbath school class goes to a nursing home to sing on a Sabbath afternoon. While you are there, you begin grumbling to a friend of yours that you wish you didn't have to come to this "smelly place full of old people." Then you turn to see one of the nurses standing behind you next to a little old woman sitting in a wheelchair. It is clear that they heard you. Then five minutes later you are singing about how God loves everyone. Don't you think the nurse and woman will be confused? First you complain about God's children, and then you sing sweet songs about Jesus' love. Your words don't match up!

It's tempting to complain, but you are representing God, and He doesn't grumble.

NEXT STOP: Banff National Park, Alberta

The Emerald Lake

Wealth is worthless in the day of wrath,
but righteousness delivers from death. **Proverbs 11:4.**

Banff National Park is stunning throughout the year, but the soaring mountains take on a majestic quality in the winter under their blanket of snow. If you've never lived in a place that gets snow, you might need to see a picture to fully appreciate how beautiful the evergreen trees and streams and mountains are all covered in white.

Lake Louise is a glacial lake located in Banff National Park. The lake was named after Princess Louise Caroline Alberta, the fourth daughter of Queen Victoria of the United Kingdom. The lake is an amazing shade of emerald; it gets its color from rock flour carried to the lake by the water that melts from the glaciers surrounding the lake. In the winter the lake is frozen and skaters can be seen twirling around on the ice. In the summer it is the backdrop for stunning pictures as hikers stop along the trails around the lake to rest and enjoy the natural beauty of the lake.

Near the edge of the lake is the Château Lake Louise. The hotel resembles a castle, and the inside is even fancier than the outside. One Christmas my husband and I flew to Alberta to visit his family, so we drove to Lake Louise. It was breathtaking! As we entered the lobby of the château, I'm sure my mouth dropped open. Huge floor-to-ceiling windows that must have been 20 feet high overlooked the lake. Plush carpet covered the floor, chandeliers hung from the ceiling, and expensive, heavy drapes framed the windows.

We walked around and enjoyed the view before returning to our "affordable" hotel. At $649 per night, the château was way out of our price range!

I will admit it—sometimes it's fun to dream about being rich and being able to stay in places like the Château Lake Louise. But I don't let myself daydream too much about riches and wealth, because if I did I would never be content with what God has given me. And He has given me plenty to be thankful for. For one thing, I'm thankful I got to see Lake Louise!

King Solomon knew exactly what kind of lifestyle riches could bring. He had it all. But he recognized that "in the day of wrath" when Jesus judges the wicked and destroys the earth once and for all, money will be of no value. But righteousness—a relationship with Jesus—will deliver us from death. It's fun to daydream, but don't get stuck living in a fairytale world.

NEXT STOP: Athabasca Glacier, Alberta

273

Hello out there!

Don't Step on the Snow

When my spirit grows faint within me, it is you who watch over my way.
In the path where I walk people have hidden a snare for me. **Psalm 142:3.**

Today is our last day in Alberta; tomorrow we will be entering Montana. But before we leave Alberta, we are visiting the Athabasca Glacier, which is the most visited glacier in North America. The reason for its popularity is that the edge of the glacier is close to the Icefields Parkway, a highway that connects Banff with the city of Jasper.

In addition to the Athabasca Glacier, seven other glaciers make up the Columbia Icefield, which is more than six times larger than the island of Manhattan in New York. Tourists wanting to see the glaciers up close and personal can book a tour and ride out onto the glaciers in snow buses with special tires.

However, because the glacier is so close to the road, many people park their cars and just walk out onto the glacier. Although people do this, they are actually urged not to, because of hidden crevasses. These crevasses can be as deep as 147 feet and as wide as 65 feet. The challenge is that snow often covers the crevasses so that you are not aware of them. Unsuspecting tourists have disappeared with one wrong step and died because of their injuries.

Instead, people are recommended to go with a professional guide who knows the glacier and has the proper equipment to make sure everyone in his or her group is safe. The guide uses a long stick to punch through the top layer of snow and ice to make sure it is solid below and isn't a crevasse.

In this life Satan sets hidden traps for us. He tries to trap us by convincing us to watch TV shows in which most of the show is good but part of it is bad. Or he traps us when we are in Sabbath school and someone says something mean about a kid at school, and everyone jumps in and starts talking about how weird he is. We can be doing something good and still fall into a hidden trap. But if Jesus is our guide, we can steer clear of these traps. Jesus knows the best path for our lives, but we have to be willing to follow it. If we do, we will avoid the hidden dangers that surround us.

NEXT STOP: Glacier National Park, Montana

The Wonder of It All

He makes springs pour water into the ravines; it flows between the mountains. **Psalm 104:10.** He makes grass grow for the cattle, and plants for people to cultivate. **Verse 14.** The high mountains belong to the wild goats. . . . He made the moon to mark the seasons, and the sun knows when to go down. **Verses 18,19.** How many are your works, Lord! In wisdom you made them all; the earth is full of your creatures. **Verse 24.**

I know I said we were leaving Canada and entering the United States again, but the national park we are visiting today in Montana actually connects to a national park in Alberta. Glacier National Park joins with Waterton Lakes National Park in Canada, forming the Waterton-Glacier International Peace Park.

Glacier National Park is the most visited location in Montana. The park runs along the state's northern border and is known as the "Crown of the Continent Ecosystem." The Rocky Mountains run through the park, which is home to hundreds of species of animals, more than 1,000 species of plants, and 131 named lakes and numerous unnamed smaller lakes. Mountain goats easily climb up the rocky cliffs that they call home. If you are lucky, you may also see a massive grizzly bear in the park, although I would hope to see one from the safety of my car while driving around and not while eating breakfast at my campsite!

When I read Psalm 104, I felt that King David could be describing Glacier National Park. He paints a picture of mountain streams and grassy fields, towering mountains and wild goats. He praises God and thanks Him for taking care of the earth and all the creatures He created, including us.

It's easy to get frustrated or discouraged when life seems to go all wrong. But when everything appears to be against us, it is important to focus on the good things God has given us. It might be something as simple as "I'm thankful that I am wearing my favorite shirt today" or "I'm thankful that the sun is shining" or "I'm thankful that I have a good friend at school," but whatever it is, focus on the positive things around you and not the negative. You can't escape this sinful world, but if you think about the good things God gives you, the crummy things won't seem so bad.

NEXT STOP: Little Belt Mountains, Montana

Hello out there!

The Crown Jewels

> The first row shall be carnelian, chrysolite and beryl; the second row shall be turquoise, lapis lazuli and emerald; the third row shall be jacinth, agate and amethyst; the fourth row shall be topaz, onyx and jasper. Mount them in gold filigree settings. There are to be twelve stones, one for each of the names of the sons of Israel, each engraved like a seal with the name of one of the twelve tribes. **Exodus 28:17-21.**

One of Montana's nicknames is the Treasure State because of the gold, silver, and sapphires that have been found in the Little Belt Mountains. In 1866 gold was discovered in Yogo Creek, and by 1878 the miners noticed some little "blue pebbles." Sixteen years later the miners figured out that the little "blue pebbles" were actually sapphires. Sapphires range in color from a brilliant cornflower blue to purple, and even yellow and green; Yogo sapphires are generally cornflower blue.

Several Yogo sapphires are on display at the Smithsonian's Natural History Museum in Washington, D.C., and Yogo sapphires even appear in the crown jewels of England. Yogo sapphires are some of the finest gems that have been found in the United States.

Gemstones are mentioned throughout the Bible, but one of the first references to them is in God's instructions concerning the breastplate that the high priest was to wear. Twelve precious stones were mounted on the breastplate, and on each stone was engraved the name of one of the 12 tribes of Israel. When Aaron went about his duties in the sanctuary, the breastplate was a constant reminder that he was bringing the children of Israel before the Lord at all times.

The breastplate and the precious stones also pointed forward to Jesus, our high priest, and His work in the heavenly sanctuary, where He is working on our behalf to judge the world and cleanse us of our sins when we ask for forgiveness. Just as Aaron carried on his chest the names of the tribes engraved in the gems, Jesus has the name of each repentant believer written on His heart. In Jesus' eyes we are more precious than any gem.

NEXT STOP: Fort Keogh, Montana

Gigantic Snowflake

For in him all things were created: things in heaven and on earth, visible and invisible, whether thrones or powers or rulers or authorities; all things have been created through him and for him. **Colossians 1:16.**

The first snow of the season sometimes covers the mountains of Montana in September, which seems strange to those of us who live in the Deep South. We don't even get snow in January!

If you live up north or have visited during a snowstorm, you know how pretty it is when little white snowflakes float down from the sky and cover the ground in a fluffy carpet of snow. I lived up north for a number of years, and I loved watching the variety of snowfalls. Some snowfalls produced little icy specks for snowflakes, while other snowfalls produced fat flakes that would stick to everything.

Well, in Fort Keogh, Montana, a rancher named Matt Coleman reported that on January 28, 1887, the snowflakes were "larger than milk pans." He claimed that one snowflake measured 15 inches wide and 8 inches thick! Of course, that was in the days before photography and the Internet, so no one can verify his statement.

Measure that with your ruler, and you'll see why most scientists and meteorologists believe that his testimony is impossible. The National Snow and Ice Data Center reports that if the conditions are just right, the largest snowflake that can form would be close to two inches across, with the average snowflake measuring approximately half an inch or less.

People can debate all they want to about the size of snowflakes or who found the largest specimen, but I know something that they may not know—God created snowflakes and designed their detailed patterns. Paul reminds us in today's text that God created *all* things. Everything was made to bring honor and glory to Him. Everything points to an all-knowing, all-powerful Creator who didn't miss anything when He made the universe and you and me!

NEXT STOP: Helena, Montana

Hello out there!

Just Perfect

Blessed are those whose ways are blameless,
who walk according to the law of the Lord. **Psalm 119:1.**

I would like to know who made these laws and what their reasoning was for such interesting rules. Listen to these: In Helena it is illegal to throw an item across a street, so that means you can't throw your ball from your yard to your neighbor's yard if they live across the road from you. It is also illegal for married women to go fishing alone on Sundays in Montana, and it is illegal for unmarried women to fish alone at all.

Here's another unique law in Montana: It is illegal to let a sheep ride in the cab of your truck if you don't have a chaperone, someone to go with you and watch after the sheep while you drive. I have to admit that I can slightly understand this one, because it doesn't seem as if it would be too safe driving with a sheep in the cab of a truck without someone else there to keep it away from the driver.

If you look up the word *law* in a thesaurus, you will find words such as *rule, regulation, principle, decree, order, statute,* and *precept.* In the book of Psalms David frequently talks about God's laws and how perfect they are. He praises God for His rules and His patience with us as we do our best to follow His commands.

Psalm 119 is the longest psalm in the Bible, but I would encourage you to read it and count all the times David references God's law. Take a look at one section, verses 10 through 16, and note the words I've italicized that refer to God's laws: "I have tried hard to find you—don't let me wander from your *commands.* I have hidden your word in my heart, that I might not sin against you. I praise you, O Lord; teach me your *decrees.* I have recited aloud all the *regulations* you have given us. I have rejoiced in your *laws* as much as in riches. I will study your *commandments* and reflect on your ways. I will delight in your *decrees* and not forget your word" (NLT).

David didn't take God's laws lightly or think they were silly or only for his grandparents. David realized he was nothing without God and His laws to govern his life.

NEXT STOP: Yellowstone National Park, Wyoming

278

No Guardrails

Act according to whatever they teach you and the decisions they give you. Do not turn aside from what they tell you. **Deuteronomy 17:11.**

Yellowstone National Park is the United States' first national park. Created in 1872, Wyoming wasn't even a state when the land was set aside as a park. Portions of the park are located in southern Montana and eastern Idaho, but the majority is in Wyoming.

The landscape of Yellowstone is very diverse and features canyons, waterfalls, lakes, and geysers throughout the park. In the northeast quadrant of the park is the Grand Canyon of Yellowstone. The Yellowstone River flows downstream and drops twice before entering the canyon. The Upper Yellowstone Falls is 109 feet tall, while the Lower Yellowstone Falls, which feeds into the canyon, is 308 feet tall, almost twice as tall as Niagara Falls, on the border of Ontario and New York.

There are multiple overlooks and trails where you can view the falls, but if you want to get up close, you can walk down a path that zigzags back and forth down the side of the mountain until you reach an observation deck at the top of the Lower Yellowstone Falls. You can hear the rushing water from the top of the trail, but the closer you get to the bottom, the more deafening the sound becomes.

As our family rounded the last bend on the trail, I noticed that there were no guardrails along the river to keep people away from the swift water. As a mom I couldn't help picturing some little kid running toward the river to explore and then slipping and falling into the raging water that plunges over the falls and drops 308 feet to the rocks below; what a horrific possibility. We stuck to the path and made our way to the observation deck, which had railings, and peered safely over the edge at the swirling whitewater.

Guardrails are meant to protect, but they aren't always there. We had to use our best judgment to decide whether it was safe to go down to the river's edge or whether we should stick to the path. You won't always have your parents there to warn you about what is good and what is bad. As you get older you will have to make decisions on your own—there won't always be "guardrails" up around you. Start making wise choices now so it will be easier in the future.

NEXT STOP: Old Faithful, Yellowstone National Park, Wyoming

279

Hello out there!

Old Faithful

The Lord has done great things for us, and we are filled with joy. **Psalm 126:3.**

We are spending a second day in Yellowstone National Park because there is so much to see. Yesterday we visited the northern section of the park with its tall evergreen trees, raging rivers, spectacular waterfalls, and deep canyons. Today we are traveling to the southwestern portion of the park, which is flatter and features open fields, mud pits, geysers, and hot springs that are the deepest turquoise and emerald colors you have ever seen.

Yellowstone National Park has approximately 10,000 active thermal features, including hot springs and mudpots, across its volcanic plain, which is the largest volcanic system in North America. Old Faithful is the most popular and consistent geyser in the park, erupting approximately every 90 minutes. When Old Faithful erupts, it shoots 3,700 to 8,400 gallons of boiling water into the air. Lasting anywhere from one and a half minutes to five minutes, the eruptions reach an average height of 145 feet, with the highest recorded eruption reaching 185 feet. Since its discovery more than 137,000 eruptions have been recorded.

The way a geyser works is that water is heated under the surface of the earth. As it boils it has to release the pressure that is building up. In the case of a boiling pot of water on your stove, the lid rattles, and steam puffs out the sides. In the case of a geyser, the boiling water and steam shoot through the small opening at the surface of the earth after enough pressure has built up.

If you compare humans to geysers, there are two types: good geysers and bad geysers. Good geysers have Jesus in their lives, and they can't help bubbling over with joy when they think about all Jesus has done for them and what He means to them. Good geysers may start singing in the middle of the day because they are thankful for Jesus' love and protection.

On the other hand, bad geysers bubble over in anger. They let things frustrate them, and as they boil inside, they get more and more angry, until they blow up and start yelling at people. You never know when they might explode next.

Which geyser are you? Which geyser do you want to be? Which geyser do people want to be around? Take time to pray and ask Jesus to help you bubble over for Him instead of bubbling over because you get angry.

NEXT STOP: Jackson, Wyoming

September 30

Ride 'em, Cowboys!

For the message of the cross is foolishness to those who are perishing, but to us who are being saved it is the power of God. **I Corinthians 1:18.**

Wyoming's unofficial nickname is the Cowboy State, and if you look at the state's license plate or the state quarter that was released in 2007, you'll see a cowboy riding a bucking bronco. According to some folks, the horse on the license plate actually has a name—Steamboat. The horse became famous in the rodeo ring, and only a handful of cowboys were able to stay on Steamboat's back as he threw himself wildly into the air trying to rid himself of the unwelcome rider.

If you hadn't guessed, rodeos are a big part of the community in Wyoming. In the Cowboy State rodeos are a way for the cowboys and cowgirls in the state to show off their skills riding, roping, and racing.

When we visited Jackson, Wyoming, we attended a local rodeo. What surprised us were the 7- and 10-year-old boys wearing football helmets and "bull riding" small calves. They would hop on their backs and be let out of the gate just like the professional bull riders. The kids would hold on for dear life and try to get the most points for staying on the longest. Of course, the men who competed in the bull riding competition were even crazier. As soon as the gate opened, 1,800 pounds of raging bull thundered into the arena, kicking and bucking and spinning in an attempt to dislodge the "thing" on its back! I caught myself squirming in my seat hoping and praying that when the rider got thrown off, he wouldn't get kicked by the bull's flying feet.

To me, bull riding seems like a foolish occupation, but for those cowboys, bull riding is a challenge. And I would dare say some of them classify it as fun!

Similarly, for some people Christianity is foolishness. Paul wrote that the message of the cross is foolish to people who are dying in their sins. People who are content with their lives without God think Jesus and Christianity are silly. But for those of us who are saved and understand the value of Christ's death, there isn't anything silly about the cross. We know that without Jesus' life, death, and resurrection, there would be no hope. The only things that are foolish are ignoring God's free gift of salvation and not sharing the good news with others.

NEXT STOP: Grand Teton National Park, Wyoming

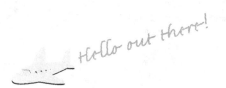

Hello out there!

The Storm Is Coming: Part One

He replied, "When evening comes, you say, 'It will be fair weather,
for the sky is red,' and in the morning, 'Today it will be stormy,
for the sky is red and overcast.'" **Matthew 16:2, 3.**

Grand Teton National Park is located in northwestern Wyoming 10 miles south of Yellowstone National Park, where we were visiting a few days ago. The park features the mountains of the Teton Range, their snowcapped peaks rising out of the scrub-brush landscape in the valley surrounding the mountains.

In the middle of July when our friends in Maryland were experiencing a heat wave with 100-degree weather, we were pulling on jackets because it was overcast and 65 degrees as we entered Grand Teton National Park. By midmorning the sun was shining, a soft breeze was blowing, and we were basking in 70-degree weather. It was perfect!

Jenny Lake is situated at the base of Grand Teton, the tallest peak in the park, and there is a two-and-a-half-mile trail that goes around the lake and slightly up the mountain, providing amazing views of the valley below. We ate lunch near Jenny Lake before grabbing our backpacks, water, and hiking poles and hitting the trail. As we hiked along the trail, we got a closer look at the snowcapped peaks, wildflowers, and quaking aspen trees, whose leaves seemed to dance in the wind.

We had heard the weather could change rapidly in the Tetons, so we had packed our rain jackets just in case. However, we didn't want to be stuck on the mountain in a storm. With about one mile to go my husband and I could see dark clouds building off in the distance. And when I say dark, I mean black! There was no way I wanted to be stuck on the trail in that storm. So we picked up the pace, keeping one eye on the trail and the other eye on the clouds. The clouds grew darker and a few fat raindrops fell, but we kept hustling, trying desperately to make it back to the car before nature unleashed its fury on the mountain . . .

NEXT STOP: Grand Teton National Park, Wyoming

The Storm Is Coming: Part Two

You know how to interpret the weather signs in the sky, but you don't know how to interpret the signs of the times! **Matthew 16:3, NLT.**

I felt a sense of relief as our feet crossed the bridge from the trail to the parking lot. We were almost safe. We continued our fast pace as we wove our way through the parking lot to our van. We quickly packed all our gear into the back, climbed in, and shut the doors. Then we sat in awe as the black clouds rolled in right behind us. The wind picked up, whipping leaves and branches off nearby trees. The clouds completely covered the towering peaks; we couldn't see anything. We were so thankful that we were safe in the car and had made it off the mountain in time!

In Matthew 16 we read about the Pharisees and Sadducees. They were such a tricky group of men, always trying to test Jesus and catch Him saying something that went against Scripture. Well, in this encounter, they asked Him for a "sign from heaven" (Matthew 16:1, NLT). Jesus told them that while they could predict the weather because they looked for the signs, they somehow could not understand the signs of the times they were living in and all of the prophecies concerning Jesus' birth and ministry. They were blinded to the truly important signs around them, and that blindness caused many of them to reject Jesus and thus His saving love.

We knew there could be a storm, so we had prepared by taking rain gear. But had we not kept our eyes open and looked for the signs of a storm, we still could have been caught off guard and surprised at the intensity of the tempest.

The Pharisees and Sadducees had spent their entire lives studying Scripture and preparing for the Messiah, but they failed to keep their eyes open for the signs.

As Jesus' disciples we have to be prepared by reading the Bible, talking to God, and worshipping Him, but we also have to watch so that we aren't surprised by events that signal Jesus' second coming is near. Don't let the "storm" catch you by surprise.

NEXT STOP: Moose, Wyoming

October 3

On a Mission

*Ask and it will be given to you; seek and you will find;
knock and the door will be opened to you.* **Matthew 7:7.**

I have traveled in Maine, Alaska, and Nova Scotia, all of which are prime moose territory, but I didn't see one single moose in any of those locations. So when I found out that Grand Teton National Park was also prime moose territory, I was very excited. I hoped that I would be able to finally see a moose in the wild.

Moose tend to keep to themselves; they don't hang out in a herd like buffalo or elk. They are often found eating in marshy areas, and it is said that the best time to see them is early in the morning. I was so determined to see a moose that I got up at 5.00 a.m. (I am not a morning person!) and drove out of our campground and down the road a little way looking for moose in the marshy valley. But I found zilch, nothing, zero!

It was our last day in the area before heading to Utah, so I was upset that I still hadn't seen a moose. We stopped at the post office in the town of Moose, and I mailed a postcard of a moose to my mom, telling her that this moose printed on a postcard was the only moose I had seen.

As we left the post office and drove back toward Jenny Lake, we saw a bunch of cars stopped alongside the road. Now, any time you see cars parked beside the road and people hanging out of them with binoculars or standing by the car with cameras, you know you've hit the animal jackpot!

We quickly pulled over and began scanning the woods where everyone else was looking. Sure enough, there was a female moose lying down in the woods! She was camouflaged pretty well, but I snapped a few pictures to prove that I had finally seen a moose. They weren't the best pictures, but I was pleased that I could check that animal off my list of wild animals I had spotted in their natural habitat.

As we drove away, I exclaimed, "Wouldn't it be cool if we saw a male moose with huge antlers? That would be awesome! But no matter what, I'm glad I got to see at least one moose."

We were headed to Jackson Hole, but my husband decided to take a shortcut on Moose Wilson Road instead of driving on the main highway. I will forever be grateful for that decision!

NEXT STOP: Moose, Wyoming

Up Close and Personal

Which of you, if your son asks for bread, will give him a stone?
Or if he asks for a fish, will give him a snake? If you, then, though you are evil,
know how to give good gifts to your children, how much more will your
Father in heaven give good gifts to those who ask him! **Matthew 7:9-11.**

What I didn't know when we headed down Moose Wilson Road was that God had a huge surprise planned for me! It was a beautiful scenic drive. There wasn't a cloud in the sky—it was one of the bluest skies I had ever seen. I kept taking pictures of the mountain range through the open window, with the blue sky forming a picture-perfect background. As we drove, I was still on the lookout for moose and any other wildlife we might see. As we rounded one bend, we saw a number of cars parked off to the side and people standing beside the road.

We stopped and jumped out of the van. Down a slope in the marshy water were a mommy moose and her baby! They were off in the distance, but unlike the moose we had seen earlier, they were standing up and were very visible. My camera clicked as fast as it could go, capturing this amazing scene. After a few minutes the mama and baby made their way off into the woods and disappeared. I was ecstatic to have seen more moose, but there was still a longing to see a male moose.

Boy, was I in for a surprise! A mile or so farther down the road was a visible traffic jam, and for good reason. Right beside the road was a marshy pond, and smack in the middle of it was a huge male moose with enormous antlers. He was up to his belly in the water, chewing contentedly. A park ranger was directing traffic and keeping everyone safe, but she allowed us to get out of our van and take pictures. We were probably 50 feet away from this massive creature!

To say the least, I couldn't stop grinning. It was only noon, and I had already had an amazing day. I had been disappointed at the beginning of the day because I hadn't seen any moose, but within a few hours I had seen two females, one baby, and one male!

God loves to give gifts to His children. Our text today is a promise to us of God's amazing love for us. He wants to make us happy and give us the desires of our heart. But He first asks us to seek Him and talk to Him about our wishes. He then asks us to trust Him that He knows what's best for us.

NEXT STOP: Cody, Wyoming

285

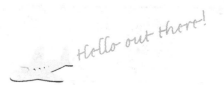

Hello out there!

What's Your Name?

No longer shall your name be called Abram, but your name shall be Abraham; for I have made you the father of a multitude of nations. **Genesis 17:5, NASB.**

Cody, Wyoming, is named after William "Buffalo Bill" Cody, a famous figure of the American West. Buffalo Bill began his claim to fame as a rider for the Pony Express at around the age of 14. He then joined the United States military and worked as a scout for the U.S. Army. He later supplied buffalo meat to the Kansas Pacific Railroad and the U.S. Army. In one 18-month time period it was reported that Buffalo Bill killed 4,280 buffalo, thus earning him his nickname!

But it was show business that really made Buffalo Bill famous. In 1872 he traveled to Chicago, where he partnered with a friend from Texas to act in *The Scouts of the Prairie*, a show about the Wild West. People were so fascinated by the Wild West that they couldn't get enough of these types of shows that depicted life and the quick shooting talents of the rough-and-tumble people who dared to tame the West.

For the next 10 years Buffalo Bill toured and entertained millions of people. Then in 1883 he founded his own show, which even traveled to Europe.

After touring for many years, Buffalo Bill helped found Cody (and settled in it), where he opened the Irma Hotel in honor of his daughter.

Would you like to have a town named after you? How about a hotel, a park, a hospital, or a school? Your name is special because it identifies who you are. Do you know what your name means? (Ask your parents to look it up if you don't know.)

In today's text we find that God changed Abram's name to Abraham. It wasn't that different, but the meaning changed. In Hebrew, Abram means "high father," whereas Abraham means "father of many." God changed his name because He wanted Abraham to be constantly reminded that he would be the father of a great nation of people, and he was. The nation of Israel came out of the lineage of Abraham and Isaac and Jacob.

If God gave me a name, I wonder what He would pick. Maybe He'll give me a new name in heaven. But if not, the most important name I will ever have from Him is "child of God."

NEXT STOP: Cheyenne, Wyoming

Anger That Kills

Saul was very angry; this refrain displeased him greatly. "They have credited David with tens of thousands," he thought, "but me with only thousands. What more can he get but the kingdom?"... [One day] David was playing the lyre, as he usually did. Saul had a spear in his hand and he hurled it.... But David eluded him twice. Saul was afraid of David, because the Lord was with David but had departed from Saul. I Samuel 18:8-12.

Robert Andrew "Clay" Allison was born on September 2, 1840. His father was a minister, but he died when Clay was only 5. Clay was born with a clubfoot, which is a deformity at birth in which one or both feet are rotated inward at the ankle. This makes it much more difficult for a child to walk. Today a baby with clubfoot will undergo surgery to correct the problem, but back in the 1800s that was not an option.

Clay grew up with a mean streak, and people were afraid of him because of his mood swings and unpredictable behavior. It is reported that one day while visiting a dentist in Cheyenne, Wyoming, he pinned the dentist down and began pulling out the dentist's teeth after the dentist accidentally drilled into the wrong molar in Clay's mouth. Fortunately, people on the street heard the screams of the dentist and came to his rescue.

It is difficult, and clearly dangerous, to be around people who don't know how to control their anger. Take, for instance, Saul. He was definitely a "loose cannon," as the saying goes. No one could predict what would set him off and when.

At first Saul loved David because David's harp music soothed him, but after David defeated Goliath and the people sang praises to him, Saul lost it. He was angry, and he let bitterness and hatred well up inside of him. Satan used those emotions to drive Saul to attempt to kill David with his spear. But God protected David, and he escaped.

The Lord was no longer with Saul, because Saul had chosen to do things his way and had turned away from God. And the more he distanced himself from God, the more he listened to Satan and took on his character. The evil spirits that plagued him drove him to be angry, jealous, and hateful, until all he could think about was killing David. Uncontrolled anger is destructive and can lead to so many problems—physical, emotional, and spiritual.

NEXT STOP: Loveland, Colorado

October 7

Hello out there!

I Love You

Three things will last forever—faith, hope, and love —and the greatest of these is love. **I Corinthians 13:13, NLT.**

Valentine's Day is another four months away, but we are visiting Loveland, Colorado, home of the Valentine Re-Mailing Program. The program began in January 1947 when the postmaster of the town received a handful of valentine cards with requests from the individuals to mail the card to their sweetheart and postmark it from Loveland. The postmaster thought that this would be a good way to advertise their town, so he designed a logo of an arrow piercing a heart over the Rocky Mountains, and he stamped this phrase on the outside of the card: "A Valentine Greeting from Sweetheart Town, Loveland, Colorado."

The post office used that phrase for two years, and then the tradition started of changing the phrase and logo each year, thus making the cards somewhat of a collector's item. On average, the post office remails more than 160,000 cards from romantic individuals in the United States and more than 110 countries.

It's fine to do something special on Valentine's Day, but if you don't show love to the people around you throughout the year, you are missing what love is all about. Check out the "love chapter" in the Bible. Paul tells us how someone who really has love behaves toward those around him or her.

"Love is patient and kind. Love is not jealous or boastful or proud or rude. It does not demand its own way. It is not irritable, and it keeps no record of being wronged. It does not rejoice about injustice but rejoices whenever the truth wins out. Love never gives up, never loses faith, is always hopeful, and endures through every circumstance. Prophecy and speaking in unknown languages and special knowledge will become useless. But love will last forever!" (1 Corinthians 13:4-8, NLT).

Read each section again and see if you love others as God wants you to love them. Are you patient with your brother or sister? Do you protect those you love? Do you forgive and not hold a grudge or keep a record of the times someone has wronged you? Loving someone as the Bible calls us to love is not always easy, but in the end you will benefit from an awesome relationship with those around you.

NEXT STOP: Dove Creek, Colorado

The Best Meal

You have a fine way of setting aside the commands of God
in order to observe your own traditions! **Mark 7:9.**

Dove Creek, Colorado, proclaims itself as the pinto bean capital of the world. Whether it actually grows the best pinto beans in the world or not, the town has claimed this honor. And if you like Mexican food you should thank the fine farmers of Dove Creek who provide you with beans for your burritos, tacos, haystacks, and anything else Mexican!

In my house haystacks are a favorite meal. In fact, they are a weekly item on the menu. Our family builds our haystacks as follows: chips, refried beans, lettuce, tomatoes, tofu sour cream, salsa, and guacamole. I have had countless plates of haystacks at potlucks, campouts, cafeterias, and other people's homes, and everyone builds their haystack a little differently. Some add onions, black olives, cheese, cucumbers, corn, or rice, while others insist that you build it in a certain order.

Haystacks are a tradition in the Adventist Church. It is reported that they were created by Ella May Hartlein in the 1950s. Mrs. Hartlein and her family enjoyed Mexican food, but when they moved from Arizona to Idaho, she invented her own Mexican dish because there were no Mexican restaurants in their area. Then when Mrs. Hartlein was a faculty member at an Adventist school in Iowa, she shared her recipe with the faculty when they were trying to decide what to serve at a Fourth of July picnic. It was originally called the "Hartlein Special," but somewhere along the way the name was changed to "haystacks."

Traditions are wonderful to have, and they create a special bond between people. For many people, haystacks are a comfort food that reminds them of good times and large get-togethers with friends and family.

The danger with traditions is that they can take the place of God's commands, which is what happened with the Pharisees. The Pharisees placed their traditions above the Word of God. They lost sight of the simple teachings of the Bible and created their own traditions and laws, which in the end took them away from God. Whatever traditions you enjoy in your church or home, make sure they never take the place of the truths in the Bible.

NEXT STOP: Colorado Rockies, Colorado

October 9

Hello out there!

The Littlest Climber

I can do all this through him who gives me strength. **Philippians 4:13.**

In the world of mountain climbing there are peaks that are known as fourteeners. These are mountains that are 14,000 feet or more above sea level. Colorado is home to the most fourteeners in North America, boasting a total of 53 peaks (although there is some debate about the actual number). The rest of the fourteeners in North America in the order of most to least are as follows: Alaska, 21; Canada, 15; California, 12; Mexico, 8; and Washington, 1.

Many mountain climbers set a goal to climb all 53 peaks in Colorado, and many have accomplished that goal. There are also plenty of records for the oldest person and youngest person to hike these enormous mountains. As I was reading about kids hiking fourteeners, I came across a 3-year-old boy named Kessler. He told his dad he wanted to hike up a big snowy mountain. Apparently this little guy liked to hike and could easily hike six miles without complaining, so his dad decided to take him up a "big snowy mountain." They began their three-day hike on July 2. (Remember, there is snow on 14,000-foot mountains in the summer!) His dad's biggest concern was the change in elevation, but Kessler did fine.

On the second day of hiking they tried to reach the summit, but at 13,750 feet there were sounds of thunder, and his dad decided they had better head back to camp. Kessler ended up 453 feet short of reaching the top, but that's quite an accomplishment for a 3-year-old kid! He hiked farther than most adults could.

If you had to hike a fourteener, would you be excited or nervous? Would you worry that you wouldn't make it? Would you think you had failed if you didn't reach the top? We often face these same questions with everyday activities or experiences. Will I pass this test? Will I remember all of my lines in the Christmas play? What will people think if I can't run a mile in under 10 minutes or can't hit the baseball or can't make a basket?

When you think you can't do something, claim the Bible promise in today's text: "I can do all this through him who gives me strength" (Philippians 4:13). There isn't anything in this world that is too hard for you to do with God by your side!

NEXT STOP: Leadville, Colorado

Melting Away

At this the hearts of the people melted in fear and became like water. **Joshua 7:5.**

Winter is approaching, and soon the mountains of Colorado will be blanketed in snow and ice. In the higher regions the first snow often falls sometime in late September or October. The snow in Colorado attracts a lot of tourists who enjoy winter sports such as snow skiing, snowmobiling, snowshoeing, cross-country skiing, and ice skating.

Well, in 1895 the town of Leadville was desperate for tourists, so they came up with an idea to attract more people to their town. The gold and silver mines had been depleted in the area, and they needed money. So the town built an ice palace that was approximately five acres in size. The walls of the palace were three feet thick, and they surrounded an ice skating rink, ballrooms, restaurants, a merry-go-round, and a toboggan slide.

The Leadville Ice Palace opened on January 1, 1896, drawing visitors from around the country as word spread about the frozen structure. But the life of the ice palace was short-lived. Unseasonably warm weather caused the ice palace to melt only three months after it opened. I'm sure it was hard for the townspeople who had worked so hard to build the ice palace to watch it melt, taking with it their dreams for more money for themselves and the town.

When you hear the word "melt," I'm assuming you think about ice or snow turning into water, but the Bible uses the word "melt" to describe the hearts of the people. In today's Bible story the children of Israel had just conquered Jericho and were feeling pumped up and very confident. So when Joshua sent them to spy out Ai, they came back and told him that only two or three thousand men needed to go fight the people of Ai, because the city would be easy to take.

Joshua followed the advice of his spies, but the Israelites lost the battle and were chased away. When the rest of the Israelites heard this, "the hearts of the people melted in fear." They went from being confident to being afraid in a matter of minutes.

So what changed? How did they go from confidently taking Jericho to melting in fear after losing the battle at Ai? The key difference is that God was fighting for them at Jericho, and they were fighting on their own at Ai. Just remember, we don't have to "melt" in fear when we are following God's plan.

NEXT STOP: Mesa Verde National Park, Colorado

October 11

Hello out there!

Where Did They Go?

Two men will be in the field; one will be taken and the other left. Two women will be grinding with a hand mill; one will be taken and the other left. **Matthew 24:40, 41.**

Mesa Verde National Park is home to the best-preserved cliff dwellings in the world, which were carved by the ancestral Pueblo people, also known as the Anasazi. Within the park are nearly 5,000 archaeological sites and more than 600 cliff dwellings.

While in Colorado we decided to visit Mesa Verde and take a tour of Cliff Palace, the largest and best-known cliff dwelling in the park. They warned us that we had to climb down a series of narrow stairways and ladders, but that was the fun part. We got to shimmy up and down ladders and descend a number of steps until we emerged at the base of the city, which was tucked under a large rock shelf. It was literally built *into* the cliff. It was fascinating to see the city with its 150 rooms (including storage rooms, open courtyards, small houses) and 23 kivas, the ceremonial rooms reserved for religious rituals. I imagined what life must have been like for these ancient people and what hardships they faced.

What baffles archaeologists is that it appears that the thousands of Pueblos who lived there suddenly disappeared. They just can't figure out what happened to them. Some speculate that they moved to another location, but no one knows for sure where they went.

People shouldn't just disappear. But did you know that some Christians believe that Jesus' followers will disappear before He comes? They use today's Bible verse to say that the Bible supports a secret rapture. The secret rapture is what people call the event they believe will occur before Christ's second coming when Christians will be secretly taken to heaven. They say, "See, two men are in the field and one is taken; he just disappears. Two women are working, and one vanishes."

When we read the Bible, we have to examine what all of the scriptures have to say about a certain subject before making a decision. This verse in Revelation clearly goes against the idea of a secret rapture: " 'Look, he is coming with the clouds,' and '*every* eye will see him' " (Revelation 1:7). Do you see why it is important to know your Bible? Without the clear Word of God, we could be very confused and lost. Read it, learn it, and memorize it so that you can stay on track!

NEXT STOP: Pit stop

Thanking God for the Harvest

I will praise God's name in song and glorify him with thanksgiving. **Psalm 69:30.**

Although we are currently traveling in the United States, we are going to take a break today to recognize Canadian Thanksgiving. On Thursday, January 31, 1957, the Canadian Parliament issued the following proclamation: "A Day of General Thanksgiving to Almighty God for the bountiful harvest with which Canada has been blessed—to be observed on the second Monday in October."

Canadian Thanksgiving corresponds with the English Harvest festival, during which churches are decorated inside and out with pumpkins, corn, wheat, and the harvest of other fall crops. Special church services are held, harvest hymns are sung, and Bible stories are told of the Jewish harvest festivals that the Israelites celebrated so many years ago.

Similar to the United States, some provinces host parades and the Canadian Football League holds a doubleheader. But unlike the United States, although the Thanksgiving holiday is officially recognized on Monday, many Canadians choose to eat their meal on any day of the three-day weekend (Saturday, Sunday, or Monday) they want to.

The Israelites celebrated many festivals in recognition of God's protection and His blessings in providing them with food. But the Israelites fell into the habit of bringing their thank offerings or saying their ritual prayers without really thanking God, the giver of all good things.

King David wrote, "I will praise God's name in song and glorify him with thanksgiving. This will please the Lord more than an ox, more than a bull with its horns and hooves" (Psalm 69:30, 31). He recognized that his words and personal songs and prayers to God were of more value to God than sacrificing an ox out of habit.

When you say the blessing over your food, do you do so as a ritual or habit? Or do you stop and think about what you are saying and truly thank God for the good things He has given you? Are your bedtime prayers a list of needs and wants? Or do you thank God for the blessings He gave you that day? Avoid the ritual and talk to God as to a friend. He would much rather hear your honest struggles, fears, joys, and needs rather than scripted, monotonous prayers.

NEXT STOP: Four Corners: Colorado, New Mexico, Arizona, Utah

Hello out there!

Everywhere at Once

Where can I flee from your presence? If I go up to the heavens, you are there; if I make my bed in the depths, you are there. If I rise on the wings of the dawn, if I settle on the far side of the sea, even there your hand will guide me, your right hand will hold me fast. **Psalm 139:7-10.**

Today you have the unique opportunity to be in four states at the same time! How? We are visiting Four Corners, where four states—Colorado, New Mexico, Arizona, and Utah—all meet at the same location.

It may seem silly to pay money to visit Four Corners, but it's fun to say that you've been in four states at the same time. The Four Corners monument features a metal plate on the ground that marks where the four states meet. Etched in the concrete surrounding the metal plate are the borders and the names of each state. When we were there, my kids both had their picture taken with a limb in each state. They had one hand in Colorado, another hand in Utah, a foot in Arizona, and another foot in New Mexico. We then took a family picture of just our feet with each of us standing in a different state.

Katelyn and Ryan were in four different states at the same time, but it was an easy accomplishment when you look at the geographic location of those states. You could never claim to be in California, Oregon, and Washington at the same time. That isn't humanly possible. But it is possible for God.

The Bible teaches us that God is omnipresent, meaning He is present everywhere. David recognized God's omnipresence. He wrote, "You know when I sit and when I rise. . . . You discern my going out and my lying down; you are familiar with all my ways" (Psalm 139:2, 3). And just as God is familiar with you, He knows all about your parents, siblings, friends, teachers, neighbors, etc.

A few verses later David wrote, "I can never get away from your presence!" (verse 7, NLT). God is everywhere; there is no place we can go where God will not be there. I'm glad God knows where I am every second of the day, watching out for me, helping me, guiding me, and providing for me, along with everyone else who calls on His name. Talk about an amazing and perfect Father!

NEXT STOP: Hay Springs Well, New Mexico

The Town Center

Now he had to go through Samaria. So he came to a town in Samaria called Sychar, near the plot of ground Jacob had given to his son Joseph. Jacob's well was there, and Jesus, tired as he was from the journey, sat down by the well. **John 4:4-6.**

The Santa Fe Trail, like the Oregon Trail, was a major route for settlers to travel from the East to the West, although this trail led into Mexico and was also used as a trade route. The trail started in Missouri and continued through Kansas, the southeast corner of Colorado, and then New Mexico, ending in Santa Fe.

The route crossed arid plains and deserts, which produced soaring temperatures during the day and cold temperatures at night. Food and water were an issue for travelers, so the Hay Springs Well in Las Vegas, New Mexico, was a welcome sight. Today it is the oldest surviving spring-fed well along the Santa Fe Trail.

Whether in the early days of the West or in Bible times, a well was very important to a community. A well not only provided a very valuable resource but also served as a community gathering spot where people could meet and discuss the news of the day as they went about the chore of gathering water for their homes.

It is at a well that we find Jesus when He meets the Samaritan woman. He is resting by the well when she approaches to draw water. It was improper for a Jew to speak with a Samaritan, but according to the culture of the day, it was even worse that Jesus talked with a woman about spiritual matters.

After offering her living water, He reveals that He knows about her life and knows that she is living with a man who isn't her husband. Then Jesus gives this woman, a sinner who, according to the Jews, is of an inferior race, a very important message. He reveals to her that He is the Messiah, a truth He did not reveal to many people during His ministry. But He chose a Samaritan woman to carry that important message into the town, which caused many more to believe and want to hear more. Jesus looked beyond what others saw and gave her a special job in spreading the gospel, and He does the same today. He looks at the heart and uses those who want to serve Him. God can use you just the way you are if you'll let Him. Try it out!

NEXT STOP: White Sands National Monument, New Mexico

October 15

 *Hello out there!*

Surprising Coolness

But to Jonah this seemed very wrong, and he became angry. **Jonah 4:1.**

If you have ever been to the beach during the summer, you know that once you take off your sandals at the end of the boardwalk you had better run for the water, because the sand is *hot!* People with tender feet can be seen hopping and scurrying across the sand in search of the cool, refreshing ocean surf.

Today we are visiting White Sands National Monument in New Mexico. These sand dunes are not made of the sand you would find at the beach. Nope, the sand is made up of white gypsum crystals. One would guess that the gleaming white sand would be blazing hot, but it isn't! Surprisingly, the gypsum does not convert the sun's energy into heat, so the sand is safe to walk on barefoot even on the hottest summer day.

If I didn't know this tidbit of information and I visited this park in the summer, I would expect to burn my feet because of previous experiences at the beach, but I would be pleasantly surprised when that wouldn't happen.

Now let's look at the story of Jonah. When Jonah was called to preach to the people of Nineveh, he expected them to kill him because they were so wicked. Jonah should have been pleasantly surprised when the people repented and turned from their wicked ways because of his warning, but he wasn't happy. In fact, he was angry at God for forgiving the people. Somehow Jonah forgot about how God had saved him and forgiven him a short time ago when he had tried to run away from God. It appears that he felt he was better than the evil people of Nineveh, even if they did repent.

Do you ever fall into the trap of thinking you are better than your siblings or classmates or friends? It's dangerous to think you are better than someone else— Lucifer had that problem, and we know what happened to him! God makes this point at the end of the book of Jonah. He told Jonah, "And should I not have concern for the great city of Nineveh, in which there are more thatn a hundred and twenty thoudand people . . . and also many animals?" (Jonah 4:11).

In God's eyes we are all equal. Remember to treat others as God treats them, and you—with love, compassion, forgiveness, and understanding.

NEXT STOP: Alamogordo, New Mexico

The Threat of Destruction

Meanwhile, Saul was still breathing out murderous threats
against the Lord's disciples. **Acts 9:1.**

The White Sands National Monument is inside the White Sands Missile Range, which is near the town of Alamogordo. In fact, the monument is closed once or twice a week when missiles are tested on the range. In November 1944 the site was selected to test the explosion of a nuclear weapon, and on July 16, 1945, the world's first atomic bomb was detonated. Less than one month later, on August 6, 1945, an atomic bomb was dropped on Hiroshima, Japan. Three days later a second bomb was dropped on Nagasaki, Japan.

Since then no nuclear weapon has been used against another country in war. However, a handful of countries—the United States, Russia, the United Kingdom, France, China, India, Pakistan, and North Korea—have tested nuclear weapons and have them in their arsenal of weapons "in case" they need to use them.

According to the Federation of American Scientists, they estimate that in 2012 there were approximately 4,300 nuclear weapons ready to be used. Part of the "game" these powerful nations play with one another and weaker countries is threatening them that if they do not listen and do what they want, they will blow them to pieces and destroy their country. It is bullying on a global scale between nations, but it is still bullying. And the majority of the bullying comes in the form of threats.

In the book of Acts we meet a bully by the name of Saul. He threatened to hunt down and capture Jesus' followers so they could be tried in Jerusalem and sentenced to death. But Saul's threats were cut short when he met the Man he was persecuting. Along the way to Damascus on his mission, "a light from heaven flashed around him. He fell to the ground and heard a voice say to him, 'Saul, Saul, why do you persecute me?' " (Acts 9:3, 4). At that moment Saul's life changed. Then, after three days of blindness, his sight was restored, and he went from being a bully to being a follower of God and one of the greatest preachers of the early Christian church. We know him best by the name he used later in life—Paul.

Never underestimate whom God will use to spread His word. The person who starts out as a bully may one day be a worker for the King of the universe!

NEXT STOP: El Morro National Monument, New Mexico

October 17

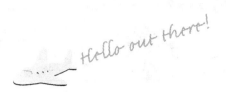
Hello out there!

For All the World to See

But Jesus bent down and started to write on the ground with his finger. **John 8:6.**

If you are on a Sabbath afternoon hike with your friends and you stop to rest at the base of a large tree, should you grab a jackknife and start carving "Samantha was here" or "James is the man" in the bark? No! That would hurt the tree, and if everyone carved a name, initial, or phrase into the trees, the forest wouldn't be natural any longer—it would look horrible. The same goes for rocks as well, although most people use spray paint or regular paint on rocks. But the end result is the same—it takes away from the beauty of nature.

We are taught this at a young age, but apparently no one taught the Indians, Spanish, and American explorers and travelers who passed by El Morro, a sandstone cliff that towered above a reliable waterhole. Because of this water source, many travelers stopped at El Morro to rest and replenish their water supply. Somehow it became a tradition to carve their names and write brief sayings in the soft sandstone cliff, which is now known as Inscription Rock. And we are not talking about 25 or 50 people who did this; we are talking about more than 2,000 people!

Although by today's standards defacing something in nature or otherwise is often considered a crime, these famous signatures and writings are now a piece of history and are preserved by the U.S. National Park Service. They are protected so that other people can see what was written so long ago.

I'm sure the men in today's Bible story were glad Jesus didn't write their sins in rock, forever listing what they had done wrong. Instead, Jesus wrote their sins in the sand and then erased them, just as He "erased" the sins of the woman caught in adultery, brought to Him by those men, when He forgave her and told her she was free to go.

In the same way that Jesus forgave the woman, He would have forgiven the men whose sins He wrote in the sand if they had asked for forgiveness. It's that simple.

When you know you have done something wrong and you feel as if your sin is written in stone and can't be erased, remember that Jesus is just waiting for you to ask Him to forgive you. Sins can be erased through the power of Jesus and His death on the cross.

NEXT STOP: Hatch, New Mexico

Red or Green?

Anyone who chooses to be a friend of the world
becomes an enemy of God. **James 4:4.**

The small town of Hatch, New Mexico, is known for its green chilies. These spicy little peppers are an important crop for the town and, in fact, for the state. One of the designated state vegetables for New Mexico is the chili—the other vegetable is frijoles, otherwise known as pinto beans. Obviously, Mexican food is a main staple in the state that bears its name.

Now, if you know anything about chili peppers, you know that they are either red or green, and they vary in how hot and spicy they are. Habanero chilies are one of the hottest peppers, but beware, your mouth might catch on fire if you eat one of these crazy chili peppers!

Because of the importance of this vegetable in New Mexico, the state has an "official" question regarding chilies, and it is simply, "Red or green?" Meaning, "Do you prefer red or green chilies?"

Chili peppers are not the only things we compare. We often compare other things of the same kind or different kinds. Do you like green apples or red apples? Do you like peaches or bananas? Do you like this shirt in blue or orange? Do you prefer math or reading class? Our world is full of choices and comparisons.

But the most important choice of all is whether you choose God or Satan. James tells us that "friendship with the world makes you an enemy of God" (James 4:4, NLT). If we choose the world, we are really choosing Satan, because he is the prince of this world. And once we choose to follow him, we naturally become enemies of God because we have joined the ranks of the fallen angel who had to leave heaven so long ago.

However, we know that we don't have to be enemies of God! In fact, we can be in God's army and fight *against* the enemy.

Red or green? God or Satan? The choice is yours.

NEXT STOP: Truth or Consequences, New Mexico

Hello out there!

Good Consequences

The one whose walk is blameless, who does what is righteous,
who speaks the truth from their heart; whose tongue utters no slander, . . .
who keeps an oath even when it hurts. . . . Whoever does these things
will never be shaken. **Psalm 15:2-5.**

Did you catch the name of the town we are visiting today? And, yes, I wrote it correctly. Truth or Consequences is really the name! The town used to be called Hot Springs, but they changed the name in 1950 when a popular game show called *Truth or Consequences* held a contest for the tenth anniversary of the show. The deal was that if a town would change its name to Truth or Consequences, the show would do their anniversary broadcast from that city.

The town of Hot Springs jumped at the opportunity because they thought it would increase the number of visitors to the town, so the town quickly held a meeting, and the majority of townspeople voted to change the name.

The show awarded the honor to the former town of Hot Springs and aired their anniversary show on April 1, 1950, although a lot of people thought it was an April Fool's joke. The show consisted of contestants having approximately two seconds to answer a goofy trivia question before the buzzer sounded. Most people could not answer the question, so they had to pay the "consequence" and do a silly stunt, such as being blindfolded and stepping over paper bags filled with water. The host often ended the show by saying, "Hoping all your consequences are happy ones."

So are there really good consequences? Yes! We often talk about bad consequences and how our poor choices can result in bad things happening, but David points out the good consequences of doing what is right in Psalm 15. Those who speak the truth will not be shaken. Those who keep their promises will not be shaken. Those who treat others with respect will not be shaken. When we get into the habit of making good choices, it is easier to push Satan away and continue making good choices even when he tempts us to do wrong. Thus, more good choices lead to more good consequences and a life centered in Jesus.

NEXT STOP: Arizona

Safety in the Thorns

The soldiers twisted together a crown of thorns
and put it on his head. **John 19:2.**

Welcome to Arizona, home of the saguaro cactus, a large cactus that can grow to be more than 70 feet tall! The cactus is native to the Sonoran Desert, and its white blossom is the official state flower.

The spines on the cactus obviously deter animals and humans from getting too close, but that is exactly why the Gila woodpeckers, purple martins, house finches, and gilded flickers make their nests in the saguaros. The birds create large holes in the saguaro and then build their nest deep inside the hole, thus hiding themselves from other animals.

I have no idea how the birds drill a hole into the cactus without getting poked by the thorns, but God obviously gave them special instincts as to how to create a safe nest for their young in these prickly giant saguaros.

As I thought about the safety these birds have by living among the thorns of the saguaro, I thought about the safety we have in "living" among the thorns that Jesus wore on His head when He was crucified for our sins. I know I do not literally have thorns around me or around my house, but when I asked Jesus into my heart, I accepted His free gift of salvation, which was given to me on the cross. And by living in Jesus, I am protected from the wages of sin—death. So I am "living" among the thorns!

If birds could talk, a cardinal or blue jay might say to the purple martin, "You are crazy for trying to build your nest among the thorns! Why not build your nest in this nice bush or tree? It will be much easier and less work."

Does this sound familiar? Do your friends ever say to you, "Why are you a Christian? You are missing out on life. Why don't you come to the party at my house? We're going to watch a horror movie. It's going to be great!"

Accepting Jesus' sacrifice does not always make sense to others, but it is the safest way to navigate through life in this messed-up world.

NEXT STOP: Yuma, Arizona

October 21

Hello out there!

Camel Train

Then the servant left, taking with him ten of his master's camels loaded with all kinds of good things from his master. **Genesis 24:10.**

There are plenty of Bible stories that feature camels. Camels were, and still are, a main form of transportation in the Middle East and desert regions around the world. But did you know that camels were used in Arizona to transport things in 1856?

In 1854 the United States purchased the land that today makes up the southern portion of Arizona and a corner of New Mexico. Because of the desert terrain, the army faced challenges defending the area and taking supplies to the various forts, since horses and mules didn't fare well in desert conditions. When someone suggested they use camels to solve their transportation problems, Secretary of War Jefferson Davis sent Major Henry Wayne to the Middle East in 1855 to purchase some camels and learn how to care for and handle them.

Major Wayne completed his assignment and brought back 33 camels with him in 1856. The camels were successfully put into service and used for a number of years until the Civil War started. When it started, the troops were pulled back east to help with the war, and the camels were left behind. Some were sold, but most were abandoned to roam the desert near Yuma, Arizona. Thus, the camel population quickly died out.

Now that you know about the history of camels in Arizona, let's look at today's Bible story, in which camels play an important role. Abraham's servant was sent on a mission to find a wife for Isaac. He took 10 camels and set out for the town of Nahor. When he arrived, he made his "camels kneel down near the well outside the town" (Genesis 24:11). It was close to evening, and, as was the custom, the women were coming to the well to draw water.

Then the servant prayed to God and asked Him for guidance. "Lord, . . . make me successful today. . . . May it be that when I say to a young woman, 'Please let down your jar that I may have a drink,' and she says, 'Drink, and I'll water your camels too'—let her be the one you have chosen for your servant Isaac" (verses 12-14). Before he even finished his prayer, Rebekah showed up at the well and said the exact words in answer to his prayer. As she cared for the needs of those thirsty camels, the servant knew that the God of heaven had heard and answered his prayer.

NEXT STOP: Kitt Peak National Observatory, Arizona

The Great Disappointment

The sun will be darkened, and the moon will not give its light; the stars will fall from the sky, and the heavenly bodies will be shaken. **Matthew 24:29.**

The Kitt Peak National Observatory is home to the largest amount of astronomical equipment in the world. The site operates 22 optical and two radio telescopes. These telescopes provide scientists brilliant images of outer space and the stars and planets and moons that make up our solar system.

The observatory is also home to the world's largest solar telescope. We most often think of looking through a telescope at night to view the moon and stars, not the sun. We've been taught not to look directly at the sun, because it will damage our eyes. But solar telescopes, according to Wikipedia, help scientists study the sun by detecting "light with wavelengths in, or not far outside, the visible spectrum." The telescope also has a special heat stop that enables it to not overheat as the intense sunlight is focused in the lenses of the telescope.

Today's trip to an observatory is very timely, since on October 22, 1844, the Millerites were waiting for Jesus to come. Why were they waiting? Because they had been studying the Bible, and they believed that Jesus would return on that date. They had read today's verse and knew that on May 19, 1780, the sun had gone black around noon over most of New England. And then on November 13, 1833, the stars fell from the sky.

The Millerites knew that these events had taken place, and after studying the prophecy of Daniel 8:14, which says that the sanctuary would be cleaned, William Miller felt that the verse was talking about the cleansing of the earth. After preaching for a number of years and warning others of Christ's soon return, he anxiously waited with other believers on October 22, 1844, for Jesus to come. But as we know from Adventist history, October 22, 1844, ended up being labeled the Great Disappointment. William Miller and other believers went back to the Bible and discovered that although the prophecies of the sun, moon, and stars had already happened, the cleansing of the sanctuary was referring to the heavenly sanctuary and the commencement of judgment.

The prophecies spoken of in Matthew 24:29 have been fulfilled, but Jesus is still judging the world and making sure everyone has a chance to make their choice before He returns.

NEXT STOP: Phoenix, Arizona

October 23

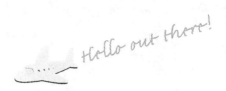

Hello out there!

All Coming Together

The Lord said to Moses, "Tell the Israelites to bring me an offering.
You are to receive the offering for me from everyone whose heart
prompts them to give. **Exodus 25:1,2.** "Then have them make a sanctuary
for me, and I will dwell among them." **Verse 8.**

The capital of a state, province, or country is an important building where government employees and administrators work to keep things running smoothly for the citizens who live within their territory. The buildings are usually ornately decorated and constructed to reflect what is important about that state, province, or country or the history about that place.

The capital of Arizona is Phoenix, and its capitol building features a copper dome, since copper is a natural metal in the area. The amount of copper that was used on the dome is equal to the amount of copper in 4.8 million pennies. One penny by itself could not be smashed into a thin circle that would cover the dome, but if you put millions of pennies together, the job suddenly seems easier and doable.

When God asked Moses to build the sanctuary in the wilderness, He told Moses to enlist the help of the whole community. He instructed Moses to ask the Israelites for an offering. God didn't force anyone to give, but He told Moses to accept gifts from those willing to give. They were asked to give gold, silver, bronze, yarn, fine linen, goat hair, ram skins, acacia wood, olive oil, spices, and precious stones and gems.

The Israelites faithfully brought their offerings to Moses until there were more than enough materials to build the sanctuary. By working together, they built their own "capitol." The sanctuary was to be God's dwelling place among them. God was to be the King and Ruler of their country.

Unfortunately, after the Israelites entered the Promised Land and, during the time of Samuel, asked for a king, things went downhill from there. Instead of relying on God to run their country, they turned to another person and put their trust in a fellow human being.

When we take our eyes off of Jesus and only look to others for answers or guidance, we are in danger of falling off the path that God has planned for our lives.

NEXT STOP: Petrified Forest National Park, Arizona

October 24

Scared Stiff

But when his heart became arrogant and hardened with pride, he was deposed from his royal throne and stripped of his glory. **Daniel 5:20.**

The Petrified Forest National Park is home to a wide variety of fossils and wood that has been scared stiff! Get it? (If you are petrified, you are scared so bad that you can't move.) The only truth in that statement is that petrified objects are very stiff because they have turned into stone. If something goes through the petrification process, the living organisms are changed into stone by minerals filling all the original pore spaces in the object until it becomes hard as a rock.

Just as wood can be hardened through petrification, people's hearts can be hardened. In a similar manner, the living organisms of goodness, kindness, love, forgiveness, and peace can give way to the "minerals" of selfishness, anger, hate, and turmoil until the person's heart is like a cold, unfeeling rock.

Nebuchadnezzar hardened his heart, and he paid the consequences of his pride. In Daniel 4 you can read about his dream, a dream in which a huge tree stood strong and tall with its branches stretching to the sky and sheltering the animals, its leaves shimmering in the breeze, and its fruit providing food for all. But the tree was cut down, and the stump was left in the ground for seven years.

Of course, Nebuchadnezzar wanted to know the meaning of the dream. God spoke through Daniel and told the king that he was the tall tree and would be cut down because of his pride, of thinking he had built by himself the beautiful kingdom he ruled. For seven years Nebuchadnezzar was to have the mind of a wild animal and crawl around on the ground and eat grass so that he would realize that God was the true God of heaven who gave him all he had.

Just as God predicted, 12 months after the dream, King Nebuchadnezzar was standing on the roof of his palace and said, "Is not this the great Babylon I have built as the royal residence, by my mighty power and for the glory of my majesty?" (Daniel 4:30). At that moment he became as a wild animal and lived in the fields. When the seven years were up, his mind was restored, and he praised the name of the Lord forever.

NEXT STOP: Grand Canyon National Park, North Rim, Arizona

Hello out there!

A Wall of Fog

Hope in the Lord and keep his way. **Psalm 37:34.**

The Grand Canyon is a massive canyon with extremely steep sides that was carved by the Colorado River. The sides of the canyon are more than a mile deep in some locations. The canyon is 277 miles long and up to 18 miles wide. The canyon walls feature layer upon layer of rock, displaying shades of reds and browns in horizontal stripes along the canyon walls.

We were traveling from Utah to Colorado at the time of our visit, so we planned to stay only one day and night at the Grand Canyon, just enough time to see the canyon, hike a few trails along the rim, camp at the North Rim campground, and then leave the next day.

Unfortunately, the closer we got to the park, the cloudier and colder it got, even though it was the middle of July. We parked at the lodge at the North Rim, and all we could see was thick fog. The rustic wood lodge with its huge floor-to-ceiling windows overlooking the canyon was beautiful, but all we could see as we peered out the windows was a wall of white clouds! We went out onto the terrace, and my kids asked me, "So where is the Grand Canyon?" To which I had to reply, "Out there!" pointing to the sea of white before our eyes. Talk about a letdown! We were all disappointed.

I spoke with a park ranger and asked if the weather was supposed to clear, and he told me he had never seen it this bad, and he didn't know when the fog would pass. That didn't give us much hope, but we decided to wait and see what would happen. After about 30 minutes, we suddenly saw a small break in the clouds. Since I didn't know if it would fully clear, I yelled to the kids, "Quick, look! There's the Grand Canyon! See the red rocks?" Then the white clouds filled back in. We continued to wait, hoping for another glimpse. Finally, another patch of fog cleared, and we could see the far wall of the canyon, only to have it disappear again behind the clouds.

But ever so slowly, the wind began to blow away the dense fog, and we could finally see the entire canyon. Waiting is hard to do, but the rewards are worth it, especially when we wait on the Lord and trust Him to lead us along the path He has planned for our lives.

NEXT STOP: Grand Canyon National Park, South Rim, Arizona

Eight Hours Versus Four Days

For everything that was written in the past was written to teach us, so that through the endurance taught in the Scriptures and the encouragement they provide we might have hope. **Romans 15:4.**

The South Rim of the Grand Canyon is far different from the North Rim. The South Rim is at a lower elevation and is much more arid and desertlike, whereas the North Rim features tall evergreen trees and cooler temperatures. The road to the North Rim even shuts down in the winter because of high accumulations of snow.

Although the vegetation and temperature are different, both rims are home to mountain lions, large cats that keep to themselves and hunt deer, elk, sheep, cattle, and even horses. For a number of years, scientists have been studying the mountain lions that call the Grand Canyon home. They have tagged many of them in hopes of learning more about their habits and hunting grounds. Because of these tags, they were able to record one young female mountain lion's trip from the South Rim to the North Rim. She descended from the South Rim, swam across the Colorado River, and made her way up the North Rim in just eight hours.

Most average hikers complete the rim-to-rim hike in three to four days, camping along the way. But those who are extremely physically fit and have diligently prepared can complete the trip in one day, which requires hiking 21 to 25 miles, depending on the trail, and descending 4,800 feet from the South Rim to the Colorado River, and then climbing 5,850 feet from the base of the canyon to the North Rim. However, because of the danger of heat exhaustion, the National Park Service strongly discourages hikers from attempting a one-day rim-to-rim trip.

Compared to a mountain lion, a hiker will never measure up to its speed and agility. Compared to Jesus, we don't measure up to His perfection. But Jesus came to this earth to teach us how to have a relationship with God. It takes endurance to be a Christian, but Paul reminds us that the Bible was written to give us encouragement and hope. All of the stories within its pages are there for a reason.

Although you may never feel as if you can be like Jesus, each day you spend time with Him will bring you closer to reflecting His image. Every day you can build a stronger relationship with Jesus!

NEXT STEP: Zion National Park, Utah

Hello out there!

Delayed Happiness

Be happy while you are young, and let your heart give you joy
in the days of your youth. **Ecclesiastes 11:9.**

Unlike the Grand Canyon, where you have to hike from the rim to the bottom of the canyon, Zion National Park is located in the bottom of a canyon, and the hiking trails traverse the canyon floor and up the steep sides, providing spectacular views.

The canyon walls are made of red and brown rock in varying shades, lending themselves to breathtaking pictures. This is especially true in the Narrows, where the Virgin River flows between the narrow canyon walls, thus earning its name. In some sections the sun barely peeks through, sending shafts of light down between the towering walls, creating shadows and sunny spots. Although one typically hikes along a trail, the Narrows is a popular hike that is mostly done in the river. In some sections you get only your ankles wet, while in other sections you are waist-deep or up to your neck in water. In a few sections, you actually have to swim.

I was really excited about this particular hike, but my son, who was 6 at the time, was not. I think if we had been able to start right at the river, he would have been happy. But in order to get to the river, we had to walk one mile along a paved path in the heat of the afternoon. A few trees offered some shade, but it was miserable, desert heat. We kept promising him that it would get better and that he would be rewarded by a cool dip in the river once we started hiking up the Narrows, but he kept dragging, going slower and slower.

At last we made it to the Narrows and began hiking up the river. By the end of our hike he proclaimed that it was the best day ever! He had found joy in the activity and was happy that he had kept going, even though for a while he wanted to give up.

Do you have a hard time being happy when things are tough or are not going your way? Solomon reminds you to be happy in your youth. (Of course, I believe this applies to older people too.) Be happy. Be joyful. Let your heart overflow with the good things of life. You have two choices in life: be grumpy and grouchy about everything or be happy and cheerful. Regardless if you are having a good or bad day, you can still choose to be happy!

NEXT STOP: Zion National Park, Utah

October 28

God's Chosen People

I say to you that many will come from the east and the west,
and will take their places at the feast with Abraham, Isaac and Jacob
in the kingdom of heaven. **Matthew 8:11.**

Zion National Park is made up of sandstone cliffs. One famous outcropping of rocks is called the Court of the Patriarchs, named after Abraham, Isaac, and Jacob. A Mormon by the name of Nephi Johnson discovered the region in 1858. (Today the denomination is also known as the Church of Jesus Christ of Latter-day Saints.)

The Mormons fled Illinois because of persecution and settled in southern Utah between 1847 and 1858. Then in 1862 Joseph Black ventured into the canyon and discovered towering sandstone formations. Some Mormons settled in the canyon in 1863 and farmed the land until 1909. While living in the valley they named some of the formations according to their religious beliefs.

Abraham, Isaac, and Jacob obviously were important biblical characters to the Mormons. But these three individuals were also very important to the Israelites, and more specifically the Pharisees of Jesus' day. They felt that because they were descendants of Abraham they were entitled to special rights or privileges.

Jesus descended from Abraham, but He did not claim any special favor because Abraham was in His lineage. In fact, He shocked the Pharisees by saying that people outside of the Jewish faith would be found in heaven. That threw the Pharisees for a loop! They believed with all their hearts that the only people who would be in heaven would be the Jews. They looked down their noses at people of other origins. They treated other people horribly.

But Jesus came to show them a different way. He came to show love and compassion to everyone. He came to share the good news of God's love with anyone who was willing to listen. And He offered the free gift of salvation to all, regardless of whether or not they were descendants of Abraham, Isaac, and Jacob. Thus He made a way for you and me to be in heaven. Maybe I'm a descendant of Abraham, but maybe I'm not. And because of Jesus, it doesn't matter. Being related to Abraham won't save me. Asking Jesus into my heart will!

NEXT STOP: Coral Pink Sand Dunes State Park, Utah

309

October 29

 *Hello out there!*

Sand in My Eye

Why do you look at the speck of sawdust in your brother's eye and pay no attention to the plank in your own eye? **Luke 6:41.**

While we were camping at Zion National Park in Utah, someone suggested we should check out Coral Pink Sand Dunes State Park. None of us had ever played around on sand dunes before, so we decided to drive to the park and explore. As we entered the park we were surrounded by a sea of pinkish-red sand, which is the result of the red sandstone cliffs characteristic of the area.

We parked the car, took off our shoes, and ran up the nearest dune to get a better view. Of course, when we reached the top, we were greeted by more sand stretching out as far as we could see. The kids ran down the hill into a valley. Then they climbed back up and ran down again. Then my husband decided that he would see how many jumps it would take him to leap from the top to the bottom. He looked like a long jumper as he wound up and jumped as far forward as he could, sinking into the sand with each jump. After he reached the bottom, both kids wanted to try.

Everyone was having fun jumping, sliding, and climbing back up the 20-foot dunes, when Ryan jumped and his feet slid out from under him and he began to roll down the hill. Of course, he didn't break a bone or cut open his skin in the soft sand, but sand was *everywhere*, including all over his face. He complained that he had sand in his eyes, but when I looked to see if I could find any, I couldn't. The specks of sand were too small for me to see, even though they were clearly bothering his eye.

After looking for a speck of sand in Ryan's eye, I find today's verse to be very interesting. Jesus is speaking about someone who finds a speck of sawdust in a friend's eye but can't seem to see that he or she has a board sticking out of his or her own eye. What?

In this verse Jesus is reminding us not to be so critical of others. Does it bother you when your little brother smacks his gum? Probably. But if you are a slob at the dinner table and chew loudly and wipe your mouth on your sleeve, should you be criticizing your brother for how he chews his gum? No. Be careful that you don't find fault in others when you are guilty of similar or worse things.

NEXT STOP: Rainbow Bridge National Monument, Utah

October 30

Bridging the Gap

Very truly I tell you, whoever hears my word and believes him
who sent me has eternal life and will not be judged
but has crossed over from death to life. **John 5:24.**

Utah is home to a number of national monuments, including the well-known Rainbow Bridge. Over a period of time, water from Bridge Creek eroded the sandstone and created an alcove in the rock wall. Then sediment, such as rock and sand, continued to wear away at the rock until the bridge stood in its current form.

Rainbow Bridge is not the longest natural rock bridge in the world, but it is the tallest. It measures 234 feet wide and 290 feet high. Standing under such a massive natural bridge is mind-boggling as you think of the amount of water it took to carve it out over the years and the length of time it took for the bridge to appear. I wonder what it looked like before the water began to eat away at the walls. And what it looked like once it was partially eroded. Maybe when I get to heaven, God can play clips from the time in history when Rainbow Bridge was formed.

Unlike a natural bridge that is just amazing to look at, manufactured bridges are put into place for a specific purpose: helping people cross from one side to another side. If you were standing on one side of a cliff and your family was on the other side getting ready to enjoy a treat at a small ice-cream parlor overlooking the valley, what would be the easiest way to get from one side of the gorge to the other? Right! A bridge would work best to get you from one side to the other. Climbing down and up sheer cliffs would be impossible.

Now think about this example in a spiritual sense. If you are on one side of a bridge and Jesus is on the other with a wrapped package for you to open, what do you have to do to get to where Jesus is? That's right: you have to cross the bridge. Jesus isn't going to force you to walk across and take the package, nor is He going to walk across and carry you over. You have to take the initiative to walk across the bridge and talk to Him, get to know Him, and accept His gift. As John says in John 5:24: When you walk across the bridge over the deep gorge below, you are crossing over "from death into life" (NLT).

NEXT STOP: Promontory, Utah

311

Hello out there!

Golden Spike

*The head of the statue was made of pure gold,
its chest and arms of silver, its belly and thighs of bronze, its legs of iron,
its feet partly of iron and partly of baked clay.* **Daniel 2:32, 33.**

In the 1800s the railroad was an exciting new invention. Although you may find it hard to imagine the excitement over a railroad because you are used to so many different forms of transportation today, back then the railroad was a major accomplishment that meant extra freedom and ease of travel. The railroad carried not only people but also all kinds of goods. Thus people and things got to their destination much faster than traveling by horse, wagon, or stagecoach.

The first railroads were built in the East, where there were a lot of people. But as people moved west, so did the railroads, until the Transcontinental Railroad was completed. This railroad, also known as the "Overland Route," connected the eastern United States with the West. And it was in Promontory, Utah, where the Transcontinental Railroad was officially completed on May 10, 1869.

A ceremony was held in honor of this accomplishment, and three special spikes were driven into the railroad ties. The most famous one was a spike made of gold. But they also drove in a silver spike and one that was a mix of gold, silver, and iron.

When I read about this special ceremony and the different spikes, I immediately thought of King Nebuchadnezzar's forgotten dream of the statue. Today's verse is Daniel's retelling of the dream just before interpreting it for the king. It tells us the different parts of the statue and the metals associated with each part. Gold represented Babylon; silver, Medo-Persia; brass, Greece; iron, Rome; and iron and clay, Europe.

Bible prophecy may seem very confusing and as if only grown-ups were meant to understand it, but you can understand things, too. The statue in Nebuchadnezzar's dream pointed forward to the different countries that would rule the world. We are currently living in the time of the mixed iron-and-clay feet, when there is not just one country, but many countries, ruling the world. If you compare history to Bible prophecy, you will find that God has predicted everything. We can trust His Word that what He says is the final outcome really will happen. In Daniel 2:45 the promise appears that God will destroy all the kingdoms of this world and set up His forever kingdom in which He will reign in honor and glory and power.

NEXT STOP: Salt Lake City, Utah

Going for Gold

Blessed is the one who perseveres under trial,
because having stood the test, that person will receive the crown of life
that the Lord has promised to those who love him. **James 1:12.**

In 2002 athletes from around the globe gathered in Salt Lake City for the Winter Olympics. Vonetta Flowers was among those athletes.

The unique thing about Vonetta's story is that she had been a sprinter and long jumper with a dream of competing in the Summer Olympics. Unfortunately, she did not make the track and field team after several attempts. Then, a few months before the 2000 Summer Olympic trials, she had to undergo her fifth surgery in eight years, which put her out of competition. She was obviously frustrated and felt that her dream of competing in the Olympics would never come true.

After the trials ended, her husband, who was also an athlete, decided to try out for the American bobsled team. He had seen a flyer inviting track and field athletes to try out for the team since they are good runners, and you need maximum speed when you take off at the beginning of the bobsled run. So Vonetta's husband went to the tryouts, and Vonetta tagged along. Unfortunately, Vonetta's husband pulled his hamstring at the trials, and he couldn't compete. So Vonetta decided to try out. In the end it was Vonetta who was chosen for the team and placed with Jill Bakken, who would become her bobsled partner.

The pair trained hard for the next year in preparation for the 2002 Winter Olympics, and against all odds they won a gold medal! Vonetta was the first African-American to win a gold medal at the Winter Olympics. And as a pair, Vonetta and Jill were the first United States bobsled team to win a medal in 46 years.

Vonetta's original plans never worked out, but she still lived her dream of going to the Olympics. And she ended up with the icing on the cake by winning a gold medal! She didn't give up and was willing to try something new, and in the end she was rewarded.

Satan tries to distract us and get us to give up. He tries to convince us that getting to heaven is impossible. But when we team up with God, we are assured our own gold medal—the "crown of life"!

NEXT STOP: Las Vegas, Nevada

November 2

Hello out there!

No Rain

> Now Elijah … said to Ahab, "As the Lord, the God of Israel, lives, whom I serve, there will be neither dew nor rain in the next few years except at my word." **1 Kings 17:1**.

Welcome to the driest state in the United States. Nevada has an average annual rainfall of seven inches. Now, that's dry! So where do they get the water for their residents and the huge tourist city of Las Vegas, which uses approximately 240 gallons per person per day? Yes, 240 *gallons* per day!

The city of Las Vegas is currently pulling water from the Lake Mead reservoir. However, there is not enough water coming into the artificially constructed lake to make up for what Las Vegas is pulling out. Some people predict that by 2021 the lake could go dry. But because the city depends on water for its huge hotels, fountains, and restaurants, it has proposed a pipeline that would travel about 263 miles to eastern Nevada. Unfortunately, this plan would hurt the natural springs that the ranchers and farmers rely on to water their animals and crops; solving one problem would create another problem.

Water is essential to life. Plants, animals, and people die without water. That's why when Elijah appeared to Ahab and pronounced that there would be no rain for the next few years, Ahab got scared, really scared. He also got really mad. He searched everywhere for Elijah, because he blamed Elijah for the drought. He failed to realize that he had to live with the consequences of promoting the worship of idols and allowing the people to turn from God. As Ahab and the nation of Israel pushed God away and put their trust in Baal for rain, food, and blessings, God left them to figure things out on their own. He let them see what it was like not to have Him providing for their needs.

As we know, it didn't work out well. Just as Elijah had said, there was a drought for three years. Rivers dried up, food became scarce, and animals and people died. When Elijah showed up in Israel at the end of the three years, Ahab and all the people were ready to listen, and after a showdown between the prophets of Baal and Elijah, the people admitted that the Lord is God of the universe.

NEXT STOP: Paradise, Nevada

Money, Money, Money . . . Money!

For the love of money is a root of all kinds of evil.
Some people, eager for money, have wandered from the faith
and pierced themselves with many griefs. I Timothy 6:10.

You may have heard this before, but Las Vegas is nicknamed Sin City, as well as the Gambling Capital of the World. Today we are actually visiting Paradise, Nevada, which is right outside downtown Las Vegas and is home to some of the largest casinos in the world.

These huge casinos offer tourists every type of gambling opportunity you can think of. You can bet money on card games, slot machines, horse races, number games, and all kinds of other games. But the slot machines seem to be a favorite, given that there are more than 160,000 machines in the state, which is one for about every 18 residents. To work a slot machine, you put in your money and either pull a lever at the side of the machine or push a button. There are three small windows with pictures in them. After you pull the lever or push the button, the pictures spin in the windows before finally stopping. If the pictures match across the three windows, you win, and money pours out. People spend hours playing this game of chance and putting in coin after coin in hopes of winning.

With approximately 40 million people visiting Las Vegas each year, Nevada pulls in most of its income from gambling. Each year players lose a total of approximately $6 billion in the casinos! As you can tell, gambling is a huge source of income for the casinos and for the state.

So what drives people to gamble? Plain and simple—the desire for money! They think, *Next time I'm going to get lucky and win. Just one more game, and I'll hit the big one and be rich!*

A lot of people want to get rich quick, and for many people gambling seems like a quick way to get some extra cash. But in their quest for riches, most people lose a bunch of money and actually become poorer instead of richer.

In his first letter to Timothy, Paul counseled him that the love of money brought about evil. So is money evil? No, but the *love* of it is. When you love something or someone, that thing or person is your priority. If you love money, your whole focus is on money, which means you're not thinking about God or your family or serving Him.

NEXT STOP: Winchester, Nevada

November 4

Hello out there!

For Life

That is why a man leaves his father and mother
and is united to his wife, and they become one flesh. **Genesis 2:24.**

Similar to the city of Paradise, the city of Winchester is located along what is known as the Las Vegas Strip and is also home to numerous casinos. In addition to the casinos, there are a lot of wedding chapels in Winchester. The city is a popular wedding destination because it is so easy to obtain a marriage license. All a couple has to do is pay $60 and show a photo ID, and within minutes they can have a marriage license.

With a marriage license in hand, couples can stop at any number of wedding chapels along the road or in the casinos and get married. The least expensive location costs $50, so getting married in Las Vegas can be really cheap. There are even drive-through wedding locations where couples can quickly say their vows and get on with life!

On average, 120,000 weddings are performed each year, which, when you do the math, is about 328 weddings per day! Maybe all of these people were madly in love and will remain married for the rest of their lives, but my guess is that many of these weddings were the result of a spur-of-the-moment decision to get married and will probably end in divorce.

God created marriage in the Garden of Eden. After forming Eve from a rib in Adam's body, Adam woke up and said, "This is now bone of my bones and flesh of my flesh; she shall be called 'woman,' for she was taken out of man" (Genesis 2:23). The next verse says, "This explains why a man leaves his father and mother and is joined to his wife, and the two are united into one" (verse 24, NLT).

Marriage is to be a special and sacred union between a man and a woman. When God is part of the relationship, there is unity and respect and love. But if God is not part of the picture, our sinful and selfish natures take over and problems arise.

You have a long time before you'll be getting married, but when the time comes, remember to make sure God and His principles are an important part of your relationship with your future spouse. That's the only way to ensure a happy marriage.

NEXT STOP: Hoover Dam, Nevada

Water Power

Then a new king, to whom Joseph meant nothing, came to power in Egypt. So they put slave masters over them to oppress them with forced labor, and they built Pithom and Rameses as store cities for Pharaoh. **Exodus 1:8-11.**

On our first day in Nevada we learned about how little rainfall there is in the state. In an effort to provide flood control, water, and electricity to the cities in the southeastern portion of the state, government officials proposed that a dam be built to hold back water in the Black Canyon on the Colorado River and trap water in Lake Mead.

The project was very controversial, but President Calvin Coolidge (1923–1929) approved it, and the project began. It wasn't an easy job; in fact, it was very dangerous. The workers used huge quantities of concrete and worked in dangerous conditions and at dizzying heights. Thousands of workers tackled the biggest public works project in the history of the United States, pouring 3.25 million cubic yards of concrete. If you spread out all that concrete, you could pave a two-lane highway from San Francisco, California, to New York, New York. The dam measures 726 feet high and is 45 feet thick at the top and 660 feet thick at the bottom, which is larger than the Great Pyramid of Cheops in Egypt.

The Hoover Dam took five years to build and thousands of workers to complete, with the highest paid workers earning $1.25 an hour and the lowest making 50 cents an hour. Compared to today's standards, that seems extremely low. But if you compare it to what the Israelites were making, which was *nothing*, it doesn't seem so bad.

After Joseph died, a new pharaoh came to power, but unlike the old pharaoh, who had a relationship with Joseph and his family, this new pharaoh didn't care who these people were. He worried that they might overthrow him and his government. So out of fear he made them slaves and forced them to work for him building cities and expanding his kingdom. But in spite of the hard labor and the pharaoh's order to kill the baby boys, God blessed the Israelites and made them increase in number and strength.

If we follow God, then even when people plan to harm us God can still bless us and give us strength to withstand the hard times.

NEXT STOP: Area 51, Nevada

November 6

Hello out there!

Secret Code

Jesus answered them, "To you it has been granted to know the mysteries of the kingdom of heaven, but to them it has not been granted." **Matthew 13:11, NASB.**

Area 51 is a top-secret area within the United States Air Force's Nevada Test and Training Range. The site is located near dry Groom Lake, although no one besides those working at the site knows exactly where it is or what goes on there. In fact, the U.S. government did not even acknowledge that the site existed until September 1995.

Even though the government has admitted to the existence of this secret site, it will not disclose anything else about it, and it is heavily guarded by security personnel with M-16s. Even military pilots who train in the area are not allowed to fly over the site.

The only thing we know about Area 51 is that it exists and is a secret military site for the U.S. government. Beyond that, we know nothing. But to those employees who work at the site, they obviously have inside knowledge about the site and its mission.

Christ's disciples had inside knowledge of His mission on earth. When they asked Him why He spoke in parables, Jesus told them that the "secrets of the kingdom of heaven" had been given to them and not the Pharisees. Why? It wasn't because God didn't love the Pharisees; it was because the Pharisees shut their hearts against Jesus' message. They really didn't want to understand. Instead, they wanted to find fault in Jesus and condemn Him.

So Jesus spoke in parables, telling stories about everyday things with important lessons woven throughout. It's interesting that the educated people—the Pharisees and Sadducees—didn't understand, but the common people did. Of course, it really didn't have anything to do with how much schooling they had received. It had to do with their hearts and how much they wanted to learn and how open they were to God.

If heaven and Christianity seem mysterious and like a big secret to you, ask God to reveal the "secrets of the kingdom of heaven" to you, and He will! He doesn't want to keep you in the dark. He would love to "let you in on the secret."

NEXT STOP: Death Valley, Nevada and California

Not One Drop

For forty days and forty nights
he fasted and became very hungry. **Matthew 4:2, NLT.**

I'm glad we are visiting Death Valley in the fall, because in the summer it is *hot!* Death Valley is the lowest point in North America, coming in at 282 feet *below* sea level. And it is the hottest place on earth, recording the highest temperature in the world—134 degrees Fahrenheit—on July 10, 1913.

Not many plants or animals live in Death Valley, but it is home to the kangaroo rat. Not actually related to the kangaroo, this creature borrows its name from the kangaroo because its back legs are long and powerful like a kangaroo's, propelling the little rat up to nine feet in one jump! The kangaroo rat also has a long tail that it uses for jumping and balancing. Although these facts are cool, what really makes the kangaroo rat special is that it can live its entire life without taking a drink of water! At first I thought this had to be a lie, because I thought nothing could survive without water. But amazingly, this little rodent gets what little moisture it needs from the different foods it eats.

So what about humans? Can humans go without water and survive? The answer is no. We must have water in order to live. Humans can go days or weeks without food, but not so without water. Someone who is dehydrated and gets lost in the woods during the summer can die within hours. And even if the person is in good shape, and it isn't too hot or too cold, he or she can only last between three and five days without any water.

After Jesus' baptism, He went into the wilderness to fast and pray. The Bible tells us He fasted for forty days and forty nights. What we don't know is if He drank any water during that time. But whether He drank water or not, God sustained Him and gave Him what He needed most—a clear mind to fight against the temptations that Satan threw at Him.

NEXT STOP: Loma Linda, California

November 8

Hello out there!

A Trip to the Hospital

On hearing this, Jesus said to them, "It is not the healthy who need a doctor, but the sick. I have not come to call the righteous, but sinners." **Mark 2:17.**

In 1905 the Adventist Church opened a sanitarium in Loma Linda, California, to care for the sick in the community. Four years later in 1909 a medical school opened to train doctors and nurses to work in the sanitarium and travel overseas as medical missionaries.

Today Loma Linda University Medical Center employs more than 400 teaching physicians and treats more than 33,000 inpatients—people who are checked into the hospital—and approximately 500,000 outpatients—people who are treated in the emergency room and sent home or who have procedures done in the hospital and are sent home the same day. The hospital is internationally recognized as the leader in infant heart transplants and proton treatments for cancer.

Jesus compared His mission on earth to that of a doctor. Just as sick people need a doctor, sinners need a Savior. And since we know we are all sinners, we all need Jesus as our Savior. Sometimes it is hard to think of ourselves as sinners. We go to church; we help people in our community; we are kind to our classmates; we do chores at home—we're good people. But the Bible tells us that we all sin and "fall short of the glory of God" (Romans 3:23).

We are all born into this sinful world, and we all struggle with sin and doing what's right. And for those reasons we all need Jesus, the Great Physician, to heal us.

If you fell off a swing and broke your arm, would you stay at home and tell yourself that it would get better on its own? No, you would go to the hospital and have them X-ray your arm to see how bad the break was, and then the doctor would put a cast on your arm to protect it and promote healing. We don't hesitate to go to the doctor when we are sick, so why do some people hesitate to give their hearts to Jesus and follow Him? As sinners we need Jesus, just as sick people need a doctor. Some people try to be "good enough" on their own, but we will never be "good enough" without Jesus.

Ask Jesus to be your Savior. Ask Him to make you well.

NEXT STOP: Hollywood, California

Glam and Glitter

Run from anything that stimulates youthful lusts. Instead, pursue righteous living, faithfulness, love, and peace. Enjoy the companionship of those who call on the Lord with pure hearts. **2 Timothy 2:22, NLT.**

Los Angeles is the second-largest city in the United States and is a leading center of the entertainment industry. One of the most famous districts in Los Angeles is Hollywood. With its name spelled out in huge white letters on a hillside overlooking the city, it is known as the center of the movie industry in the United States. Huge movie budgets, talented actors, elaborate sets and wardrobes, and expensive film equipment are the norm in Hollywood. That's why it's nicknamed Tinseltown, because of all the glitz and glamour that surrounds the movie industry and the stars who work in Hollywood and the studios in Los Angeles.

Translated from Spanish into English, Los Angeles means City of Angels, but many say it is a city of wickedness, based on the movies and television shows that are produced there. I would agree that the majority of what Hollywood produces does not uphold biblical standards and is certainly not pure and good and right, which is what Paul tells us to think about in Philippians 4:8. But there are still true followers of God who live and work in Hollywood and who are letting their lights shine for Jesus in an industry that tries to forget that there is a God.

DeVon Franklin is a Seventh-day Adventist, and he is the vice president of production at Columbia Pictures. In August 2012 DeVon appeared on Oprah Winfrey's talk show to discuss a new book he had written. During the interview she asked him what religion he was. DeVon immediately told Oprah he was a Seventh-day Adventist, and he went on to tell her about the Sabbath and why he keeps it holy. He told her that he puts away his cell phone and unplugs from everything so that he can spend time with God and his family.

Oprah proceeded to tell DeVon that that kind of devotion to his faith and setting one day aside for God was unheard-of in Hollywood.

Paul told Timothy to flee from evil and pursue what is good. Whether we are in Hollywood or a small town of a few hundred people, Satan tries to suck us into a world of impure images and messages. But we can resist! With God as our guide, we can keep our hearts pure and be a witness to others of our devotion to God and His commandments.

NEXT STOP: Mount Whitney, California

November 10

Hello out there!

Old Age

Moses was a hundred and twenty years old when he died,
yet his eyes were not weak nor his strength gone. **Deuteronomy 34:7.**

Mount Whitney is the highest peak in the contiguous United States, meaning the lower 48 states minus Alaska and Hawaii. At 14,505 feet mountain climbers enjoy conquering this mountain, which was first climbed to the peak in August 1873.

Twenty-three years after the first ascent, Hulda Crooks was born in what is now Saskatchewan, Canada. One of 18 children, she grew up eating lots of meat and candy. With such a poor diet she weighed 160 pounds by the time she was 16. Two years later Hulda became a Seventh-day Adventist and adopted a vegetarian diet. It was then that the 18-year-old moved to California and attended Pacific Union College and then Loma Linda University. With a change in her lifestyle, the weight came off.

Hulda enjoyed being outdoors and exercising, but hiking and climbing became even more important after the death of her husband and, 19 years later, her only son. In 1962, at age 66, Hulda climbed Mount Whitney for the first time. Each year after that, she climbed Mount Whitney, with her last climb taking place at the age of 91. This earned her the nickname "Grandma Whitney." In recognition of her accomplishment, a southern peak on Mount Whitney was named Crooks Peak in her honor. She died at the age of 101.

You may think your grandparents are really old, but age is just a number. Hulda didn't let old age slow her down. In fact, it was when she was older that she accomplished some pretty amazing things. Not every old person is stuck in a hospital or nursing home waiting to die.

Moses died at age 120, but right up until his death he served God by leading the children of Israel. He didn't make the excuse that he was too tired and old to work for God. Grandma Whitney didn't make any excuses that she was too old to climb a mountain.

Whether we are young or old or somewhere in the middle, we can choose to make excuses so that we don't have to serve God and do anything that is hard, or we can jump in with the determination of Grandma Whitney and Moses and do our best. And when we do our best, God takes it from there and helps us to succeed.

NEXT STOP: Sequoia National Park, California

322

Walking Trees

He looked up and said, "I see people;
they look like trees walking around." Mark 8:24.

Sequoia National Park is home to some of the largest trees in the world. An average height for a sequoia tree is 160 to 279 feet tall and 62 to 81 feet around. The largest recorded tree measured 311 feet tall and 175 feet around.

If the average person has an arm span of five and a half feet, then it would take 32 people to stand fingertip to fingertip around the base of the largest tree! That gives you some sense of how huge the tree trunks are on these giant sequoias. They are massive!

Obviously the blind man in today's story was not comparing the people he saw to the giant sequoia, because he did not see giants when Jesus opened his eyes. Had he seen giants, he might have been scared!

In this story Jesus arrived in Bethsaida, and some people brought a blind man to Him to be healed. Jesus took the man by the hand and led him out of the village, where He then "spit on the man's eyes and put his hands on him," asking, "Do you see anything?" (Mark 8:23). That is when the man said, "I see people. . . . They look like trees walking around" (verse 24, NLT).

I'm guessing the man had had his sight at one time; otherwise, how could he have known what people and trees looked like? But clearly his eyes weren't focusing properly when Jesus first spit on them. So "once more Jesus put his hands on the man's eyes. Then his eyes were opened, his sight was restored, and he saw everything clearly" (verse 25).

In this case the healing was not instant, but Jesus never leaves things half done. He began the process of restoring sight to the blind man, and by the power of God He returned the man to full health.

Have you ever prayed for healing for yourself or someone in your family or church? It's hard when God doesn't heal someone who is sick right away. But God's timing is always perfect, and even if He doesn't heal the person on this earth, we will all receive perfect, healthy bodies when we go to heaven.

NEXT STOP: Alcatraz Island, California

Hello out there!

Escape!

So Peter was kept in prison, but the church
was earnestly praying to God for him. **Acts 12:5.**

Alcatraz Island is located in the San Francisco Bay just one and a half miles off the shore of the city of San Francisco. The island is nicknamed The Rock because it was said to be impossible to escape from the prison located on the island. Prisoners who caused problems at prisons across the country were shipped to Alcatraz.

The prison was in operation for 29 years, and during that time it is claimed that no prisoner successfully escaped. It is recorded that 36 prisoners, on different occasions and some working together as a team, tried to escape 14 times. But everyone was caught or shot or drowned in the rough waters surrounding the jagged, rocky cliffs that plunge into the bay from the island.

Most inmates who try to escape from prison, whether from Alcatraz in the past or another prison, fail to actually make it to freedom without being caught or killed. It is difficult to get by the guards.

That's why the Bible story of Peter escaping from prison is so miraculous. He had been arrested by Herod and was going to be put on trial the next day. These were scary times for the early church as they dealt with persecution on all sides, so when Peter, one of their main leaders, was arrested, they quickly pulled together for an all-night prayer session.

As they prayed, Peter was sleeping between two guards. He was also bound with chains, and there were two other guards stationed at the door of his cell. Talk about maximum security! Suddenly an angel appeared and flooded the cell with light. He then told Peter to get up. The chains fell off, Peter grabbed his clothes, and he followed the angel outside the prison (Acts 12:6-11).

God protected Peter because He still had a job for him to do. But Peter was at peace no matter what was going to happen. He placed his whole trust in God. That's why he was able to sleep while in prison. He trusted God with his life, even if that meant dying for Him.

Do you trust God when things are going good *and* when they are going bad? Being thrown in prison is pretty bad, but Peter still trusted God, and so can we.

NEXT STOP: San Francisco, California

Don't Do It!

Saul said to his armor-bearer, "Draw your sword and run me through . . . ." But his armor-bearer was terrified and would not do it; so Saul took his own sword and fell on it. When the armor-bearer saw that Saul was dead, he too fell on his sword and died with him. **I Samuel 31:4, 5.**

What is the fastest way to get from one landmass to another landmass separated by water? Today we would say a bridge, but in the 1800s and early 1900s, it was by ferry. San Francisco's ferry service, started in 1867, became the world's largest ferry operation by the late 1920s. In 1916 it was proposed that a bridge be built, although many people were concerned about the safety of building such a bridge. They worried that the swift currents and tides and the strong winds in the bay would destroy any bridge they built.

It was finally decided to build a suspension bridge across the 6,700-foot strait. Construction began on January 5, 1933, with a price tag of $35 million. Four years later the Golden Gate Bridge was completed and opened for pedestrian and motor traffic. The bridge was a major accomplishment and a great time-saver for travelers. But the bridge also turned into a good place to end a person's sorrow and pain.

What am I talking about? I'm talking about committing suicide, meaning killing oneself. Since the bridge opened in 1937, more than 1,200 people have jumped off the bridge and fallen 245 feet to their death. Why would someone do that? How could someone stand on the edge of the bridge, look down, and jump to his or her death? It just doesn't make sense, but some people just can't imagine living another day on this earth, whether it is because they don't feel as if anyone loves them or they feel as if they have messed up too much or they are sick and dying already.

King Saul was losing the battle, and he didn't want the enemy to catch him and torture him. He was afraid of the unknown, so he fell on his own sword and killed himself when his armor-bearer refused to do the job. Then the armor-bearer killed himself too, probably out of fear of being killed when someone found out the king was dead. It is such a sad story.

Suicide is never the answer—it only causes pain and suffering for the people left behind. When life seems like too much to handle, we need to turn to Jesus for the answers. He created us for life and hope, not death and despair.

NEXT STOP: Napa Valley, California

November 14

Hello out there!

Wine Country

On the third day a wedding took place at Cana in Galilee. Jesus' mother was there, and Jesus and his disciples had also been invited to the wedding. When the wine was gone, Jesus' mother said to him, "They have no more wine." **John 2:1-3.**

Welcome to Napa Valley, a beautiful section of California that is home to countless vineyards. California produced a record 4 million tons of grapes in 2012. As you drive through the rolling countryside, you can see red, green, and purple grapes growing in long, straight rows. During the harvest, workers walk up and down the rows cutting bunches of grapes from the vines with a knife and collecting the fruit for processing.

The grapes are then used to make grape juice or wine. But Napa Valley is not known for Welch's grape juice; it is known for its wine. In fact, each year California produces more than 17 million gallons of wine, which is a lot of alcohol.

The Bible teaches that wine and alcohol are not good for the body or mind. Ellen White tells us the same thing. So why, then, would Jesus turn water into wine at the wedding feast in Cana, which was His first miracle on earth? Good question.

The Greek word for wine that is used in the Bible actually can mean both alcoholic and regular grape juice. So what did Jesus serve? Ellen White tells us in *The Desire of Ages* that Jesus provided the wedding guests with grape juice to drink (p. 149). Jesus would not have contradicted the Bible or gone against God's own counsel by serving wine when the Bible teaches us not to drink alcohol.

Another clue to help us understand what Jesus served is the reaction of the master of the banquet. When he tasted the wine, he commented that the best wine had been saved for last (John 2:9, 10). If the wedding guests had been drinking alcoholic wine instead of grape juice, we can assume that they wouldn't have been able to tell the difference, because they would have been drunk.

Jesus' first miracle shows how much He cares about people. He cares about the happy occasions in life and the things that matter to us, such as wedding celebrations. He cares about what we need for food and drink. But most important, He cares about our feelings.

NEXT STOP: San Andreas Fault, California

Beware of the Shaking

About midnight Paul and Silas were praying and singing hymns to God, and the other prisoners were listening to them. Suddenly there was such a violent earthquake that the foundations of the prison were shaken. At once all the prison doors flew open, and everybody's chains came loose. **Acts 16:25, 26.**

Today we are not visiting a city in California. Instead, we are talking about an important geological phenomenon that effects the majority of California. The San Andreas Fault extends from southern California by the Salton Sea to northern California at Cape Mendocino, which is about 250 miles north of San Francisco. The fault is where two tectonic plates meet—the Pacific Plate and the north American Plate. As these plates slide and shift and bump into each other, they create tremors, or earthquakes, on the surface of the earth. It is estimated that southern California experiences approximately 10,000 earthquakes each year!

Just like most schools have fire drills, students in California also have earthquake drills. During an earthquake drill, students crawl under their desks and curl up in a ball with their hands over their heads to protect themselves from falling debris should the building shake so much that it begins to collapse. Fortunately, most earthquakes are small and result in minor damages to property. Of course, big earthquakes can cause a lot of damage and loss of life when buildings collapse and trap people beneath piles of rubble.

In Bible times they didn't rate earthquakes on a scale, but the one that hit while Paul and Silas were in prison was forceful enough to shake the foundation of the prison and cause the doors to fly open and everyone's chains to fall off. When the jailer discovered that the prison doors were wide open, he feared for his life and was about ready to kill himself, when Paul shouted, "Don't harm yourself! We are all here!" (Acts 16:28).

I don't know what Paul said to the other prisoners to keep them from running away, but everyone was there. Then the jailer ran to Paul and Silas and asked, "Sirs, what must I do to be saved?" (verse 30). That night Paul told the jailer and his family about Jesus, and the family was baptized. All because of an earthquake! This is just one example of how God used the forces of nature for His purposes. I'm glad God controls the universe and everything in it.

NEXT STOP: Mount Shasta, California

Hello out there!

The Promised Land

So I have come down to rescue them from the hand of the Egyptians and to bring them up out of that land into a good and spacious land, a land flowing with milk and honey. **Exodus 3:8.**

Did you know that one of California's nicknames is the Land of Milk and Honey? It is a reference to the Promised Land in the Bible. Some people feel that California has it all—great climate, mountains, beaches, the ocean, money, good soil for farming, and so on. Of course, when the gold rush hit California in 1848, it was really considered the Promised Land.

On our last day in California we are visiting Mount Shasta. Located in the Cascade Range in northern California, the mountain is 14,179 feet tall and is the fifth-highest mountain in California. It is considered a dormant volcano and is popular with mountain climbers and backcountry skiers. Because it isn't connected to any other mountains, it dominates the horizon.

I love the mountains. If I had my choice, I would visit the mountains instead of the beach or any other place, any day. Of course, you might feel differently. Maybe you love the beach, and the ocean spray, the openness of the prairies, or even the sandy desert. The mountains are my "promised land."

For the children of Israel, the Promised Land was filled with good food and plenty of land for them to spread out and raise their families and animals and crops. In addition to the good things about the area, it was the Promised Land because it was God's plan for their lives.

Your "promised land" may be in Canada, the United States, Mexico, Brazil, or Kenya. It may be in the mountains or near the beach. It may be in a community with a lot of Adventists or someplace where you are the only kid in your church. But when God places you and your family in an area, He is giving you your own "promised land."

Of course, the ultimate Promised Land for each of us as followers of God is heaven. But until that time when Jesus returns to take us home, I hope you are living and serving God wherever He has placed you.

NEXT STOP: Hawaii

Way Out There

*Joseph's master took him and put him in prison,
the place where the king's prisoners were confined.* **Genesis 39:20.**

Aloha ("Hello" in Hawaiian)! Many people consider Hawaii to be a tropical paradise. Located in the middle of the northern Pacific Ocean, the island chain was formed by volcanic eruptions, resulting in large mountains that descend into lush valleys that eventually turn into sandy beaches.

Although some people find Hawaii to be the perfect island getaway, it is also expensive to travel to and live there because it is so isolated. Hawaii is 2,390 miles from California; 3,850 miles from Japan; 4,900 miles from China; and 5,280 miles from the Philippines. Everything costs more because everything has to be grown on the island or shipped in by boat or plane.

In Hawaii you can't decide just to hop in the car and drive to your grandparents' home in Nevada. You are separated from the mainland of the United States by a vast ocean, which makes travel more difficult. People living in Hawaii are somewhat isolated from the rest of the world.

Being isolated from the people you love and care about can be tough. Some missionaries and military personnel struggle with being so far away from home when they serve overseas. But when we feel isolated and cut off from the rest of the world, God is still right there beside us.

Look at the story of Joseph. He was in a foreign country far from his family and friends when he was thrown into prison for a crime he didn't commit. He was isolated from everything and everyone who was familiar to him. But God blessed Joseph, and the warden put him in charge of all the other prisoners. Joseph was not immediately freed or removed from the situation, but God brought him some comfort and peace in the midst of suffering.

Do you ever feel isolated and alone? You don't have to be on the other side of the world to feel alone. Sometimes when friends or family pick on you and treat you unkindly, you may feel as if you are all alone with no one to talk to. Just remember, you can always talk to Jesus. He will gladly listen to your problems and troubles. He knows how you feel. He felt alone on this earth when His disciples left Him right at the moment He needed their support the most. He cares, and He will help see you through whatever challenges you are facing.

NEXT STOP: Hawaiian Volcanoes

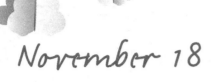

November 18

Hello out there!

Don't Let It Blow!

"In your anger do not sin": Do not let the sun go down while you are still angry, and do not give the devil a foothold. **Ephesians 4:26, 27.**

The Hawaiian Island chain is spread out over 1,500 miles. At the southern tip of the island chain lie the eight main islands of Hawaii. From west to east they are Niʻihau, Kauaʻi, Oʻahu, Molokaʻi, Lānaʻi, Kahoʻolawe, Maui, and the island of Hawaiʻi, which is often called the Big Island to avoid confusion over its name compared to the name of the state.

As we mentioned yesterday, Hawaii was formed because of volcanic activity. It is interesting to note that Hawaii's tallest mountain, Mauna Kea, is taller than Mount Everest if measured from the base of the mountain. You see, from the surface of the ocean to the peak of the mountain it is 13,796 feet, which is shorter than Everest, but if you measure from the base of the mountain, which is at the bottom of the Pacific Ocean, the mountain is about 33,500 feet tall!

The Hawaiian Island chain is scattered with dormant volcanoes, but there are still a few active ones. The Kīlauea volcano is one of the most active volcanoes in the world, having erupted 61 times since 1823. Its longest eruption began on January 3, 1983, and was still going as of January 2011. Over the years the eruption has shifted from one vent to another, but Kīlauea is still sending lava flows down the slopes of the volcano. In January 2011 it was calculated that the eruption had produced one cubit mile of lava, destroyed 213 structures, and created lava as thick as 115 feet on a nearby highway.

Some people have a temper like a volcano. They let anger build up inside of them until it comes spewing out, covering anyone who happens to be nearby when they blow. They don't think about whom they are hurting with their angry words or the objects they throw around in their anger; they just react. And in the process of letting out all their stored up anger, they may hurt people physically or emotionally.

The Bible instructs us to not sin when we get angry. We need to control our anger and express ourselves in ways that don't hurt others. We also need to make things right if we do get angry and apologize or discuss the situation as soon as possible with the person we hurt. Anger is a natural feeling, but we need to express it appropriately.

NEXT STOP: Oʻahu, Hawaii

Don't Be Swayed

And you will know that I am the Lord, for you have not followed
my decrees or kept my laws but have conformed to the standards
of the nations around you. **Ezekiel 11:12.**

If you visit Hawaii, most people will tell you that you need to attend a luau. This traditional Hawaiian party or feast features lots of food, music, and the hula. The hula is a dance native to Hawaii, which is supposed to be representative of the islands. The hula dancers move their hands and bodies in graceful movements to the rhythm of the music.

The interesting thing is that before the luau became a tourist event that brought in a lot of money from people who wanted to see what traditional Hawaiian culture was all about, the hula was a sacred dance. Hawaiians believe that the first person who performed the hula was a goddess, hence the reason it is special. And yet this sacred ritual and event has turned into something that is performed at hotels and resorts across the island of O'ahu as entertainment.

Since we don't believe in other gods or goddesses, the hula has no special significance to us as Christians in a spiritual sense. However, if the Hawaiian people really believe it is a sacred ritual, are they conforming to the world by performing it at nightly shows? Are they selling themselves out to earn money?

The children of Israel struggled throughout their existence with standing firm for what they believed and not bending to the surrounding countries. It was a constant battle for them to remain true to God and not worship the idols of the neighboring nations. Time and time again they failed to follow the Lord's decrees and keep His laws.

Did they sell themselves out for riches and fame or supposed peace? In some instances, they took what they considered to be the easy road, not relying on God for guidance or protection.

Do you conform to the world? Do you shift your beliefs to fit with the lifestyles of the friends around you? Or do you plant your feet firm on God's law and the truth of the Bible and not move? I hope you choose to stand firm and hold to your standards, no matter what.

NEXT STOP: Ni'ihau, Hawaii

Hello out there!

November 20

The Legend of Pele

Therefore rebuke them sharply, so that they will be sound in the faith and will pay no attention to Jewish myths or to the merely human commands of those who reject the truth. **Titus 1:13, 14.**

The island of Ni'ihau is a privately owned island to the southwest of the island of Kaua'i. Elizabeth Sinclair purchased Ni'ihau in 1864, and since that time it has been passed down to her relatives. Its nickname is "The Forbidden Isle" because it is only open to invited guests, government officials, U.S. Navy personnel, and a small number of tourists on approved hunting safaris or helicopter tours. The total population on the island was 130 people as of June 2009.

Another unique characteristic of the island is that legend claims that the goddess Pele was befriended by a queen on this island. Pele is the goddess of fire, lightning, wind, and volcanoes, which fits perfectly into Hawaii's terrain. But that's not where the legend stops. Hawaiian mythology also claims that Pele is full of passion and love. Therefore, every volcanic eruption is a show of Pele's passion for her true love, a young chief named Lohiau.

The interesting thing about legends is that there are often a variety of versions, which is the case with Pele. Legends and myths cannot be trusted for that very reason—there are just too many different versions.

During the time of the early Christian church, Greek mythology was a powerful influence in the towns and cities Paul visited, but here in his letter to Titus we find that there were also Jewish myths that were causing problems. Paul speaks strongly to Titus to express his strong disapproval of their beliefs and actions so that they will stand firm in the faith. If Titus did not point out the errors of their ways, Paul warned that they would fall further away from the church.

When you are faced with a legend, myth, or new idea, always test it against the Bible. We often don't want to hurt people's feelings by telling them they are wrong, but Paul reminds Titus how important it is to point out false teachings and get rid of the people causing the trouble before the whole church is infected. This is what Paul wrote: "For there are many rebellious people, full of meaningless talk and deception. . . . They must be silenced, because they are disrupting whole households by teaching things they ought not to teach" (Titus 1:10, 11). Don't be afraid to stand up for what you believe. It is your right and duty as a child of God.

NEXT STOP: Pearl Harbor, Hawaii

Revenge!

*Dear friends, never take revenge. Leave that
to the righteous anger of God. For the Scriptures say,
"I will take revenge; I will pay them back," says the Lord.* **Romans 12:19, NLT.**

The United States Navy operates a naval base in Pearl Harbor, Hawaii, which is the headquarters of the U.S. Pacific Fleet. The navy established its presence in Pearl Harbor in 1899, but on December 7, 1941, everything changed for the naval base. World War II had begun two years before, on September 1, 1939, but the United States had managed to stay out of the war thus far. On the fateful morning of December 7 the Imperial Japanese Navy launched a devastating surprise attack.

Beginning at 6:00 a.m., six Japanese aircraft carriers launched 181 bomber planes. Shortly before 8:00 a.m., the first planes simultaneously attacked the ships in the harbor and the military airfields. A second wave of 170 bombers arrived in the harbor about 8:40 a.m. One ship in particular, the U.S.S. *Arizona*, sank within minutes after it was hit by a bomb and exploded.

When the fighting finally stopped, more than 2,300 Americans had lost their lives, including 48 to 68 civilians, and more than 1,100 soldiers and civilians were wounded. The death toll on the *Arizona* alone totaled 1,177. Twenty-one U.S. ships were sunk or damaged. After the attack, posters were printed with the words "Avenge December 7" on them as a battle cry to inspire the soldiers to fight their hardest and remind Americans what the war was all about.

When people hurt us, our family, or our country, we want to get back at them and make the wrong right. We want to teach them a lesson and make sure they know they can't treat us that way. We want to make them pay for what they did.

But God teaches us a different way. Romans 12:17 says, "Never pay back evil with more evil. Do things in such a way that everyone can see you are honorable" (NLT). Two verses later we find today's memory text, which talks about not taking revenge on others but leaving it to God to handle. Verses 20 and 21 give us even more detail as to how we are to treat those who hurt us: "Instead, 'If your enemies are hungry, feed them. If they are thirsty, give them something to drink. In doing this, you will heap burning coals of shame on their heads.' Don't let evil conquer you, but conquer evil by doing good" (NLT). It may seem hard to do, but the more we become like Christ, the more we will adopt His character—a character of love.

NEXT STOP: Kalaupapa, Hawaii

Hello out there!

A Thankful Heart

As he was going into a village, ten men who had leprosy met him.
They stood at a distance and called out in a loud voice,
"Jesus, Master, have pity on us!" **Luke 17:12, 13.**

Leprosy in Bible times was a horrible disease to contract. There was no cure, and because it was so highly contagious, as soon as a person was diagnosed with leprosy, that person had to leave his or her family and go live in a leper colony with other lepers so that the disease would not spread in the community.

But leprosy affected more than just people in Bible times. In 1873 Father Damien, a Roman Catholic priest and missionary, settled in Kalaupapa and began ministering to the lepers whom the government had sent there to isolate them from the rest of the community. At one point 1,200 men, women, and children with leprosy lived in the village; a total of about 8,000 people with leprosy have lived there. Up until the late 1930s, when a treatment was discovered, if you got leprosy your life was ruined and you were cut off from the rest of society.

There are a few references in the Bible of Jesus healing people with leprosy, but one in particular has always stood out to me. Ten lepers see Jesus off in the distance, and they yell to Him, "Have mercy on us!" (Luke 17:13, NLT). Jesus then says, "'Go, show yourselves to the priests.' And as they went, they were cleansed" (verse 14).

The men obviously had faith, for they were healed as they turned to go show themselves to the priest. But only one man came back, "praising God in a loud voice. He threw himself at Jesus' feet and thanked him—and he was a Samaritan" (verses 15, 16). Remember, Samaritans and Jews didn't like each other, so that makes his return and offer of thanks even more special.

All 10 were healed, but only one came back to say thank you. Saying thank you is a sign of good manners, but many forget to say it and still others don't seem to mean it when they say it. Jesus healed the lepers, and only one returned. Jesus died for the sins of the world, but how many people tell Him thank you for His sacrifice? If you haven't done that yet, take the time to really tell Jesus thank you for His gift of life. He'll appreciate it!

NEXT STOP: Kaua'i, Hawaii

Which Way?

Now Jacob sent Judah ahead of him to Joseph
to get directions to Goshen. **Genesis 46:28.**

How would you give directions in Bible times? In today's Bible text Judah goes ahead of Jacob and the rest of the family to get directions from Joseph as to the best route to travel to Goshen. Maybe they sounded like this: "Travel straight for one day until the sun sets on the horizon. Then stop and camp at the oasis. The next morning turn west and travel until the sun is directly overhead. Then turn south and continue until you reach the tents of the family of Zebel."

Those are obviously imaginary directions, but I'm sure their directions were much more visual than "turn left on Peanut Street, travel two miles and turn on Milky Avenue, and then arrive at house number 298." And we all know they didn't have a GPS to program their final destination into! In those days they gave directions based on landmarks.

So I found it interesting that in Hawaii there are two typical ways that local residents give directions. If we were visiting Kaua'i— which is considered the garden island, with its lush vegetation, mountains, and waterfalls— and we asked for directions to Waimea Canyon State Park, a local would say, "Mauka," meaning toward the mountains. If we were trying to get to the beach, they would say "Makai," meaning toward the sea. Hopefully they also give specific road names and other landmarks to help travelers, but they've developed a system that points in one of two directions, to the mountains or the sea.

Good directions get you to where you need to go—bad directions just get you lost. Whether people give you directions or you print them off the Internet or you follow the GPS, there is always a chance you may get lost. None of these methods is foolproof, though. The only way to ensure you don't get lost is to have someone in the vehicle who knows where you are going and tells you where to turn.

The same is true with our walk with God. We may get lost if we look to other people for direction or read books or things on the Internet as to how we should interpret the Bible. However, if we read the Bible and ask the Holy Spirit to direct us, we are sure to make all the right turns that lead us to the ultimate destination—heaven!

NEXT STOP: Guam

Hello out there!

It Must Be a Trick

For the appeal we make does not spring from error or impure motives, nor are we trying to trick you. On the contrary, we speak as those approved by God to be entrusted with the gospel. **I Thessalonians 2:3, 4.**

Although Guam is approximately 3,800 miles west of Hawaii in the vast Pacific Ocean, it is a United States territory and is part of the North American Division of the Seventh-day Adventist Church. The largest island in Micronesia, Guam came under United States control in 1898 during the Spanish-American War, and it soon became a U.S. military base for ships patrolling the waters of the Pacific Ocean.

On December 8, 1941, one day after Japan attacked Pearl Harbor, Japanese forces invaded Guam and took over the island. For two and a half years the Japanese oppressed the citizens of Guam until the U.S. military launched an attack on July 21, 1944. In one day of fighting the American forces defeated the Japanese, killing more than 18,000 soldiers who refused to surrender.

But 10 Japanese soldiers went into hiding in the jungles of Guam after the battle. One of the soldiers was Shoichi Yokoi. For 28 years Yokoi lived in seclusion in a cave, hunting at night and making clothes and utensils out of plants in the jungle. Then on January 24, 1972, two fishermen bumped into Yokoi in the jungle. They thought he was a villager, but Yokoi attacked them, so they fought back and dragged him out of the jungle. It was then that the story came out, and they discovered that he had been hiding all those years, fearing that the war was not over and that his life would be in danger should he be discovered. Even though he had found leaflets declaring that World War II had ended, he thought the information was a trick.

Many people think the gospel is a trick and that the gift of salvation is a scam. Paul ran into that problem in Thessalonica, and Christians who share their faith today run into this same problem. People simply do not want to believe the good news, or they think there is some catch. But we believe in the truth of the Bible! Maybe you can share Yokoi's story with someone who is skeptical and encourage them to believe instead of living in fear and missing out on the best gift this world has to offer—salvation and a life with Jesus.

NEXT STOP: Guam

His Church

Then he said to his disciples, "The harvest is plentiful
but the workers are few. Ask the Lord of the harvest, therefore,
to send out workers into his harvest field." **Matthew 9:37, 38.**

Jesus told His disciples that the "harvest" of people who were ready to hear the gospel and follow Jesus was plentiful. There were many whose hearts were open to learning more about Jesus, but sadly not many people were willing to take the message of God's love to those who were eager to hear it. The same problem exists today. And yet God still has people who are willing to tell others about the love of Christ, as is evident in the story of the formation of the Adventist Church in Guam.

During World War II seven Adventist military personnel were sent to Guam. Before leaving Hawaii, where they were stationed, Bob Beckett's pastor encouraged him not only to serve his country but also to serve his church by working to establish an Adventist church on the island. So Bob was deployed to Guam with two missions.

Upon arriving, Bob brought together the small group of Adventists to worship on the first Sabbath in their new military location. Attendance grew, and Henry Metzker soon asked Bob if he could invite the Chamorros, a name for the native people of Guam. Bob thought it was a great idea, so Henry ventured into the community in search of people who might be interested in the Bible.

Henry came across an island family who didn't know about the Adventist Church but who were interested in a church that kept the Bible Sabbath. The Ulloa family agreed to study the Bible with Henry, and soon they opened their home to the Adventists as a place of worship. Shortly after that members of the Ulloa family asked to be baptized, and the beginnings of a permanent Adventist church in Guam were under way.

The harvest is still plentiful, but Jesus needs more workers. What can you do to share Jesus with those around you? Could you share your *Guide* with a friend who doesn't come to church? Could you invite someone over to your house to watch a Bible video? Could you raise money to send Bibles overseas? There are so many ways that you can help Jesus bring in the harvest. Be creative. Pray for ways to share with others. And then get to it!

NEXT STOP: Pit Stop

Hello out there!

True Thankfulness

Enter his gates with thanksgiving and his courts with praise;
give thanks to him and praise his name. **Psalm 100:4.**

What are you thankful for this year? Although maybe not in this order, would your list look something like this?

- God
- a warm bed and house
- clothes
- parents and siblings
- pets

Many of us have it pretty good and live in relative comfort. We have much to be thankful for. But now I want you to think about things a little differently. I want you to think of something bad that happened this year and how you can be thankful for that. David praised God through the good and the bad, and Paul wrote that we should give thanks at all times (1 Thessalonians 5:18).

So what is there to be thankful for when your dad loses his job or your classmate dies in an accident or your best friend won't speak to you? It's hard to be thankful in these situations, but that's what God wants us to do. He wants us to trust Him in the good and bad. He wants us to find the good in all situations.

So what could be good about your dad losing his job? Maybe it will make you more compassionate toward others who don't have much. What about a classmate dying? Maybe it will help you yearn for heaven and share with others the good news of Jesus' return. What about losing a good friend? Maybe you will become friends with someone else who is lonely and looking for a friend.

When bad times come, you have a choice. You can get mad and wish for everything to return to normal, or you can accept it and look for the good in the situation. So what are you thankful for? This year I challenge you to think about something bad that happened and the good that God has brought out of it. You can do it! Give thanks—always!

NEXT STOP: Sea Lion Caves, Oregon

Stuck in a Cave

When Joshua was told that the five kings had been found hiding in the cave at
Makkedah, he said, "Roll large rocks up to the mouth of the cave,
and post some men there to guard it." **Joshua 10:17, 18.**

Welcome back to the mainland. We have spent the past week visiting Hawaii and Guam, but today we are in the Pacific Northwest in the state of Oregon visiting the coast and a place called Sea Lion Caves. As you can imagine, Sea Lion Caves got its name from the sea lions that make their home in the cave and near its entrance. The cave system is one of the largest sea caves in the world. The main cavern is roughly the size of two acres, with a 125-foot-high vaulted ceiling. There are three entrances to the cave and its system of tunnels, but explorers have to be careful not to get caught in the cave during high tide or rough weather, as the waves are constantly crashing into the main cavern.

Throughout history, caves have served as natural homes, storage areas, hiding places, and burial sites. In today's Bible text we discover a story where a cave was used as a temporary jail.

Joshua and the Israelites were fighting the five kings of the Amorites. In fact, God caused the sun not to set until the Israelites defeated the army of the five kings. (Read Joshua 10 if you don't remember this story.) The five kings tried to escape, and they hid "in the cave at Makkedah" (Joshua 10:16). When Joshua found out where they were, he sent some troops to place large stones in front of the entrance so they could not escape. He also posted a few guards, and then he sent the troops to continue pursuing the fleeing soldiers.

I have no idea what the five kings were thinking, but I'm guessing they knew they didn't have long to live. Sure enough, after defeating the enemy armies, Joshua returned and ordered that the stones be removed and the kings brought out. Before killing the kings, he told the people, "Do not be afraid; do not be discouraged. Be strong and courageous. This is what the Lord will do to all the enemies you are going to fight" (verse 25).

Joshua knew he didn't have any power by himself. The power over his enemies came because God gave him the victory. With God on his side, he wasn't afraid. With God on our side, we don't have to be afraid either. We too can stand strong and be courageous!

NEXT STOP: Eugene, Oregon

Hello out there!

Practice Makes Perfect

Share with the Lord's people who are in need. Practice hospitality. **Romans 12:13**.

When did you learn to ride a bike? Did you learn when you were 4 or 5, or not until you were 8 or 9? Were you scared or nervous the first time you tried to ride without training wheels? Were you afraid you would fall over and crash? Regardless of how you felt, you were probably like my two children. At first they had a hard time balancing, and they crashed a few times, but once they figured out how to balance, they took off! There was no stopping them as they pedaled down the road at full speed.

Kids aren't the only ones who like to ride bikes. Many adults enjoy biking, or cycling, as it is known in the sports community. And apparently Eugene, Oregon, is a favorite destination for cyclists. According to *Bicycling Magazine* the city is known as one of the 10 best cycling communities in the United States. The weather is ideal for biking, and there are plenty of paths to explore and bike lanes to keep cyclists safe on the road.

Enthusiastic cyclists will often ride between 30 and 60 miles each ride. I'm sure that seems like a lot for your legs, but for adults who have been biking for the past 10 to 20 years, those miles are nothing compared to the thousands of miles they've ridden in their lifetimes. The more time they spend on their bikes, the easier it is to ride longer distances.

If you wanted to ride longer distances on your bike, you would need to begin by practicing riding 10 miles, then 15 miles, then 20 miles, and so on. That old saying is true, practice makes perfect.

Does practice work with kindness toward others? Of course! Paul told the church in Rome to share with others who were in need and "practice hospitality" (Romans 12:13). If you were to practice being kind to your brother or sister or classmates, it would become easier until you wouldn't even have to think about being kind; it would be second nature to treat others as Christ would treat them. Like Paul, I urge you to practice hospitality, kindness, thankfulness, and generosity until these character traits define who you are.

NEXT STOP: Crater Lake, Oregon

Majestic Beauty

The foundations of the city walls were decorated
with every kind of precious stone. The first foundation was jasper,
the second sapphire, the third agate, the fourth emerald,
the fifth onyx, the sixth ruby, the seventh chrysolite, the eighth beryl,
the ninth topaz, the tenth turquoise, the eleventh jacinth,
and the twelfth amethyst. **Revelation 21:19, 20.**

I can't even begin to describe the beauty of Crater Lake and the deep blue color of the lake. It reminds me of the richest blue sapphire I've ever seen, which was at the Smithsonian Natural History museum in Washington, D.C.

The lake was first named Deep Blue Lake because of its color. It was later changed to Blue Lake and Lake Majesty before finally being named Crater Lake. The unique thing about the lake is that it is not fed by a river or any other body of water. The lake is located in the crater of what used to be a volcano, and its water supply is replenished by rain and melted snow.

When I look at the natural beauty and color of Crater Lake, I can't wait to see the jewels of heaven. In Revelation 21 we find a description of the city walls of the New Jerusalem, which will be decorated "with every kind of precious stone" (Revelation 21:19, NASB). The second layer will be of sapphire, which I'm sure will be more stunning than anything we have ever seen on earth and will outshine the beauty of the blue waters of Crater Lake. The rest of the jewels in the foundation will be equally exquisite.

God has so much planned for us. He loves us and wants to give us good things. The original splendor of the Garden of Eden will be restored when He comes again, and I think that the magnificence of the New Jerusalem and the new earth will astound us because we are used to a sick, sin-filled earth. Are you excited about heaven and what the future holds? I hope so, because it's going to be amazing!

NEXT STOP: Portland, Oregon

November 30

Hello out there!

An Important Name

One of you says, "I follow Paul"; another, "I follow Apollos"; another, "I follow Cephas"; still another, "I follow Christ." **I Corinthians 1:12.**

If you haven't heard of Nike, it is an international company that specializes in sports apparel and accessories. The company was formed in 1964 by Phil Knight and Bill Bowerman and was originally named Blue Ribbon Sports. A few years later in 1971 Carolyn Davidson, who was a student at Portland State University, was asked to design a logo for the company.

Carolyn submitted a number of designs to Phil for consideration. It is reported that Phil actually did not like any of the designs, but he selected the "swoosh," saying that maybe he would get used to it. The company stuck with the design, and in 1978 they changed their name to Nike, which means "victory" in Greek.

Today the company is a leading supplier of athletic shoes, outfitting star athletes throughout the sporting community. From basketball players to Olympic runners and track and field stars, athletes from around the world can be seen wearing Nike shoes.

Maybe it's because I grew up owning a few pairs of Nike shoes, but I can't imagine wearing Blue Ribbon Sports shoes. The name just doesn't seem to fit.

Likewise, it would seem weird if we were "Paulians" or "Apollians"! We are Christians because we follow Christ, our Savior and leader. And yet the early Christian church struggled with division in the church and the desire of some members to follow the teachings of one apostle or another. Paul quickly addressed the growing division and reminded the church at Corinth that we are all part of Christ.

He wrote, "Is Christ divided? Was Paul crucified for you? Were you baptized into the name of Paul?" (1 Corinthians 1:13). His point was that no one should be following or worshipping him. Jesus was the head of the church, not one of the apostles.

Jesus is still head of the church. We don't follow Mark Finley, Dwight K. Nelson, Derek Morris, Ted N. C. Wilson, or any other church leader or evangelist. It is fine to look up to and respect godly men and women in the church, but they can never take the place of Jesus. He is the one whose name we take when we become Christians!

NEXT STOP: Oregon City, Oregon

Father Abraham

Against all hope, Abraham in hope believed and so became the father of many nations, just as it had been said to him, "So shall your offspring be." **Romans 4:18.**

John McLoughlin was born and raised in Quebec. Upon becoming a licensed physician in 1803, he moved to a trading post in Ontario, where, although I'm sure he used his medical skills, he became a successful trader for the North West Company. In 1821 when the North West Company was bought by the Hudson's Bay Company, he was promoted to a new district within the Hudson's Bay territory.

In 1824 John moved to the Pacific Northwest, where he built Fort Vancouver as part of the Hudson's Bay Company's expansion into new fur trading territory. As the Americans began pushing west, John assisted some of the new settlers who made it across the Oregon Trail. This was in direct disobedience to the orders of the Hudson's Bay Company (which was operated by the British) not to assist the Americans in any way. There was definitely tension between the British and the Americans, but John kept the peace. In fact, it was noted that he treated everyone fairly whether they were British, American, or native to the Northwest.

John retired from the Hudson's Bay Company in 1846 and moved to Oregon City. There he opened a store to supply settlers with food and tools and equipment after the long journey across the United States from the East. Because of his contributions to the early formation of Oregon, the Oregon Legislative Assembly voted in 1957 to honor him with the title "Father of Oregon," in memory of his death 100 years before.

As I read about John McLoughlin, the "father of Oregon," I thought about Abraham, the father of many nations. John died 100 years before he received recognition from the government for his role in the establishment of Oregon. But his reward is simply an earthly reward. Abraham, too, received recognition for his faith and the establishment of the Jewish nation after his death, but unlike John's, Abraham's reward is laid up in heaven. His faith and devotion to God were recognized by Paul in the New Testament and have certainly been recorded in the book of life in heaven.

Earthly treasures such as fame and fortune fade away, but heavenly rewards last forever.

NEXT STOP: Twin Falls, Idaho

December 2

Hello out there!

Foolish Stunts

*A foolish son brings grief to his father
and bitterness to the mother who bore him.* **Proverbs 17:25.**

Evel Knievel was a daredevil known for doing reckless and dangerous things such as jumping his motorcycle across anything you could stack on top of something else or line up end to end with a ramp on either side. Then Evel Knievel changed his focus to jumping over a canyon.

To keep himself in the news, Evel Knievel began to plan for a jump across the Grand Canyon. In an interview he stated that he didn't care if he died; he was just determined to be the first person to attempt such a jump. He tried to negotiate with the U.S. government to secure a jump site, but in the end he was denied. So he changed directions and decided to jump over the Snake River Canyon near Twin Falls, Idaho.

Evel Knievel had a special rocket built with a steam-powered engine that would carry him across the canyon, since the jump would not be possible on a motorcycle. On September 8, 1974, he attempted the jump. The rocket fired, and the parachute deployed as projected. However, he missed the north rim of the canyon by a few feet because of the drag of the parachute. He floated to the bottom of the canyon with only minor injuries.

The failed Snake River Canyon jump was actually one of his safer jumps. A few years prior to the canyon jump, he crashed while trying to jump over the fountains in front of Caesars Palace in Las Vegas and spent the following 29 days in a coma. During his career he crashed countless other times, breaking 35 bones a total of 433 times during his career and earning him the title of the survivor of the most broken bones in a lifetime in the *Guinness Book of World Records*.

Solomon reminds us how important wisdom is and that when kids, or adults, are foolish, it makes their parents sad. It can be hard to say no when your friends want you to do something foolish like jump off a 20-foot cliff into the river without a life jacket on and without knowing how deep the water is. But in the end you, and your parents, will be happier when you make good decisions and don't put yourself in danger. Spending months in the hospital, or worse, dying, because you made a poor decision and followed the crowd will only cause pain and suffering. Think before you act! Be wise instead of foolish!

NEXT STOP: Spencer, Idaho

Buried Treasure

The kingdom of heaven is like treasure hidden in a field.
When a man found it, he hid it again, and then in his joy went
and sold all he had and bought that field. **Matthew 13:44.**

Grab a metal detector, because we are going on a treasure hunt! There is a rumor that buried treasure lies in Beaver Canyon near Spencer, Idaho, and the treasure is none other than gold. It is thought that an outlaw by the name of Henry Plummer stole gold during a stagecoach robbery and then buried the gold in the canyon while trying to escape the authorities.

What would you do if you found gold? Would you buy a bunch of electronics? Would you help your parents pay for your school bills or the house or food? Would you take your family on a vacation? Now, think about this. What if you found the treasure on land that was owned by the government? Would you try to buy the land so that you could have the treasure?

That's exactly what the man did in the parable of the hidden treasure. After finding the treasure, he "sold everything he owned . . . to buy the field" (Matthew 13:44, NLT). Jesus compared the man's discovery of hidden treasure to discovering the truth of God's love in the Bible. People who find Christ are willing to give up everything on this earth to follow Him because they realize that nothing on this earth will ever bring them true happiness. The "treasure" of heaven is what brings them joy.

Have you discovered the "treasure" of a relationship with Jesus? Would you do anything for Jesus, even giving up your life if you were faced with choosing this world and denying that you worship God or standing firm and admitting that you follow a risen Savior? Those are hard questions I think we all hope we never have to face, but the early Christians didn't have the luxury of living in a world that practiced religious freedom. Many died because of their faith in Jesus, and yet they knew that their treasure was in Jesus and they would be rewarded at Jesus' second coming.

Are you willing to sacrifice everything for the treasure of eternal life? Make a commitment to follow Jesus, even if it means losing everything.

NEXT STOP: Hells Canyon Wilderness, Idaho

Hello out there!

December 4

Dropping Into Hell

Then he will say to those on his left, "Depart from me, you who are cursed,
into the eternal fire prepared for the devil and his angels. For I was hungry and
you gave me nothing to eat, I was thirty and you gave me nothing to drink, I was a
stranger and you did not invite me in, I needed clothes and you did not clothe me,
I was sick and in prison and you did not look after me." **Matthew 25:41-43.**

Welcome to Hells Canyon Wilderness! Doesn't that sound like a wonderful place to visit? While making our way through the mountain region, we will certainly want to stop at the Seven Devils. You may even want to climb some of the peaks in the Seven Devils mountain range. How about He Devil, She Devil, Devils Throne, the Tower of Babel, or Mount Baal?

I know it is just a mountain range, but I find these names disturbing. It's just strange to have things in God's creation named after the devil. Instead, I would prefer to visit Heaven's Gate Overlook, which gives you views into four states, including a view into the Hells Canyon Wilderness. At the end of time the righteous will be in heaven overlooking the destruction of the wicked. There is no way I want to be on the other side and experience the wrath of God as it falls on all those who have rejected Him.

Hell is not a physical location that is currently burning with fire waiting to consume the wicked. No, hell will be the fire that destroys the wicked for good. After Jesus' second coming, the righteous will spend a thousand years in heaven and then will return to this earth with Jesus. As the New Jerusalem descends from heaven, the wicked dead will be raised to life, and Satan will convince them to march against God and the righteous. But before they attack the city, the dead will be judged, and they will see the error of their ways and the fairness of God's laws. All will admit that God has been just in His dealings with the wicked. After the books have been opened, the wicked will be thrown into the lake of fire, and sin will be destroyed forever. You can read about all of this in Revelation 20.

Satan wants to entice us into "playing around" in Hells Canyon, but don't fall for his trap. The only safe place to pitch your tent is at heaven's gate!

NEXT STOP: Rigby, Idaho

December 5

You Are What You Watch

For in my inner being I delight in God's law; but I see another law at work in me, waging war against the law of my mind and making me a prisoner of the law of sin at work within me. **Romans 7:22, 23.**

Philo Farnsworth and his family moved to Rigby, Idaho, in 1918 when Philo was 12 years old. Philo had a knack for mechanical and electrical engineering, and he was very excited to find the family's new home wired for electricity. The home had a generator that operated a few pieces of equipment, and when the generator broke, Philo quickly learned how the machinery worked and fixed it himself.

At Rigby High School, Philo really enjoyed his chemistry and physics classes, and he did well in them. It was here that he first shared his idea of an electronic television set with his high school science teacher. Over the next few years Philo worked on his idea of an electronic device that could display motion pictures and sound. In 1927 Philo was able to display the first signal, which was a straight line, across the screen. In 1928 he displayed his first image, a dollar sign. In 1929 he produced the first live picture of a human on the screen.

Today there are hundreds of television channels and programs, and the average American watches almost three hours of TV per day. So is TV good or bad? The answer has to do with what and how much you watch. That's what makes TV good or bad. There are plenty of educational shows on TV that are great, but there are some really bad shows that show people killing other people, committing adultery, lying, or yelling at each other.

I hope you don't have this problem, but I've seen Christians who say they don't want to watch the trashy stuff on TV, but when they are channel surfing, their remote seems to stop on these nasty shows, and they don't change the channel.

Paul talks about knowing God's law and wanting to follow it but getting sucked into the world of sin. It's a battle we all have to fight. Whether it is TV, music, books, or after-school activities, we are all tempted at times to go along with the ways of the world, but we must wage war within ourselves and beat back the devil so that God's law remains first in our lives.

NEXT STOP: Shelley, Idaho

December 6

The Importance of Roots

Jesus replied, "Every plant not planted
by my heavenly Father will be uprooted." Matthew 15:13, NLT.

Idaho produces approximately 13 billion pounds of potatoes each year! That's a lot of potatoes, but think about all the ways you eat them. There are baked potatoes, french fries, potato chips, tater tots, scalloped potatoes, hash browns, mashed potatoes, and so on.

In Shelley, Idaho, the town hosts the Idaho Annual Spud Day each September. The event began in 1927 and has been held every year since then. The day features a parade, free baked potatoes, and a tug-of-war contest with a pit of mashed potatoes between the two teams—I think you get the picture as to what happens to the losing team! It's a fun day celebrating the harvest of the state's most important crop.

If you were to go into a potato field after the farmer planted the seeds and plant carrots alongside the potatoes, do you think the farmer would notice once the plants started to grow? Of course! A potato farmer knows what his crop looks like. The leaves of the carrot plant look very different from that of the potato plant.

In the same way, God knows who are His children and who are not. You can act like you're a Christian on the outside. You can dress a certain way, say the right words, and go to church every week. You can fool your parents and teachers and pastors, but you can't fool God. He knows if you really love Him or not. He knows what is in your heart, and those who reject Him will be "uprooted" (Matthew 15:13, NLT).

You can't trick God, but you can be honest with Him. Talk to Him. Argue with Him if you don't understand something. Cry to Him when you are hurt and alone. Share each day with Him. When you make Him part of your life, you will know Him, and He will know you. Instead of your roots being pulled up, they will remain firmly planted in God, and you will stand strong until His coming.

NEXT STOP: Mount St. Helens, Washington

You've Been Warned

Warn a divisive person once, and then warn them a second time. After that, have nothing to do with them. **Titus 3:10.**

Mount St. Helens is an active volcano located in the Cascade mountain range in Washington, and on May 18, 1980, it erupted after an earthquake. For two months smaller earthquakes had occurred in the area, causing magma to be pushed toward the surface of the volcano. A bulge had appeared on the north slope of the volcano, which eventually created a graben, or trench, in the surface of the volcano. Scientists were worried about the possibility of an eruption, so they closed the area to the general public and urged residents to evacuate. They warned the people living near Mount St. Helens about the possibility of an eruption.

When the earthquake hit, the whole north side of the mountain gave way and lava and rock exploded from the open cavity. The blast and avalanche that followed snapped trees off at the base and sent mud and debris hurtling down the mountain at deadly speeds. In addition, an 80,000-foot column of ash rose into the atmosphere, and high winds carried ash to 11 states—ash was seen as far away as Minnesota and Oklahoma!

Sadly, some people didn't heed the warning, and they died in the eruption. One man had lived near the mountain for 54 years, and he refused to leave, even though he was urged to do so. His body was never found.

The Bible is full of warnings. There are warnings about the end of time and Christ's coming. There are warnings about false prophets. There are warnings about what will happen if we don't follow the law. But I found the warning in today's verse to be very interesting.

It talks about a divisive person, someone who causes disagreements or stirs up trouble between people. You can find these people at church, at school, and sometimes in your home. So how do you handle people like this? Paul's advice is to talk to the person about the problem. If the person doesn't listen or change, Paul recommends distancing yourself so that you don't get sucked into the person's negative behavior. I would then urge you to pray. Pray that the person will change. God is the only one who can change someone who likes to cause trouble into someone who loves peace. Prayer is a powerful thing that can change lives. Trust me!

NEXT STOP: Seattle, Washington

349

December 8

Hello out there!

Pie in the Sky

*Consequently, you are no longer foreigners and strangers,
but fellow citizens with God's people and also members of his household,
built on the foundation of the apostles and prophets, with Christ Jesus himself
as the chief cornerstone.* **Ephesians 2:19, 20.**

At 605 feet high, the Space Needle towers above Seattle, Washington, and has an observation deck at 520 feet and a rotating restaurant at 500 feet. When construction was completed in 1961, it was the tallest structure west of the Mississippi.

How would you like to eat lunch 500 feet in the air? The outside wall of the SkyCity restaurant features spacious windows, which provide diners with a view of Seattle from any table or booth in the whole restaurant. Another neat feature of the restaurant is that every 47 minutes the restaurant completes a full revolution. So, in the course of your lunch you should be able to see the whole city as you slowly spin around in the sky while enjoying your meal.

If you were eating lunch at SkyCity and an earthquake began shaking the ground, how safe would you feel? Or what if a sudden storm with wind gusts of 75 miles per hour hit? Would you feel safe? I'm guessing you answered no. But what if I told you the Space Needle was built on a solid foundation and could withstand up to 200-mile-per-hour wind gusts or a 9.1-magnitude earthquake. Would you feel safer?

A good foundation makes all the difference in the world when you are talking about the stability of a structure. In writing to the church at Ephesus, Paul reminded the church members that they were no longer Ephesians or Gentiles or Jews or Romans. They were now citizens of God's kingdom—they were God's children.

What have you built your foundation on—Christ or the world? If you have chosen Christ, He promises to fill you with His Spirit and live in you. He promises to help you make wise decisions. He promises to be your friend and walk beside you through life. That way when the "winds" blow or an "earthquake" hits, such as the death of a family member or being bullied at school, you stand on the firm foundation of Jesus.

NEXT STOP: Seattle, Washington

Living in a Boat

Immediately Jesus made the disciples get into the boat and go on ahead of him to the other side, while he dismissed the crowd. **Matthew 14:22.**

Before Peter and John left their fishing boats to follow Jesus, they spent their nights out on the water in their boats. They spent so much time in their boats working and fishing and sleeping that we would probably say they "lived" in their boats. But they didn't really live in it the way people in Seattle live in boats.

Seattle is home to approximately 500 houseboats. At one time the city had about 2,000 houseboats, but over time the number of people living on the water has decreased. If you've never seen a houseboat, it is exactly what it sounds like. It is a small house, sometimes two stories, but more often just one, that floats on a flatboat. The rooms aren't very large, and the ceilings are lower than in a normal house, but if you love the water, you might enjoy living in a houseboat. Every night you could fall asleep to the sound of water gently lapping against the side of the boat and the gentle movement of the boat rocking slightly. Of course, you might not like living in a houseboat in the middle of a storm! I'm sure that could be a scary experience.

In the course of their work as fishermen, I'm guessing the disciples experienced plenty of storms, but one night they saw something they had never seen before. The disciples had just witnessed Jesus feeding the five thousand. They were pumped because of the miracle. But as they rowed to the other side of the lake, they got caught in a storm. Life suddenly took a turn for the worse. Life was no longer good! As they fought against the storm, they saw something on the lake that scared them half to death! They saw the form of a person, which they thought was a ghost. They "cried out in fear. But Jesus immediately said to them: 'Take courage! It is I. Don't be afraid'" (Matthew 14:26, 27).

Jesus could have kept quiet and made them think it really was a ghost. He could have teased them and scared them even more, but Jesus isn't like that. He will never try to trick us or scare us. When we are afraid, he says, "Don't be afraid. Be strong. Take courage. Stand fast. It is I, and I am on your side!"

NEXT STOP: Seattle, Washington

Hello out there!

Giving to God

*So when you give to the needy, do not announce it with trumpets,
as the hypocrites do in the synagogues and on the streets, to be honored
by others. Trulyl tell you, they have received their reward in full. But when you give
to the needy, do not let your left hand know what your right hand
is doing, so that your giving may be in secret. Then your Father,
who sees what is done in secret, will reward you.* **Matthew 6:2-4.**

We are spending one more day in Seattle before leaving the city for the mountains. Today we are visiting the headquarters of the Bill and Melinda Gates Foundation. Although visiting an office building probably doesn't sound like much fun, check out this information.

The foundation was started by Bill Gates, the founder of Microsoft, and after making billions of dollars, Bill and his wife, Melinda, decided to start a charitable foundation to help others. With the money the Gateses donated, plus donations from their wealthy friends and colleagues, as of December 31, 2012, they had $36.4 billion!

The focus of their foundation is to reduce poverty, promote education, and make health care better around the world. The foundation is required to give away at least 5 percent of its assets, which totals approximately $1.5 billion each year. Talk about a lot of money!

So why do people give money to others? Some do it because they care and want to help others who don't have as much as they do. Others do it because they want to look good to those around them. In essence they are saying, "Look at me. I am special; I gave money to a needy family. I'm such a good person!" Some people give quietly, while others make a big show of it.

Jesus tells us to help the needy, but He instructs us to do so quietly. We shouldn't make a big deal about it or brag to our friends that our family gave $50, $100, or even $1,000 to a family whose dad lost his job. When we give quietly and humbly, we point people to our Father in heaven instead of to ourselves. No matter how much you give to others or do for others, do it for Jesus. He sees your deeds. He knows your heart. And He has your reward set aside for you in heaven!

NEXT STOP: Mount Rainier, Washington

The Big Plan

"All this," David said, "I have in writing as a result of the Lord's hand on me, and he enabled me to understand all the details of the plan." **I Chronicles 28:19.**

Mount Rainier is the tallest mountain in Washington, with the summit elevation reaching 14,411 feet. Large portions of Mount Rainier are covered in glacial ice. Climbers who attempt to reach the summit of Mount Rainier need ice axes and crampons, which are spikes that clip on to your boots to provide traction in the snow and ice.

In 2006 my husband and brother and a group of their friends climbed Mount Rainier. But they didn't just fly to Washington, rent ice axes, boots, and crampons, and begin climbing. Their trip involved almost a year of planning. They read books about climbing Rainier. They determined the best time to go and when the weather was most favorable so they could reach the summit. They began training so they would have enough endurance to complete the climb. They swam, ran, hiked, and biked to get their bodies in top physical condition. Since they would all be tied together on the final ascent to the summit, they practiced self-arrests and rescue techniques so that if someone fell they would know what to do. All of their planning paid off, and they reached the summit and watched the sunrise as it glistened on the snowfields surrounding them.

Planning takes time, and sometimes it is hard to wait for the planning to be done so you can move on to the actual activity. But oftentimes planning can be the difference between having a good time and total chaos.

David and Solomon knew the importance of planning and following God's lead. Before David died, he gave Solomon the detailed plans for the Temple. It was a *huge* project, and David knew that even though there was a plan, it might be overwhelming for Solomon to think of tackling such a large building project. That's why he told him the following: "Be strong and courageous, and do the work. Do not be afraid or discouraged, for the Lord God, my God, is with you. He will not fail you or forsake you until all the work . . . is finished" (1 Chronicles 28:20).

These same words apply to us when we are afraid to tackle something big, even if we've planned for it. When we follow God's plan, He promises to help us complete it.

NEXT STOP: Washington

Hello out there!

December 12

Call Before You Act

For the third time he spoke to them: "Why? What crime has this man committed? I have found in him no grounds for the death penalty. Therefore I will have him punished and then release him." **Luke 23:22.**

Today is our last day in Washington before we venture into Canada and on to our final destination, Alaska. We are not visiting a specific city or landmark today. Instead, we are talking about a law that is on the books in Washington that states the following: "It is mandatory for a motorist with criminal intentions to stop at the city limits and telephone the chief of police as he is entering the town."

Apparently the law was put into place because of increased crime in the state, but I bet you can guess how many criminals have followed this law—zero, zilch, nada! If you want to break the law, why would you call the police beforehand to alert them to the fact that you are going to rob a bank? If you did, that would mean they would be waiting for you at the bank. The whole point of committing a crime is trying to get away with breaking the law. Criminals purposefully try to do something wrong and then avoid getting caught.

On the flip side, there are unfortunate circumstances in which people are falsely accused of a crime and are punished for something they never did. Jesus found Himself caught in this situation. He didn't break any laws. He didn't commit any crimes. He was falsely accused of stirring up the people, which, in my estimation, were silly charges.

I think Pilate knew these charges were false, but he was afraid of the people. Although he was supposed to be a mighty Roman in control of the region, he was scared, and he gave in to the people. Pilate listened to their cries to crucify Jesus, and he folded.

I'm guessing you don't like it when the whole class has to stay in for recess because one person was caught talking. It doesn't seem fair! Or maybe you've gotten into trouble for something your brother or sister did in the house and you lost part of your allowance for their bad choice. It doesn't seem fair! But was it fair for Jesus to die for *your* sins? He didn't commit any crimes; in fact, He lived a perfect life. He didn't sin. He didn't deserve to die, but He still gave His life so *you* can live. That's perfect love!

NEXT STOP: Abbotsford, British Columbia

Raspberry Goodness

Like newborn babies, long for the pure milk of the word,
so that by it you may grow in respect to salvation,
if you have tasted the kindness of the Lord. **I Peter 2:2, 3, NASB.**

The Fraser Valley, which includes the city of Abbotsford, British Columbia, is home to 5,000 acres of raspberry fields. Each year the farmers harvest more than 26 million pounds of raspberries! Just think of all the treats that could be made with that many raspberries: jam, sherbet, pie, cheesecake, or frozen yogurt. I don't know about you, but I like them picked fresh off the bush!

Juicy, delicious, plump red raspberries are a favorite treat in my house, but if we had to choose between frozen or fresh, we would all choose fresh raspberries. If you have never eaten a fresh raspberry, the frozen ones would probably be good enough, but after you've enjoyed the sweet goodness of a fresh raspberry, nothing else compares.

In today's verse Peter used food to describe our experience with God. Check it out. Babies want their mother's milk when they are little. It fills their tummies and helps them grow healthy and strong. If you gave water to a baby for a few days instead of milk, what do you think he or she would do? After feeding two hungry babies of my own a few years ago, I can tell you there would have been plenty of fussing and complaining if I had taken away the nutritious milk my babies had grown to love and replaced it with water.

Fresh raspberries are better than frozen ones. Mother's milk is better than water. And a life with Jesus is better than a life in this world. Once "you have tasted the kindness of the Lord" (1 Peter 2:3, NASB) and you understand that His gift of salvation means freedom, you won't want to go back to a life without Jesus. I hope you've already asked Jesus into your life and that you realize the value of a relationship with Him. If not, keep reading and studying until you are ready. A decision to follow Jesus is the best decision you will ever make!

NEXT STOP: Okanagan Valley, British Columbia

Hello out there!

God's Blessings

The Lord blessed the latter part of Job's life more than the former part. He had fourteen thousand sheep, six thousand camels, a thousand yoke of oxen and a thousand donkeys. And he also had seven sons and three daughters. **Job 42:12, 13.**

The Thompson Okanagan region, also known as the Okanagan Valley, is located in the Interior of British Columbia. In this area Canada's largest working cattle ranch operates on more than 500,000 acres of land. The Douglas Lake Ranch owns approximately 20,000 cattle! That's a lot of animals to take care of and round up when it comes time to sell some at auction. But sitting in the saddle and riding the open range in search of cattle are all in a day's work for the ranch hands.

When I read about the amount of cattle at this ranch, I immediately thought of Job and how many animals he had at the end of his life. If you remember, he lost everything—his children, his livestock, his servants—in one day. Satan was allowed to take everything away from him as a test of his faith and obedience to God. And although all of these rotten things happened to Job, he never cursed God. He prayed to God and argued with Him, but he never lost faith that God was in heaven and everything was under His control.

After allowing Job's faith to be tested, God rewarded Job for his obedience and faithfulness. In fact, he "gave him twice as much as he had before" (Job 42:10). Job was blessed with 14,000 sheep, 6,000 camels, 1,000 yoke of oxen, and 1,000 donkeys (verse 12). That's a lot of animals! He was also blessed with "seven more sons and three more daughters" (verse 13, NLT).

I don't know what kind of hard times you may be going through right now. Maybe your parents are struggling financially. Maybe your best friend isn't speaking to you. Or maybe you are having a hard time in school. Whatever challenge you are facing, keep turning to God. Keep talking to Him, because He will see you through this difficult time. And He will bless you for faithfully serving Him and praising His name. It might not happen right away, but it will happen!

NEXT STOP: North Vancouver, British Columbia

December 15

Snow Limousines

But he brought his people out like a flock; he led them like sheep through the wilderness. He guided them safely, so they were unafraid; but the sea engulfed their enemies. And so he brought them to the border of his holy land, to the hill country his right hand had taken. **Psalm 78:52-54.**

British Columbia has a number of ski resorts that offer winter enthusiasts such as skiers and snowboarders an outdoor playground. One of the most famous ski resorts is the town of Whistler, which was one of the skiing venues for the 2010 Winter Olympics held in nearby Vancouver. However, we are going to visit Grouse Mountain, which is located in North Vancouver, about 75 miles south of Whistler.

If you have never learned how to snow ski or if your grandma wanted to experience the thrill of skiing but would probably break her neck on skis, Grouse Mountain has the perfect means of allowing people to travel down the slopes safely without learning how to ski. It is called the Snow Limo. Invented by a ski instructor by the name of Paul Auger, the Snow Limo could be compared to a dog sled. The person going for the ride sits in the sled, which is attached to two runners, or skis. The guide then stands on the skis at the back and steers the sled down the mountain.

Whether you know how to ski or not, would you like to ride in the Snow Limo with me guiding you—someone who has gone skiing 25 times—or would you prefer to go with a professional skier who skis every day and knows each trail like the back of his or her hand? If I were you, I would pick the professional skier. I sure would!

As you go through life, whom are you going to follow? Your friends? Your favorite singer? Your favorite sports star? Or are you going to pick God? In Psalm 78 David wrote about the children of Israel and how God brought them out of Egypt. He said, "He kept them safe, so they were not afraid" (verse 53, NLT).

Just as you wouldn't want me to be your guide on the ski slope, you don't want a TV actor to be your guide in life. Let God be your guide. Let Him lead you safely through life on this earth.

NEXT STOP: Nanaimo Harbour, British Columbia

December 16

Hello out there!

Scrub-a-dub-dub

But when he saw the wind, he was afraid and, beginning to sink,
cried out, "Lord, save me!" **Matthew 14:30.**

We are going to spend the next three days visiting different cities on Vancouver Island. Located off the coast of British Columbia, the island is home to the capital city of the province, Victoria. The island is 290 miles long and 50 miles wide, and it is the largest island in the Pacific Ocean east of New Zealand.

Today we are visiting Nanaimo Harbour, the site of the International World Championship Bathtub Race. The race began in 1967 as a way to attract attention to the city of Nanaimo, and the plan worked! Every year since then on the last weekend in July, "tubbers" arrive in Nanaimo from as far away as Australia to compete in the race. A more traditional style boat can be built around the bathtub and a small engine can be installed, but a bathtub must still be the main part of the boat.

Although today's boats look pretty sophisticated, I can imagine that the early boats were anything but seaworthy. I'm sure a lot of them sank and the participants needed to be rescued, kind of like Peter in today's Bible story.

Earlier this month we talked about the story of Jesus walking on the water and how the disciples thought they had seen a ghost. Well, after Jesus told them not to be scared, bold Peter said, "If it's you . . . tell me to come to you" (Matthew 14:28). So Jesus told him to come. Peter stepped out of the boat and miraculously began walking on the water toward Jesus. Unfortunately, he got distracted by the wind and waves, and he took his eyes off Jesus. As soon as he did, he started to sink. So he cried out, "Save me, Lord!" (verse 30, NLT). Of course, Jesus reached down His hand and pulled Peter out of the water, and they walked to the boat together.

Do you ever feel like you are drowning in schoolwork or in the worries of this life? Don't wait to cry out to Jesus until you are completely under the water. As soon as you feel as if you are sinking, ask Jesus for help. Talk to your parents or another adult you trust. Jesus doesn't want you to drown in this life. That's why He is right beside you, and that's why He has placed people in your life who care about you.

NEXT STOP: Chemainus, British Columbia

December 17

Under the Sea

You alone are the Lord. You made the heavens, even the highest heavens, and all their starry host, the earth and all that is on it, the seas and all that is in them. You give life to everything, and the multitudes of heaven worship you. **Nehemiah 9:6.**

On January 14, 2006, near the town of Chemainus, the Artificial Reef Society of British Columbia sank a Boeing 737 airplane more than 60 feet below the surface a little more than half a mile from shore. The plane was part of an overall project to establish an artificial reef for divers to explore.

I've never been scuba diving, but I've talked to people who have gone, and they say it looks like a totally different world under the surface of the water. The colorful fish, sharks, turtles, stingrays, and other marine life they have seen all point to a wonderful Creator who formed each unique creature. I've heard more than one diver say they feel close to God when they are under the water and are looking at all of the things He made when He created the world.

Throughout the Bible, the writers of Scripture remind us that God made *everything.* Nehemiah points to the sky and the earth and the sea. I really like the last part of Nehemiah 9:6. He wrote, "You gave life to all. The heavenly powers . . . worship you" (TEV).

The angels in heaven and all creation worships God and recognizes that He made everything. Sadly, there are many people on this earth who do not give glory to God for the world He made. They fail to thank Jesus for the food He provides, the air He gives us to breathe, and the water He supplies us with.

Do you thank God for the things He has created? Do you take time to look around you and give Him praise for the good things on this earth? In one week it will be Christmas Eve, a time of celebration for many people. What will you celebrate and be thankful for? More electronics? A new video game? New clothes? Or will you thank God for the things in life that we often take for granted every day. Look around you. Then make a list of all the things you are thankful for that God created. Finally, place the list where you will look at it every day. May your list serve as a daily reminder of all the good things God gives us, especially the gift of nature.

NEXT STOP: Pacific Rim National Park Preserve, British Columbia

December 18

Hello out there!

A Looonnng Trip

Here are the stages in the journey of the Israelites when they came out of Egypt.... At the Lord's command Moses recorded the stages in their journey. **Numbers 33:1, 2.**

In October, when the ice begins to form in the northern waters of Alaska, eastern Pacific gray whales, which average 40 to 50 feet in length, begin their 5,000- to 6,800-mile trip south to the warm waters of the Gulf of California and the Baja peninsula of Mexico. But the best time to see these whales from the Pacific Rim National Park Preserve is in the springtime when the whales are migrating back to their arctic feeding grounds.

Scientists estimate that there are 20,000 to 22,000 whales that make the long round-trip each year. It is believed that gray whales have the longest annual migration route of any mammal on earth. It is reported that the whales travel night and day, although I'm not sure how they swim and sleep at the same time! Averaging approximately 75 miles a day, the whales take two to three months to make the trip.

If the gray whale qualifies for the longest migration route, I wonder if the Israelites qualify for the longest backpacking trip! I would like you to get out your Bible and look up Numbers 33. You don't have to read every word of the chapter because it is literally a list of cities, but I want you to get a sense of how many places the Israelites camped. They set up and tore down camp so many times that I bet they could have done it in their sleep!

The crazy thing is that although they were probably sick of camping and wandering in the desert, they thought they knew better than God. Instead of trusting Him, they relied on their own "wisdom," and they ended up backpacking for 40 more years.

Is there something that makes you nervous? Maybe God has asked you to befriend the new girl in class. Maybe He's given you the opportunity to sing at church. Maybe He's asked you to share with your brother or sister. But what if you don't want to do what God has asked you to do? If you aren't following God's plan or doing what He has called you to do, stop! Don't be like the Israelites. When they didn't follow God's plan, they got into a heap of trouble. If you don't believe me, read about their wanderings in the book of Deuteronomy.

It's your choice; will you follow God all the way, even when His plan doesn't fit into your desires or time frame? I hope so!

NEXT STOP: Yukon

Light Show

A rainbow that shown like an emerald encircled the throne. **Revelation 4:3.**

The Yukon is the smallest of the three territories in Canada. In 2011 only 33,897 people lived in the entire territory! That's about double the amount of people who live in my town of Calhoun, Georgia. The crazy thing is that we are comparing the population of a city with that of a whole territory! About two thirds of the total population of the territory lives in the capital city of Whitehorse; the rest live in much smaller towns and villages.

With very few people in the territory, there aren't a bunch of bright cities or streetlights lighting up the night. Without the presence of artificial light, the stars and aurora borealis, otherwise known as the northern lights, dominate the sky and present a vivid and beautiful light show. Ask your parents to show you pictures of the aurora borealis, because it is amazing! Words cannot come anywhere close to describing how colorful the aurora borealis is.

The easiest explanation as to how the green and red colors appear in the night sky is that the auroras borealis are created by an electrical charge near the magnetic pole. When oxygen is emitted, a green or brownish-red color appears. If nitrogen is emitted, a blue or red light appears. The lights flicker and dance across the night sky.

I was fortunate to see the aurora borealis from a plane. As I looked out my window, the night sky danced and flashed red and green. It was amazing!

In Revelation 4, John gives us a glimpse of the throne of heaven, and verse 3 tells us that a rainbow that is green like an emerald encircles the throne. As I peered out the small airplane window, the auroras borealis were the most stunning green, but I know those colors will pale in comparison to the dazzling emerald-colored rainbow that surrounds God's throne.

I'm looking forward to seeing all the splendor of heaven and God in His glory. I hope you are, too!

NEXT STOP: Watson Lake, Yukon

December 20

Hello out there!

The Christian Sign

However, if you suffer as a Christian, do not be ashamed,
but praise God that you bear that name. **1 Peter 4:16.**

Approximately 1,200 people live in the little town of Watson Lake, Yukon, which is located along the Alaska Highway near the border of British Columbia. What makes Watson Lake unique is its Signpost Forest, which was started by a man named Carl Lindley.

Carl was in the U.S. Army, and he was assigned the duty of helping to build the Alaska Highway in 1942. Homesick, Carl put up a sign with the name of his hometown of Danville, Illinois, and the distance to Danville from Watson Lake. Not wanting to be left out, other people followed his lead and posted signs. Today, more than 70 years later, the tradition lives on. The Signpost Forest has more than 76,000 signs posted with names of cities from around the world.

Names are important to us. People tell where they are from because they are proud of the town they live in. Some people share the name of the school they graduated from because they are proud of their school. Others are quick to mention their last name and the important descendents who make up their family tree.

What about the title of Christian? Are we quick to tell others we are followers of Jesus? Are we proud of that name? Or are we sometimes afraid of the title of Christian because we don't want to be persecuted and suffer for our faith?

When you decided to follow Jesus, did you hope it would be smooth sailing and nothing but good times? Did you think that all the bumps in life would be smoothed out because you were now a son or daughter of the King of the universe? It would be nice if that were true, but we are still in the midst of the big showdown between God and Satan. If God were to make our lives easy, then Satan would accuse Him of being unfair and bribing His followers with gifts. God has to prove that the reason Christians follow Him is that we love Him, even if that means suffering for our faith while here on earth. Our reward isn't on this earth anyway; our reward is waiting for us in heaven.

NEXT STOP: Whitehorse, Yukon

The Ultimate Dogsled Race

I have fought the good fight, I have finished the race,
I have kept the faith. **2 Timothy 4:7.**

The Yukon Quest 1,000-mile International Sled Dog Race begins in Whitehorse, Yukon, and travels through desolate terrain until it reaches the finish line in Fairbanks, Alaska. In odd-numbered years, that is. In even-numbered years, the race begins in Fairbanks and ends in Whitehorse. The race is run every February, during some of the harshest winter weather. Blizzard conditions are very common, with wind gusts between 20 and 50 miles per hour. Temperatures are in the negative digits. It is very common to experience minus 40-degree-Fahrenheit temperatures on the trail.

Because of the terrain, the weather, and the limited support to the dogsled teams, many people consider the race to be the most difficult dog sled race in the world. In spite of the challenge of the race and the potential for death, people sign up every year to compete. The fastest time for a team took place in 2010 when the race was finished in nine days and 26 minutes, while the longest run took 20 days, eight hours, and 29 minutes.

Think about this for a minute. Why would someone sign up for a dangerous race without the assurance of a prize? Death is possible, and there is no guarantee of winning.

Being a Christian could be compared to the Yukon Quest race. It is obvious from Paul's situation that being a Christian is dangerous. Paul was persecuted from all sides, and he often did not know if he would live or die. But he chose to run the race before him. He chose to follow Jesus all the way and keep the faith. Why? Because Paul loved Jesus and was willing to run the same race Jesus ran.

But unlike competitors in the Yukon Quest, Paul knew a reward was waiting for him. In the Christian faith, we can all be winners. Paul wrote, "Now there is in store for me the crown of righteousness, which the Lord . . . will award to me on that day—and not only to me, but also to all who have longed for his appearing" (2 Timothy 4:8).

Although the race of life is hard, we are guaranteed the prize if we finish. Don't give up! Don't get swallowed in Satan's "blizzard." He tries to trap us with lies and tricks, but if we stick close to Jesus, we won't stumble.

Are you ready to finish the race? Let's go!

NEXT STOP: Alaska

Hello out there!

December 22

The Last Frontier

And the gospel must first be preached to all nations. **Mark 13:10.**

Alaska is often called America's Last Frontier. It is a huge landmass that is more than twice the size of Texas. In fact, Alaska is larger than the total combined land of the 22 smallest states. Needless to say, it is an extremely large area, with most of it being untouched land.

Although Alaska has plenty of land, there aren't many people living there. The total population of Alaska was more than 730,000 as of July 2012, which is only about 100,000 more people than the total population of Washington, D.C. Comparing one city to a whole state is crazy!

It takes a special person to live in Alaska. It takes people who have a sense of adventure and don't mind living without all of the comforts of life. It takes people who are willing to deal with freezing temperatures and long periods of time without sun. It takes people who are not afraid to give it their all. It takes people who don't mind being isolated from the rest of society.

When the disciples asked Jesus what signs they should look for that would signal the end of the world, He told them that the gospel "must first be preached to all nations" (Mark 13:10, NLT). The gospel has to reach the last frontiers of the world, the remote villages and towns where people may have never seen a Bible before or heard about the saving power of Jesus' death on the cross.

Just as people go to Alaska for the adventure of taming the wild or striking it rich mining for gold or fishing in the deadly ocean waters, missionaries risk their lives and leave all the comforts of home behind to take the gospel to the unreached people of the world. Is God calling you to be a missionary someday? Maybe. As you continue to grow, listen to His voice. God will reveal His plan for your life at the right time. Whatever God's plan is, give it your all and remember that you can always share God's love with others, no matter what job you have. You don't have to be a missionary or pastor to tell others about Jesus. Let's keep preaching and sharing the good news with others so that we can finish the work and go to heaven!

NEXT STOP: Seward, Alaska

Seward's Folly

Please pay no attention, my lord, to that wicked man Nabal. He is just like his name—his name means Fool, and folly goes with him. **I Samuel 25:25.**

Alaska was purchased from the Russians in 1867 for $7.2 million, which worked out to two cents per acre. The man who was responsible for the purchase of the land was then Secretary of State William H. Seward. Many Americans thought the deal was crazy, and they called the purchase Seward's Folly. To many it seemed foolish to have this huge amount of unusable land that wasn't even connected to the rest of the United States.

I'm guessing that many of those Americans who thought the deal was crazy considered the man a genius when gold was discovered near the Klondike River in 1896. With the announcement of gold, the Alaska gold rush was on! Since mining began in 1896, it is estimated that more than 1.25 million pounds of gold have been extracted from the Klondike. Seward's Folly turned out to be Seward's Wisdom, and in honor of the man who purchased Alaska, the state named a city after him.

In today's Bible story, Abigail, the wife of Nabal, came to David and begged him not to destroy her husband or her household for her husband's folly, or foolishness. You see, David and his men had protected Nabal's shepherds and treated them with kindness without being asked. Since they had to rely on others for food, David sent a message to Nabal asking him for some food in exchange for their protection. But Nabal was greedy and mean. He was a foolish man who only thought of himself, so he refused to give them any food or water.

In anger David decided he would teach Nabal a lesson. Fortunately Abigail heard about the whole situation, and she gathered up supplies and went to meet David. When they met on the road, Abigail told David that her husband's name meant "fool." Then she presented David with the food she had brought and asked him to forgive her husband's ungratefulness. By taking action, Abigail saved David from his own folly. Her wisdom brought him to his senses.

Do you ever make foolish decisions? I'm sure you do—we all do. Just remember that when you make a bad choice, you can turn things around with God's help. He'll give you the wisdom you need to fix the problem.

NEXT STOP: North Pole, Alaska

Hello out there!

Christmas Legends

Have nothing to do with godless myths and old wives' tales; rather, train yourself to be godly. **I Timothy 4:7.**

If you still believe in Santa Claus, I hate to break it to you, but he isn't real. He is a fictional character who is said to live at the North Pole and deliver presents to children around the world on Christmas Eve, December 24, with the help of his elves. (They aren't real either, in case you were wondering.)

Santa is big business, so most people jump all over the legend and keep it going. Parents lead their kids to believe that Santa is real and that he is the one who brings them presents, and stores do their best to use the Santa story to sell more gifts.

Although North Pole, Alaska, is not really at the North Pole, it has capitalized on the fact that its name is the supposed home of Santa. The town built the world's largest fiberglass statue of Santa, which is outside a store called Santa Claus House that sells all kinds of gifts and gadgets. The streetlights look like candy canes, and many of the local businesses decorate their storefronts in a Christmas theme all year long.

Before you begin to think I'm Scrooge and that I don't celebrate Christmas, I do. But I think we need to celebrate the real meaning of Christmas and leave all the legends and myths out of the season. Paul urged Timothy not to "waste time arguing over godless ideas and old wives' tales." Instead, he told him to be "training for godliness" (1 Timothy 4:7, NLT).

Do you find it easy or hard to think about Jesus at Christmas when you are surrounded by Santa and Rudolph and Frosty the Snowman? Is it easy or hard to focus on Jesus when you are surrounded by a pile of gifts?

Christmas is about the ultimate gift of God's Son, who came to this earth as a helpless baby to live among evil men and women who would eventually kill Him. He came to reveal God's character of love. It is about sharing that good news with others. It is about giving and not worrying about what we get in return. It is about love for God and for one another. That's what Christmas is about.

NEXT STOP: Pit Stop

God With Us

Do not be afraid, Mary; you have found favor with God. You will conceive and give birth to a son, and you are to call him Jesus. He will be great and will be called the Son of the Most High. The Lord God will give him the throne of his father David, and he will reign over Jacob's descendants forever; his kingdom will never end. **Luke 1:30-33.**

As you celebrate Christmas today with family, and as you open gifts and eat yummy food, I hope you will take the time to think about Jesus' birth. You've probably heard the story since you were a baby—how Mary and Joseph traveled to Bethlehem, how there was no room in the inn, how Jesus was born in a stable, how the angels appeared to the shepherds in the field and told them to follow the star and worship the newborn King—but I want you to think about it in a new way.

We often focus on that last part of the miracle story of Jesus' birth, but today I want us to think about Mary's reaction to the news that she was going to give birth to the Messiah. One day an angel appeared to Mary and said, "Greetings, you who are highly favored! The Lord is with you" (Luke 1:28). The angel probably scared her to death, because his next words were "Don't be afraid" (verse 30, NLT). Then he told her that she would give birth to the Promised One.

Can you imagine all the questions that probably went through Mary's mind? *Why me? What will my friends and family think? What will Joseph think? Everyone in town will think I cheated on Joseph, but I've remained pure. I haven't been with any man.*

Mary asked the angel, "How will this be . . . since I am a virgin?" (verse 34). Then he told her that the Holy Spirit would come over her, and she would be pregnant with the Son of God. "For no word from God will ever fail" (verse 37). After hearing those words, Mary said, "I am the Lord's servant. . . . May your word to me be fulfilled" (verse 38).

Mary believed the angel's words and submitted herself to following God's plan, even though it wasn't easy, even though she didn't know how everything was going to work out with her family or with Joseph. She trusted God's word and that He would take care of everything.

Do you trust Jesus with your life? Do you trust Him to take care of the challenges you face? Your life will never be free of problems and pain—Mary's life certainly wasn't—but you can trust Jesus to be right there beside you.

NEXT STOP: Nome, Alaska

December 26

Hello out there!

Mush!

She will give birth to a son, and you are to give him the name Jesus, because he will save his people from their sins. **Matthew 1:21.**

Dog mushing is the official state sport of Alaska, and in the winter of 1925 a group of dogsled teams saved the lives of children in the village of Nome. Known as the Great Race of Mercy, the teams raced 674 miles from Nenana to Nome in five and a half days to deliver medicine to the dying children.

A diphtheria epidemic had broken out among the Inuit children in Nome, but blizzard conditions across much of Alaska prevented anyone from flying the medicine from Anchorage to Nome. Thus, a plan was devised to take the medicine by train to Nenana, where it was then passed off to the first of 20 dogsled teams who raced through the blinding snow and bitter cold to deliver the life-saving medicine. In memory of the Great Race of Mercy, the Iditarod Trail Sled Dog Race began in 1973. Each year teams race more than 1,000 miles across the snow and ice to Nome.

In 1925 a group of men and their dogs took it upon themselves to save the dying children of Nome. More than 2,000 years ago Jesus took it upon Himself to save humanity. His name literally means "savior." The Greek form of the name Jesus is Joshua, which means "the Lord saves."

Now think about this. What if the men had risked their lives to deliver the medicine and all the families refused to give the medicine to their children? Would the fact that the medicine was in their village help their children without their taking it? Of course not! The same principle applies to Jesus' gift of salvation. We are dying, but if we do not accept His gift, it won't do us any good. Jesus came to the earth and gave Himself for us that we might live, but we have to confess our sins and ask Him into our life in order to have salvation. Please "take the medicine" before it's too late!

NEXT STOP: Denali National Park and Preserve, Alaska

Alaskan Wildlife

The wolf and the lamb will feed together,
and the lion will eat straw like the ox. **Isaiah 65:25.**

Denali National Park and Preserve is home to a variety of wildlife. Grizzly bears, black bears, moose, gray wolves, and herds of caribou roam the park. Smaller animals such as beavers, arctic ground squirrels, pikas, foxes, wolverines, and snowshoe hares also make their home in the shadow of Mount McKinley, the highest mountain in North America.

Although I was unable to travel to the interior of Alaska and visit the famous Denali National Park, I did have the privilege of taking an Alaskan cruise with my family and seeing many of the coastal cities. While on the cruise, I spent most of my time looking for wildlife. I stood for hours on the deck of the ship with my binoculars as the cold wind blew around me, looking for killer whales and seals. When we took a train ride through the mountains, I kept my eyes glued to the window in search for grizzly bears.

Unfortunately, at the end of our seven-day cruise I hadn't seen a grizzly bear or a killer whale, two of the largest and fiercest animals in Alaska. Of course, I wouldn't have wanted to see them face to face, but from the safety of the boat or train, I was eager to catch a glimpse of these powerful creatures God made.

I hope that someday soon I will be able to see these animals up close without fear of them attacking me. I look forward to heaven when I will be able to pet a grizzly bear and swim with a killer whale.

The second-to-last chapter of the book of Isaiah contains a passage about the new heaven and new earth that God has planned for us, and at the end, Isaiah included today's text about the wolf and the lamb, and the lion and the ox. Scripture tells us that the animals will be tame in heaven and will no longer kill one another for food. As someone who loves animals, I can't wait until the day when I will no longer have to be afraid of wild animals.

NEXT STOP: Barrow, Alaska

Hello out there!

December 28

In the Light

Then Jesus told them, "You are going to have the light just a little while longer. Walk while you have the light, before darkness overtakes you. Whoever walks in the dark does not know where they are going. Believe in the light while you have the light, so that you may become children of light." **John 12:35, 36.**

Barrow, Alaska, is the northernmost city in the United States and the ninth northernmost city in the world. Barrow is 320 miles north of the Arctic Circle, so in addition to extremely cold weather, the city experiences extended periods of darkness or light, depending on the tilt of the earth.

On November 18 or 19 the sun sets and doesn't reappear for 65 days. So from the middle of November until January 22 or 23, the residents of Barrow live in darkness, which is called a polar night. Five months later the opposite happens and the sun doesn't set for approximately 80 days, beginning on May 11 or 12 and lasting until July 31 or August 1.

If you lived in Barrow, what would you do on the last day before the sun set for more than two months? Would you spend all day outside, soaking up the last of the sun's rays, knowing you wouldn't see full daylight for 65 days?

Jesus told His disciples that they needed to take advantage of the time they had with Him, because He knew He wouldn't be with them forever. He told them, "Walk in the light while you can, so the darkness will not overtake you" (John 12:35, NLT).

Are you walking with Jesus now? Are you reading the Bible and learning as much as you can about Him while you have time? We know a day is coming when we will not be able to freely worship Jesus, so we need to prepare now while we have the freedom and liberty to do so.

I'm sure the disciples wished they had paid closer attention to Jesus' teachings after He was gone. I bet they wished they could talk to Him directly again and ask Him more questions. But they couldn't go back. They had to rely on their memory and the things He had taught them.

Read and study the Bible while you can. Hide God's Word in your heart so you will be ready when Satan tries to trick God's people. Take advantage of the Light while you can!

NEXT STOP: Prince William Sound, Alaska

Toxic Waste

Create in me a pure heart, O God,
and renew a steadfast spirit within me. **Psalm 51:10.**

Prince William Sound, which is slightly smaller than a bay, shelters the town of Valdez, Alaska. In order to enter Prince William Sound, ships must pass through a channel between two islands. Once inside the sound, ships must still carefully navigate along the rocky coast before reaching port.

Unfortunately, on March 24, 1989, an accident of epic proportion happened. An oil tanker named the *Exxon Valdez* left Valdez and headed for the open sea, but it never made it. The tanker ran aground on Bligh Reef within Prince William Sound, resulting in the second largest oil spill in U.S. history. The ship was fully loaded and carrying 53.1 million gallons of oil at the time of the accident. It is estimated that the ship lost between 10.8 million and 32 million gallons of oil.

If you have ever conducted a science experiment with oil and water, you know that the two do not mix. Now imagine millions and millions of gallons of oil floating on the surface of the ocean and washing ashore as the tide rolls in and out. I remember seeing pictures on the news of birds with black, sticky oil covering their wings. There were also pictures of dead seals and whales washed up on shore because they ate contaminated fish that were filled with toxic oil. In total, it is estimated that up to 250,000 seabirds, 3,000 sea otters, 300 harbor seals, 250 bald eagles, and 22 killer whales died as a result of the spill.

Environmentalists worked day and night after the spill to try and contain the oil, clean up the shore, and save as many lives of the animals as they could.

Sin is like the sticky oil that covered those poor animals. They could not clean themselves up on their own. They had to rely on others to wash off the oil and cleanse them of the toxic mess. Similarly, Jesus is the only one who can clean us up and remove the sin from our lives. David wrote, "Create a pure heart in me" (Psalm 51:10, TEV)—some translations use the word "clean" instead of "pure." David knew God was his only hope when it came to forgiving his sins.

Have you asked Jesus to forgive your sins? Have you asked Him to clean you and make you new? It doesn't matter what you've done in the past; today is a new day. Jesus is waiting for you to come to Him and ask Him for a new heart—a clean heart—a heart dedicated to Him.

NEXT STOP: Pit Stop

December 30

Hello out there!

Another Year

"For I know the plans I have for you," declares the Lord, "plans to prosper you and not to harm you, plans to give you hope and a future." **Jeremiah 29:11.**

It's hard to believe January 1 is only two days away, but it is. There's no stopping time; the clock keeps ticking. So, was 2014 a good year? If so, what made it good? If it was a bad year, what made it bad? If it was a great year, you're probably hoping that the good times keep coming and that 2015 is as good as or better than this year. If it was bad, I'm sure you're hoping that good things are right around the corner.

It is natural to want good things to happen to us. We want life to be peaceful and smooth. We want the happy moments of life, the moments filled with laughter, to never end. But I'm guessing you've lived long enough to figure out that life isn't always filled with balloons and candy and presents and trips. Nope, life is also filled with rotten things like broken bones and death and hurt feelings.

I wish I could protect my kids and the kids I work with at church from ever having to go through the tough times of life, but I can't. The only thing I can do is point them to Jesus. The Bible repeats the promise five times that God will never leave us nor forsake us. God never lies. What He says, He does. My favorite Bible text is Jeremiah 29:11, because this verse fits right into the promise that God will never leave me. "For I know the plans I have for you. . . . They are plans for good and not for disaster, to give you a future and a hope" (NLT). God has a plan for your life and mine—a plan that involves hope and prosperity and protection.

You might be saying, "Yeah, right! I'm not rich, and I get hurt all the time. God isn't keeping His promise." Even when it doesn't feel like it, God has a plan. Noah spent 120 years building the ark and preaching and being made fun of before God sent the flood. Abraham wandered to an unknown land and had to wait until he was 100 years old before Isaac was born and the promise that he would become the father of a great nation was fulfilled. Joseph was a slave and spent years in prison before he became a ruler next to Pharaoh.

I don't know what is in store for your life in 2015 and beyond, but I know that God has a plan. He loves you more than you can ever imagine, and He promises never to leave you.

FINAL DESTINATION: Heaven

Almost Home

Look, I am coming soon! My reward is with me, and I will give to each person according to what they have done. I am the Alpha and the Omega, the First and the Last, the Beginning and the End. **Revelation 22:12, 13.**

We have spent the last 364 days traveling throughout the United States and Canada, including side trips to Bermuda and Guam, on the ultimate vacation! As we've traveled, I hope you've enjoyed "seeing" the sights, but beyond that, I hope each destination has brought you closer to Jesus and to our final destination—heaven.

A friendship with Jesus and a willingness to follow Him are the only things that matter in this life. Everything on this earth will fade away in the end, but a relationship with Jesus assures us of salvation and eternal life.

Jesus may return in 2015, or He may not come until 2020 or 2028. We don't know the exact date of His return, but the signs are pointing to His soon coming. Whether He comes this year or 10 years from now, Jesus tells us that we need to be ready, and He asks us to share the good news with others.

The last chapter of Revelation contains the words of Jesus and the promise of His return. "Look, I am coming soon, bringing my reward with me" (Revelation 22:12, NLT). Those who have chosen to follow Christ will be taken home to heaven, and those who have chosen to live life their own way will be destroyed. This is not a game, and there are no second chances. This is the real deal.

Jesus loves you, and He wants you in heaven. It's your choice. Are you willing to accept His free gift, a ticket to heaven? If so, pack your bags. Just remember, there isn't a scheduled departure date, so you must be ready at all times. How do you do that? Spend time with Jesus, read His Word, fill your mind with good things, surround yourself with godly friends, get involved in your church, show others how much God loves them—all these things will help you prepare for the ultimate trip, a trip beyond the stars to heaven, where Jesus has prepared a home for those who love and obey Him.

Hello out there!

Hello out there!

Hello out there!

Amazing
True Stories
you'll Enjoy . . .

Guide's Greatest Stories Series

Guide's Greatest Narrow Escape Stories
978-0-8280-2040-4
Guide's Greatest Mystery Stories
978-0-8280-2038-1
Guide's Greatest Animal Stories
978-0-8280-1944-6
Guide's Greatest Christmas Stories
978-0-8280-1802-9
Guide's Greatest Prayer Stories
978-0-8280-1647-6
Guide's Greatest Prayer Stories Audio CD
978-0-8280-1862-3
Guide's Greatest Sabbath Stories
978-0-8280-1814-2
Guide's Greatest Change of Heart Stories
978-0-8280-2697-0

Guide's Greatest Miracle Stories
978-0-8280-1575-2
Guide's Greatest Angel Stories
978-0-8280-1880-7
Guide's Greatest Escape From Crime Stories
978-0-8280-1753-4
Guide's Greatest Grace Stories
978-0-8280-2390-0
Guide's Greatest Mission Stories
978-0-8280-2501-0
Guide's Greatest Rescue Stories
978-0-8280-2259-1
Guide's Greatest Hero Stories
978-0-8280-2637-6

Availability subject to change.